AF835757

User-Centered Design of Online Learning Communities

Niki Lambropoulos
London South Bank University, UK

Panayiotis Zaphiris
City University, London, UK

INFOSCI Information Science Publishing
Hershey • London • Melbourne • Singapore

Acquisitions Editor: Kristin Klinger
Development Editor: Kristin Roth
Senior Managing Editor: Jennifer Neidig
Managing Editor: Sara Reed
Assistant Managing Editor: Sharon Berger
Copy Editor: Maria Boyer
Typesetter: Amanda Appicello
Cover Design: Lisa Tosheff
Printed at: Yurchak Printing Inc.

Published in the United States of America by
Information Science Publishing (an imprint of Idea Group Inc.)
701 E. Chocolate Avenue
Hershey PA 17033
Tel: 717-533-8845
Fax: 717-533-8661
E-mail: cust@idea-group.com
Web site: http://www.idea-group.com

and in the United Kingdom by
Information Science Publishing (an imprint of Idea Group Inc.)
3 Henrietta Street
Covent Garden
London WC2E 8LU
Tel: 44 20 7240 0856
Fax: 44 20 7379 3313
Web site: http://www.eurospan.co.uk

Copyright © 2007 by Idea Group Inc. All rights reserved. No part of this book may be reproduced, stored or distributed in any form or by any means, electronic or mechanical, including photocopying, without written permission from the publisher.

Product or company names used in this book are for identification purposes only. Inclusion of the names of the products or companies does not indicate a claim of ownership by IGI of the trademark or registered trademark.

Library of Congress Cataloging-in-Publication Data

User-centered design of online learning communities / Niki Lambropoulos and Panayiotis Zaphiris, editors.
p. cm.
Summary: "This book is anchored in the concept that information technology empowers and enhances learners' capabilities adopting a learning summit on using the machine for the augmentation of human intellect for productivity, improvement, and innovation at individual, organizational, societal, national, and global levels" --Provided by publisher.
Includes bibliographical references and index.
ISBN 1-59904-358-0 -- ISBN 1-59904-359-9 (softcover) -- ISBN 1-59904-360-2 (ebook)
1. Distance education--Computer-assisted instruction. 2. Educational technology. 3. User interfaces (Computer systems) 4. Computer software--Development. I. Lambropoulos, Niki, 1966- . II. Zaphiris, Panayiotis.
LC5803.C65U72 2007
371.35'8--dc22
2006027716

British Cataloguing in Publication Data
A Cataloguing in Publication record for this book is available from the British Library.

All work contributed to this book is new, previously-unpublished material. The views expressed in this book are those of the authors, but not necessarily of the publisher.

User-Centered Design of Online Learning Communities

Table of Contents

Foreword

User-Centered Design for Quality in Online Learning Communities

This collection makes a valuable contribution to the already large literature of online learning communities. The 16 chapters come from diverse international sources, but they are satisfyingly narrow in their focus on user-centered design, analysis, and evaluation.

The opening chapter provides a role model for what follows: good reviews of the literature, description of technology, compelling principles, and evidence-based reports. It is gratifying to see that this community of researchers has made the transition from controlled experiments to strategies that blend quantitative, qualitative, and ethnographic methods. The multiple strategies, ranging from observations and interviews with small groups to automated logging and surveys of multiple courses, seem well matched with the high-level goals of these researchers, even though there will always be questions of adequate controls and replicability.

These authors are deeply interested in intention, self-reflection, creativity, and community, and they demonstrate admirable attention to contemporary topics such as trust, privacy, empathy, and personal responsibility. Several authors applied advanced interfaces concepts related to collaboration strategies, visualization tools, and social network analysis, thereby contributing to progress in those fields.

Readers will be pleased to find that this group of chapters emphasized practical implementations in functioning classrooms and online courses. This demonstrates the advancing nature of the online learning research community, which has moved from utopian promises of what might be implemented to realistic field studies of interfaces in use. As a result the design principles and usage recommendations often have greater authority and utility than earlier work. There are helpful, and numerous take home messages for teachers, guidance for implementers, and provocative questions for researchers.

Of course, some themes might have been more prominent, such as universal usability. By applying methods that enable easy usage with small and large displays, as well as fast and slow networks, the goal of broad dissemination is more effectively supported. Other universal usability issues include ease of conversion across languages, accommodation for multiple platforms, browser independence, minimal use of plugins, and user control of font size, color, and contrast. As universal usability becomes a design expectation, the good news is that software development tools increasingly facilitate the process, thereby reducing the burden on developers. The other good news about planning for universal usability is that with a modest additional effort by developers, they can achieve better interfaces for all users while gaining greater flexibility in accommodating modifications.

Overall, this collection presents positive progress on the state of online learning communities, leaving us to consider what aspirations we have for the next generation of projects. I believe that powerful technologies enable online educators to raise their expectations of what students can do. These educators in technology-rich environments can set ambitious goals for their students to write poems, paint murals, compose music, and perform plays. Some educators are already pushing further to have student teams design Web sites, edit videos, develop animations, build robots, and conduct research projects. In the best situations, students are engaging in meaningful environmental research, promoting neighborhood improvements, or supporting school activities in sports, theater, music, or hobby groups. These active learning tasks are gaining acceptance as service-oriented projects. They give students opportunities to practice planning carefully, collaborating effectively, and communicating constructively. They also help students develop their social skills in forming teams, resolving differences, and mediating disputes. These experiences build self-confidence, raise awareness of what is important, and help our students to contribute to their families, communities, and countries. It also makes them more ready to enter the workplace, take on leadership responsibilities, or become politically engaged.

As educators and interface designers, our roles include the noble goal of making the world a better place. We have the opportunity and responsibility to guide students as they develop their personalities and intellects. By giving students the experience of working with and helping others, we shape the directions of their lives.

Among educators we can accelerate the acceptance of these goals by discussing the values we see as important and writing about how we have designed our courses around our values. Then with a clear mind and confident tone, we can convey them effectively to our students.

Ben Shneiderman
University of Maryland, USA

Preface

User-centered design (UCD) has gained popularity as online learning has been attracting the interest in both the educational and business sector. This is due to the fact that UCD sheds light on the entire process of planning, designing, developing, and evaluating computer-based learning.

To now, this process is divided into parts, and different groups of stakeholders work in their areas of specialization. The result is environments where, technically, all parts exist; however, there are areas that are vague, missing, or do not work and create boredom and fatigue to the learners. Thus, the problem is not only connected to the technologies used in online learning, but also it is a decision-making problem, distributing responsibility for failure and success to all stakeholders.

User-Centered Design: Focus on Users/Learners

A problem indicates its own solution or at least the context for solutions. As such, human-computer interaction (HCI) by definition fits planning and design to its purpose of use. This is because HCI is an interdisciplinary area concerned with the analysis, design, and evaluation of interactive computing systems for human use and with the study of major phenomena surrounding them (ACM SIGCHI, 1992). Furthermore, HCI pioneers seemed to adopt a learning summit on using the machine for the "augmentation of human intellect" (Engelbart, 1962). User-centered design proposes that the designers need to enable human capabilities (Shackel, 1991). Norman (1986) stressed that the purpose of a UCD system is to serve the user. The users/learners' needs should dominate the design of the interface, and the needs of the interface should dominate the design of the rest of the system. The importance of following the social turn in learning technology with Vygotsky (1978) and Lave and Wenger (1991) was apparent in computer-supported collaborative learning (CSCL) and networked learning. However, UCD in education is still related to easy-to-use (usability) issues, without integrating the learning and social parameters in analysis, design, and evaluation.

Learning tools appeared to enhance the social character of learning, most of the times having astonishing results in controlled environments such as laboratories and case studies. In the real world, the repetition of the same interface pattern is found in widely used socio-based learning environments. This is due to the fact that alignment between all stakeholders' needs and visions is still missing. The physical and conceptual distance between all groups participating in learning, as well as the distance between the 'ideal' environment provided by the theories and what is really happening in learning environments, makes it difficult to provide adequate solutions as adequate descriptions of the processes are still missing. Even though technology changed the way we work, learn, and entertain ourselves, we still live outside the control rooms.

Description of Chapters

This edition aims to illuminate aspects of online learning communities' reality by employing methodologies that achieve gaining a better understanding of the users/learners. A UCD approach focuses on the description and understanding the needs and visions of the users as learners for analysis, design, and evaluation. Thus, our book is structured in four broad areas: Section I introduces UCD and identifies the problem of quality in online learning communities. Section II refers to analysis and design, and Section III presents case studies, as well as evaluation of online learning communities.

The book includes 16 chapters from prominent international collaborating authors from Australia, China, Greece, Ireland, Iceland, Japan, Poland, Switzerland, Taiwan, the United Kingdom, and the United States.

The following section presents an overview of each chapter.

Organization of the Book

Section I: UCD for Quality in Online Learning Communities

In Chapter I, Lambropoulos introduces user-centered design and its basic concepts associated with online learning communities. Another aim is to search for guidelines to ensure quality in online learning. Seven guidelines for experts' evaluation are proposed as signposts to ensure quality: intention, information, interactivity, real-time evaluation, visibility, control, and support.

In Chapter II, Schwier and Daniel employ a variety of user-centered evaluation approaches to examine methods for determining whether a community exists, and if it does, to isolate and understand interactions among its constituent elements, and ultimately to build a model of formal virtual learning communities. This chapter presents multiple methods for identifying a community and its constituent elements in formal online learning environments.

In Chapter III, Daniel, O'Brien, and Sarkar examine current research on online learning communities aiming to identify user-centered design principles critical to the emergence and sustainability of distributed communities of practice. The investigation aims to improve awareness, research, and sharing data and knowledge in the field of governance and international development. It argues that the sociotechnical research program offers useable insights on questions of constructability, performance, and sustainability. The authors conclude with a framework of principles to support the construction and deployment of online learning communities.

In Chapter IV, Law and Hvannberg search for quality models on exploration, evaluation, and exploitation of online community systems. Their review includes: (a) review of key theoretical models underpinning the design, (b) identification and evaluation of quality models, (c) an understanding of the importance of the feedback loop between evaluation redesign, and (d) the development of a generic framework for user interface quality models which comprises the four levels of factors, criteria, guidelines, and metrics.

Section II: Analysis and Design of Online Learning Communities

In Chapter V, Mowbray designs online learning communities to encourage participation and discourage uncooperative or antisocial behavior. She touches on aspects of the governance, social structure, moderation practices, and technical architecture of online learning communities. The first half of the chapter discusses why people behave antisocially in online learning communities, and ways to discourage this through design. The second half discusses why people behave cooperatively in online learning communities, and ways to encourage this through user-centered design, applying some results of experiments in social psychology.

In Chapter VI, Newman, Barbanell, and Falco document online users' interactions in videoconferencing communities. Working on a multi-year national program, the authors investigated and developed multiple methods by which videoconferencing could be used to expand PK-12 educational communities. They identify four major types of videoconferencing communities, and common patterns within each that help to support effective use of the process. The authors also examine the nature and structure of these videoconferencing communities, provide examples of successful use, summarize key user variables that impact on the process, and make recommendations for methods applied when studying videoconferencing communities.

In Chapter VII, Jelfs, Harvey, and Jones provide results from a study on communities of practice and their implementation on the development of two blended communities supporting a portal for science teachers in Ireland and Bulgaria. They discuss the communities in relation to recognized criteria and features that may be conducive to the success of small communities, and specifically online communities, and how these relate to the different stages of resource development. Sociotechnical findings indicate the need to blend the face-to-face meetings with electronic communications. The role of a key respected teacher/educator was also a pivotal feature in gaining the trust and respect of other participants at an initial stage.

In Chapter VIII, McNaught, Cheng, and Lam present evidence-based criteria for the design and use of online forums in higher education in Hong Kong anchored in the evaluation of 13 educational online forums. The study provides empirical data across multiple online forum experiences to better inform the pedagogy of using online forums. They propose three key factors that tend to affect forum success: ease of use, clear facilitation, and motivation to engage. The centrality of the role of the teacher was confirmed.

Section III: Evaluation and Case Studies

In Chapter IX, Bell, Zaitseva, and Zakrzewska stress the importance of evaluation as a link in the chain of sustainability. Models, based on the literature, were used to analyze and support the design and evaluation on the EU-funded project for Collaboration Across Borders (CAB). They present a case study of the development of the CAB community and offer practical advice for developing online learning communities.

In Chapter X, Rigou, Sirmakessis, Stavrinoudis, and Xenos review tools and methods for supporting online learning communities and their evaluation. The authors de-

scribe types and core functionalities, and suggest a set of general purpose evaluation methods suitable for assessing quality aspects of these tools, along with a method for the statistical analysis of the derived data.

In Chapter XI, Laghos and Zaphiris evaluated attitudes towards thinking and learning in a computer-aided language learning Web site via computer-mediated communication (CMC). The authors provide an overview of the models and frameworks available that are being used for analyzing CMC in e-learning environments. The significance of the proposed presentation is that it aims to provide the reader with up-to-date information regarding these methods, and based on the advantages and disadvantages of each of the CMC analysis methods, suggestions are applied to a characteristic scenario in e-learning.

In Chapter XII, Hartnell-Young, McGuinness, and Cuttance describe the analysis, design, development, and evaluation of Australia's National Quality Schooling Framework (NQSF), created particularly for teachers and others involved in improving school education. Funded by the Australian government, NQSF was developed as a means of building and testing knowledge. The authors, using Wenger's framework for communities of practice, evaluated the NQSF in light of its capacity for engagement, imagination, and alignment. The authors provide meaningful insights regarding engagement, shared purpose, as well as responsibility between the stakeholders.

Chapter XIII, Nguyen-Ngoc, Rekik, and Gillet present a model for the evaluation of Web-based experimentation environments based on an iterative paradigm. They integrate different analysis methods including quantitative and qualitative analysis, and Social Network Analysis. The approach is illustrated with the iterative user-centered design and development of the eMersion environment carried out at the Ecole Polytechnique Fédérale de Lausanne between 2002 and 2005. The authors investigate issues on participation, flexibility, learning performance, collaboration, and community social structure.

In Chapter XIV, Prammanee presents a study of online interaction based on identifications of users' needs. He implemented successfully Hillman et al. and Moore's four types of interaction and Henri's analytical model as a framework to guide the investigation in order to understand the nature of interaction in an online course. The author provides recommendations and practices for designing and delivering online courses effectively.

In Chapter XV, Brook and Oliver explore the influence of instructor actions on learning communities' development in online settings. They used their Learning Community Development Model to guide a multi-case study and measured the individuals' community experience using the Sense of Community Index supported by observations and open-ended questions.

In Chapter XVI, Mochizuki and his colleagues from different universities in Japan, working from a multiple-perspective framework, studied the promotion of self-

assessment in collaborative discussion using visualization software. The authors developed and evaluated self-assessment using a software program in order to visualize the discussion on a bulletin board system. The software, referred to as the "Bulletin board enrollee envisioner" (i-Bee), can visually display the co-occurrence relation between keywords and learners, as well as the recent level of participation of each learner and the frequency of the learner's use of each keyword. The authors provide results on this study regarding students' self-assessment and reflection, as well effectiveness on learning community sustainability.

References

ACM SIGCHI (Association for Computing Machinery Special Interest Group on Computer-Human Interaction Curriculum Development Group). (1992). *Curricula for human-computer interaction.* Retrieved February 8, 2004, from http://sigchi.org/cdg/

Engelbart, D. C. (1962). A conceptual framework for the augmentation of man's intellect. In P. Howerton (Ed.), *Vistas in information handling* (Vol. 1). Washington, DC: Spartan Books.

Lave, J., & Wenger, E. (1991). *Situated learning. Legitimate peripheral participation.* Cambridge: University of Cambridge Press.

Norman, D. A. (1986). Cognitive engineering. In D. A. Norman & S. W. Draper (Eds.), *User-centered system design: New perspectives on human-computer interaction* (pp. 32-65). Hillsdale, NJ: Lawrence Erlbaum.

Shackel, B. (1991). Usability—Context, framework, definition, design and evaluation. In B. Shackel & S. J. Richardson (Eds.), *Human factors for informatics usability* (pp. 21-37). Cambridge: Cambridge University Press.

Vygotsky, L. S. (1978). *Mind in society.* Cambridge, MA: Harvard University Press.

Niki Lambropoulos
London South Bank University, UK

Panayiotis Zaphiris
City University, London, UK

Acknowledgments

The editors would like to acknowledge the help of everyone involved in the collation and review process of the book without whose support the project could not have been satisfactorily completed. This book would not be in our hands without Xristine Faulkner, reader at the Centre for Interactive Systems Engineering, London South Bank University, and Sara Martin at the Institute of Jewish Studies, University College London. Special thanks also go to the publishing team at Idea Group Inc., in particular to Jan Travers, who facilitated this process enormously, and our editor Kristin Roth, who got through all the interesting situations with us. We are grateful to them for their expert guidance, support, and incredible spirit.

In closing, we wish to thank all authors who sent proposals for their willingness to follow our advice and contribute to shape this book.

Niki Lambropoulos
London South Bank University, UK

Panayiotis Zaphiris
City University, London, UK

June 2006

Section I:

UCD for Quality in Online Learning Communities

Chapter I

User-Centered Design of Online Learning Communities

Niki Lambropoulos, London South Bank University, UK

Abstract

This chapter aims to introduce user-centered design and its basic concepts associated with online learning communities. Another aim is to search for guidelines to ensure quality in online learning. Human-computer interaction for education provides the missing holistic approach for online learning. Functioning in a sociotechnical framework, online learning communities combine information and knowledge stores situated in shared social spaces using social learning software. In recent years, educational technologists linked theory and systems design in education. However, several disciplines combine in online learning. User-centered design provides the cross-disciplinary approach that appears to be essential for quality in online learning design and engineering. Thus, seven guidelines for experts' evaluation are proposed as signposts: intention, information, interactivity, real-time evaluation, visibility, control, and support.

Copyright © 2007, Idea Group Inc. Copying or distributing in print or electronic forms without written permission of Idea Group Inc. is prohibited.

Introduction

As computers invaded our lives, education adapted a protean nature moving into time and space. Technology and culture have co-evolved, and computer professionals catalysed this process (Bruckman, 2004). Technology in the workplace and at home needed to be different from the provision of a raw technology that could be used only by computer experts. The shift from machine-centered automation to user-centered services and tools is enabling users to be more creative and achieve more. In other words, this shift to human factors is redirecting the focus from what machines can do to what users can do (Shneiderman, 2002). The human-computer interaction (HCI) community searched for common places between behaviourally and technically oriented research that might lead to more productive end results *for every user* (Karat & Karat, 2003). The concept *"education with computers for all"* drives some major research centres nowadays (e.g., $100 dollar laptop—see http://laptop.media.mit.edu/).

In 1963, in the Lincoln Labs MIT, Sutherland (1980) designed the Sketchpad, a revolutionary computer program written in the course of his PhD thesis, changing the way people interacted with computers. One of his colleagues, Baecker, paved the way of modern HCI involving trained animators in the development and testing process in 1969. Xerox PARC furthered the work in Lincoln Labs suggesting sociotechnical implications for design and utilities to date (Buxton, 2005). HCI considers the interaction between the human and the computer within a complex multidisciplinary framework; HCI is "concerned with the design, evaluation and implementation of interactive computing systems for human use and with the study of major phenomena surrounding them" (ACM SIGCHI, 1992, p. 6). While engaging with computers, users, especially the younger ones, juggle more than one task simultaneously to achieve their goals, for example doing homework, listening to Mp3s, and chatting with friends (Dede, 2005). Technology provided the users with flexible ways to learn (flexible learning) by managing their tasks and freeing them in terms of time and space. Flexibility and learners' control were related to critical thinking, enhanced by comparison of multiple sources of information, individually incomplete and collectively inconsistent. Dede (2005) defined the new ways of learning as the *neo-millennial learning* (NL). NL is found in multi-user learning environments and augmented realities that are supported by the physical plant, technology infrastructure, and research, inducing learning. Personalisation of educational products and services tailored to individual needs insists on equal responsibility between all involved stakeholders. NL styles promoted cross-age social learning styles in:

- fluency in multiple media and simulation-based virtual settings;

Copyright © 2007, Idea Group Inc. Copying or distributing in print or electronic forms without written permission of Idea Group Inc. is prohibited.

- communal learning involving diverse, tacit, situated experience, with knowledge distributed across a community and a context, and the learner;
- a balance among experiential learning, guided mentoring, and collective reflection;
- expression through nonlinear, associational webs of representations; and
- co-design of learning experiences personalized to individual needs and preferences (learner-centered design, LCD) (Soloway, Guzdial, & Hay, 1994).

NL involves all stakeholders in the design experiences, seeing the learner as a learner and a user, as well as a consumer. Thus, one aim of this chapter is to seek the cross-discipline view in user-centered design (UCD). A second aim is to search for best practices and solutions, suggesting them as guidelines for experts' evaluation as one of the ways to ensure stakeholders' return of investment. The criteria for categorisation of OLCs provides the map for their evaluation (e.g., Chapter X, this volume), however without being designed for OLC evaluation as such. Alem and Kravis (2005) used Preece's (2000) sociability and usability framework for iterative community-centered development process successfully. This was to design and evaluate OLC success related to the number of participants and the volume of e-mails, the frequency of each reference, the focus on discussion, the value the participants saw in the discussion, and overall satisfaction. Silius, Tervakari, and Pohjolainen (2003) developed a multidisciplinary online tool for ease of use (usability) and functionality (utility), the later defining the pedagogical value. Usability evaluation that focuses on usability for effectiveness, efficiency, satisfaction, and enjoyability provides feedback for learning and design by employing several evaluation methods (Zaharias, 2004):

- *Formative and summative evaluation,* has a criterion on the time of evaluation related to the completeness of the online learning system design. Formative evaluation is conducted before and during the design, and development and summative after.
- *Objective and subjective evaluation,* is based on performance measures. Objective evaluation reflects on users' capabilities, whereas subjective refers to users' enjoyability.
- *Analytic and empiric evaluation,* has a criterion of who is doing the evaluation and how. Analytic refers to the design presentation before use, whereas empirical to design in use (by the learners). For analytic evaluation, expert reviews provide the reports based on the following methods (Shneiderman, 1987): heuristic evaluation, *guidelines review,* consistency inspection, cognitive walkthrough, and formal usability inspection.

Copyright © 2007, Idea Group Inc. Copying or distributing in print or electronic forms without written permission of Idea Group Inc. is prohibited.

Comparative analysis on studies revealed that both experts' and users' reviews are of equal importance (e.g., Jeffries, Miller, Wharton, & Uyeda, 1991; Karat, Campbell, & Fiegel, 1992). This chapter proposes a set of guidelines for system design characteristics based on sociotechnical design for experts' inspection, anchored in the dual identity of the student as a user and a learner in OLC. This expert's review aims to identify design elements for intention, information, interactivity, real-time evaluation, visibility, control, and support.

In the next section, affective learning is proposed to be the missing link for systems and individual learnability in OLC connecting the individual with the social unit. Collaborative learning then provides the conceptual foundation for the guidelines, and we conclude by introducing UCD and pedagogical usability (PU).

Collaborative and Affective Learning in Online Learning Communities: The Road to Social Capital

Effective OLCs have the properties of a social organisation, such as networks, norms, and trust that facilitate coordination and collaboration for mutual benefit (Putnam, 1993). OLCs functioning as communities of practice (CoP) (Lave & Wenger, 1991) bond members with the links of collaborative and affective learning, enabling social capital (Coleman, 1998) to be formed. Here, the concept of social capital is the manifestation of the potential of OLC when identity reconstruction via active engagement develops a degree of cohesion and immersion within OLC. This is visible on the alignment of individual assets with the OLC targets. However, the ability of open and distance learning and OLC to contribute to social capital is extremely limited (St. Clair & Fite, 2005). Still, if socio-emotional elements provide the bonds, then manifestation of the OLC potential in the form of social capital is possible. This is the reason why sociotechnical design is important to facilitate the process of engagement. Due to its social bases, the aim of sociotechnical design is to fit the process of design into the framework of the needs of the organisation, designing for the user and the task. It endeavours to design within the structure of the organisation and the way in which it operates (Faulkner, 1998, p. 134). In this context, sociotechnical design is related to CoP and social capital for members' bond building with the aid of the catalysts of intention, information, interactivity, real-time evaluation, visibility, control, and support.

After the latest Piagetian psychology of the individual, the educators turned to a sociological model, as the human was considered to exist within a situated social unit (Garfinkel, 1967). However, the individual disappeared within this unit, which

Copyright © 2007, Idea Group Inc. Copying or distributing in print or electronic forms without written permission of Idea Group Inc. is prohibited.

took responsibility for her activities, actions, resources, amusement, and learning. This stripped the individual of her responsibility for her own learning, as the learning environments were usually built, so when individualistic learning is present the social is lacking and vice versa. In online environments, the analytic reconstruction of work activities into ever more finely grained components removes the essential "real-world" affective features, which make them practices within a socially organised setting. In other words, breaking down tasks into smaller tasks removes the overall picture, and therefore the problems associated with the job in its entirety. This complaint attacks the individualistic slant of the cognitivism which underlies analytic approaches (Bentley et al., 1992). According to Bentley and his colleagues, the activities are performed within an organised environment which is composed of other individuals. It is this that gives shape to the activities, as "real-world" situated activities; the focus is on the social practises and the relationships between the individuals and their tasks. The properties of affective learning link the individual with the community as emotions, attitudes, interest, attention, awareness, trust, motivation, or empathy enabling communication, consultation, and participation. However, affective learning is yet to be part of learning technologies.

After the introduction of computer networks, new tenets appeared related to the social property of the networks such as the division of labour and conflict resolution that were hitherto the subjects of sociology (Durkheim, 1893; Arensberg & Kimball, 1968). One of the first attempts to humanise collaborative work combined systems design and ethnography, and coupled ergonomics and human factors engineering (Hughes, O'Brien, Rodden, Rouncefield, & Blythin, 1997) indicating the need for multidisciplinary frameworks. In the field of education, two approaches considered a cross-disciplinary framework, computer-supported collaborative learning (CSCL) (McConnell, 2000) and network-supported collaborative learning (NSCL) (Steeples & Jones, 2002). Sfard (1998) separated learning from information and practice, and distinguished between two metaphors of learning: (a) the knowledge acquisition metaphor based on information acquisition and internalisation of information, and (b) the participation metaphor that needs resources background as the message for interactivity. Koschmann's research questions for CSCL were: (a) CSCL tends to focus on process rather than outcome; (b) there is a central concern on grounding theories in observational data, in that CSCL studies tend to be descriptive rather than experimental; and (c) there is an expressed interest in understanding the process from a participant's viewpoint (1996, p. 15). Consequently, CSCL provided a more inclusive approach and forwarded crucial issues regarding the role of the individual within a social unit and the social unit itself. OLCs were an essential part of CSCL in online courses.

In an OLC the knowledge acquired by the individual is based on the alignment of asymmetrical interactions between learners and more capable peers (Vygotsky, 1978). Knowledge is shaped through the active engagement of diverse perspectives within a community, as men live in a community in virtue of the things which they

Copyright © 2007, Idea Group Inc. Copying or distributing in print or electronic forms without written permission of Idea Group Inc. is prohibited.

have in common (Dewey, 1916). The distance between them, for example between novices and other learners, signifies their potential development or learning distance. Knowledge alignments to shorten the distance are built by the negotiation of meaning and the resolution of conflicts as disagreements in discussions (Crook, 1994). Thus, collaborative learning occurs when these conflicts are resolved, tagging members and communities' growth points. This disturbs equilibrium, which occurs when knowledge held by diverse individuals and comes into contact—and conflicts—, is the necessary grounding for true learning and change in a democratic society (Glassman, 2001). However, in recent research, students have been observed to be reluctant to take part in this kind of collaborative learning experience (Lambropoulos, 2002; Rozaitis, 2005).

OLCs are hosted in learning management systems' (LMSs') either open source or purchased products. Despite the socio-cultural shift in education, LMS design for wider use is still techno-centric. Technologists tend to build systems for academics, thus integrating several levels of functionality, which is geared towards the teachers rather than the learner. In addition, they are not familiar with HCI heuristics and more specifically with pedagogical usability measurements. Intuition and experience have proved poor guides for design (Landauer, 1993). In the networked-supported collaborative learning conference held in Salford, UK (2004), the problem of definition of this area of specialisation was addressed with wry humour in the session "Learning Technologists: Split Personality or Community of Practice?" Thus, a narrowed instructional teaching style and design is not efficient anymore for neo-millennial learning, as the following tenets appear to be essential for systems design:

- co-design by involvement of all stakeholders in the process of design (cross-disciplinarity);
- user-centered design (the learner as a user);
- learner-centered design (the user as a learner);
- the learner as a consumer;
- sociotechnical design; and
- freedom and flexibility for creativity and imagination.

The following guidelines try to fill the existing gaps by proving a map to facilitate the interactions between the individual, the social, and the medium of computer. Intention, information, interactivity, real-time evaluation, visibility, control, and support are found essential signposts for the road of OLC to social capital.

Copyright © 2007, Idea Group Inc. Copying or distributing in print or electronic forms without written permission of Idea Group Inc. is prohibited.

Intention

Intention proposes the importance of the shared purpose in OLC for planning and maintaining the mental effort that keeps the commitment (Dennett, 1983). Setting intention is a cognitive process that strengthens the focus on the initial learning purposes, and provides continuum despite the fact that the members and the community are in a state of constant change and development.

Information

Access to information as a web of integrated and external resources includes organisations' purposes as well as resources and information derived from social interactivity in the form of text messages. Community inquiry theory (Peirce, 1868; Dewey (1916), considers inquiry or investigation as the result of the natural desire to learn. Peirce (1868, cited in Shields, 1999) suggested that human inquiry requires a cooperative community of minds and has a public character. Idea gathering and information flow, as well as presentation of the content, needs to be relevant and suitable for a given learning context (Liu, 2001).

Interactivity

Interactivity involves two ways of activity, and action is prerequisite to interaction; however, *public participation is not prerequisite although necessary.* This is the social contribution paradox. If interactivity and participation increase, the learner's knowledge deepens, allowing a grasp of more difficult and complex ideas. Interactivity is central in situated learning and engagement stages via legitimate peripheral participation (Lave & Wenger, 1991). Norman (1988) proposed seven stages in his Action Cycle Model, three internal to the individual, one external, and another three internal: forming the goal, forming the intention, specifying the action, executing the action, perceiving the state of the world, interpreting the stage of the world, and evaluating the outcome. For Shneiderman (2002), the road from activity to interactivity has the following stages (p. 113):

- **Collect:** Gather information and acquired resources.
- **Relate:** Work in collaborative teams.
- **Create:** Develop ambitious projects.
- **Donate:** Produce results that are meaningful to others.

Copyright © 2007, Idea Group Inc. Copying or distributing in print or electronic forms without written permission of Idea Group Inc. is prohibited.

Norman's first three stages and Shneiderman's first two stages suggest that a lot of work has to be done before an action is initiated. However, Norman does not believe that the stages are discrete nor that they necessarily are done in order. Some stages may be missed out completely. For Lambropoulos (2005), the decision of taking an action is the crossroads between meaning internalisation and own understanding externalisation.

Real-Time Evaluation

Real-time evaluation is seeing the window for immediate space of use related to situated learning. In addition, it is explicitly connected to quality measurements in online learning. The situated present requires a spotlight to be seen since online learning is a time-based process, and every moment is anchored in the situated learning activity. Depending on the targets, this point in time provides the signposts for benchmarking. Real-time evaluation offers stakeholders adequate information, real-time data gathering, data analysis, and design interventions. As a result, decision making is on time and appropriate to the given situation.

Visibility

OLC activities, interactivities, and cognitive, social presence and co-presence can be visible to "present" the community. Social presence and co-presence enhance the sense of community and the sense of belonging to a community (Beer, Slack, & Armitt, 2003). Garrison (2003) suggests that cognitive presence concerns the process of both reflection and discourse in the initiation, construction, and confirmation of meaningful learning outcomes. In OLC there are two properties—reflection and collaboration—that shape cognitive presence in ways unique to this medium. According to Law and Hvannberg (Chapter IV, this volume), visibility is an important feature for all conceptual frameworks underlying the design of OLC.

Control

Control facilitates self-directed and self-organised learning for self development (Garrison, 2003). For Garrison, self-directed learning assumes greater control of monitoring and managing the cognitive and contextual aspects of learning. Educators share the responsibility to provide structure and guidance that will encourage and support students assuming increased control of their own learning. The conduit to link internalisation and externalisation processes is the affective learning attributes. Being in control of our own personal learning brings a sense of confidence, keeps the

Copyright © 2007, Idea Group Inc. Copying or distributing in print or electronic forms without written permission of Idea Group Inc. is prohibited.

initial intention and purpose for coming to the learning community, and facilitates externalisation of learning experiences as active and public participation.

Support

Peer-to-peer support, task support, and learner support are considering the essential triangle for students' interpersonal growth and promote the intellectual development for authentic online learning. A study at the Hellenic Open University searched for the support students require from their tutors as well as the tutors' views on the support they believe is required from them (Papageorgiou-Vasilou & Vasala, 2005). This survey showed that the students require their tutors to possess communication skills and particularly, friendliness, availability, and understanding for students' problems, knowledge of the subject, and provision of quality feedback. The tutors on the other hand believed that their students' priority is to have very good scientific knowledge of their field. It appears students think that support is more important than mere acquisition of knowledge, as support will enhance the latter.

Garrison and Baynton (1987, p. 7) considered that learners' support has a broader definition, for example having access to services in order to carry out the learning processes. Furthermore, Garrison (1989, p. 29) suggests that support is concerned with a range of human and non-human resources to guide and facilitate the educational transaction, and they could be library facilities, various media and software programs, or community leaders. In addition, they could be various socio-economic variables such as students' financial self-sufficiency and capacity to cope with their roles and responsibilities in the family and community. Furthermore, Garrison stresses the importance of the teacher as the most important form of support in an educational transaction, who through guidance and direction can assist the students to achieve their goals and develop control of the educational process. Thorpe (2003) proposed the idea of the "third-generation student support"; online learning blurs the conceptual distinction between course development and learner support by using the learners themselves as a resource, to build on their experience, reading, and perspectives. But having a good knowledge of the subject increases the ability to learn. The problem is to teach anyone how to learn, as it is pre-supposed that students already posses the skills to learn. This is not always the case.

In identifying sociotechnical deign elements for OLC, the previous OLC guidelines were seen in the conceptual framework. Now the aim is to translate them in design elements to ensure quality in OLC. According to the Council for Higher Education Accreditation in its glossary for International Quality Review, quality refers to "fitness of purpose—meeting or conforming to generally accepted standards..." (CHEA, 2001). From an educational UCD point of view, the learner needs to use the system without physical and cognitive effort *to learn*. In other words, all of their learning energies should be directed towards the chosen area of study, not towards the learning

Copyright © 2007, Idea Group Inc. Copying or distributing in print or electronic forms without written permission of Idea Group Inc. is prohibited.

environment (i.e., the tool). The next section discusses the development of UCD in Education and the previous OLC guidelines as quality measure elements.

The Development of UCD and Usability for Educational Purposes

Over the last 10 years, ubiquitous technology brought a dramatically growing number of users. The technologists faced a reality they did not expect; a large number of users were unable to use their systems because they were unfamiliar with computer systems. In order to improve this state of affairs, the end product evaluation based on users' needs and suggestions seemed to be crucial. Approaches such as participatory design and interaction design aimed to solve the problem of failing prototypes for wide use by engaging the users in the early stages of product design and evaluation. Therefore, the context of use was defining the system's use as designers observed that the development of interactive technologies increasingly relies upon an appreciation of the social circumstances in which systems are deployed and used. The International Organisation for Standardisation (ISO) defined usability as a measure of quality of user's experience when interacting with a system, in terms of effectiveness, efficiency, and satisfaction (ISO FDIS 9241-11, 1997). Shackel's (1991) definition suggests that the designers have the power to enable human capabilities:

...capability in human functional terms to be used easily and effectively by the specified range of users, given specified training and user support, to fulfil the specified range of tasks, with the specified range of environmental scenarios.

User-centered design focus is in the process of change and development by being context sensitive. Gould and Lewis (1985) suggested four principles for useful and easy ways to use computer systems. These were: (a) early focus on the users and tasks, (b) empirical measurement for evaluation, (c) iterative design, and (d) integrated design. The latter suggests that when problems are found in user testing, then interactions are needed and observations need to be carried out to see the effects of the fixes. Referring to everyday product design, Norman and Draper suggested that UCD points at an interaction triad between the designer, the user, and the product (1986, pp. 31-61). The needs of the users and help to achieve more should dominate the design of the interface, and the needs of the interface should dominate the design for the rest of the system. For people to use a product successfully, they must have the same mental model (the user's model) as the system's image as that of the designer (the designer's model). If there is no explicit communication and interac-

Copyright © 2007, Idea Group Inc. Copying or distributing in print or electronic forms without written permission of Idea Group Inc. is prohibited.

tion between the user and designer, the user talks to the designer about the product via the product (i.e., if the users buy the product and design is deemed). This is an expensive process in terms of time and money, and not exact. Several end products are needed to achieve the desired one with the necessary levels of usability. The easiest way to jump to the desirable stage is to involve the users in the early stages of design. To Karat and Bennett (1991), user-centered means that:

...the total system function is crafted to meet requirements for effective user learning and efficient user access to that function. That is, the eventual users must see the system as useful and usable in their ongoing environment. (p. 270)

Landauer (1995) defines UCD as "design driven, informed, and shaped by empirical evaluation of usefulness and usability" (p. 221). However, Bannon (1991) proposed that although these abstract definitions suggest systems to be useful and usable to their users, "exactly what the term user-centered system design means, and how it can be achieved, is far from clear" (p. 38). Karat (1997), after years of research, concluded that:

UCD is an iterative process whose goal is the development of usable systems... achieved through involvement of potential users of a system in system design. It captures a commitment the usability community supports—that you must involve users in system design. (p. 38)

Yet, methods to achieve this are not defined. Among several attempts to contextualise UCD, Preece, Rogers, and Sharp (2002) aimed to apply ethnography in design. They extended Gould and Lewis' principles of the early focus on the user and insisted on the importance of sociability. The interaction design (ID) approach is used when a system fits within a use context, combining the understanding of the users and their environment with effective social interaction online (sociability) as well as the system's ease of use (usability). Sociability includes all stakeholders, their purposes, and practices. Usability seeks the minimum cognitive and physical effort required to use a system. ID for designing interactive products supports people in their everyday and working lives, by creating user experiences that enhance and extend the way people learn, work, communicate, and interact (2002, p. v).

One of the aims of UCD for OLC is sociotechnical design. Mumford and Sutton proposed eight principles for sociotechnical design on (1991, cited in Faulkner, 1998, pp. 134-136): compatibility, minimum critical specifications, sociotechnical criterion, multifunction, boundary location, information flow, support congruence, design and human values, and design incompletion. They recommended that sociotechnical systems should:

Copyright © 2007, Idea Group Inc. Copying or distributing in print or electronic forms without written permission of Idea Group Inc. is prohibited.

- support users in their tasks by being easy to learn, easy to use, and easy to understand;
- provide all information a user needs without expecting the user to change his or her work practices to fit the system;
- support scheduling and multitasking to facilitate neo-millennial learning; and
- support group work within the users' context, their work, and their environment.

In the search for personalised sociotechnical designs, the organisation sets the initial intentions and purposes. Despite the fact that several attempts were made to include all stakeholders in systems design, the widely used learning management systems still exist as artefacts rather than environments for collaborative activities. This is due to the fact that the engagement of the stakeholders and especially the learners in the early stages of design is still neglected. These tools are the product medium that allow or restrict the learners to a degree in their activities. However, most work on development and evaluation of online tools for online learning has been done in experimental projects, vulnerable to the Hawthorne effect, so that there is little evidence of how to use the technology effectively in real-life settings. In addition, these tools do not provide adequate help in rethinking the design and quality in online learning and are not widely incorporated in LMSs. Management, learning, and system evaluation have several levels of disfunctionality and success, and more important, the identification of the problems and the provision of solutions are not feasible. Also, the dual identity of the learner as a user is ignored. As a result, quality and benchmarking for online learning cannot be defined in clear stages. Some solutions for the aforementioned problems appeared in the design of online courses, usability (Chapter IX, this volume), and the introduction of pedagogical usability.

From Usability to Pedagogical Usability

When designing sociotechnical systems for online learning environments, forming the goal, the intention, and specifying the tasks are essential to collect and relate relevant information. This is because the learners as users are free to justify the reasons they use the application, and these reasons need to match some of the organisation's intentions. This will provide the starting point of ensuring quality. On a second level, several usability evaluation frameworks—known as heuristics—can be used. On a third level there are pedagogy-oriented heuristics. Heuristics provided a map to work on, as inspection methods, without the need for extensive users' evaluations—in other words, without end-users. Norman (1998), Shneiderman (1987), and Nielsen (2005) tried to help designers and evaluators to design systems for the users by

Copyright © 2007, Idea Group Inc. Copying or distributing in print or electronic forms without written permission of Idea Group Inc. is prohibited.

providing general guidelines. Even though Norman did not use the term heuristics (1988), he proposed "seven principles for transforming difficult tasks into simple ones." These are mostly used as system evaluation tools and are the following:

1. Use both knowledge in the world and knowledge in the head.
2. Simplify the structure of tasks.
3. Make things visible: bridge the gulfs of Execution and Evaluation.
4. Get mappings right.
5. Exploit the power of constraints, both natural and artificial.
6. Design for error.
7. When all else fails, standardise.

A second set of heuristics comes from Shneiderman's 8 Golden Rules. These can be applied during or after the system is designed, and can be used as an evaluation tool and as usability heuristics:

1. Strive for consistency.
2. Enable frequent users to use shortcuts.
3. Offer informative feedback.
4. Design dialogues to yield closure.
5. Offer simple error handling.
6. Permit easy reversal of actions.
7. Support internal locus of control.
8. Reduce short-term memory load.

The most widely used usability heuristics for user interface design come from Nielsen. He considers them usability guidelines, but they are more general rules:

1. Visibility of system status.
2. Match between system and the real world.
3. User control and freedom.
4. Consistency and standards.
5. Error prevention.
6. Recognition rather than recall.
7. Flexibility and efficiency of use.

Copyright © 2007, Idea Group Inc. Copying or distributing in print or electronic forms without written permission of Idea Group Inc. is prohibited.

8. Aesthetic and minimalist design.
9. Help users recognize, diagnose, and recover from errors.
10. Help and documentation.

After the migration of the sociotechnical environments on the Net, new heuristics to support the social nature of the systems were needed. For example, usability for online communities is translated into navigation, access, information design, and dialogue support (Preece, 2000). For computer-mediated communication (CMC), Suleiman (1998) suggested checking user control, user communication, and technological boundary. When online learning environments appeared in the mid-1990s, new usability heuristics were needed with a social and pedagogical orientation. Laurillard, Preece, Shneiderman, Neal, and Waern (1998) identified the needs for pedagogical perspectives at the CHI'98 Conference to articulate a true learner-centered philosophy of online learning. Laurillard suggested a technology-driven attitude in online learning, focusing on user interface, learning activities design, performance assessment, and evaluation in the form of checking whether the learning objectives have been met (Q&A with Diana Laurillard; Neal, 2003). The existing heuristics failed to address issues on usability and learning. Squires and Preece (1999) provided the first set of learning with software heuristics from a socio-constructivist perspective:

- match between designer and learner models;
- navigational fidelity;
- appropriate levels of learner control;
- prevention of peripheral cognitive errors;
- understandable and meaningful symbolic representations;
- support personally significant approaches to learning;
- strategies for cognitive error recognition, diagnosis, and recovery; and
- match with the curriculum.

"Learning with software" heuristics opened the way to *pedagogical usability* (PU). PU evaluation denotes whether the tools, content, interface, and tasks support learners to learn (Silius et al., 2003). Silius and his colleagues constructed an online usability and pedagogical usability evaluation tool based on questionnaires, involving all stakeholders and providing easy ways for evaluation. PU is based on Muir, Shield, and Kukulska-Hulme's (2003) concept on the PU Pyramid (PPU), integrating focuses as added values borrowed from Silius. Muir takes on the human networks that the technology rests on and provides a map to separate different types of users' needs. Also, the PU Pyramid identifies the people who make and use the technology (A.

Copyright © 2007, Idea Group Inc. Copying or distributing in print or electronic forms without written permission of Idea Group Inc. is prohibited.

Muir, personal communication, March 23, 2005). Seeds of the concept of PUP exist in Muir's master's thesis on online music education software (Muir, 2001). Later, Muir and his colleagues involved all stakeholders in the evaluation process, as the problem is still about the difficulty for all stakeholders to get involved in the process of producing and approving learning and learning resources, as well as ensuring pedagogical design adjusted to the level of study. The authors specified PPU for online learning as the educational effectiveness, practical efficiency, and general enjoyability of a course-related Web site (see Figure 1).

PUP consists of two parts with several levels resting on the previous. The part of the pyramid above the ground consists of four levels of usability—technical, general, academic, and context specific. The base, which is the foundation of the pyramid, suggests the involvement of the users of the course Web sites—that is, the Web site development team and the technical and maintenance team, the local support, the institutional support, and the external support. Thus, PUP suggested the involvement of all stakeholders—the people for organisation, management, technical development, and learning—and their purposes and practices. Muir's co-authors, Kukulska-Hulme and Shield (2004), forwarded the research and proposed four learning principles: flexibility, control, creativity, and imagination.

The next section finds the previous guidelines within UCD in an effort to find middle ground between Education and HCI, and HCI and Education for OLC.

Figure 1. The Pyramid of Pedagogical Usability (adapted from Muir et al., 2004)

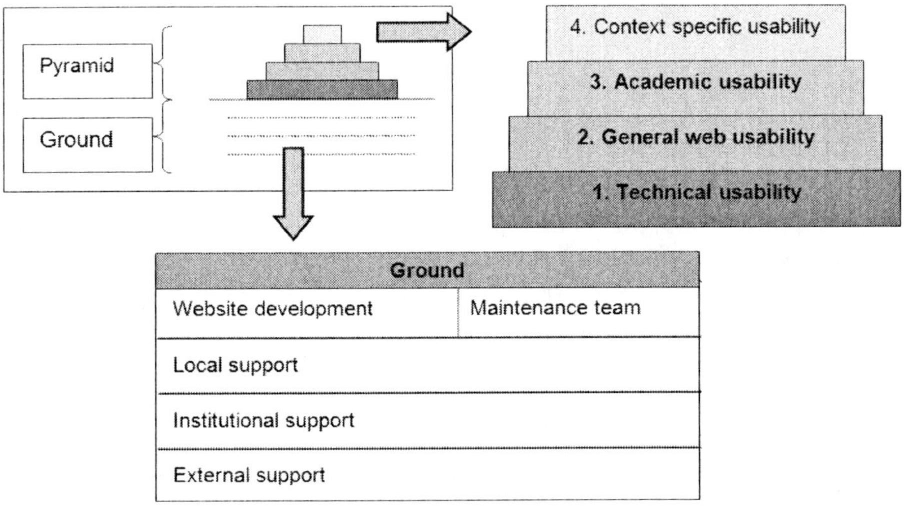

Copyright © 2007, Idea Group Inc. Copying or distributing in print or electronic forms without written permission of Idea Group Inc. is prohibited.

Seven Guidelines for User-Centered Design of Online Learning Communities

This section aims to provide experts with guidelines as part of OLC's quality check. If accurate description of people, tasks, and their relationships can provide signs for benchmarking depending on stakeholders' objectives, then these guidelines are useful as they integrate design, evaluation, and use. Therefore, intention, information, interactivity, real-time evaluation, visibility, control, and support can be part of ways for ensuring quality in OLC. Then benchmarking can be built on the information provided and organisation's objectives.

Intention

Building intentional online learning courses is a process that requires initial setting of intentions, planning, designing, developing, and sustaining OLC, as well as the systems used. Students are motivated to adopt technology in online learning when they perceive reasonable effort for inclusion in the design process and rely on potential benefits. The community needs are assessed prior to making decisions about the technology and designing usability; sociability is planned for, and the needs of the community are reassessed. In an *advanced interactive discovery environment* (AIDE) developed using IBM Lotus QuickPlace (Odom-Reed, Hancock, & Gay, 2005), researchers found that the early immersion is crucial in hybrid space bulletin boards, threaded discussions, and shared file structures, and facilitates audio-video conferences using desktop computing. This is the only significant predictor of the learning experience in terms of both satisfaction and performance. This finding represents a fundamental issue for designers and instructors to consider when developing learning spaces in order to retain the intention to learn and to motivate students into immersing themselves early on.

Information

Setting intentions is grounded in the purposes, goals, and targets of the community, and requires transparent information and meta-information to enable interactivity. Information and meta-information refers to access to resources and information about the online learning environment: the who, what, how, when, and why (Bharadwaj & Reddy, 2003). In addition, informational content and learning resources need to meet the criteria of accuracy, authority, objectivity, currency, and coverage (Silius et al., 2003). The organisation purposes define the intentions, goals, and strategies for all stakeholders. This information needs to be transparent for all the members

Copyright © 2007, Idea Group Inc. Copying or distributing in print or electronic forms without written permission of Idea Group Inc. is prohibited.

of the community so that people can decide to join some communities and not others, since decision rests with the will of the individual (Tönnies, 1955; Lave & Wenger, 1991). Transparency in purposes and practices provide clear understanding, enhance productivity, and minimise the "cost-of-not-knowing". Early analyses of social computing often focused on how information can support individuals' knowledge and power (Kling, 1980). In online discussions, the learners actively "foreground" and "background" information according to their own purposes and measures, and the system could provide them with tools to facilitate their strategies. In other words, they decide for themselves the relative importance and urgency of the information they access.

Interactivity

In OLC, interactivity is defined to the degree a medium facilitates: (a) potential levels of activity between the learners; and (b) levels of activity between the learners to control information, flexibility, range of choices, and feedback, having reactive, proactive, and interactive characteristics (Thomson & Jorgensen, 1989). The degree of interactivity has three dimensions (Kettanurak, Ramamurthy, & Haseman, 2001, pp. 548-549): (a) frequency of user inputs/responses made using interactive features during the dialogue, (b) range of choices in interactive features available to users at a given time during the interaction, and (c) modality of transformation/presentation of information. Observation is an active and strong mode of learning in online environments however, having a passive interactive property. Rewards and consequences from social interaction increase, decrease, or suppress active participation and learning. To now, these attributes are not adequately translated into systems settings and tools.

Real-Time Evaluation

There are several evaluation layers (see chapter introduction) as regards to the pedagogical and technological levels. To date, product evaluation is conducted within laboratories, thus vulnerable to the Hawthorn effect. Evolving design methods and conceptual developments for evaluation and feedback are imported and adapted from other fields such as ethnography, information design, cultural probes, and scenario-based design (Rogers, 2004). For example, social network analysis has proven successful for viewing social networks and relationships between members (Laghos & Zaphiris, Chapter XI, this volume; Koku & Wellman, 2004). Herring (2004) uses computer-mediated discourse analysis for researching online learning behaviour in online discussions. Different lenses can be used, as the purposes are different. The time-based life of the online learning community makes evaluation

Copyright © 2007, Idea Group Inc. Copying or distributing in print or electronic forms without written permission of Idea Group Inc. is prohibited.

and assessment a difficult and expensive process in terms of time, effort, and money. Not only this, the results acquired with common methodological instruments suggest solutions to past problems. Traditional ethnographers immerse themselves in cultures for weeks or months, user interface designers need to limit this process to a period of days or even hours, and they still need to obtain the relevant data needed to influence a redesign (Shneiderman, 1987).

Thus, the key concept is evaluation and assessment in real time, supporting the constant change of computing and the lifecycle of the community. Ethnography has been used in HCI to capture events as they occur. Ethnography is a time-based methodology, aiming to provide a description of a process in order to understand the situation. It captures data about an environment over a period of time, providing descriptions of the individuals and their tasks. It is not simply a snapshot on one given day, and this is the reason it was used to understand a developing context. Furthermore, time-series data gathering and analysis offer accurate representations of reality for the designer's model, the system image, and the user's model. In OLC for example, visualisation of OLC attributes and real-time content analysis with themes tree analysis can provide spatial representation of the OLC and its social space, actually giving a *picture* of the community. All stakeholders get real-time data, and experts are able to interpret the data according to their own expertise and work together on solutions. Evaluation and assessment connected to benchmarking reveals imperfections and strengths to each discipline for correct interpretation and understanding that makes precise help and support possible.

Visibility

Visibility applies to both learning and interface design. Provided the cognitive presence, proximity is perceived as approaching cognitively other learners' thoughts, expressed as contextual communication. Visibility assists proximity as it enhances awareness of one's self, other people, the learning environments, as well as the project as a whole (Bharadwaj & Reddy, 2003). As cognitive proximity is the only visible way to be aware of other people's existence, visibility of this proximity will enhance participation as learners are visible to each other, similar to a discussion in the real world. Information and social and temporal structures become observable and reportable when patterns of communicative exchange emerge in online discussions. Donath has worked on several projects for discussion visualisation (2005). Social presence and co-presence are visible to the degree a medium facilitates awareness of the self, the other person, and interpersonal relationships, and represents traces of information by situating the text and its author within the messages exchanged. In Chat Circles, a synchronous graphical chat system, the system administrators can place images and texts in the chat space to serve as conversational foci. The participants, the texts, and the images have a "hearing range"; one must be physi-

Copyright © 2007, Idea Group Inc. Copying or distributing in print or electronic forms without written permission of Idea Group Inc. is prohibited.

cally near a person to converse or to view an image. Users' movements leave trails in space, enabling people to perceive and establish presence. Loom is a series of visualization of Usenet newsgroups that explores both what information is most useful to depict and what vocabulary should be used to depict it. Mochizuki and his colleagues (Chapter XVI, this volume) investigated self-assessment in online discussions using a bulletin board for context awareness. i-Bee (Bulletin board Enrollee Envisioner) co-occurrences relations between keywords and learners, displaying the recent level of participation of each learner and the frequency of the learner's use of each keyword. The evaluation showed that i-Bee enabled students to assess and reflect upon their discussion, understand the condition, and reorganize their commitment in a discussion that reflects their learning activity.

Linking the individual with OLC via affective factors, learners need to trust each other, feel a sense of warmth and belonging, and feel close to each other before they are willing to offer ideas, critique peer ideas, or consider others' critiques as valuable (Rourke, Anderson, Garrison, & Archer, 2000). In other words, there needs to be a social environment in which learning can take place. Design for OLC needs to facilitate the emergence of a social structure and to *show that structure can and does exist.* It needs to allow and encourage learners to construct social networks in order to facilitate their learning. It is essential for systems design to support these aspects of affective learning, as these are the connectors between the individual and the community. As a result, learning is visible and measurable in the changes of behaviour for identity reconstruction.

Control

Based on information provision via real-time evaluation, there are several layers and levels of control to support all stakeholders in the process of learning design. Interactivity with the system for operational efficiency, locating information and network resources, interface configurations, corporate policy, and security control enhance networking and paths for communication aimed at self-maintained systems. Self-control and locus control with the aid of the technical environment is important for self-regulation and self-organisation. In turn, self-organisation is required for self-evaluation, leading to self-efficacy closely related to task performance and active participation in the community.

Support

Support for efficiency is referred to as a 24/7 and Just-in-Time technical support, as well as performance support and instructional design, related to quality assurance and immediate feedback. Support is related to usability for process simplification,

Copyright © 2007, Idea Group Inc. Copying or distributing in print or electronic forms without written permission of Idea Group Inc. is prohibited.

reducing complexity, decision support, representation of tasks sequences by use and meaning, facilitation of community roles, or simplifying workflow. Lastly, support is about dealing with pedagogical usability, ergonomics, implementation strategies, as well as reducing administrative overheads. Efficiency is assisted by a set of support services, and in their absence, individuals become frustrated and dissatisfied (Mumford, 1983).

Overall, the UCD guidelines for OLC do not propose a nebulous and convoluted sociotechnical system. Complex and sophisticated interfaces can interrupt the flow of interaction, and this is the reason that they need to be kept in a very simple format (Alty, 1993). In addition, the guidelines do not mean that uncontrolled environments enhance flow. On the contrary, when properly implemented, they facilitate creativity and imagination for enjoyable engagement and experiences of group intelligence and collective knowledge production.

Discussion and Conclusion

With the turn of the century, many new technologies emerge and evolve in real time so their structures are partially a product of their evolution. Had we predicted the power of the Web at the time, we might have structured it differently. However, technologies very rarely remain in the laboratory and are products for use. It is the "in use" situation which aids their future development. There are some design decisions which it is very unlikely to undo, so all that can be done is to minimise the disadvantages of such designs or to provide a structure that is more convenient from a human-centered perspective rather than from a machine or technological perspective. User-centered design of online learning communities is a multidisciplinary approach anchored in human factors. UCD of OLC involves all stakeholders from the process of requirements acquisition and evaluation, to user-acceptance testing for educational effectiveness, practical efficiency, and general enjoyability. A "community-centered design" will emphasise the social character of learning and the embedded activities, taking into account the "real-world" individual users and OLC, contact with situated activities, and recognise the way users acquire expertise through experience (see Bannon & Hughes, 1993).

The seven UCD guidelines for OLC are intention, information, interactivity, real-time evaluation, visibility, control, and support. The limitation of the proposition is that results come from only one study (Lambropoulos, 2006). From this perspective, HCI is still concentrated on the creation of theoretical frameworks, methods, and usability heuristics to ensure quality, rather than integrating these principles directly into the software engineering process. One of the attempts to tackle this

Copyright © 2007, Idea Group Inc. Copying or distributing in print or electronic forms without written permission of Idea Group Inc. is prohibited.

problem was conducted by Faulkner and Culwin (2000) at the Centre for Interactive Systems Engineering, London South Bank University. The authors proposed that usability engineers need to know the feasibility of their designs and build from a user-centered perspective. The process to achieve these goals by knowing the users and their objectives and knowing their tasks is *usability engineering* (UE) (Faulkner, 2000). In a pedagogical usability framework, the process is the instructional engineering employing ethnomethodology, targeting to know the users-learners and their tasks to fulfil their purpose to learn. Pedagogical usability goes beyond usability taking account of both user and learner identities. The users, not having to spend all their potential to learn about the system as the system is already easy to use, they are free of restrictions to their own learnability. The guidelines are proposed as examples of best practices and solutions to bridge the gap between the development and OLC context in sociotechnical design. Pedagogical usability engineering is recommended as the process to ensure their functionality for design, use, and evaluation. Implications in online learning entail all stakeholders by the provision of transparent and visible information on people, purposes, and practices; facilitate interactivity for engagement and social transformation; support all styles of learning; provide support; facilitate evaluation and assessment; and help all members to reach their potential.

Acknowledgments

Special thanks to Sara, Jenny, and Xristine. Sara for her support to overcome difficulties I could never do without her, Jenny for her support and expertise that make me be keen on the HCI community; and Xristine for her expert advice, guidance, and support, as well as her patience with me. Xristine Faulkner and Fintan Culwin gave me back my dreams, lost for some time. Last but not least, Alexander Muir for his permission to adopt the Pyramid of Pedagogical Usability figure.

References

ACM SIGCHI (Association for Computing Machinery Special Interest Group on Computer-Human Interaction Curriculum Development Group)0. (1992). *Curricula for human-computer interaction.* Retrieved February 8, 2004, from http://sigchi.org/cdg/

Alem, L., & Kravis, S. (2005). Design and evaluation of an online learning community: A case study at CSIRO. *ACM Siggraph Bulletin (Special Issue on Online Learning Communities), 25*(1), 20-24.

Copyright © 2007, Idea Group Inc. Copying or distributing in print or electronic forms without written permission of Idea Group Inc. is prohibited.

Alty, J. L. (1993). Multimedia: We have the technology but do we have the methodology? In H. Maurer (Ed.), *Proceedings of Euromedia'93* (pp. 3-10).

Arensberg, C. M., & Kimball, S. (1968). Community study: Retrospect and prospect. *American Journal of Sociology,* 691-705.

Bannon, L. (1991). From human factors to human actors: The role of psychology and human-computer interaction studies in system design. In J. Greenbaum & M. Kyng (Eds.), *Design at work: Cooperative design of computer systems.* Hillsdale, NJ: Lawrence Erlbaum.

Bannon, L. J., & Hughes, J.(1993, February). Introductory paper. In K. Schmidt (Ed.), *Developing CSCW systems: Design concepts.* Report of COST14 "CoTech" Working Group4 (1991-1992) (pp. 9-36).

Beer, M. D., Slack, F., & Armitt, G. (2003, January 6-9). Community building and virtual teamwork in an online learning environment. *Proceedings of the 36th Hawaii International Conference on System Sciences*, Big Island, HI (HICSS-36 2003).

Bentley, R., Hughes, J. A., Randall, D., Rodden, T., Sawyer, P., Shapiro, D. et al. (1992). Ethnographically informed systems design for air traffic control. *Proceedings of the 1992 ACM Conference on Computer-Supported Cooperative Work,* Toronto, Ontario, Canada.

Bharadwaj, V., & Reddy, Y.V.R. (2003). A framework to support collaboration in heterogeneous environments. *ACM SIGGROUP Bulletin, 24*(3), 103-116.

Bruckman, A. (2004). Co-evolution of technological design and pedagogy in online learning community. In S.A. Barab, R. Kling, & J. H. Gray (Eds.), *Designing for virtual communities in the service of learning* (pp. 239-255). New York: Cambridge University Press.

Buxton, W. (2005). Interaction at Lincoln Laboratory in the 1960s: Looking forward—Looking back. Panel introduction. *Proceedings of the ACM Conference on Human Factors in Computing Systems* (CHI'05). Retrieved November 17, 2005, from http://www.billbuxton.com/LincolnLab.pdf

CHEA. (2001, January 23). *Proceedings of the CHEA Annual Conference,* New Orleans, LA. Retrieved November 17, 2005, from http://www.chea.org/international/barblan.html

Coleman, J. S. (1988). Social capital in the creation of human capital. *American Journal of Sociology, 94*(supplement).

Crook, C. (1994). *Computers and the collaborative experience of learning.* London: Routledge.

Dede, C. (2005). Planning for neomillennial learning style: Shifts in students' learning style will prompt a shift to active construction of knowledge through mediated immersion. *Educause, 28*(1). Retrieved April 4, 2005, from http://www.educause.edu/apps/eq/eqm05/eqm0511.asp?bhcp=1

Copyright © 2007, Idea Group Inc. Copying or distributing in print or electronic forms without written permission of Idea Group Inc. is prohibited.

Dennett, D. C. (1983). The intentional stance. *Behavioral and Brain Sciences, 3,* 343-350.

Dewey, J. (1916). *Democracy and education: An introduction to the philosophy of education* (p. 4f). New York: MacMillan.

Donath, J. (2005, April 3). Words as landscape: Beyond threaded conversation. *Proceedings of the CHI Workshop,* Portland, OR.

Durkheim. (1893). *The division of labor in society.* New York: The Free Press (reprint 1997).

Faulkner, X. (1998). *The essence of human-computer interaction.* Harlow, UK: Prentice-Hall.

Faulkner, X. (2000). *Usability engineering.* New York: Palgrave MacMillan.

Faulkner, X., & Culwin, F. (2000). Enter the usability engineer: Integration of HCI and software engineering. *Proceedings of ITiCSE* (pp. 61-64). Helsinki: ACM.

Garfinkel, H. (1967). *Studies in ethnomethodology.* Englewood Cliffs, NJ: Prentice-Hall.

Garrison, D. R. (1989). *Understanding distance education: A framework for the future.* London: Routledge.

Garrison, D. R. (2003). Cognitive presence for effective asynchronous online learning: The role of reflective inquiry, self-direction and metacognition. In J. Bourne & J. C. Moore (Eds.), *Elements of quality online education: Practice and direction* (Vol. 4 in the Sloan C Series). Needham, MA: The Sloan Consortium.

Garrison, D. R., & Baynton, M. (1987). Beyond independence in distance education: The concept of control. *American Journal of Distance Education, 1*(3), 3-15.

Glassman, M. (2001). Dewey and Vygotsky: Society, experience, and inquiry in educational practice. *Educational Researcher, 30*(4), 3-14.

Gould, J. D., & Lewis, C. (1985). Designing for usability: Key principles and what designers think. *Communications of the ACM, 28*(3), 300-311.

Herring, S. (2004). Computer-mediated discourse analysis: An approach to researching online behaviour. In S. A. Barab, R. Kling, & J. H. Gray (Eds.), *Designing for virtual communities in the service of learning.* New York: Cambridge University Press.

Hughes, J. A., O'Brien, J., Rodden, T., Rouncefield, M., & Blythin, S. (1997). Designing with ethnography: A presentation framework for design. *Proceedings of the Symposium on Designing Interactive Systems of the Conference on Designing Interactive Systems: Processes, Practices, Methods, and Techniques,* Amsterdam, The Netherlands.

Copyright © 2007, Idea Group Inc. Copying or distributing in print or electronic forms without written permission of Idea Group Inc. is prohibited.

ISO FDIS 9241-11. (1997). *Ergonomic requirements for office work with visual display terminals (VDTs), part 11: Guidance on usability specification and measures.* Technical Report.

Jeffries, R., Miller, J. R., Wharton, C., & Uyeda, K. M. (1991, April 28-May 2). User interface evaluation in the real world: A comparison of four techniques. *Proceedings of the ACM CHI'91 Conference,* New Orleans, LA *(pp. 119-124).*

Karat, C., Campbell, R. L., & Fiegel, T. (1992, May 3-7). Comparison of empirical testing and walkthrough methods in user interface evaluation. *Proceedings of the ACM CHI'92 Conference*, Monterey, CA (pp. 397-404).

Karat, J. (1997). Evolving the scope of user-centered design. *Communications of the ACM, 40*(7), 33-38.

Karat, J., & Bennett, J. L. (1991). Using scenarios in design meetings: A case study example. In J. Karat (Ed.), *Taking software design seriously: Practical techniques for human-computer interaction design* (pp. 63-94). Boston: Academic Press.

Karat, J., & Karat, C. M. (2003). The evolution of user-centered focus in the human-computer interaction field. *IBM Systems Journal, 42*(4), 532-541. Retrieved September 4, 2005, from http://www.research.ibm.com/journal/sj/424/karat.pdf

Kettanurak, V., Ramamurthy, K., & Haseman, W. D. (2001). User attitude as a mediator of learning performance improvement in an interactive multimedia environment: An empirical investigation of the degree of interactivity and learning styles. *International Journal of Human-Computer Studies, 54*(4), 541-583.

Kling, R. (1980). Social analyses of computing: Theoretical perspectives in recent empirical research. *Computing Surveys, 12,* 61-110.

Koku, E. F., & Wellman, B. (2004). Scholarly networks as learning communities. In S. A. Barab, R. Kling, & J. H. Gray (Eds.), *Designing for virtual communities in the service of learning* (pp. 299-337). New York: Cambridge University Press.

Koschmann, T. (Ed.). (1996). *CSCL, theory and practice of an emerging paradigm* (pp. 1-23). Mahwah, NJ: Lawrence Erlbaum.

Kukulska-Hulme, A., & Shield, L. (2004). Usability and pedagogical design: Are language learning Web sites special? *Proceedings of the World Conference on Educational Multimedia, Hypermedia and Telecommunications 2004* (pp. 4235-4242). Retrieved August 28, 2005, from http://www.aace.org/dl/files/EDMEDIA2004/paper_3016_9574.pdf

Lambropoulos, N. (2002). *Collaborative and individualistic learning in a situated, computer-supported cooperative environment for multimedia constructions.*

Copyright © 2007, Idea Group Inc. Copying or distributing in print or electronic forms without written permission of Idea Group Inc. is prohibited.

Unpublished master's thesis, Institute of Education, University of London, UK.

Lambropoulos, N. (2005, July 22-27). Sociability and usability for contribution based on situated informal learning and consensus knowledge building in online communities. *Proceedings of the 1st Conference on Online Communities and Social Computing at the 11th International Conference on Human-Computer Interaction,* Las Vegas, NV.

Lambropoulos, N. (2006). *Integration of pedagogical and operational levels for quality assurance in instructional design: A Moodle example.* Online conference 'VLEs: Pedagogy and Implementation: The Theory and Practice of Learning Platforms and Virtual Learning Environments (October 16-19). Retrieved July 29, 2006, from http://www.online-conference.net/vle2006/programme.htm

Landauer, T. K. (1993). *The trouble with computers.* Cambridge, MA: MIT Press.

Landauer, T. K. (1995). User-centered design methods. In T. K. Landauer (Ed.), *The trouble with computers.* Cambridge, MA: MIT Press.

Laurillard, D., Preece, J., Shneiderman, B., Neal, L., & Waern, Y. (1998). Distance learning: Is it the end of education as most of us know it? *Proceedings of the CHI'98 Summary Conference on Human Factors in Computing Systems* (pp. 86-87).

Lave, J., & Wenger, E. (1991). *Situated learning. Legitimate peripheral participation.* Cambridge: University of Cambridge Press.

Liu, M.-C. (2001). A systematic Web-course development process: User-centered requirements. *Educational Technology, 41*(6), 15-22.

McConnell, D. (2000). *Implementing computer supported cooperative learning* (2nd ed.). London: Kogan Page.

Muir, A. (2001). *Guidelines for developers of online music education software.* Unpublished master's thesis, Napier University, UK.

Muir, A., Shield, L., & Kukulska-Hulme, A. (2003, June 15-18). The pyramid of usability: A framework for quality course Web sites. *Proceedings of 12th Annual Conference of the European Distance Education Network, the Quality Dialogue: Integrating Quality Cultures in Flexible, Distance and E-Learning* (pp. 188-194), Rhodes, Greece.

Mumford, E. (1983). *Designing human systems—The ETHICS method.* Retrieved December 20, 2005, from http://www.enid.u-net.com/C1book1.htm

Mumford, E., & Sutton, D. (1991). Designing organisational and over-coming the failings of current IT methodologies. *Computer Bulletin,* (August), 12-14.

Neal, L. (2003). *Q&A with Diana Laurillard.* Retrieved September 14, 2004, from http://www.elearnmag.org/subpage.cfm?section=articles&article=14-1

Copyright © 2007, Idea Group Inc. Copying or distributing in print or electronic forms without written permission of Idea Group Inc. is prohibited.

Nielsen, J. (2005). *Ten usability heuristics.* Retrieved November 29, 2005, from http://www.useit.com/papers/heuristic/heuristic_list.html

Norman, D.A. (1988). *The psychology of everyday things.* New York: Basic Books.

Norman, D. A., & Draper, S. W. (1986). *User centered system design.* Hillsdale, NJ: Lawrence Erlbaum.

NSCL. (2005). Learning technologists: Split personality or community of practice? *Proceedings of the Networked Learning Conference 2004.* Retrieved September 14, 2005, from http://www.shef.ac.uk/nlc2004/Proceedings/Symposia/Symposium1/index.htm

Odom-Reed, P. D., Hancock, J., & Gay, G. (2005). Presence, community and immersion in hybrid learning environments. *Proceedings of the HCI International Conference 2005,* Las Vegas, NV.

Papageorgiou-Vasilou, V., & Vasala, P. (2005, November 11-13). Supporting postgraduate students in distance education: What do students need and what do tutors believe they need. *Proceedings of the 3rd International Conference on Open and Distance Learning: Applications of Pedagogy and Technology,* Patras, Greece (pp. 124-134).

Peirce, C. S. (1868). Some consequences of four incapacities claimed for man. *Journal of Speculative Philosophy, 2,* 140-157.

Preece, J. (2000). *Online communities: Designing usability and supporting sociability.* New York: John Wiley & Sons.

Preece, J., Rogers, Y., & Sharp, H. (2002). *Interaction design: Beyond human-computer interaction.* Chicester, UK: John Wiley & Sons.

Putnam, R. D. (1993). The prosperous community: Social capital and public life. *American Prospect, 4*(13).

Rogers, Y. (2004). New theoretical approaches for human-computer interaction. *Annual Review of Information, Science and Technology, 38,* 87-143.

Rourke, L., Anderson, T., Garrison, D.R., & Archer, W. (2001). Assessing social presence in asynchronous text-based computer conferencing. *Journal of Distance Education, 14*(2). Retrieved September 14, 2005, from http://cade.icaap.org/vol14.2/rourke_et_al.html

Rozaitis, B. (2005). *Scenes from a classroom: Making active learning work.* Retrieved September 14, 2005, from http://www1.umn.edu/ohr/teachlearn/workshops/activelearning/resistance.html

Sfard, A. (1998). On two metaphors for learning and the dangers of choosing just one. *Educational Researcher, 27*(2), 4-13.

Copyright © 2007, Idea Group Inc. Copying or distributing in print or electronic forms without written permission of Idea Group Inc. is prohibited.

Shackel, B. (1991). Usability–Context, framework, definition, design and evaluation. In B. Shackel & S. J. Richardson (Eds.), *Human factors for informatics usability* (pp. 21-37). Cambridge: Cambridge University.

Shields, P. (1999, March 23-25). The community of inquiry: Insights for public administration from Jane Addams, John Dewey and Charles S. Peirce. *Proceedings of the Public Administration Theory Network Meeting,* Portland, OR.

Shneiderman, B. (2002). *Leonardo's laptop: Human needs and the new computing technologies.* Cambridge, MA: MIT Press.

Shneiderman, B., & Plaisant, C. (2005). *Designing the user interface: Strategies for effective human-computer interaction* (4th ed.). Reading, MA: Addison-Wesley.

Silius, K., Tervakari, A.-M., & Pohjolainen, S. (2003, June 28-July 1). A multidisciplinary tool for the evaluation of usability, pedagogical usability, accessibility and informational quality of Web-based courses. *Proceedings of the 11th International PEG Conference: Powerful ICT for Teaching and Learning,* St. Petersburg, Russia.

Soloway, E., Guzdial, M., & Hay, K. (1994). Learner-centered design. The challenge for HCI in the 21st century. *Interactions, 1*(2), 36-48.

St. Clair, R., & Fite, S. (2005, November 11-13). Far off voices: Social capital and distance education. *Proceedings of the 3rd International Conference on Open and Distance Learning: Applications of Pedagogy and Technology*, Patras, Greece (pp. 13-18).

Steeples, C., & Jones, C. (Eds.). (2002). *Issues in networked learning.* Berlin: Springer-Verlag.

Suleiman, S. (1998). *Heuristics for evaluating the usability of CMC systems.* MPhil thesis, South Bank University, UK.

Sutherland, I. E. (1980). *Sketchpad: A man-machine graphical communication system.* New York: Garland Publishers. Retrieved September 14, 2005, from http://www.cl.cam.ac.uk/TechReports/UCAM-CL-TR-574.pdf

Thorpe, M. (2003). Collaborative online learning: Transforming learner support and course design. In A. Tait & R. Mills (Eds.), *Rethinking learner support in distance education: Change and continuity in an international context* (pp.182-211). London: Routledge Falmer.

Tönnies, F. (1955). *Community and association* (C. P. Loomis, Trans.). London: Routland & Kegan Paul.

Vygotsky, L. S. (1978). *Mind in society.* Cambridge, MA: Harvard University Press.

Copyright © 2007, Idea Group Inc. Copying or distributing in print or electronic forms without written permission of Idea Group Inc. is prohibited.

Zaharias, P. (2004). *A usability evaluation method for e-learning courses.* Unpublished PhD Thesis, Athens University of Economics and Business, Greece.

Copyright © 2007, Idea Group Inc. Copying or distributing in print or electronic forms without written permission of Idea Group Inc. is prohibited.

Chapter II

Did We Become a Community? Multiple Methods for Identifying Community and Its Constituent Elements in Formal Online Learning Environments

Richard A. Schwier, University of Saskatchewan, Canada

Ben K. Daniel, University of Saskatchewan, Canada

Abstract

To understand the nature of formal virtual learning communities in higher education, we are employing a variety of user-centered evaluation approaches to examine methods for determining whether a community exists, and if it does, to isolate and understand interactions among its constituent elements, and ultimately to build a model of formal virtual learning communities. This chapter presents the methods we are employing to answer these seemingly simple questions, including user perceptions of community (Sense of Community Index, Classroom Community Scale), interaction analysis (density, reciprocity), content analysis (transcript analysis,

Copyright © 2007, Idea Group Inc. Copying or distributing in print or electronic forms without written permission of Idea Group Inc. is prohibited.

interviews, focus groups), paired-comparison analysis (Thurstone scaling), and community modeling techniques (Bayesian Belief Network analysis).

Introduction

This chapter grew out of a growing concern we had about whether "community" was a useful metaphor for understanding online learning environments, and whether there was any precision in the application of the metaphor. It seems as though the label of learning community is used widely and indiscriminately to describe a variety of online learning environments, from rigid prescribed online classrooms to completely voluntary chatrooms. In addition, while there have been a number of solid and valuable contributions to methods for evaluating online learning environments, they necessarily focus very sharply on specific perspectives of community such as overall user perceptions of community (e.g., Chavis & Wandersman, 1990; Rovai & Jordan, 2004), content analysis of transcripts (e.g., Jeong, 2004; Rourke, Anderson, Garrison, & Archer, 2001), measures of interaction (Fahy, Crawford, & Ally, 2001; Prammanee, Chapter XIV, this volume), or reports of experiences and difficulties by participants and instructors (e.g., Dykes & Schwier, 2003; Murphy & Coleman, 2004). While each of these approaches provides a useful lens into the operation of an online learning environment, none provides a complete picture of how online learning communities operate. We sensed that these approaches could be used in concert with others to address the questions of whether online communities exist, what their constituent parts are, and how these elements interact. Ultimately, we hope to create a method of modeling formal online learning communities that is drawn from experience, and robust enough to be adapted to a range of online learning communities.

The notion of using community as a framework for understanding group learning is largely drawn from social learning theory (Lave & Wenger, 1991; Vygotsky, 1978; Wenger, 1998). Learning is proposed to be occurring in all kinds of communities, formal or informal, physical or virtual (Wenger, 1998; Schwier, 2001). Currently, virtual learning communities are gaining wider recognition among researchers as vehicles for knowledge creation and transformation (Daniel, Schwier, & McCalla, 2003; Daniel, Schwier & Ross, 2005; Paloff & Pratt, 1999; Preece, 2000; 2002). Despite this growing interest, there are limited theories informing our understanding of what comprises community. In addition, the over-reliance by researchers on transcript analysis to the exclusion of other methods of evaluation results in a limited lens through which to view community. We contend that community can be best understood through the members of the community, and more specifically through a combined analysis of their perceptions, interactions, and artifacts, and by using models to interpret the interactions among emergent community variables.

Copyright © 2007, Idea Group Inc. Copying or distributing in print or electronic forms without written permission of Idea Group Inc. is prohibited.

Our analysis was initially informed by a model of virtual learning communities (VLCs) proposed by Schwier (2001) that includes catalysts, elements, and emphases of VLCs (see Figure 1). The purpose was not to validate the model, but to use the elements proposed in it as a starting point for understanding the nature of community that developed in the formal learning environments we observed. Ultimately, our goal is to build a new model of formal VLCs that grows out of practice and the comprehensive observation and analysis of online learning environments. In this chapter, we will use preliminary data to illustrate the procedures we are using, but it is premature to draw firm conclusions from the data at this point; analysis is at an early stage, and we are using the data to make sense of the methods we are employing.

So this chapter proposes and describes a set of approaches that can be used to measure and understand the characteristics of community. The categories of analysis include identifying a sense of community, isolating characteristics of community, comparing characteristics of community, and modeling community. There is an intentional "flow" to the analysis and the combination of methods described here, and we have attempted to map the methods of analysis we employed onto the categories of analysis we intended to conduct (see Table 1). First, we wanted to employ a measure of the perceived existence of community by participants in the community. Our contention is that summative judgments by participants, however flawed and limited, provided an important initial perspective on the question. Then, we turn our attention to isolating characteristics of community, and once characteristics are identified, we use paired comparison techniques to determine the relative importance of the various characteristics. Finally, we attempt to build a model from the data—one that not only represents the interrelationships among variables, but

Figure 1. Model of virtual learning community from Schwier (2001)

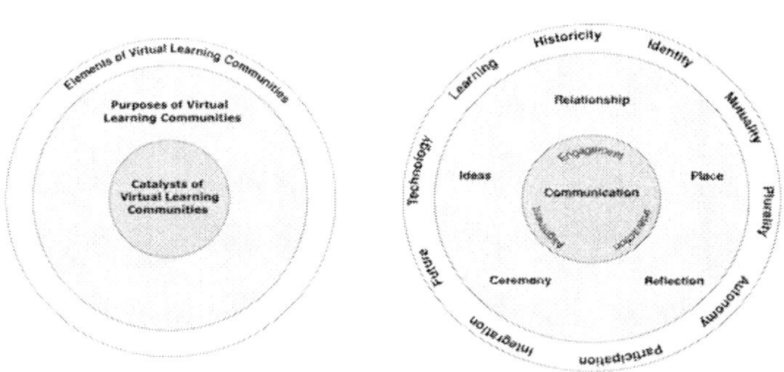

Copyright © 2007, Idea Group Inc. Copying or distributing in print or electronic forms without written permission of Idea Group Inc. is prohibited.

Table 1. Questions and associated methods of analysis for examining elements of community in online learning environments

Intention of Analysis	Method of Analysis
Identifying a sense of community: Did participants develop a sense of community? Did the group patterns of interaction suggest that a community might exist?	-Sense of community indices -Density and intensity of peripheral participation
Isolating characteristics of community: What characteristics of the online learning communities were manifest in the groups?	-Transcript analysis of online discussions, chat sessions, and e-mail -Frequency count of characteristics -Interviews with participants
Comparing characteristics of community: What was the relative importance of each community characteristic?	-Thurstone paired comparison analysis
Modeling community: How can the observed community characteristics be used to model the relationships among and influence of significant elements on community?	-Bayesian belief network

that can also be used to project the effect on the community when the constituent elements are changed.

Examples of these analyses draw from three years of online communication among cohorts of graduate students in educational communications and technology as they participated in seminars on the foundations of educational technology and instructional design. Each course spanned an entire semester or academic year. The courses were small graduate seminars with enrollments from six to thirteen students, and each class met primarily online, but with monthly group meetings. While most students were able to attend the group meetings regularly, every cohort had members who participated exclusively or mostly from a distance. Given the blended nature of all of the courses, we confine our conclusions to similar environments, and acknowledge that these results cannot be generalized to environments that are entirely online or entirely face-to-face.

In the remainder of this chapter, we elaborate on the approaches we used to address each of the four categories and questions. Each approach includes a discussion of the procedure, an example of its application from our data, and a description of its strengths and weaknesses.

Copyright © 2007, Idea Group Inc. Copying or distributing in print or electronic forms without written permission of Idea Group Inc. is prohibited.

Sense of Community Indices

The first challenge we faced was to obtain some indication that the groups we were observing could be characterized as communities. Did participants consider their groups "communities," and did the groups exhibit patterns of communication that suggested a community might exist?

Sense of Community Index

As a rough measure of sense of community, we employed the "Sense of Community Index" (Chavis, n.d.), a classic instrument employed broadly in the field of community psychology (Chavis & Wandersman, 1990; Chipuer & Pretty, 1999; Obst & White, 2004) and revised to examine online learning communities (Brook & Oliver, Chapter XV, this volume). The Sense of Community Index (SCI) measures an individual's psychological sense of community. The survey is comprised of 12 true/false items that measure four dimensions of the overall construct: membership, influence, reinforcement of needs, and shared emotional connection. Some attention has been given to revising the dimensions of the construct (Chipuer & Pretty, 2004), but normative data were not available beyond reliability estimates (Chronbach's alpha = .72 and .78) provided in two investigations (Pretty, 1990).

We used the index for the first time in the most recent group studied, so parallel data are not available for groups from previous years. We administered the SCI at the beginning and end of a year-long course, and ran a simple t-test on the data to see if there was any change in measures of the group's sense of community by the end of the course (see Table 2). The results of the t-test indicated that there was

Table 2. T-test of "Sense of Community Index" scores at the beginning and end of the course

T-Test: Two-Samples Assuming Equal Variances		
Mean	41.70	48.40
Variance	31.12	22.04
Observations	10.00	10.00
Pooled Variance	26.58	
df	18.00	
t Stat	-2.91	
P(T<=t) one-tail	0.005	

Copyright © 2007, Idea Group Inc. Copying or distributing in print or electronic forms without written permission of Idea Group Inc. is prohibited.

significant positive growth in the SCI scores from the beginning to the end of the course ($p < .01$).

Given the questionable reliability of the SCI, despite its long use, we are have begun using the Classroom Community Scale (CCS) proposed by Rovai and Jordan (2004) as a second measure. The CCS is similar in format and intent to the Sense of Community Index, but it boasts a higher reliability estimate for the full scale (Chronbach's alpha = .93) and the subscales (connectedness = .92; learning = .87).

Patterns of Prescribed and Peripheral Interaction

Fahy et al. (2001) proposed several useful measures of describing interaction that they called collectively the Transcript Analysis Tool (TAT). The TAT includes methods of measuring density, intensity, and persistence of interactions in transcripts of online discussions. We drew on their recommendations and extended some of them to analyze interactions in our data, particularly transcripts of asynchronous discussions.

Density

Fahy et al.'s (2001) definition of density was "the ratio of the actual number of connections observed, to the total potential number of possible connections." It is calculated by using the following formula: Density = $2a/N(N-1)$, where "a" is the number of observed interactions between participants, and "N" is the total number of participants. Density is a measure of how connected individuals are to others in a group, and the idea is that a higher degree of connection is a positive indicator of community. Fahy et al. (2001) caution that the measure of density is sensitive to the size of the network, so larger groups will likely exhibit lower density ratios than will smaller groups.

For our own calculations, we included only peripheral (voluntary or additional) communications between people by eliminating all instances of required postings and responses. We felt that peripheral interaction would provide a stronger measure of community, given that required communications among students might inflate the actual density value. In the case of one of our groups, we discovered a density ratio of .78, suggesting that 78% of the possible connections were made.

$$\text{Density} = 2(122)/13(12) = .782$$

Copyright © 2007, Idea Group Inc. Copying or distributing in print or electronic forms without written permission of Idea Group Inc. is prohibited.

Although there are no baseline data to make judgments about the existence of community, this level of density did seem to suggest a strong level of connection among participants.

Intensity

Fahy et al. (2001) also recommend using measures of intensity to determine whether participants are authentically engaged with each other, not merely carrying out their responsibilities in a course. They argue that it is a useful measure of involvement because it involves measures of persistence and dedication to being connected to others in the group.

One measure of intensity is "levels of participation," or the degree to which the number of postings observed in a group exceeds the number of required postings. In this case, students were required to make 490 postings as part of the course requirements, and they actually made 858 postings, yielding a level of participation ratio of 1.75. While this is a useful measure, it is inflated by the number of responses that were quick, brief, and relatively thoughtless replies to postings, such as, "Yes, I agree with you. Good point." It was also not useful for a group we studied that created and maintained its own community without the direction of the instructor. In this case, the course was problem based and the students were engaged, as a team, in solving an authentic problem with an actual client. They posted more than 800 messages, often with thread lengths exceeding 20 and without the direct intervention of the instructor. There is little doubt that an "intense" community was at play, but "levels of participation" was not a useful measure of that intensity.

Another measure of intensity employed by Fahy et al. (2001) is persistence, or the level to which participants pursue topics. Persistence is operationalized by measuring the number of levels of communication in a particular discussion thread from the first posting to the last. We chose not to employ a measure of persistence at this stage of analysis, as we felt it was a stronger measure of engagement of participants with topics than necessarily engagement with each other. We may revisit this decision in subsequent analyses.

Reciprocity

A particularly important TAT measure for the purpose of understanding community was "S-R ratio," a formula to measure the parity of communication among participants. We referred to this as a measure of "reciprocity," and we felt that truly engaged groups who form communities will exhibit high degrees of reciprocity. Given its importance to our investigation, we will describe our analysis in somewhat more detail, and also describe a few approaches we used to augment the strategy.

Copyright © 2007, Idea Group Inc. Copying or distributing in print or electronic forms without written permission of Idea Group Inc. is prohibited.

Once again, we employed only peripheral communication to obtain a measure of the reciprocity of communication among the group. By peripheral interaction, we mean those interactions that took place outside of the required communications that were a part of the course. For this analysis we only included interactions that were not directed to the group. Any topics of messages were included, but in each case, the communication was directed to a particular person, instead of to the group or to nobody in particular. Peripheral interaction is one measure of voluntary interpersonal communication within the group, and we contend that it is a stronger indication of community than is required interaction. In one class, for example, the total number of postings was 858, but the number of peripheral messages was 368. Our assumption is that peripheral participation gives a more legitimate measure of social engagement and community involvement than does required participation.

As an initial step in the analysis, we charted the number of peripheral messages sent and received among participants in the class (see Table 3). The S/R ratio (sent to received messages) is an indication of the reciprocity of messaging within the group. Ratios approaching 1.0 indicate a high degree of reciprocity. Ratios considerably higher or lower than 1.0 indicate disparity in the communication. High numbers indicate that the individual was communicating to others, but not receiving as many communications in return. A low number indicates that a higher number of messages were received than were sent in response. It is our supposition that a healthy community exhibits a high amount of reciprocity among members of the group.

As a second step in the reciprocity analysis, we illustrated the messages sent and received by drawing line graphs and sociograms of the interactions with each

Table 3. Table of messages sent and received within a group, and resultant reciprocity ratios

		Received													
		Inst	DM	CM	WR	HK	DP	SD	CB	DT	GD	TD	TC	HJ	Tot Received
	Inst	NA	0	6	3	1	1	0	0	0	0	0	0	1	12
	DM	0	NA	7	4	1	0	0	0	0	0	1	0	0	13
	CM	7	2	NA	5	2	3	3	2	3	1	3	5	1	37
	WR	5	4	12	NA	6	1	1	4	1	1	1	1	2	39
Sent	HK	7	1	5	7	NA	2	3	1	0	0	0	3	1	30
	DP	5	2	4	0	2	NA	0	0	2	1	3	4	0	23
	SD	6	3	5	3	4	2	NA	2	4	0	2	0	3	34
	CB	4	3	5	4	0	3	1	NA	2	0	2	3	0	27
	DT	4	2	11	2	1	0	2	1	NA	1	1	2	5	32
	GD	1	1	1	3	3	2	2	1	1	NA	1	0	0	16
	TD	6	4	4	1	3	4	2	2	2	1	NA	2	2	33
	TC	0	2	3	2	1	2	1	3	2	1	0	NA	1	18
	HJ	2	3	2	1	4	1	0	2	4	0	4	2	NA	25
	Tot Sent	47	27	65	35	28	21	15	18	21	6	18	22	16	
		3.92	**2.08**	**1.76**	**0.90**	**0.93**	**0.91**	**0.44**	**0.67**	**0.66**	**0.38**	**0.55**	**1.22**	**0.64**	

Copyright © 2007, Idea Group Inc. Copying or distributing in print or electronic forms without written permission of Idea Group Inc. is prohibited.

participant as the focal point of communication. For example, from the reciprocity data in Table 3, we concentrated on the interactions between the instructor and the students in one course, and generated a line graph and sociogram that illustrate the pattern of engagement with the students individually and collectively (see Figure 2). These two approaches to illustrating the same data offer unique perspectives.

The sociogram is drawn by drawing a circle on a large piece of paper. Plotting the data starts at the outside and works toward the inside of the circle, starting with the student who received the fewest messages at the outside. Subsequent participants are located proportionally closer to the center of the circle, with the person receiv-

Figure 2. Sociogram and line graph illustrations of patterns of peripheral interactions between the instructor and students

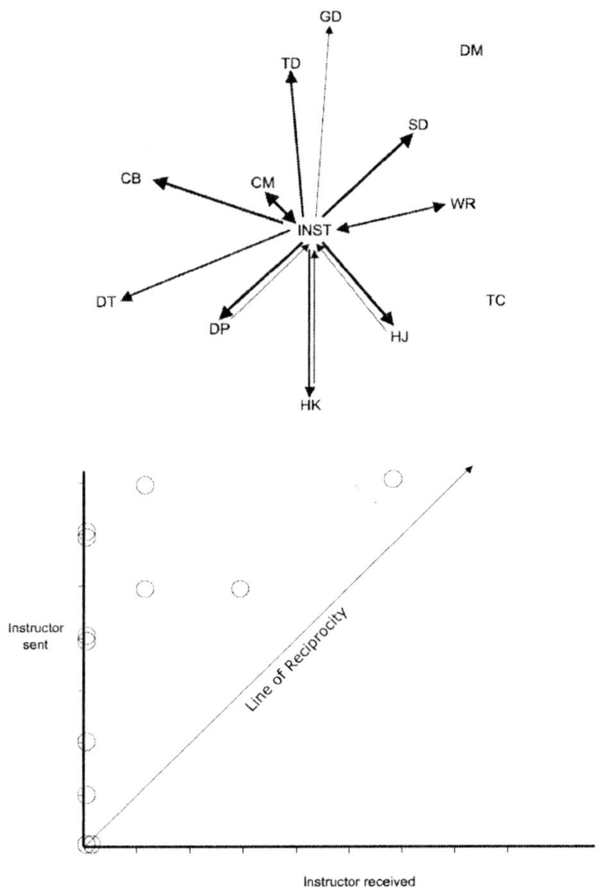

Copyright © 2007, Idea Group Inc. Copying or distributing in print or electronic forms without written permission of Idea Group Inc. is prohibited.

ing the most messages in the center. This procedure roughly represents the relative number of interactions among students as the distance between them.

In the example illustrated in Figure 2, we have used line density to represent the relative density of interaction between two people, so as people interact more often, the lines become increasingly dense. As an alternative, and to increase precision, the total number of messages sent and received can be included next to the initials of each participant.

For Figure 2, we graphed the number of messages sent from the instructor to each student on the Y axis, and the messages sent to the instructor from each student on the X axis of the graph. The vector dividing the graph is the reciprocity line—the locations where messages to and from the instructor and students would be equal in number. For the group, as the distribution of points coagulates around the median, it suggests reciprocity of communication. Distribution of points above the median, such as we see here, indicates that the instructor sent more messages to students than he received from students. Is this an indication of voice, authority, favoritism, or disengagement? Were students reluctant to engage the instructor in conversation, or was the instructor trying to drive discussion? The illustrations are mute on these important points. It is necessary to read these messages in context to understand how they represent the relationships between the students and the instructor, so in order to understand the meaning of the pattern, we needed to review the patterns within the context of the conversations. But it is interesting to examine the pattern that emerges from the data, and as we examine the patterns of reciprocity in the group, we can use the analysis as an indication of how strong the mutual engagement was among participants in the community by taking each participant in turn and examining the reciprocity of that person's engagement with other members of the group.

For the purpose of analysis, we found that these two approaches, when used in concert, provided a useful way to think about the data we observed. First, the sociogram provided a graphic sense of distance among students in relation to the person who was the focal point (in this example, the instructor). It visually reinforced the apparent isolation of two members of the group (TC and DM had no peripheral interaction with the instructor), and it also underscored the dominant outflow of messages in this example.

The line graph, on the other hand, provides a visual snapshot of reciprocity from the way messages cluster around the reciprocity vector. It also gives a sense of the distribution of the amount of communication across the group from the scatter of points across the area of the graph. If the points clustered somewhere close to the line and huddled together more closely, it suggests that peripheral communication within the group is balanced.

While these are useful tools, they should not be used in isolation of the actual communications, and it is possible, even likely, to misinterpret the data if they are considered out of context. For example, a bullying instructor might browbeat students

Copyright © 2007, Idea Group Inc. Copying or distributing in print or electronic forms without written permission of Idea Group Inc. is prohibited.

into responding to challenges, and while such a graph might indicate a high degree of reciprocity, there is the likelihood that this type of reciprocity would damage the sense of community shared by the group. Another caution is that these tools are not as precise as they might appear. While they are useful for conveying trends, there are no post-hoc methods for isolating significant differences.

Characteristics of Community

Once we were satisfied that users felt a sense of community, and we examined patterns of their interactions to reinforce and qualify their perceptions, we wanted to investigate what the key features of that community might be. Beyond users' sense of community, we wanted to know if there was any evidence of community manifest in the artifacts of interaction in the community, and then to confirm our observations with participants through follow-up interviews and focus group sessions. In order to get a sense of what were the manifest characteristics of online learning communities, we turned our attention to transcript analysis, a compelling source of data because we had a relatively complete and comprehensive verbatim record of interactions among the students and the instructor.

Content Analysis

Transcripts of all asynchronous and synchronous events, as well as transcripts of interviews and focus group sessions, were analyzed using a grounded theory approach (Strauss & Corbin, 1997) and Atlas ti™ software, with the purpose of extending, refining, and/or altering our understanding of the role played by online discussion in the development of virtual communities. One researcher coded transcripts, and a second researcher reviewed the coding scheme as it emerged. Inter-coder reliability estimates were not calculated; however codes were subjected to negotiation between researchers. The unit of analysis employed was "unit of meaning," which seemed reasonable initially, but was later subject to criticisms of its reliability and labor intensiveness by other researchers. In retrospect, we would have used sentences or messages as the units of analysis, but given our intention to surface elements of community, the meaning unit of analysis was acceptable, albeit very time consuming to perform.

While an "emergent fit" strategy was used in this study, our model of community (see Figure 1) constituted a starting place. Therefore, as data were coded, the emerging themes were compared and contrasted with the model using constant comparative analysis, and caution was taken to ensure that theoretical views were not imposed on the data.

Copyright © 2007, Idea Group Inc. Copying or distributing in print or electronic forms without written permission of Idea Group Inc. is prohibited.

Ultimately, a preliminary level of analysis was used to select characteristics we would investigate further—frequency counts of characteristics within transcripts. The data were rich, but in order to focus the remainder of our analysis, we needed to isolate those characteristics that were more prevalent than others, and simple frequencies afforded one convenient measure. Sources of data included transcripts of asynchronous discussions, transcripts of synchronous chat sessions, and e-mail correspondence that was copied to the instructor (private e-mail was excluded).

Interviews and Focus Groups

These characteristics, and their relative frequencies, became one focus of interviews and focus groups so we could attempt to identify which were significant characteristics and which were trivial or insignificant by comparing them to characteristics that emerged from conversations we held with participants. Primary data from interviews and focus groups were gathered though semi-structured interviews, each of which lasted approximately one hour, and which were initially structured to address the sense of community, relationships within the community, and learning. Participants were sent interview questions ahead of time, but they were not required to confine themselves to these questions, nor were they required to address all of them. Participants were encouraged to digress and to ignore questions that were not important to their experiences. The goal was to provide structure to verify and elaborate on known variables associated with online learning communities, but still promote each participant's control over her/his own story. Interviews were conducted conversationally, and the intention was to explore the questions that had the most meaning to the participants, and that they were able to comment on with the most authority. In other words, we were more interested in the directions that the participants steered the conversations than we were in a prescribed set of questions.

The interviews were very useful for refining and elaborating our understanding of characteristics we discovered in the transcript analyses. In fact, four additional key characteristics—trust, intensity, awareness, and reflection—were drawn primarily from the interviews and focus groups that were not immediately apparent in the transcripts of online conversations. The participants also identified how these characteristics, particularly awareness and trust, introduced a temporal and developmental theme that we feel is critical to understanding how communities form. From a methodological perspective, we found that these types of observations were often embedded in the stories of the participants about their experiences, and a narrative approach added a very rich layer of understanding to our other observations.

Copyright © 2007, Idea Group Inc. Copying or distributing in print or electronic forms without written permission of Idea Group Inc. is prohibited.

Comparison of Characteristics

At this stage of the analysis, we had identified 15 characteristics of community that grew out of the theoretical model, from the analysis of interactions among participants, from a content analysis of transcripts of communication among community participants, and from interviews and focus groups. We were also able to generate operational definitions of each of these characteristics (see Table 4). While the process to this point was disciplined at each step, the intention was to draw out characteristics that might be important in formal virtual learning communities; the purpose was not to validate or compare the relative significance of any of the characteristics. The next step in the process was to try to determine the relative importance of the characteristics that were drawn from these various sources. We had a good sense of what many of the characteristics were that comprised the communities we observed, but we did not have any reliable information about which characteristics were important, which were trivial, and which might be more important than others.

To address this question, we developed a paired-comparison treatment that asked participants to compare each characteristic of a VLC to every other characteristic and choose the characteristic they believed was more important to the community (see

Table 4. Characteristics of formal virtual learning communities and operational definitions drawn from models, interaction analysis, content analysis, and interviews

Characteristic	Operational Definition
Awareness	Knowledge of people, tasks, environment—or some combination of these.
Social Protocols	Rules of engagement, acceptable and unacceptable ways of behaving in a community.
Historicity	Communities develop their own history and culture.
Identity	The boundaries of the community—its identity or recognized focus.
Mutuality	Interdependence and reciprocity. Participants construct purposes, intentions, and the types of interaction.
Plurality	"Intermediate associations" such as families, churches, and other peripheral groups—other communities that individuals use to enrich the new community.
Autonomy	Individuals have the capacity and authority to conduct discourse freely, or withdraw from discourse without penalty.
Participation	Social participation in the community, especially participation that sustains the community.
Trust	The level of certainty or confidence that one community member uses to assess the action of another member of the community.
Future	The sense that the community is moving in a direction, typically toward the future.
Technology	The role played by technology to facilitate or inhibit the growth of community.
Learning	Formal or informal, yet purposeful, learning in the community.
Reflection	Situating previous experiences or postings in current discussions, or grounding current discussions in previous events.
Intensity	Active engagement, open discourse, and a sense of importance or urgency in discussion, critique, and argumentation.

Copyright © 2007, Idea Group Inc. Copying or distributing in print or electronic forms without written permission of Idea Group Inc. is prohibited.

Figure 3. Example of screen from paired-comparison treatment

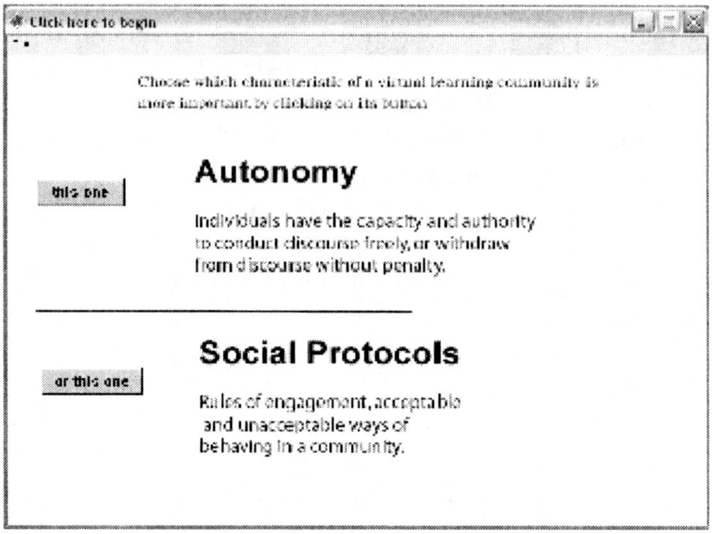

Table 5. Thurstone Scale rankings and scale points for each of the 14 VLC characteristics

Characteristic	Thurstone Scale Ranking	Thurstone Scale Point
Trust	1	**0.7341**
Learning	2	**0.5806**
Participation	3	**0.3182**
Mutuality	4	**0.2671**
Intensity	5	**0.2425**
Social Protocols	6	**0.1852**
Reflection	7	**0.1523**
Autonomy	8	**0.0155**
Awareness	9	**-0.0785**
Identity	10	**-0.1939**
Future	11	**-0.2474**
Technology	12	**-0.5033**

Figure 4. Graphic interval representation of the Thurstone Scale points for the 14 VLC characteristics

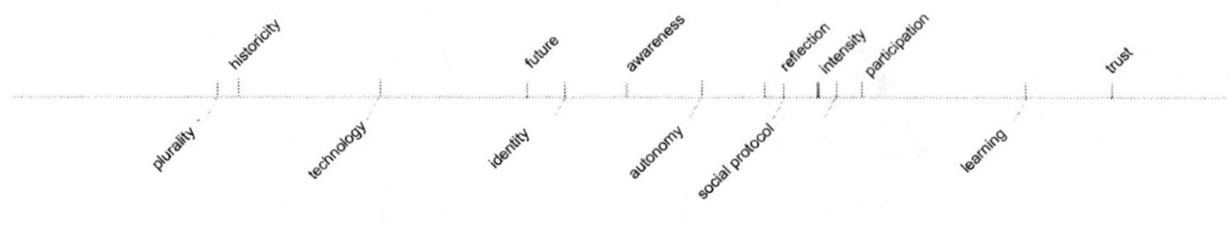

Copyright © 2007, Idea Group Inc. Copying or distributing in print or electronic forms without written permission of Idea Group Inc. is prohibited.

Figure 3). Twenty-three students who had completed their coursework volunteered to participate in the study. The 14 characteristics were compared against each other, resulting in 91 paired-comparisons in the treatment. Authorware Professional™ was used to develop the treatment, and the treatment was administered on Windows-based PC workstations. In the design of the treatment, care was taken to avoid response bias and contamination from fatigue by presenting each pair in random order and by alternating the upper-lower orientation of each characteristic in relation to the characteristic against which it was being compared. After completing the comparisons, participants were asked to describe how they made their decisions generally, and if there were factors that influenced their decisions.

The raw data collected were used to construct a Thurstone Scale (see Table 5 and Figure 4). The Thurstone Scale is a common example of a differential scale, using paired comparisons to derive relative preferences among a set of items. Thurstone (1927) postulated that for each of the items being compared and among all subjects, a preference will exist, and that for each item the preference will be distributed normally around that item's most frequent or modal response. A person's preference for each item vs. every other item is obtained, and the more people that select one item of a pair over the other item, the greater the preference for, or perceived importance of, that item, and thus the greater its scale weight. Thurstone's Law of Comparative Judgment circumvents potential ceiling effect problems by forcing individuals to rank items two at a time rather than all at once (Manitoba Centre for Health Policy, 2005).

Thurstone's Law of Comparative Judgment is able to transform rank order comparative judgments by individuals in a group to a single-group-composite interval scale. Binary or ordinal scale data can be turned into interval scale data, which can illustrate the relative distances between the objects that have been judged by participants. There are important practical reasons to employ the method. For one thing, the Thurstone scaling method does not assume that each stimulus always evokes the same discrimination for different individuals or even for the same individual at different times. Also, when comparing lists of complex characteristics, it is comparatively more accurate to ask individuals to rank order items than to ask for interval or ratio measures. In many cases, such as our study, the judgment we wish to solicit from an individual is a ranking (i.e., ordinal scale measurement) of individual items. A person can decide that one particular characteristic is more important than another one; however, it is much more difficult to consistently estimate how much more important a characteristic is from among a group of characteristics. A scaling method such as Thurstone's Law of Comparative Judgment can transform individual ranking judgments and produce an interval scale rather than a rank-ordered scale, which allows the individuals to detect the extent to which certain characteristics are clearly distinct from other characteristics, and which are proximal more reliably. Merely providing an averaging of the ranking scale does not contribute this added insight to the group as a whole (Li, Cheng, Wang, Hiltz, & Turoff, 2001).

Copyright © 2007, Idea Group Inc. Copying or distributing in print or electronic forms without written permission of Idea Group Inc. is prohibited.

So, in essence, Thurstone scaling graphically represents groups of comparative judgments linearly. It allows the researcher to convert paired comparisons into a graphical representation of distance between variables under study. In this study, each VLC characteristic was compared with the others in sequence, following procedures outlined by Misanchuk (1988). The data were then converted into a line drawing that depicted differences between elements along a line. Greater differences were shown spatially as larger distances between points on the line.

The main advantage of Thurstone scaling is that it provides a method for representing distances meaningfully. Graphically, it is easy to describe the relative positions of the combined choices (Schwier & Misanchuk, 1997). At the same time Thurstone scaling is limited to description, as there are no known methods for testing whether points along the line are significantly different from each other statistically. One can describe points along the line as different from each other descriptively, but when points cluster, it is not reasonable to speak of them as significantly different from each other statistically.

As a result of this analysis, we were able to obtain measures that could be used to understand the association and interplay of community characteristics in a VLC, and we could also use the Thurstone Scale points to assign weights to these characteristics when we attempted to construct a dynamic model of virtual learning communities. Reviewing the results, it is apparent that there are at least three clusters of characteristics. Trust and learning were considered by the participants to be the most important characteristics of a VLC. A large cluster of characteristics gathered around the mean scale point, and while they differed from each other, we treated them as a group because of their central position relative to the other points. Technology, historicity, and plurality were ascribed much lower status than the other characteristics, and one might argue as a result that they should be eliminated from the model entirely. A review of the comments provided by participants gives a qualified view however. For example, when discussing the relative importance of technology, this was a typical response:

"I also always chose Technology as my second choice because all of the other characteristics seemed more important in terms of building community. Yes the technology makes it possible but it is the vehicle...not the destination or goal."

In this case, it appears that technology was viewed primarily as a prerequisite condition for virtual communities to form. After reviewing comments, it was apparent that even those characteristics that were positioned at the low end of the Thurstone Scale still had a role to play in the construction of community, however marginal that influence might be.

We were also reluctant to eliminate characteristics at this point in the research because we are still gathering primary data from new groups. Our confidence in the

Copyright © 2007, Idea Group Inc. Copying or distributing in print or electronic forms without written permission of Idea Group Inc. is prohibited.

relative positions of these characteristics, and ultimately our judgments about their inclusion in a model of VLC, will grow as our analysis continues. At what point will we be satisfied that we have identified the important characteristics and measured their relative importance? Probably never, given that VLCs are dynamic environments that are also situated in particular learning contexts. But we will continue to gather data to develop and refine models, and our tools and the sophistication of our observations will mature over time too.

Modeling Community

A Bayesian Belief Network (BBN) is one of several techniques for building models. BBNs are graphs composed of nodes and directional arrows (Pearl, 1988). Nodes in BBNs represent variables, and the directed edges (arrows) between pairs of nodes indicate relationships between the variables. The nodes in a BBN are variables usually drawn as circles or ovals. The arrows between pairs of nodes that indicate relationships between the variables can be assigned different states, such as positive, null, or negative. A BBN is a mathematically rigorous way to model a complex environment, and it is flexible, able to mature as knowledge about the system grows, and computationally efficient (Druzdzel & Gaag, 2000; Rusell & Norvig, 1995).

In Bayesian statistics, the expression of prior beliefs about a given situation (before collecting any data) is required. This degree of belief is normally expressed in terms of a probability distribution, and then Baye's theorem is used to update the beliefs in light of the information provided by the data. BNs enable reasoning when there is uncertainty, and they combine the advantages of an intuitive visual representation with a sound mathematical basis in Bayesian probability. The use of a Bayesian network makes it possible to articulate experts' beliefs about dependencies between different variables, and naturally and consistently propagate the impact of the evidence on probabilities of uncertain outcomes.

The structure of a Bayesian network can also be viewed as a graphical, qualitative illustration of the interactions among a set of variables within a network. The interactions of the variables in a network model can be quantified to predict the consequences of observable behaviors in a model. Research suggests that BBN techniques have significant power to support the use of probabilistic inference to update and revise belief values (Pearl, 1998). They can readily permit qualitative inferences without the computational inefficiencies of traditional joint probability determinations (Niedermayer, 1998). The casual information encoded in BBN facilitates the analysis of actions, sequences of events, observations, consequences, and expected utility (Pearl, 1998).

Copyright © 2007, Idea Group Inc. Copying or distributing in print or electronic forms without written permission of Idea Group Inc. is prohibited.

Building the Bayesian Belief Network

The first step in creating a BBN is to identify the key variables that represent a domain (Druzdzel & Gaag, 2000; Rusell & Norvig, 1995). The variables used to build the network here are based upon the results of the Thurstone analysis described previously in this chapter. The goal of using the BBN is to obtain measures that can be used to understand the critical casual relationships among the characteristics of a VLC. The variables identified by the participants and their relative locations along the scale were assigned weights based on both the Thurstone value and qualitative reasoning. For instance, observation of the Thurstone Scale suggests that there are at least three clusters of characteristics, where trust and learning were considered by the participants to be the most important characteristics of a VLC (see Table 4 for the variables used to build the BBN).

The second step is to map out the variables into some structure based on logical and coherent qualitative reasoning. During the qualitative reasoning, causal relationships among the variables are conjured, resulting in a cyclical graph. For instance, in virtual learning communities, participation and learning are essentially mediated by technology (i.e., it is unimaginable to be able to learn online without any mediation of technology), and therefore, technology is assigned a strong positive (S+) influence on the level of participation. Similarly, participation can influence awareness in a strong and positive manner, which in turn can lead to the development of trusting relationships. Since awareness can contribute to both trust and distrust, the link influence is medium (M+). Furthermore, technology can influence awareness in a positive and strong manner (S+). For example, imagine a learning environment in which each individual has a profile (electronic portfolio) and the information is made available to others in the community; this can create sense of awareness about who is who, or who knows what, in that community. Similarly, technology may influence intensity in a weak positive manner (W+), since availability of technology alone does not guarantee that people will be actively engaged in discussions. Extending this type of qualitative reasoning resulted in the BBN shown in Figure 5. In the model, those nodes that contribute to higher nodes align themselves in "child" to "parent" relationships, where parent nodes are super-ordinate to child nodes. For example, trust is the child of mutuality, awareness, and intensity, which are in turn children of participation and technology (see Figure 5).

The third step in building the BBN involves assigning initial probabilities to the network. In general, BBN initial probabilities can be obtained from domain experts, secondary statistics, or they can be taken from observations and subjective intuition. It is also possible that initial probabilities can be learned from raw data. In addition to learning prior probabilities, it is sometimes necessary to examine the structure of the network. In our case, the initial probabilities were assigned by examining the distances between the variables of virtual learning communities along the Thurstone

Copyright © 2007, Idea Group Inc. Copying or distributing in print or electronic forms without written permission of Idea Group Inc. is prohibited.

Figure 5. BBN representation of relationships among virtual learning community variables

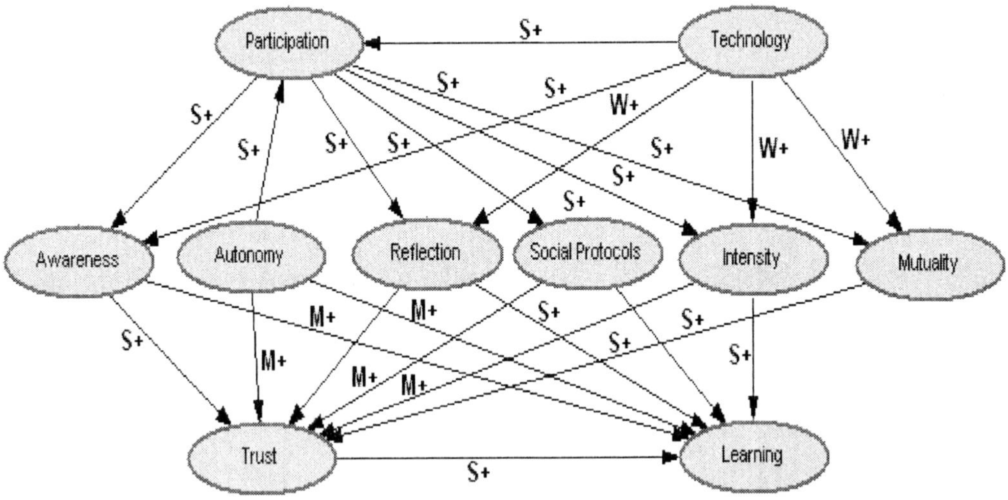

Scale. This approach enables us to cluster those variables that were closely aligned on the Thurstone Scale. We have also introduced the degree of influence among the variables to qualitatively describe relationships among the variables.

Generating the Conditional Probability Table

The initial conditional probabilities were also generated by examining qualitative descriptions of the influence between two or more variables and the strength of their relationships in the model (Daniel, Zapata-Revera, & McCalla, 2003; Daniel, McCalla, & Schwier, 2005). Each probability describes the strength of relationship. For instance, various degrees of influence among variables are represented by the letters S (strong), M (medium), and W (weak). The signs + and - represent positive and negative relationships. The probability values were obtained by adding weights to the values of the variables depending on the number of parents and the strength of the relationship between particular parents and children. For example, if there are positive relationships between two variables, the weights associated with each degree of influence are determined by establishing a threshold value associated with each degree of influence. The threshold values correspond to the highest probability value that a child could reach under a certain degree of influence from its parents; that is, assuming that participation and technology have positive and strong relationships with Awareness, evidence of good technology and high participation will result in a conditional probability value of 0.98 (i.e., Awareness=Exist). This value

Copyright © 2007, Idea Group Inc. Copying or distributing in print or electronic forms without written permission of Idea Group Inc. is prohibited.

Table 6. Threshold values and weights with two parents

Degree of Influence	Thresholds	Weights
Strong	1-α = 1 - 0.02 = 0.98	(0.98-0.5) / 2 = 0.48 / 2 = 0.24
Medium	0.8	(0.8-0.5) / 2 =0.3 / 2 = 0.15
Weak	0.6	(0.6-0.5) / 2 =0.1 / 2 = 0.05

Table 7. Example of a conditional probability table for two parents with strong, positive relationships

Participation	High		Low	
Technology	Good	Bad	Good	Bad
Awareness Exists	0.98	0.74	0.74	0.5
Awareness Does Not Exist	0.02	0.26	0.26	0.5

is obtained by subtracting a base value (1/number of parents—0.5 in this case with two parents) from the threshold value associated to the degree of influence (i.e., threshold value for strong = 0.98) and dividing the result by the number of parents (i.e., (0.98 - 0.5)/2 = 0.24). Table 6 lists threshold values and weights used in this example. The value $\alpha = 0.02$ leaves some room for uncertainty when considering evidence coming from positive and strong relationships.

This assumes that participation and technology have positive strong relationships with awareness, and there is evidence of positive participation and technology in a particular community. Given these assumptions, weights will be added to the conditional probability table of awareness every time participation = high or technology = good. For example, the conditional probability value associated with awareness given that there is evidence of participation = high, and technology = good is 0.98. This value is obtained by adding to the base value the weights associated with participation and technology (0.24 each). Table 7 shows a complete conditional probability table for this example.

The calculation of the various states of the relationships among the three variables (awareness, participation, and technology) and their corresponding values used in Table 7 are given:

P (Awareness= Exist | Participation = High & Technology = Good) = 0.5 + 0.24 + 0.24 = 0.98

P (Awareness= DoesNotExist| Participation = High & Technology = Good) = 1 - 0.98 = 0.02

Copyright © 2007, Idea Group Inc. Copying or distributing in print or electronic forms without written permission of Idea Group Inc. is prohibited.

P (Awareness= DoesNotExist | Participation = High & Technology = Bad) = 1 - 0.74 = 0.26

P (Awareness= Exist| Participation = Low & Technology = Good) = 0.5 + 0.24 = 0.74

P (Awareness= DoesNotExist | Participation = Low & Technology = Good) = 1 - 0.74 =0.26

Querying the Network

Querying a BBN refers to the process of updating the conditional probability table and making inferences based on new evidence. One way of updating a BBN is to develop a detailed number of scenarios that can be used to query the model. A scenario refers to a written synopsis of inferences drawn from observed phenomenon or empirical data. Further, updating a BBN is an attempt to understand the statistical significance of various relationships among variables in a network. Based on the results of Thurstone scaling, we have observed a large cluster of variables around the mean scale point. Although they can be treated as a group because of their central position relative to the other points, it is difficult to tell their individual relative importance to others in the same cluster or in other clusters in the VLC model. We build simple scenarios based on the results of Thurstone analysis to infer relative importance of individual variables in the network, and we can refer to the relative distances between variables to provide a quantitative measure of the differences.

In one case, for example, we were interested in observing changes in the state of the variable learning as a result of changes in the state of the variable awareness. Since learning is a grandchild of awareness, and awareness is a parent of trust, and trust is a parent of learning, any changes in the value of awareness will naturally propagate to learning. Awareness is given a binary state ("exist" with a value 0.98 or "does not exist" with a value of 0.02). Imagine a scenario in a VLC where students are not aware of each other. This would mean the value of awareness is set at "does not exist" and assigned a probability of 0.02. Say we are interested in determining what effects low probability of awareness can have on learning. Querying the model with this information resulted in a high (learning is high) value of learning dropping to 0.14, and a low value of learning (learning is low) increasing to 0.85. Propagating backwards, it can be observed that the parents of awareness assume certain values. For instance, awareness has three parents—no autonomy, low participation, and bad technology.

Querying the BBN in this way offers a disciplined method of examining the cumulative effect of making changes anywhere in the network and also for speculating about how any particular change can alter the values of related variables. The BBN is still, at its core, a tool for speculation, but over time and as data are added to inform the variables and their interrelationships, the network can be "tuned" to provide robust and precise ways to make decisions about the design and operation of formal learning communities.

Copyright © 2007, Idea Group Inc. Copying or distributing in print or electronic forms without written permission of Idea Group Inc. is prohibited.

Summary

The central point of this chapter is that we need to use a variety of methods to analyze anything as complex as an online learning community. The methods we propose flow from definition to analysis to prediction, so they have some intuitive and practical appeal. But we must recognize that we are at the beginning of learning about how to understand online learning communities as organisms, and so we make no claims that these methods represent a definitive set of tools for that job.

But regardless of the specific tools used to determine whether virtual communities exist, our experience has led us to a few key principles or ideas. First, considering the full cycle from definition to modeling is important, much of the research to date looks closely at a few variables in communities and much of the literature is speculative. We think that there is a need to isolate features of communities, try to determine their relative importance, and then build models that can be used to test inferences in new environments and inform design science in distance learning. However, we acknowledge that this type of cyclical investigation is difficult, labor intensive, and time consuming. The strategies we describe in this chapter are drawn from an array of options available to researchers and designers, and we use them more to illustrate the process than to advocate for any particular tools. We did find that a combination of descriptive, qualitative, experimental, and inferential approaches provided us with the kind of precision and insight we wanted. Along the way, we have developed a hunger for replication and baseline data. We noticed that many very useful approaches, such as the Sense of Community Index and the TAT, would benefit from having many researchers use them to develop a body of comparative data in the literature over time. In addition, the Bayesian Belief Network approach introduced in this chapter can enable researchers to isolate the most important variables of virtual learning communities, given N-Case scenarios. This in turn will enable them to develop robust procedures and tools to enhance our understanding of virtual learning communities and support their development. But perhaps the most important thing we can do at this stage of development is to open a conversation about these important issues, and look for creative and imaginative answers.

Acknowledgments

The authors acknowledge and thank Heather Ross for her transcript analysis and associated contributions to the ideas offered in this chapter. This research is funded by a grant from the Social Sciences and Humanities Research Council of Canada.

Copyright © 2007, Idea Group Inc. Copying or distributing in print or electronic forms without written permission of Idea Group Inc. is prohibited.

References

Chavis, D.M. (n.d.). *The sense of community index.* Retrieved August 31, 2005, from http://www.capablecommunity.com/pubs/SCIndex.PDF

Chavis, D. M. et al. (1986). Sense of community through Brunswick's lens: A first look. *Journal of Community Psychology, 14*(1), 24-40.

Chavis, D. M., & Wandersman A. (1990). Sense of community in the urban environment. A catalyst for participation and community development. *American Journal of Community Psychology, 18,* 55-81.

Chipuer, H. M., & Pretty, G. M. H. (1999). A review of the sense of community index. *Journal of Community Psychology, 27,* 246-658.

Daniel, B. K., McCalla, G. I., & Schwier, R. A. (2005, July 18-22). Data mining and modeling social capital in virtual learning communities. *Proceedings of the 12th International Conference on Artificial Intelligence in Education* (pp. 200-208), Amsterdam.

Daniel, B. K., Schwier, R. A., & McCalla, G. I. (2003). Social capital in virtual learning communities and distributed communities of practice. *Canadian Journal of Learning and Technology, 29*(3), 113-139.

Daniel, B. K., Schwier, R. A., & Ross, H. (2005). Intentional and incidental discourse variables in a virtual learning community. *Proceedings of E-Learn 2005,* Vancouver, British Columbia.

Daniel, B. K., Zapata-Rivera, D. J., & McCalla, G. I. (2003). A Bayesian computational model of social capital in virtual communities. In M. Huysman, E. Wenger, & V. Wulf (Eds.), *Communities and technologies* (pp.287-305). London: Kluwer.

Druzdzel, M. J., & Gaag, L. C (2000). Building probabilistic networks: "Where do the numbers come from?" Guest editor's introduction. *Data Engineering, 12*(4), 481-486.

Dykes, M. E., & Schwier, R. A. (2003). Content and community redux: Instructor and student interpretations of online communication in a graduate seminar. *Canadian Journal of Learning and Technology, 29*(2), 79-99.

Fahy, P. J., Crawford, G., & Ally, M. (2001). Patterns of interaction in a computer conference transcript. *International Review of Research in Open and Distance Learning, 2*(1). Retrieved August 28, 2005, from http://www.irrodl.org/content/v2.1/fahy.html

Fahy, P. J., Crawford, G., Ally, M., Cookson, P., Keller, V., & Prosser, F. (2000). The development of testing of a tool for computer-mediated conferencing transcripts. *Alberta Journal of Educational Research, 46*(1), 85-88.

Copyright © 2007, Idea Group Inc. Copying or distributing in print or electronic forms without written permission of Idea Group Inc. is prohibited.

Heckerman, D., Geiger, D., & Chickering, D. (1995). Learning Bayesian networks: The combination of knowledge and statistical data. *Machine Learning, 20,* 197-243.

Jeong, A. (2004). Message content on growth patterns of discussion threads in computer-supported collaborative argumentation. *Journal of Distance Education, 19*(1), 36-53.

Lave, J., & Wenger, E. (1991). *Situated learning: Legitimate peripheral participation.* New York: Cambridge University.

Li, Z., Cheng, K. E., Wang, Y., Hiltz, S. R., & Turoff, M. (2001). Thurstone's Law of Comparative Judgment for group support. *Proceedings of the 7th Americas Conference on Information Systems.* Retrieved August 1, 2005, from http://web.njit.edu/~zxl8078/Publication/BB004.PDF

Manitoba Center for Health Policy. (2005). *The Thurstone manual.* Retrieved August 31, 2005, from http://www.umanitoba.ca/centres/mchp/concept/thurstone/background.shtml

Misanchuk, E. R. (1988). Step-by-step procedure for constructing a Thurstone Scale. *Proceedings of the Annual Management Program of the Canadian Association for University Continuing Education,* Halifax, Nova Scotia.

Murphy, E., & Coleman, E. (2004). Graduate students' experiences of challenges in online asynchronous discussions. *Canadian Journal of Learning and Technology, 30*(2), 29-46.

Niedermayer, D. (1998). *An introduction to Bayesian Networks and their contemporary applications.* Retrieved May 6, 2004, from http://www.niedermayer.ca/papers/bayesian/bayes.html

Obst, P. L., & White, K. M. (2004). Revisiting the sense of community index: A confirmatory factor analysis. *Journal of Community Psychology, 32*(6), 691-705.

Paloff, R. M., & Pratt, K. (1999). *Building learning communities in cyberspace: Effective strategies for the online classroom.* San Francisco: Jossey-Bass.

Pearl, J. (1988). *Probabilistic reasoning in intelligent systems: Networks of plausible inference.* San Mateo, CA: Morgan Kaufmann.

Preece, J. (2000). *Online communities: Designing usability and supporting sociability.* New York: John Wiley & Sons.

Preece, J. (2002). Supporting community and building social capital. *Communications of the ACM, 45*(4), 37-39.

Pretty, G. H. 1990. Relating psychological sense of community to social climate characteristics. *Journal of Community Psychology, 18,* 60-65.

Copyright © 2007, Idea Group Inc. Copying or distributing in print or electronic forms without written permission of Idea Group Inc. is prohibited.

Rourke, L., Anderson, T., Garrison, D. R., & Archer, W. (2001). Methodological issues in the content analysis of computer conference transcripts. *International Journal of Artificial Intelligence in Education, 12,* 8-22.

Rovai, A. P., & Jordan, H. M. (2004, August). Blended learning and sense of community: A comparative analysis with traditional and fully online graduate courses. *International Review of Research in Open and Distance Learning.* Retrieved April 26, 2005, from http://www.irrodl.org/content/v5.2/rovai-jordan.html

Russell, S., & Norvig, P. (1995). *Solution manual for artificial intelligence: A modern approach.* Englewood Cliffs, NJ: Prentice-Hall.

Schwier, R. A. (2001). Catalysts, emphases and elements of virtual learning communities: Implications for research and practice. *The Quarterly Review of Distance Education, 2*(1), 5-18.

Strauss, A., & Corbin, J. (Eds.). (1997). *Grounded theory in practice.* Thousand Oaks, CA: Sage.

Strauss, A., & Corbin, J. (1998). *Basics of qualitative research: Techniques and procedures for developing grounded theory* (2nd ed.). Thousand Oaks, CA: Sage.

Thurstone, L. L. (1927). A law of comparative judgment. *Psychological Review, 34,* 273-286.

Vygotsky, L. S. (1978). *Mind in society: The development of higher psychological processes.* Cambridge, MA: Harvard University Press.

Wenger, E. (1998). *Communities of practice: Learning, meaning, and identity.* Cambridge, UK: Cambridge University Press.

Copyright © 2007, Idea Group Inc. Copying or distributing in print or electronic forms without written permission of Idea Group Inc. is prohibited.

Chapter III

User-Centered Design Principles for Online Learning Communities: A Sociotechnical Approach for the Design of a Distributed Community of Practice

Ben K. Daniel, University of Saskatchewan, Canada

David O'Brien, University of Saskatchewan, Canada

Asit Sarkar, University of Saskatchewan, Canada

Abstract

This chapter examines current research on online learning communities (OLCs), with the aim of identifying user-centered design (UCD) principles critical to the emergence and sustainability of distributed communities of practice (DCoPs), a kind of OLC. This research synthesis is motivated by the authors' involvement in constructing a DCoP dedicated to improving awareness, research, and sharing data and knowledge in the field of governance and international development. It argues that the sociotechnical research program offers useable insights on questions of constructability. Its attention in particular to participatory design and human-computer interaction are germane to designing user-centered online learning communities.

Copyright © 2007, Idea Group Inc. Copying or distributing in print or electronic forms without written permission of Idea Group Inc. is prohibited.

Aside from these insights, research has yet to probe in any systematic fashion the factors affecting the performance and sustainability of DCoP. The chapter concludes with a discussion of UCD principles for online learning community to support the construction and deployment of online learning communities.

Introduction

Increasingly, distributed communities of practice (DCoPs) are attracting attention for their potential to enhance learning, to facilitate information exchange, and to stimulate knowledge creation across cultural, geographical, and organizational boundaries. Research shows the utility of DCoP on their members is positive (Daniel, Sarkar, & O'Brien, 2004a; Daniel, Poon, & Sarkar, 2005; Schwier & Daniel, Chapter II, this volume). Their allure aside, experience indicates that they may not emerge or flourish even in the presence of demand from users. In fact the process of constructing DCoP is not well understood, and factors influencing sustainability merit further research attention.

This chapter introduces the authors' involvement in the development of a DCoP. The DCoP in question is the Governance Knowledge Network (GKN). This project began in 2001 with the aim of assessing the interest of academics and practitioners in Canada to develop an online learning community (OLC) for systematizing the exchange of information at the intersection of governance and international development (Daniel et al., 2004a). The surveys of key Canadian stakeholders in the project indicated considerable data existed, and recommended the proposed GKN to: actively engage in dissemination and archiving of data not widely accessible in the public sphere, profile community members, promote social network building and collaboration, and inform members of current events and opportunities.

Following the identification of the demand and interest, the second stage of our research involved the development of a GKN prototype. In this unchartered course, we were guided by enabling technology and other DCoP models (World Bank, UNDP).[1] We also turned to research to inform our efforts on how to effectively sustain the project. Our synthesis of research in the area identified promising insights from studies we refer to as the sociotechnical approach. As applied to DCoP, the sociotechnical approach aims at understanding people's interaction with technology and the ensuing communication, feedback, and control mechanisms necessary for people to take ownership of the design and implementation process.

This chapter focuses on this interaction, as it is germane to the development and sustainability of the GKN, in particular, and DCoP more generally. The chapter is divided into the following sections. The next section outlines relevant research on DCoPs and the sociotechnical approach. We next provide an overview of the GKN

Copyright © 2007, Idea Group Inc. Copying or distributing in print or electronic forms without written permission of Idea Group Inc. is prohibited.

OLC project and present key results from the research that informed the design of the GKN. A discussion of various human and technology elements we consider critical to the initiation, development, growth, and sustainability of the GKN follows, and in the next section, we revisit the key human and technology design issues. Finally, we conclude the chapter and present UCD principles for OLCs drawn from the sociotechnical approach.

Related Work

Daniel, Schwier, and McCalla (2003b) observe that online learning communities have attracted diverse disciplinary interest, but that it is possible to identify two dominant perspectives—technological determinism and social constructivism. The basic tenet of the technology determinism research is that technology shapes cultural values, social structure, and knowledge. In technology-related fields, such as computer science and information systems, significant attention has been given to understanding technological developments and how these changes influence social structures.

The social constructivism perspective, on the other hand, posits that knowledge and world views are created through social interaction. Social constructivism theories have inspired research on knowledge construction within communities of practice. Lave and Wenger (1991) assert that a society's practical knowledge is situated in relations among practitioners, their practice, and the social organization and political economy of communities of practice. For this reason, learning should involve such knowledge and practice (Lave & Wenger, 1991). Between these heuristic poles there are cross-disciplinary perspectives, of which it is possible to further discern them into four subcategories:

1. **Applied Technology Perspective:** Much of the work on OLC by computer scientists and information systems researchers is driven by a desire to understand and improve computational approaches. Studies in computer science, information systems, and educational technologies are mainly aimed at understanding technology to develop tools and systems that support learning environments (Daniel, Zapata-Rivera, & McCalla, 2003a; Preece, 2002; Schwier, 2001). Findings have been utilized for building technologies that support OLC. For instance, a growing number of developers and researchers in industry and universities are investigating ways to create software packages that add new functionality to systems supporting interaction, collaboration, and leaning in online learning communities (Kim, 2000; McCalla, 2000; Preece, 2000; Resnick, 2002; Schraefel, Ho, Milton, & Chignell, 2000).

Copyright © 2007, Idea Group Inc. Copying or distributing in print or electronic forms without written permission of Idea Group Inc. is prohibited.

2. **Ethno-Narrative Perspective:** Ethno-narrative research is devoted to revealing personal experiences of being a member of an OLC. Most studies adopt a narrative approach, similar to participant observation inquiry used in anthropology. Researchers in this tradition have undertaken comparative analysis of both online learning and temporal communities (Schwier, 2001). Critics have disparaged ethno-narrative studies on the grounds that findings tend to be anecdotal and lack external validity; their conclusions are tentative and limited to the groups under study (cf. Downes, 2001; Rhiengold, 1993, 1999, 2002). Stolterman, Croon, and Argren (2000) argue that although the generalization and validity of such studies is limited, understanding personal perceptions of learning in OLC is essential. It is difficult to imagine how one can improve the learning environment of OLC without the subjective feedback of the learners.
3. **Cultural Studies Perspective:** Cultural studies have contributed enormously to understanding online learning communities. For instance, research by Brook and Boal (1995), Dery (1994), and Hershman and Leason (1996) investigate the relationship between the virtual and the physical, and they fall within the context of cultural interpretation research. Approaches employed in this category include experimental studies, with an emphasis on cultural events in online environments. The background disciplines of this group are diverse, including social psychology, philosophy, psychology, and fine arts.
4. **Sociotechnical Perspective:** The sociotechnical research tradition argues for a balanced approach to integrating cognitive and technical dimensions of OLC. This approach emerged from the extension of sociology, anthropology, and psychology to the study of HCI. Subsequently this research informed disciplines, including computer science and information systems (Heylighten, 1999). Research in sociotechnical areas addresses issues such as:
    - **User-Centered Design:** Moving the focus of interest to learners and away from technology in the design of online learning (Norman, 1996).
    - **Contextual Enquiry:** Understanding the user's context and its potential influence on the use of technology (Preece, 2000).
    - **Sociability:** Appreciating the importance of community policies for interactions, governance, and social protocols in OLC (Preece, 2000).
    - **Participatory Design:** Involving user participation in the design of OLC and the effects on learning outcomes (Mumford, 1987; Nguyen-Ngoc, Rekik, & Gillet, Chapter XIII, this volume).
    - **Direct-Manipulation:** Creating tools for users to create their online learning environment and exploring the effects of functional options such as menu-driven and graphical interfaces (Shneiderman, 1998).

Copyright © 2007, Idea Group Inc. Copying or distributing in print or electronic forms without written permission of Idea Group Inc. is prohibited.

Common to this growing body of research issues is the need for the interplay of human and technology factors to guide the design, development, deployment, and evaluation of online learning communities.

Formal and Informal Online Learning Communities

There are numerous computational tools that support social learning across time and place (Laghos & Zaphiris, Chapter XI, this volume). New tools and patterns of communication have enabled social engagement, information, and knowledge sharing within social systems now referred to as OLC. Unlike a temporal community that resides in a fixed locale and whose members often know each other well enough to carry effective interactions, OLCs exist in cyberspace and may or may not be aware of each other (Daniel, Schwier, & McCalla, 2003). The character of an OLC is influenced by structural features, which may include: community size, duration of interaction and anticipated lifespan, location or distribution of the community, the homogeneity/heterogeneity of members, and breadth or narrowness of subject area. Variation of these features gives rise to diverse OLCs.

In Table 1, we simplify this diversity by distinguishing between formal and informal online learning communities. Formal online learning communities have explicit

Table 1. Features of online learning communities and distributed communities of practice (adapted from Daniel et al., 2003b)

Formal: Online Learning Communities (OLCs)	**Informal: Distributed Communities of Practice (DCoPs)**
• Membership is explicit and identities are generally known	• Membership may or may not be made explicit
• Participation is often required	• Participation is mainly voluntary
• High degree of individual awareness (who is who, who is where)	• Low degree of individual awareness
• Explicit set of social protocols for interaction	• Implicit and implied set of social protocols for interactions
• Formal learning goals	• Informal learning goals
• Possibly diverse backgrounds	• Common subject matter
• Low shared understanding of domain	• High shared understanding of domain
• Loose sense of identity	• Strong sense of identity
• Strict distribution of responsibilities	• No formal distribution of responsibilities
• Easily disbanded once established	• Less easily disbanded once established
• Low level of trust	• Reasonable level of trust
• Lifespan determined by extent in which goals are achieved	• Lifespan determined by the instrumental/expressive value the community provides to its members
• Pre-planned enterprise and fixed goals	• A joint enterprise as understood and continually renegotiated by its members

Copyright © 2007, Idea Group Inc. Copying or distributing in print or electronic forms without written permission of Idea Group Inc. is prohibited.

learning goals and evaluation criteria. Examples would include courses/programs offered by education institutions or companies (McCalla, 2000; Schwier, 2001). In contrast, informal OLCs achieve learning outcomes through social learning. Examples would include distributed communities of practice (Daniel, O'Brien, & Sarkar 2004b). A unique feature of DCoPs is the absence of a teacher or instructor; rather, in a DCoP, the learners are also teachers, as members collectively determine the content and support each other throughout the learning process. Further differences are contrasted in Table 1.

A growing body of research identifies the contribution of DCoPs to facilitating information exchange and knowledge creation, thereby enriching the work of the collective (Brown & Duguid, 1991; Hildreth, Kimble, & Wright, 1998; Lesser & Prusak, 2000). These positive outcomes have caught the interest of scholars and knowledge managers. And yet, there is little comparative research on the correlates of DCoP performance or sustainability. We find this surprising, given the fact that OLCs emerged and proliferated with the advent of the Internet and then World Wide Web over a decade ago. The case-study foundations for comparative research are certainly present, however (Kalaitzakis, Dafoulas, & Macaulay, 2003; Hartnell-Young, McGuinness, & Cuttance, Chapter XII, this volume).

Germane to the topic of DCoP emergence and sustainability is the question of "constructability". Can the DCoP features listed in Table 1 be built, or have DCoPs simply migrated from the temporal to the online world? If we return to the literature review briefly touched on earlier, perhaps not surprisingly we would find a different answer to this question depending on the literature consulted. For example, the sociology and cultural studies literature tends to be skeptical of the view that DCoPs can be constructed (Kollock & Smith, 1996). By contrast, the computer science and information systems research, on the whole, seem more optimistic that robust DCoPs can be constructed (Preece, 2000; Daniel et al., 2003b; McCalla, 2000).

Further, informed by user-centered design principles, Preece formulated the community-centered development (CCD) framework to guide practitioners in the field (Preece, 2000). CCD provides a blueprint for building a DCoP. The framework encourages designers to: (1) assess members' interests, (2) identify community norms and appropriate technology, (3) involve stakeholders in prototype design and testing, (4) correct for poor usability, and (5) foster community network building and identity. Literature informed by this approach draws attention to the interaction between human and technology dimensions in setting the context for the development and sustainability of DCoPs.

CCD integrates a sociotechnical perspective and pays attention to HCI. On the human dimension side, attention has been drawn to understanding participants' goals, motivations, and perceptions of the learning environment (Daniel et al., 2003b); trust (Preece, 2002); and culture and learning needs (Daniel et al., 2004a). On the technology side, issues include privacy and security, usability, scalability, and authenticity (Daniel et al., 2003a; Preece, 2000).

Copyright © 2007, Idea Group Inc. Copying or distributing in print or electronic forms without written permission of Idea Group Inc. is prohibited.

The attention paid by a sociotechnical approach to HCI makes this framework particularly well suited to understanding the development and sustainability of DCoPs. In particular, the relevance of a sociotechnical approach to the evolution of the GKN project results from the attention to, and monitoring of, feedback loops to inform design and subsequent operation. For example, a sociotechnical approach cautions against a "build it and wait till they come" approach, and favors a co-design process that enables potential users to define their goals and areas of concerns. Joint construction can be regarded as fostering a shared identity and building networks necessary for the development of trust and effective ICT-mediated interaction.

Our Current Research

The GKN project was launched to address a perceived need to span geography and cross-organizational boundaries to enhance the scholarship on, and the practice of, governance and its role in advancing international development. The underlying challenge of praxis is not unique to this particular subject area. A consultation document issued by the Social Science and Humanities Research Council of Canada, for example, re-stated the networking challenge for advancing collaboration and innovation in the humanities and the social sciences in the following terms:

"Canada is a will against geography. It has a relatively small population, mostly scattered across more than 5,000 kilometres. It has no centres equivalent to Paris or London that naturally draw the best minds and greatest talents...to meet and interact on a regular basis. It does not have the numerous institutions...the Americans have to move people and ideas around. The net result...is that it is hard for people to know each other well, to trust each other and to work together over time and distance." (SSHRC, 2004)

With the emergence of ICTs, these obstacles to the exchange of information and collaboration were no longer permanent fixtures, though they have tended to endure.

Research Approach to the Design of User-Centered Online Learning Communities

We began our effort to overcome these obstacles through a participatory design approach (PDA). Key to PDA is an iterative process that seeks to address users' needs and promotes their involvement in project development (Schuler & Namioka, 1993).

Copyright © 2007, Idea Group Inc. Copying or distributing in print or electronic forms without written permission of Idea Group Inc. is prohibited.

A PDA, also known as a cooperative design approach, shares numerous similarities with Preece's (2000) community-centered approach.

The first step identified potential technologies capable of spanning geography and nurturing collaboration in a DCoP. Working on the human dimension, the project team created a profile of key stakeholders of 200 individuals from academia, government, and the non- and for-profit sectors. This list represented our target population for the survey of potential users' views on knowledge sharing in the field and interest in participating in the development of a DCoP.

The users' assessment was divided into three sections:

- an assessment of existing communication/networking mechanisms among potential community users,
- an assessment of the level of awareness of work undertaken by users and their affiliated organizations, and
- users' perceived value of a DCoP and what services would contribute to its potential value.

The goal of the users' assessment was to identify a target group's interests, perceived knowledge gaps, thematic content, and potential design models for the proposed GKN portal.

Following the analysis of the assessment, we identified design features that matched identified services together with appropriate technological requirements. We further contacted those who had completed the survey by telephone for a follow-up interview. The goal of the interview was to elicit further information regarding individuals' preferences for content and portal design. These steps also served the equally important objective of engaging potential community participants. In addition, we were able to gauge the reaction to the objectives of the GKN project and method of development and implementation. In addition, the telephone follow-up was an opportunity to initiate informal connections among various individuals working in the same area of research.

Results and Discussion

The target population for the survey was close to 200 organizations identified as working in the field of international development and governance. The response rate to the survey was 25%. Of those responding, 38% were university based, 23% were from provincial and federal government institutions, 30% were from non-

Copyright © 2007, Idea Group Inc. Copying or distributing in print or electronic forms without written permission of Idea Group Inc. is prohibited.

governmental and research organizations, and 9% were from private consulting firms. The respondents were distributed across Canada: 45% from western Canada, 53% from central Canada, and only 2% from the eastern part of the country. These figures reflect the geographical and sectoral diversity of our sample. Four out of five respondents were interested in applied research and technical assistance in this area, and a similar proportion were interested in influencing, contributing, or participating in the policy-making process. In addition, over 80% of respondents revealed that it is important for them to keep current on new developments in research and practice. Depending on their organizational affiliation, 50% to 80% of the respondents were interested in building collaborative partnerships for research and technical assistance

We also asked respondents what kind of research (applied vs. basic research) they were interested in, and if they were willing to share a range of potential outputs with potential GKN members. The majority (90%) responded that they were interested in applied research. They were also willing to contribute to, and participate in, policymaking processes. Participants identified the potential for the GKN to support their interest in keeping abreast of current research and practice in their fields. In terms of collaboration, a large number of the respondents viewed the GKN as a potential mechanism to facilitate information exchange and knowledge sharing among members. These findings were encouraging for, as Lave and Wenger (1991) suggest, CoP development when individuals realize the potential to benefit by sharing knowledge, insights, and experiences with each other, and enhance their practices and performances.

Survey data and follow-up interviews revealed low levels of awareness of contemporary research and practice in the field. At the same time informants commented on the specialized nature of their work and the limited number of organizations active in the field, they also reported that they were largely unaware of contemporary contributions to knowledge and action that their counterparts have made. Though establishing a benchmark of awareness is problematic, our results indicated a considerable lack of awareness among researchers and practitioners working on governance and international development in Canada. The majority of the participants described current knowledge on governance and development as fragmented, and said that there was a serious lack of awareness among people working on similar issues across provinces and between organizations. Similarly, it was observed that a considerable amount of publicly funded research, reports, and policy documents are not exchanged in a systematic manner. Respondents identified the potential of a GKN initiative to facilitate relations among public, private, non-governmental organizations and academia.

Though overall results revealed that information sharing and knowledge awareness were fragmented, there was a pattern to the responses. First, organizations within a sector were more knowledgeable of current work undertaken by their counterparts within the same sector than organizations in different sectors. Second, there were

Copyright © 2007, Idea Group Inc. Copying or distributing in print or electronic forms without written permission of Idea Group Inc. is prohibited.

marked differences in the level of awareness among counterparts within provinces compared to those operating outside their provinces. Although there was a high utilization of information and communication technologies as means to exchange information and data, they were not used systematically to break down the information barriers across organizations and across geographic jurisdictions.

Consistent with previous findings (Wenger, McDermott, & Snyder, 2000), geographic distance is considered an obstacle to knowledge sharing and utilization, even by those who are active users of ICTs. Moving from geographic to language barriers, several respondents underscored the importance of Canada's two official languages as a potential barrier. Language is critical to any community, since it is deemed as a part of a community identity: identity fosters collaboration and shared understanding within a community (McCalla, 2000). Turning to services, the following list identifies the top four stakeholder recommendations:

- Design a DCoP to facilitate information exchange and knowledge sharing.
- Provide a platform for sharing lessons, experiences, and best practices.
- Identify and nurture collaboration among government, research community, academia, NGOs, and development practitioners.
- Build linkages and partnerships with other international research communities to advance policy and practice.

Following the analysis of the data and feedback to respondents, we identified and profiled different technologies capable of supporting a DCoP that would perform to stakeholder expectations. Once the technological elements were identified, feedback was sought again from participants on the relevance of these models. This feedback was integrated in the prototype development of the GKN portal, which is currently in its formative stages. As the GKN project moved from a needs assessment to co-development with interested partners, human and technology interaction issues are gaining more importance.

At present, the GKN team has implemented a beta version of the system, while at the same time pursuing research into social and technical means to nurture and support an evolving community. Currently, we are experimenting with the use of blended strategies of face-to-face workshops and videoconferencing as additional avenues to encourage integration of human and technology factors. We are also developing an evaluation plan to assess the importance of the factors identified earlier to developing and sustaining the GKN project. In the following section, we describe the dimensions of HCI that have the potential to affect the viability and robustness of the GKN project.

Copyright © 2007, Idea Group Inc. Copying or distributing in print or electronic forms without written permission of Idea Group Inc. is prohibited.

Emergent Human and Technology Issues

There are multiple factors affecting the emergence and sustainability of a DCoP. Drawing from the GKN experience and insights from the sociotechnical approach outlined previously, we maintain that the following set of factors are important to HCI. Their influence and relative importance to the emergence and sustainability of a DCoP is introduced briefly in the following:

- **Didactics:** Learning is a shared experience, and by extension DCoPs are learning communities. Some OLCs have explicit learning goals (e.g., formal OLCs created around WebCT courses), while others have more implicit goals of sharing ideas, practices, and knowledge (e.g., DCoPs among corporate-oriented/professional communities). The technology must therefore enable learning, and perceptions of learning feedback would likely affect participation.
- **Trust:** Stakeholder surveys revealed that a key attraction of the proposed GKN online community would be the ability to share and retrieve archived data that was not widely available. The creation of this shared resource would depend on the willingness of these stakeholders to contribute their data. Their decision to share data would likely be influenced by their trust in others in the community as well as the environment in which they interact, for instance, questions such as: How would community members treat my data? Would my research be reproduced without my permission or quoted out of context? Creating generalized trust within a DCoP is difficult to "engineer", but likely a pre-requisite condition for the sharing and accumulation of data.
- **Privacy and Security:** Privacy and security tools address individual perceptions of safety in the community. In an environment where a person feels their privacy threatened, declining participation is anticipated. In this regard, computational tools that protect the privacy and security of individuals must be provided.
- **Scalability and Authenticity:** Scalability expresses the ability of a system to accommodate multiple users, and authenticity refers to the ability of a system to protect individuals in a community from outsiders. A DCoP must encourage entrants and their participation. This dimension is critical to the growth of the DCoP, whereas authenticity appears more important to sustainability. For example, an open system that does not protect users (e.g., from hackers) is susceptible to negative feedback and eventual decline of member participation.
- **Sociability:** Sociability relates to the protocols in use for communication and interaction in the community (Preece, 2000). These protocols may be imposed

Copyright © 2007, Idea Group Inc. Copying or distributing in print or electronic forms without written permission of Idea Group Inc. is prohibited.

in the first instance, but will likely shift in response to community dynamics. Sociability is of particular importance to "constructed" online communities that do not inherit protocols in use, as would temporal communities that have migrated to an ICT-mediated environment. This dimension is likely critical to the sustainability of a DCoP, as protocols in use will need to reflect members' preferences and practices. As new protocols emerge, technology must accommodate such changes.

- **Usability:** Our research indicated that interest in the GKN initiative centered on the promise of instrumental outcomes (e.g., access to information, new insights, and expanded contacts). Here, technology and human interaction are clearly linked, as relevant content is dependent on member input and its ease of retrieval is dependent on technology. User-centered interface design and continuous involvement of users are critical to both the emergence and sustainability of the GKN project.
- **Culture:** An explicit objective of the GKN project was to bridge organizational and linguistic boundaries. As organizational theory suggests that organizations inculcate and perpetuate cultures that may promote or discourage inter-organizational information sharing and/or collaboration. Once organizational or individual participation is present (a human, not a technical issue), we are uncertain of how technology may shape or accommodate different culture(s). Though others suggest that the viability of DCoPs depends on the development of a shared culture, our project is not sufficiently far advanced to comment on this hypothesis.
- **Awareness:** The ability of ICT tools to provide awareness among its members is predicted to have a powerful impact on members' interactions in the community. More specifically, awareness (e.g., awareness about who is who, and who does and knows what) can have a significant positive feedback that would in turn promote participation and contribute to sustainability.

These elements highlighted exert different forces on technology and human interaction. For reasons stated, we anticipate that each will have a bearing on the emergence and sustainability of the GKN initiative and DCoP more generally.

Discussion

The sociotechnical approach to the development of a DCoP suggests that human and technical factors are interlinked and they co-determine the emergence, evolution, growth, and sustainability of DCoPs. For practitioners involved in designing

Copyright © 2007, Idea Group Inc. Copying or distributing in print or electronic forms without written permission of Idea Group Inc. is prohibited.

or developing a DCoP, the variables outlined previously will likely provide a useful starting point for guiding implementation and identifying key relationships. For researchers, our preliminary exploration of these relationships creates a number of hypotheses for future investigation. As these relationships have a bearing on both practice and research, we intend to track these relationships through user evaluations and internal monitoring. We anticipate that these findings will work toward a framework for comparative research on factors affecting the emergence and sustainability of a DCoP.

By way of conclusion, we offer the following general UCD principles for designing and sustaining online learning communities based on the sociotechnical approach.

Design Principles

- Assessing needs of actual or potential users/learners.
- Identifying the gap between what is and what needs to be.
- Understanding users and usage contexts.
- Profiling learning styles.
- Benchmarking existing community models.
- Identifying existing technological tools.
- Maintaining an iterative design and development processes that keep users/learners informed.
- Providing appropriate tools to support and mediate learning, social interaction and facilitate a sense of togetherness.
- Exploring navigation tools to enable members to gather information about others and have access to community interactions traces of activities.

Didactic Principles

- Nurturing open and informal discourse as members interact to satisfy their own personal and community learning needs.
- Encouraging learners to become active users and contributors of content.
- Supporting different learning styles.
- Encouraging participation and discourse around central themes, ideas, or purposes.
- Guiding participants throughout the interaction process, and providing them with clear directions to attainment of learning goals.

Copyright © 2007, Idea Group Inc. Copying or distributing in print or electronic forms without written permission of Idea Group Inc. is prohibited.

- Understanding unique individual learning needs differences, and encouraging participants to construct their own meaning based on unique individual experiences.

Sociability Principles

- Establishing a clear set of social protocols for interactions.
- Encouraging informal interaction and an environment conducive to learner/user interaction so that members have opportunities to test the trustworthiness of others.
- Supporting shared objectives—which creates a rationale for belonging to the community.
- Maintaining relevant content and context for interaction throughout the lifespan of the community.
- Encouraging ongoing active dialogue among members.
- Maintaining different forms of awareness (who is who, who knows what, who knows who knows what, etc.) in the community to lubricate effective interaction.

Acknowledgments

The research reported in this chapter has been supported financially by the Policy Branch of the Canadian International Development Agency (CIDA), the Social Sciences and Humanities Research Council of Canada (SSHRC), and the International Center for Governance and Development at the University of Saskatchewan.

References

Brook, J., & Boal, I. A. (Eds.). (1995). *Resisting the virtual life: The culture and politics of information.* San Francisco: City Lights Books.

Brown, J. S., & Duguid, P. (1991). Organizational learning and communities of practice: Towards a unified view of working, learning and innovating. *Organization Science, 2,* 40-57.

Cothrel, J. (1999). Virtual community today. *The Journal of AGSI, 7,* 52-55.

Copyright © 2007, Idea Group Inc. Copying or distributing in print or electronic forms without written permission of Idea Group Inc. is prohibited.

Daniel, B. K., O'Brien, D., & Sarkar, A. (2004b, July 21-25). The cybernetics of distributed communities of practice. *Proceedings of the Joint International Conference on Education and Information Systems, Technologies and Applications* (EISTA 2004) *and the International Conference on Cybernetics and Information Technologies, Systems and Applications* (CITSA 2004), Orlando, FL.

Daniel, B. K., Poon, N., & Sarkar, A. (2005, June 27-July 2). Analysis of patterns of interactions in video-chat supported virtual communities to model social capital. *Proceedings of the World Conference on Educational Multimedia, Hypermedia and Telecommunications* (ED-MEDIA 2005), Montreal, Canada.

Daniel, B. K., Sarkar, A., & O'Brien, D. (2004a, June 21-26). A participatory design approach for a distributed community of practice on governance and international development. *Proceedings of the World Conference on Educational Multimedia, Hypermedia and Educational Telecommunications* (pp. 4606-4613), Lugano, Switzerland.

Daniel, B. K., Schwier, R. A., & McCalla, G. I. (2003b). Social capital in virtual learning communities and distributed communities of practice. *Canadian Journal of Learning and Technology, 29*(3), 113-139.

Daniel, B. K., Zapata-Rivera, D. J., & McCalla, G. I. (2003a). A Bayesian computational model of social capital. In M. Huysman, E. Wenger, & V. Wulf (Eds.), *Communities and technologies.* London: Kluwer.

Downes, S. (2001). *Learning communities.* Retrieved May 1, 2003, from http//www.atl.ualberta.ca/downes/future/communities.htm

Gutwin, C., & Greenberg, S. (1998). Design for individuals, design for groups: Tradeoffs between power and workspace awareness. *Proceedings of the ACM Conference on Computer-Supported Cooperative Work* (pp. 207-216).

Heylighten, F. (1999). *What are socio-technical approaches and systems science? Principia socio-technical approach Web.* Retrieved from http://pespmc1.vub.ac.be/CYBSWHAT.html

Hildreth, P., Kimble, C., & Wright, P. (1998). Computer-mediated communications and international communities of practice. *Proceedings of the 4th International Conference on Ethical Issues of Information Technology* (Ethicomp98), Rotterdam, Holland.

Kalaitzakis, E., Dafoulas, G., & Macaulay, L. (2003, June 22-27). Designing online communities: Community-centered development for intensively focused user groups. *Proceedings of the 10th HCI International Conference,* Greece.

Kim, A. J. (2000). *Community building on the Web: Secret strategies for successful online communities.* Berkeley, CA: Peachpit Press.

Kim, E.E. (2003). *An introduction to open source communities*. Retrieved May 1, 2003, from http://www.blueoxen.org/research/00007/

Copyright © 2007, Idea Group Inc. Copying or distributing in print or electronic forms without written permission of Idea Group Inc. is prohibited.

Kollock, P., & Smith, M. (1996). Managing the virtual commons: Cooperation and conflict in computer communities. In S. Herring (Ed.), *Computer-mediated communication: Linguistic, social, and cross-cultural perspectives.* Amsterdam: John Benjamins.

Krippendorf, K. (1984). Epistemological foundation for communication. *Journal of Communication, 84.*

Lave, J., & Wenger, E. (1991). *Situated learning: Legitimate peripheral participation.* New York: Cambridge University Press.

Lesser, E. L., & Prusak, L. (2000). Communities of practice, social capital and organizational knowledge. In E. L. Lesser, M. A. Fontaine, & J. A. Slusher (Eds.), *Knowledge and communities.* Boston: Butterworth Heinemann.

Lesser, E., & Storck, J. (2001). Communities of practice and organizational performance. *IBM Systems Journal, 40*(4).

McCalla, G. (2000). The fragmentation of culture, learning, teaching and technology: Implications for artificial intelligence in education research. *International Journal of Artificial Intelligence, 11*(2), 177-196.

Mumford, E. (1987). Socio-technical systems design: Evolving theory and practice. In P. Ehn & M. Kyng (Eds.), *Computers and democracy: A Scandinavian challenge* (pp. 59-76). London: Avebury.

Norman, D.A. (1996). Cognitive engineering. In D. A. Norman & S. W. Draper (Eds.), *User-centered systems design new perspectives on human-computer interaction* (pp. 31-61). Hillsdale, NJ: Lawrence Erlbaum.

Preece, J. (2000). *Online communities: Designing usability and supporting sociability.* New York: John Wiley & Sons.

Preece, J. (2002). Supporting community and building social capital. *Communications of the ACM, 45*(4), 37-39.

Resnick, P. (2002). Beyond bowling together: Socio-technical capital. In J.M. Carroll (Ed.), *HCI in the new millennium* (pp. 247-272). New York: Addison-Wesley.

Rheingold, H. (1993). *The virtual community: Homesteading on the virtual frontier.* New York: Addison-Wesley.

Riedl, M. O. (2001, January 14-17). A computational model and classification framework for social navigation. *Proceedings of the International Conference on Intelligent User Interfaces 2001* (pp. 137-144), Santa Fe, NM.

Schraefel, M. C., Ho, J., Chignell, M., & Milton, M. (2000). Building virtual communities for research. *Proceedings of the International Working Conference and Industrial Expo on New Advances and Emerging Trends in Next Generation Enterprises,* Buffalo, NY.

Copyright © 2007, Idea Group Inc. Copying or distributing in print or electronic forms without written permission of Idea Group Inc. is prohibited.

Schuler, D., & Namioka, A. (Eds.). (1993). *Participatory design: Principles and practices.* Hillsdale, NJ: Lawrence Erlbaum.

Schwier, R. A. (2001). Catalysts, emphases, and elements of virtual learning communities. Implication for research. *The Quarterly Review of Distance Education, 2*(1), 5-18.

Sclove, R. E. (1995). *Democracy and technology.* New York: The Guildford Press.

Shneiderman, B. (1998). *Designing the user interface. Strategies for effective human-computer interaction.* Boston: Addison-Wesley.

Smith, M. (1992). *Voices from the WELL: The logic of the virtual commons.* Master's thesis, Department of Sociology, UCLA, USA.

SSHRC. (2004). *From a granting to a knowledge council.* Ottawa: Social Sciences and Humanities Research Council of Canada.

Stolterman, E., Croon, A., & Argren, P.-O. (2000). *Virtual communities□Why and how they are studied.* Working paper, Department of Informatics, Umeå University, Sweden.

Wenger, E., McDermott, R., & Snyder, W. M. (2002). *Cultivating communities of practice: A guide to managing knowledge.* Boston: Harvard Business School Press.

Wickre, K. (1995). *Virtual communities: Are they real? Are they real enough?* Retrieved May 1, 2003, from http://www.thenet-usa.com/mag/back/0995/community.html

Endnote

1 Presenters at the *1st GKN Workshop on Building Distributed Communities of Practice for Enhanced Research-Policy Interface,* May 28-31, 2004. Presentations available at http://www.icgd.usask.ca/workshopPlan.html

Copyright © 2007, Idea Group Inc. Copying or distributing in print or electronic forms without written permission of Idea Group Inc. is prohibited.

Chapter IV

Quality Models of Online Learning Community Systems: Exploration, Evaluation and Exploitation

Effie Lai-Chong Law, Swiss Federal Institute of Technology, Switzerland

Ebba Thora Hvannberg, University of Iceland, Iceland

Abstract

The main goal of this chapter is fourfold: to review key theoretical models underpinning the design of online learning community systems (OLCSs); to identify and evaluate quality models for OLCSs; to better understand the feedback loop between evaluation of OLCSs and their redesign; and to develop a generic framework for user interface quality models for OLCSs. Specifically, we have reviewed a set of software quality standards, quality models, and literature on human-centered design, usability, information technology quality assurance, accessibility, security, and trust. Several empirical case studies are described to illustrate our arguments and views. We have developed the generic framework that comprises four levels—factors, criteria, guidelines, and metrics.

Copyright © 2007, Idea Group Inc. Copying or distributing in print or electronic forms without written permission of Idea Group Inc. is prohibited.

"Where technology separates us from challenges, meaning, purpose and alignment with nature, it brings a type of death."

—paraphrased from W. Brian Arthur (2005)

Introduction

It is a well-recognized fact that there are two major critical success factors for online communities (OCs)—high usability and good sociability (Preece, 2000)—with each of them comprising a set of attributes and corresponding measures. Whereas usability is primarily concerned with how users interact with technology, sociability is concerned with how members of a community interact with each other through the supporting technology. Another well-recognized fact is that there are a variety of OCs, being defined by their specific goal, composition of membership, and technological support. In particular, OCs for learning (or online learning communities, OLCs) are distinct from other OCs in a way that learning objects or knowledge resources are essential elements that coalesce, mediate, and sustain interactions and communications among members. In contrast, OCs grounded in economic relationships (e.g., eBay) are bound by members' bargaining power.

Presumably, easy, effective, and flexible access to quality learning objects is imperative for the advancement of an OLC whose members collaboratively build knowledge. Sociotechnical systems (Mumford & Beekman, 1994) that enable online exchanges of knowledge resources are basic infrastructures for knowledge-building community. OLC members range from students, teaching and administrative staff of primary schools as well as of higher education institutions, to professionals in different workplaces of public as well as private sectors. Given the broad scope and complexity of issues pertaining to OLCs and the limited space of this chapter, it is very difficult, if not impossible, to take into account all relevant issues of OLCs. Consequently, we selectively focus on addressing *usability* issues of software systems that support the development of OLCs in the context of *higher education institutions* and of workplace learning. Specifically, members of these OLCs archive, retrieve, reuse, and more importantly discuss as well as reflect on learning objects *per se* and on associated problems arising from their usages. These learning activities can lead not only to the enrichment of knowledge of individual members, but also to the consolidation of the community built on topics of interest. Put concisely, the focus of the chapter is on the *technicality* of OLC systems. Nevertheless, we are fully aware of the very significance of sociability of OLCs and the interdependence between these two dimensions. Whereas other chapters in this volume address sociability issues of OLCs thoroughly and insightfully, this chapter presents complementary as well as supplementary views on intriguing issues pertinent to design and evaluation of OLC systems.

Copyright © 2007, Idea Group Inc. Copying or distributing in print or electronic forms without written permission of Idea Group Inc. is prohibited.

The mission of this chapter is fourfold:

- to review key theoretical models underpinning the design of online learning community systems (OLCSs);
- to identify and evaluate quality models for basic components of OLCSs;
- to better understand the feedback loop between evaluation of OLCSs and their re-design; and
- to develop a generic framework for user interface quality models for OLCSs.

Design and evaluation are two faces of the same coin. Two major components of an OLCS are human users and software systems. We attempt to understand the former with germane theories in cognitive psychology, and the latter with relevant quality models and standards established in HCI and software/Web engineering. Further, we believe that the success of OLCS should go beyond usability to include other significant quality factors, namely security, privacy, credibility/trust, accessibility, and pleasure (i.e., funology; Blythe, Hassenzahl, & Wright, 2004). Deeper understanding of intricate interactions among these quality factors can definitely lead to further insights into success and failure of OLCSs. Further, inability to integrate evaluation results effectively into system redesign undermines the very goal of software validation and verification. To bridge the gap in the lifecycle of OLC system development, we examine the role of defect classification schemes in system redesign.

Theoretical Models

An online community is a group whose members are connected by means of information and communication technologies (ICTs), typically the Internet (cf. McGrath & Hollingshead, 1994; Rheingold, 1994). Online communities can be categorized in terms of user, task, goal, context of use, frequency of use, and so forth (see Figure 1). Specifically, an online learning community aims to achieve certain learning outcomes or effects (Barab, Kling, & Gray, 2004).

Since the early 1990s, the two interdisciplinary fields computer-supported collaborative work (CSCW) and human-computer interaction (HCI) have been progressing almost in parallel. Both fields strive to bridge the gaps between theories and practices, and between the social and the technical (cf. Bannon, 1997; Grudin, 2004). The basic assumptions underpinning the research work of CSCW and HCI are that social interactions, be they between peers or between learners and their

Copyright © 2007, Idea Group Inc. Copying or distributing in print or electronic forms without written permission of Idea Group Inc. is prohibited.

Table 1. continued

Learning Theories	Basic Tenets	Implications to Design of OLCSs
Schön's (1987) Theory of Reflective Practitioner	Reflection-*on*-action and reflection-*in*-action are essential for the development of professional artistry. The effectiveness of training depends on social interaction, especially reciprocally reflective dialogues between coach and student, and on an individual's reflective conversation with the situation. The ability to communicate in the form of telling and listening and demonstrating and imitating is essential for acquiring reflective skills.	• A conversation space where dialogues can efficiently be exchanged and moderated by a more knowledgeable user. • A facility for documenting floating questions and their multi-perspective answers from different community members to facilitate reflective thinking. • High bandwidth is required to enable creation of 3D worlds for visualization and demonstration of certain professional skills, online auditoriums, conference rooms, and so forth.
Situated Action (SA) models (Lave, 1988; Suchman, 1987)	According to SA, the structuring of activity is not something that precedes it, but it can only grow directly out of the immediacy of the situation. The inquiry takes place at a very fine-grained level of minutely observed activities. The unit of analysis is a relation between the individual and the environment. In focusing on improvisation and response to contingency, SA de-emphasizes study of more durable, stable phenomena that persist across situations.	• Information architecture is so designed that users can best orient themselves to sources of information required for tasks at hand and get instant access to such resources (e.g., access to help messages), • Users can navigate in the Web site housing the community with great ease to enable them to respond promptly and appropriately to activities of other users (i.e., gestures of avatars). • An effective search engine enables users to locate resources efficiently to address situational demands.
Distributed Cognition (DC) (Salomon, 1993)	DC is concerned with structures—representations inside and outside the head—and the transformations these structures undergo. DC tends to provide finely detailed analyses of particular artifacts and aims to identify stable design principles that are widely applicable across problems. DC strives to understand how individual agents align and coordinate within a distributed process. Shared goals and plans as well as specific features of the artifact in use are important determinants of the interactions and the quality of collaboration.	A set of principles of DC on three major themes (Blandford & Furniss, 2005), including: • *physical layout,* (e.g., naturalness principle; i.e., fidelity of representations for real objects), situation awareness (i.e., access to common information to keep track of happenings); • *information flow,* (e.g., buffering; i.e., holding up new information until a suitable time to avoid loss or confusion), informal communication (e.g., a chat-room-like feature with the possibility to archive the communication); • *design and use of artifacts,* (e.g., representation-goal parity; i.e., explicit representation of the current state and a goal state) and coordination of resources (including plans, goals, affordance, history, and action-effect).
Activity Theory (AT) (Leont'ev, 1974)	A key idea of AT is the notion of *mediation* by artifacts such as "computer-mediated activity." Another key notion is to equate activity with context, which is constituted through the enactment of an activity involving people and artifacts. AT holds that the constituents of an activity system (i.e., object, actions, and operation) are not fixed, but can dynamically change as conditions change. In AT, one's ability to organize and use resources is the result of specific historical and developmental processes in which a person is changed.	• Enables smooth flow of *activities* by ensuring reliability of data transfer, compatibility of different software modules imported, and consistency in interaction style between these modules and the Web site housing the community. • Supports creation and management of sub-communities to meet dynamic evolution of the community. • Provides a shared workspace to facilitate co-authoring and peer review, and a private workplace to allow individuals to marshal personal resources.

Copyright © 2007, Idea Group Inc. Copying or distributing in print or electronic forms without written permission of Idea Group Inc. is prohibited.

(1983) theory of reflective practitioner. More recently several theories have been embraced by the HCI community, including situated action (Lave, 1988; Suchman, 1987), distributed cognition (Salomon, 1993), and activity theory (Leont'ev, 1974, cited in Nardi, 1994). Essentially they are grounded in social constructivism and are pertinent to understanding the functioning of OLCSs. However, these frameworks are rather abstract and generic. The challenge is how to translate them into practical guidelines for the design and evaluation of an OLCS. Subsequently, we highlight the basic tenets of each of these relevant theoretical models and draw implications how they can inform design of OLCSs (see Table 1).

Clearly, the list of technology supports for OLCSs derived from the related theoretical frameworks in Table 1 is not exhaustive (cf. Wenger, 2001). Figure 2 illustrates basic components of an OLCS, including digital libraries, learning content management systems, vide-conferencing tools, wiki, blogs, other synchronous and asynchronous communication tools, and authoring tools. These technology supports entail high demand on a set of software quality. We highlight several quality attributes that can commonly be derived from the aforementioned theoretical models:

- Usability
  - **Information Management:** Concerns the presentation, integrity, currency, and scope of information presented.
  - **Ease of Use:** Concerns whether users can navigate the system effectively and efficiently. and achieve their goals error-free and satisfactorily.
- Functionality
  - **Interoperability:** Concerns whether the components of the system are compatible and operate seamlessly.
  - **Stability:** Concerns whether the system can function reliably and predictably.
- Interactivity
  - **Communicativity:** Concerns whether the system can support different types of communication, irrespective of the modality.
  - **Responsiveness:** Concerns whether the system can heighten users' awareness to respond to situational demands, be they system-generated or user-submitted requests.
- Naturalness
  - **Authenticity:** Concerns whether the system can support problem-oriented learning in terms of making sense of the situation with reference to perceived contextual data.
  - **Presence:** Concerns whether the system can enable the user to develop a sense of co-location.

Copyright © 2007, Idea Group Inc. Copying or distributing in print or electronic forms without written permission of Idea Group Inc. is prohibited.

Figure 2. Basic components of an OLCS

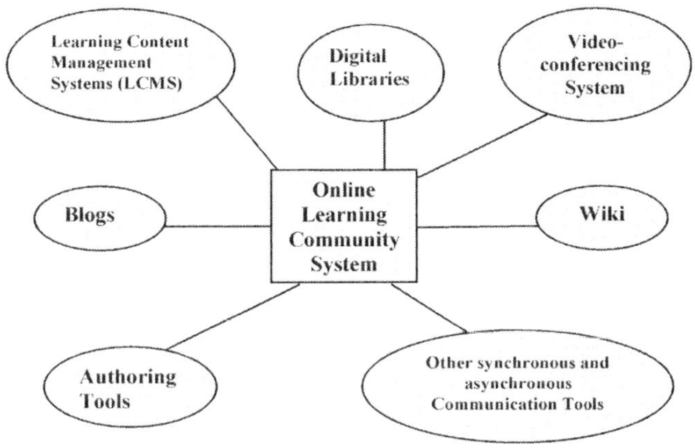

Quality Models and Standards

Relevant theoretical models can inform design of OLCSs in terms of providing practical guidelines and requirements, which can be distilled in the form of quality models and standards. Subsequently, we first define the key notion: *quality model.* Then we investigate a set of selected standards to assess their roles in designing and evaluating OLCSs. Different case studies are described to illustrate our arguments.

Definitions and Instances

A *quality model* (QM) is to make the general term "quality" specific and useful when engineering requirements. Another significant purpose of a QM is to understand, control, and improve a product or a process by determining usability problems or performance bottlenecks, determining a baseline for comparison, assessing the progress, and predicting certain attributes from others (Brajnik, 2001). A QM first decomposes the general concept of quality to create a hierarchy of component quality factors/characteristics. It then provides specific quality criteria and metrics that can be used to determine, with appropriate analysis methods and tools, whether certain quality actually exists. A QM may involve a large set of interdependent attributes (cf. an 80-attribute quality requirement tree; Olsina, Lafuente, & Rossi, 2001) and

Copyright © 2007, Idea Group Inc. Copying or distributing in print or electronic forms without written permission of Idea Group Inc. is prohibited.

must take into account the particular usage of the product for which quality is being modeled. Design guidelines as well as usability evaluation techniques and tools are powerful ingredients of quality models. Since McCall, Richards, and Walters' (1977) pioneering work, various QMs have been defined, adopted, and enhanced, especially in the fields of HCI, software engineering, and Web engineering (Vanderdonckt, Law, & Hvannberg, 2005). While developing and documenting a QM is advocated as a crucial and foremost step for producing a complete and consistent set of quality requirements (Firesmith, 2003), many projects fail to undertake this process.

Standards are published when a discipline has reached a consensus on subjects of interest. Standards are seen as a useful source of best practices and can represent external authority or credibility for recommendation. The role of standards for designing OLCSs is twofold. One role is to enforce quality through specification of minimum requirements and by giving guidelines on how to implement individual quality characteristics. A second role is to set standards for technology implementation, such as data exchange or services. Since this chapter is not concerned with technology implementation, the latter type of standards is not discussed further.

Applicability of Quality Models and Standards to OLCS Components

The applicability of quality models and standards to the ever-changing IT products cannot be taken for granted, considering that standards normally need to go through lengthy ratification processes and thus may not be able to keep in sync with the rapid IT development. Further, innovative IT leads to an escalation of new opportunities for augmenting, extending, and supporting learning and teaching in a diversity of contexts, especially in the form of OLC.

In the last decade online education or e-learning has drawn a lot of research as well as practical concerns and efforts in the academic community and industry. Digital library (DL) is broadly defined as "information systems (IS) and services that provide electronic documents—text files, digital sound, digital video—available in dynamic and archival repositories" (Elliot & Kling, 1997, p. 1023). It is an integral part of an OLCS (see Figure 2). As pointed out in the foregoing discussion, knowledge resources being exchanged via a DL of an OLCS are important cultural artifacts that foster interactions and communications of the community members. Concomitantly, a quality model is deemed necessary to engineer usability as well as other requirements of a DL: the quality of knowledge resources, the efficiency and reliability of searching and downloading resources of interest, the ease with which the facility to enable online discussions on the resources selected can be deployed, the effectiveness of the facility to thread and document such discussions, and the level of interoperability with other DLs of interest.

Copyright © 2007, Idea Group Inc. Copying or distributing in print or electronic forms without written permission of Idea Group Inc. is prohibited.

We aim to explore how the existing software quality standards can inform the design and evaluation of DL as a crucial component of an OLCS. To meet this aim, we have identified several software quality standards because of specific qualities they address, their wide adoption, high popularity, or recency. Further, we have performed different empirical studies on different DLs of interest to illustrate our arguments. In the ensuing text, we present a brief description of each of the standards selected and report some case studies of their applications.

Human-Centered Design Standards

ISO/IEC 13407:1999 Human-Centered Design Processes for Interactive Systems

ISO TR 18529:2000 Human-Centered Lifecycle Process Descriptions

User-centered design (UCD) is the key notion of this volume. UCD refers to a design process that takes account of users of a system. According to Bevan (2001), taking a user-centered approach to design can lessen development times and rework for new versions, improve the productivity of users, and reduce training, documentation, and support costs. The publication of ISO 13407 and the associated ISO TR 18529 represents a maturing of the discipline of UCD. The term *human-centered design* (HCD) is coined to refer to the particular design process defined in ISO 13407 and ISO TR 18529.

ISO TR 18529 provides a comprehensive basis for *process assessment* and *improvement* by identifying improvement priorities (i.e., formative evaluation) through a scale of capability (cf. Capability Maturity Model) and by describing what should be done to make a system lifecycle human centered. The standard addresses several important activities that are missing from traditional software and usability engineering, such as consideration of organizational requirements and processes, verification of context of use, definition of the overall experience of use of the system, and so forth. In short, ISO 13407 and ISO TR 18529 provide guidance for designing usability and are basically management standards. However, they have several shortcomings: methodologies are too general to adapt to a particular project; statements on HCI/human factors techniques are difficult to understand because they are too techno-centric and detailed (Earthy, Jones, & Bevan, 2001); and limited guidance is provided for the descriptions of user goals and usability measures in particular, and for the process of producing various outcomes in general.

The availability of a process model for HCD eases its inclusion in the scope of continuous improvement. Surely, OLC cannot be formed in a vacuum. The organization, namely a university, where an OLC is taking root, should have the capability (i.e., adequate personnel and infrastructure) to sustain the running of the OLC. If

Copyright © 2007, Idea Group Inc. Copying or distributing in print or electronic forms without written permission of Idea Group Inc. is prohibited.

an OLC is employed as a formal instrument of teaching and learning, application of standards such as ISO 13407 and ISO TR 18529 to access the usability maturity of the system can lead to the effectiveness and efficiency of the learning process, and to the satisfaction of teachers as well as learners.

Usability Standards

ISO 9241-11: 1998 Ergonomic Requirements for Office Work with Visual Display Terminals (VDTs)—Part 11: Guidance on Usability

This standard defines usability as "the extent to which a product can be used by specified users to achieve specified goals with *effectiveness, efficiency,* and *satisfaction* in a specified context of use." The three usability metrics are defined as follows:

- **Effectiveness:** The accuracy and completeness with which users achieve specified goals.
- **Efficiency:** The resources expended in relation to the accuracy and completeness with which users achieve goals.
- **Satisfaction:** The comfort and acceptability of use.

To operationalize the terms, effectiveness and efficiency are the function of unassisted task completion rates and task completion times, respectively. These metrics, however, may not be valid for academic DLs. A common usage scenario can well illustrate the point. Whether DL users are asked to locate known items or some items relevant to topics of interest, it is highly probable that the search result will modify their needs and goals, especially when they locate extra items that were not originally included as targets. In this case, it is difficult to define the cutting point for task completion. Some attempts to refine these metrics (cf. "search efficacy"; Kelly & Cool, 2002) have been made. However, these metrics are not single-dimensional; combinatorial measurements taking all contributing contextual factors into account are yet to develop. Identifying such factors is already a challenge, let alone translating them into computational terms. For instance, it was shown that users' search behavior would vary substantially with the testing environment (e.g., with or without the presence of an experimenter), especially when the searching task was open ended—that is, no constraint on specific topical areas, no time limit, and so forth (Schulte & Huber, 2003).

Copyright © 2007, Idea Group Inc. Copying or distributing in print or electronic forms without written permission of Idea Group Inc. is prohibited.

Case Study: Correlations Between Objective and Subjective Measures

How the three usability measures correlate with each other is another question to explore. We illustrate this issue with the results of usability tests on EducaNext (http:www.educanext.org), which is a multilingual academic portal supporting the sharing of knowledge resources for higher education institutions. It is open to any members of the academic and research community. In particular, the portal allows users to create a community on a specific topic and in a selected European language, and to offer knowledge resources within a selected community (see Figure 3).

Twenty-two users from two European universities were recruited in usability tests on EducaNext. Each user was required to perform 10 tasks and to complete an "After Scenario Questionnaire" as well as a "Computer System Usability Questionnaire" (Lewis, 1995) to measure their subjective perception and satisfaction. Objective measures included time-on-task (i.e., efficiency) and number of usability problems identified (i.e., effectiveness). The two types of measures were not consistent with each other. According to *ISO/IEC 9241-11 (1998) Section 5.4.1 Choice of Measures,* "If it is not possible to obtain objective measures of effectiveness and efficiency, subjective measures based on the user's perception can provide an indication of effectiveness and efficiency." This statement implies that objective usability measures

Figure 3. The community feature of EducaNext

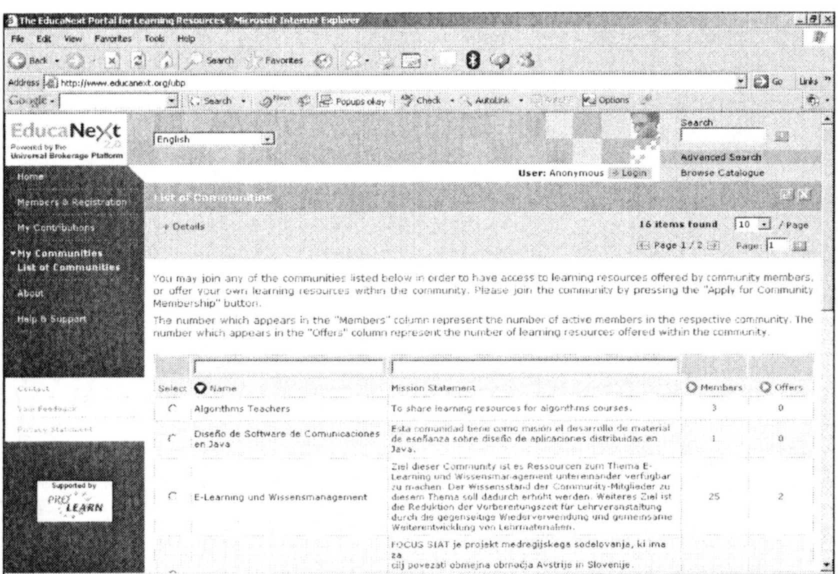

Copyright © 2007, Idea Group Inc. Copying or distributing in print or electronic forms without written permission of Idea Group Inc. is prohibited.

should significantly correlate with subjective ones, but our empirical findings tend to refute this implication.

In summary, there are two major issues with ISO/IEC 9241-11 (1998): the ambiguous cut-off point for defining task completion that is related to the measures of effectiveness and efficiency, and the lack of correlation between objective and subjective usability measures.

Software Quality Standards

ISO/IEC 9126-1: 2001 Software Engineering—Product Puality—Part 1: Quality Model

According to ISO/IEC 9126, usability is defined as "a set of attributes of software which bear on the effort needed for use and on the individual assessment of such use by a stated or implied set of users." Interestingly, this definition does not explicitly address the key notion *goals,* as it does in ISO 9241-11. In addition, "the effort needed for use" and "the individual assessment" somewhat correspond to objective (i.e., efficiency) and subjective measures (i.e., satisfaction) specified in ISO 9241-11. Furthermore, usability as defined in ISO 9241-11 depends on software qualities which are distinct from usability as defined in ISO 9126-1.

Figure 4. An exemplified quality model adapted from ISO/IEC 9126-1

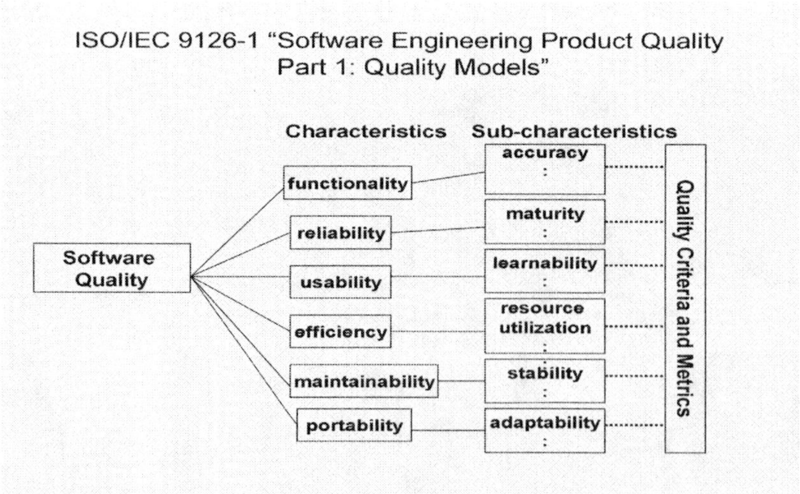

Copyright © 2007, Idea Group Inc. Copying or distributing in print or electronic forms without written permission of Idea Group Inc. is prohibited.

Specifically, ISO 9126-1 provides a hierarchical quality model comprising six broad categories of quality factors, which are divided into sub-characteristics (see Figure 4). Subsequently, we delineate the quality model of EducaNext and then analyze to what extent it is compliant with the standard. Further, we extrapolate the analysis to other DLs.

Case Study: Quality Model of EducaNext

The effectiveness model portrayed in Figure 5 is a form of quality model. The quality factor at the highest level is *effectiveness*, which is the major yardstick for assessing whether the portal can attain its ultimate goal, as reflected subjectively by the level of satisfaction that users experience when using the portal and objectively by usage frequency. Further, the quality factor *effectiveness* is related to two sets of quality factors subsumed by the two categories: *brokerage systems* and *users*.

Brokerage Systems

The quality factor *functionality* refers to the features that are currently available and those that will be built into the portal contingent on users' emerging needs. The quality factor *performance and reliability* refers to the general response time for queries being submitted to the system, and to the stability and consistency of the system's behavior. The quality factor *ease of use* denotes how simple it is as perceived by users to operate the system. The quality factor *trust and security* refers to the gen-

Figure 5. The EducaNext Effectiveness Model (adapted from Simon, 2001)

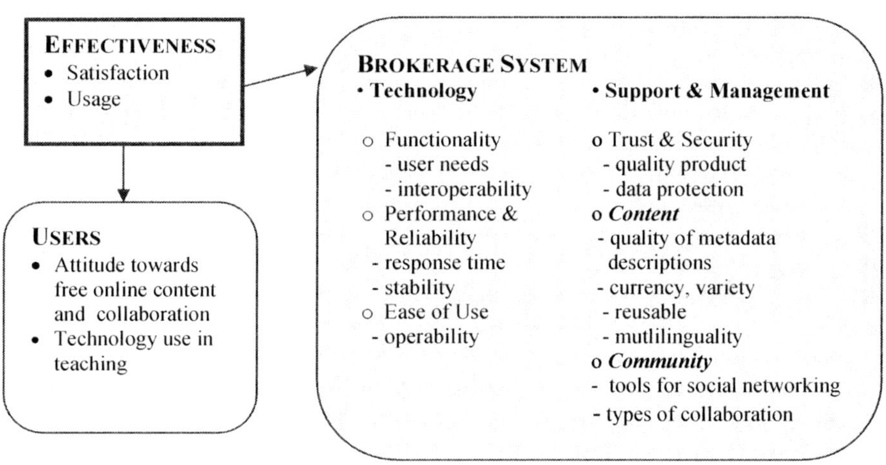

Copyright © 2007, Idea Group Inc. Copying or distributing in print or electronic forms without written permission of Idea Group Inc. is prohibited.

eral image and reputation of the organization as perceived by users for delivering quality products and services, and to the policy for protecting intellectual property rights and personal data. Indeed, issues of credibility and security are becoming more critical in the increasingly popular Web-based transactions. The quality factor *content* is actually composite, subsuming a set of interrelated attributes influencing the quality of learning objects offered in the portal.

We have evaluated the compliance of the EducaNext effectiveness model with ISO 9126-1 by identifying so-called *mapped* and *extra* quality factors, which are and are not addressed in the standard, respectively. Several mapped quality factors (e.g., *effectiveness*, *safety*, and *usability*) and three extra quality factors (i.e., *trust*, *content*, and *community*) were also identified.

Case Study: Quality Models of Other Digital Libraries

The EducaNext effectiveness model can well exemplify quality models of other DLs. We look into three different non-European-based DLs, namely **MERLOT** of the USA, **eduSource** of Canada, and **EdNA Online** of Australia. For content quality control, both MERLOT and eduSource adopt a sophisticated peer review system. The three basic evaluation criteria are quality of content, potential effectiveness as a teaching tool, and ease of use. In addition, eduSource has developed a set of criteria for evaluating quality of learning objects, such as interaction usability, accessibility, and reusability. Similar to EducaNext, EdNA Online puts emphasis on metadata quality, currency, and variety of learning objects and multi-linguality.

Given that most users of DLs are knowledge workers for whom the knowledge-building community is a significant channel for them to share expertise and material, the quality factor *community* is deemed essential. MERLOT communities and EdNA Online communities are built on disciplines and educational sectors, respectively, whereas eduSource communities, like EducaNext, are thematic, being defined by users themselves. Further, the three DLs address the quality factor *accessibility* and emphasize compliance with the related guidelines and standards (e.g., W3C-WAI Web Content Accessibility). Besides, the three DLs adopt a user-centered design approach by involving users in all stages of development.

To summarize, ISO 9126-1 is primarily concerned with qualities of software systems, which serve as a vehicle or medium to convey or store contents. Obviously, the quality of the vehicle does not necessarily relate to the quality of the content it carries. As a given standard cannot be all-encompassing to include everything, it is understandable that attributes pertinent to content quality controls are not addressed in ISO 9126-1. This quality factor is extensively addressed in ISO/IEC 19796-1. The quality factor *community* addresses interactions between users. The question concerned is: How can a system enable user interactions that are essential for community building? The attribute *interactivity* needs to be introduced under the quality

Copyright © 2007, Idea Group Inc. Copying or distributing in print or electronic forms without written permission of Idea Group Inc. is prohibited.

factor *usability* and be specified with reference to supporting features required for effective communication. On the other hand, the quality factor *accessibility* by itself is so complex as to call forth a separate set of guidelines.

Information Technology Standards

ISO 19796-1: 2005 Information Technology – Learning, Education, and Training – Quality Management Assurance and Metrics – Part 1: General Approach

The final committee draft (FCD) of this standard was released in February 2005. It is especially relevant to DLs as it addresses the quality factor *content* rather extensively. Aligning with the conceptual model of existing DLs, peer review is deployed as the main mechanism for quality control. Besides, this standard explicitly addresses the issue of metadata quality—a core concern in the library science. Of particular interest is the framework for metadata creation, which is built upon Svenonius's (2000) Principles of Bibliographic Description and Access, including the principles of *user convenience, common usage, representation, accuracy, sufficiency and necessity, standardization,* and *integration***.** These principles are philosophically and academically grounded, and highly applicable to evaluating the catalogue of a DL and to addressing the quality factor *content*. Nonetheless, meaningful metrics for assessing the compliance with these principles have not yet been available. This is a challenge facing DL designers, information science professionals, and the like.

Further, ISO 19796-1 addresses the attribute *collaboration* that is somewhat related to the quality factor *community* mentioned earlier. Specifically, *collaboration*—together with other associated attributes such as communication, interaction, and experience exchange—is mapped to the category *responsiveness*, which is based on the Chinese E-Learning Technology Standard Committee. Specifically, *responsiveness* is measured in terms of average reply time to requests of different actors involved, and more interestingly, average complaints by student as well as complaints per course. These quantitative measures are apparently inadequate, because the quality of reply and reasons underlying complaints are more relevant. Furthermore, caution needs to be exercised when borrowing concepts across cultures, that is, the Asian standards may not be applicable to the Western contexts, and vice versa.

Accessibility Standards

Accessibility to an OLC is an essential quality factor because of diverse capabilities of users who are involved in such a community. Several projects are underway within the standardization community on accessibility. Among others, there is work on general guidelines (ISO/AWI 9241-20) for development of ICT products (i.e.,

Copyright © 2007, Idea Group Inc. Copying or distributing in print or electronic forms without written permission of Idea Group Inc. is prohibited.

software and hardware) and services to ensure their accessibility by people with a range of abilities, including perceptual, motor, and cognitive, focusing on disabilities that are either permanent or temporary. The standard also concerns the purchase and evaluation of products for users with disabilities. The scope of ISO/CD 9241-171: draft (*Ergonomics of Human-System Interaction—Part 171: Guidance on Software Accessibility*) includes requirements and recommendations for design of accessible software, be it at work, at home, in educational institutions, or in public places. The aim of the standard is to complement general design for usability covered by ISO 9241-110:draft (*Part 110: Dialogue Principles*), ISO 14915:2002 (*Software Ergonomics for Multimedia User Interfaces*), and ISO 13407.

Security Standards

ISO 17799: 2000 – Code of Practice for Information Security Management

ISO 15408:1999 – The Common Criteria for IT Security Evaluation

The most widely used security standard is ISO 17799, which is a management standard that helps an organization set a security policy, analyze risks and threats, and react to them in a timely manner. The standard contains a set of controls that consist of best practices in information security. The standard is organized into 10 major sections: *Business Continuity Planning, System Access Control, System Development and Maintenance, Physical and Environmental Security, Compliance, Personnel Security, Security Organization, Computer and Network Management, Asset Classification & Control,* and *Security Policy.* The coverage of this standard is extensive, from physical access, human errors, theft, fraud, managing information security within a company, compliance with regulations and civil laws, to security of operations of information systems. For instance, the *System Development and Maintenance* covers topics on ensuring confidence, authenticity, and integration of information. An organization can get certification for compliance with ISO 17799, but this can be very tedious since every information system needs to be examined.

The challenge of distributed systems such as OLCs is that security is not supposed to be centrally managed, but is at the discretion of each participant to enforce. Security is about privacy on the one hand (protecting resources from loss, corruption, and other abuses)and authentication on the other hand (knowing who the interacting actor is). In ISO 9126-1, Security is a sub-characteristic of *functionality*, together with *accuracy, suitability, and interoperability*, and is measured with the extent to which the software product implements security functions and an event trail of how many times security has been breached during operation.

Whereas ISO 17799 is a management standard, ISO 15408 is a technical standard. The standard supports the specification and implementation of security features of

Copyright © 2007, Idea Group Inc. Copying or distributing in print or electronic forms without written permission of Idea Group Inc. is prohibited.

an IT product. A certification scheme is described that evaluates a software product against security levels. The standard provides seven *evaluation assurance levels.* The lowest is functionally tested, the next is structurally tested, then methodically tested and checked, and the highest (i.e., seventh) is formally verified, designed, and tested. The levels are suitable for different requirements, ranging from level one where threats to security are not considered serious to level four where maximum assurance is ensured based on good commercial development practices. Level four is the highest level that can be achieved in an economical way. Level seven, the highest level, is required in extremely high-risk situations and where the high value of assets justifies the cost. For an online community for learning resources, there is hardly a need to go above level four.

Online Trust

The definition of trust has evolved (Golbeck & Hendler, 2004). When we make a *commitment* to a particular action or entity based on a *belief* that this action or entity will behave as we expect, we trust in it. Corritorea, Krachera, and Wiedenbeck (2003) have stated that online trust based on the definition of off-line trust is to be the expectation of confidence that one's vulnerabilities are not violated in a risky situation. Further, their model of online trust includes three perceived quality factors that influence the decision on trust: *credibility*, *ease of use*, and *risk*. Each of these quality factors can be measured with different instruments. One quality criterion of credibility is *predictability.* If you get good consistent feedback from the system and experience few errors, you tend to perceive the system as being predictable. Other quality criteria of credibility are *expertise, reputation,* and *honesty.* The second quality factor of the model—*ease of use*—can be measured with Davis' (1989) technology acceptance model or other forms of user-based evaluation. Concerning the quality factor Risk, a good sense of control can lead to less risk. Risk assessments can be performed; for instance, in security management such assessment is a major component. Then the threats, vulnerabilities, and possible intruders are analyzed.

Trust and Nature

Arthur (2005) discusses that technologies are becoming more and more organic, intelligent, and biological. He further claims that people are uncomfortable about this, because there are two major forces—nature and technology—that are in collision. The reason he states is that we put our hope in technology and trust in nature. We constantly ask ourselves whether the forces of technology are natural and whether to trust them. Is it natural to communicate with the aid of technologies, where you cannot see or feel the other person's presence? We know that we have no desire

Copyright © 2007, Idea Group Inc. Copying or distributing in print or electronic forms without written permission of Idea Group Inc. is prohibited.

to be without technology, but want to hold onto the nature. Arthur thus brings our attention not only to trust but also to naturalness (cf. user credibility and sense of realness; Fogg et al., 2001).

Trust and Security

Trust can be related to security in that the more you trust the entity, the less security you need to implement. Paradoxically, the more security functionality is implemented, the more you can trust it. Figure 6 illustrates how one can build trust when the security level is high and no incidence occurs, and consequently decides to lower the security level, for example, for economical reasons.

When security is breached, trust is lowered and one sees again the need to raise the level of security. It then takes some time for one to gain confidence in the system. A security breach is not the only thing that can lower one's security; another is some bad experience that the user associates with the product being of lower quality than expected. It can be a message or some status of the system from which the user infers that security can be threatened. For example, if the performance of the system becomes low, the user may infer that a denial of service attack has occurred, regardless of its existence or not. Trust is a perceived subjective quality. Hence, it is difficult to measure trust reliably, especially when a human user tends to have different levels of trust in different parts of technology.

Figure 6. A theoretical relationship between trust and security

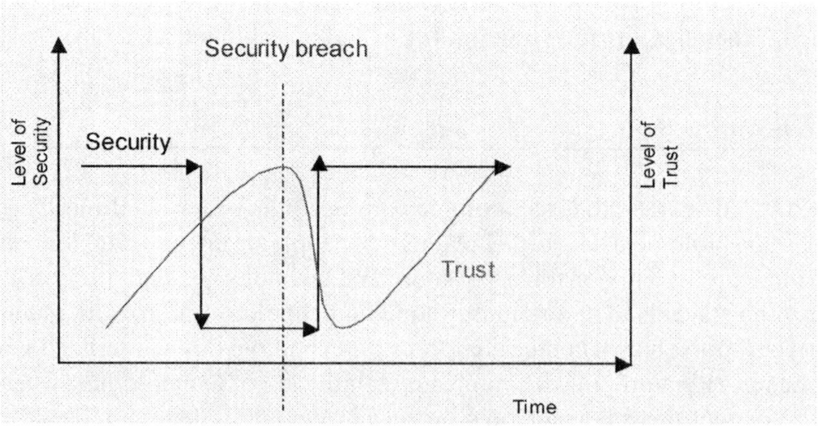

Copyright © 2007, Idea Group Inc. Copying or distributing in print or electronic forms without written permission of Idea Group Inc. is prohibited.

Case Study: An Online Community System for Workplace Learning

The ELENA-HCD Suite (http://www.hcd-online.com/HCDExp) is a tool that aims to support continuing development of human capital through goal-oriented learning processes. The suite implements a workflow that engages potential learners, trainers, Human Resource (HR) managers, and software developers in a collaborative decision process on the type of training needed, where to find it, and how to assess its performance.

The quality goals of the suite are open, intelligent, and effective. Open means access to a variety of repositories, integration of heterogeneous systems, and a simple query language. Intelligent means personalized querying based on profiles including background, goals, and learning history. Effective means an optimized planning of human capital development, including goal-driven learning that is met by learning resources that fit personal and corporate needs and strategies.

A community can be built within a company department, a company division, a site, or across professional sectors. The role of the community is to connect learning resources to the goals of the community and to assess the quality of the resources. In the early phases of the suite's development, we proposed 15 design features to human resources managers and asked for their opinions on positive and negative feedback. Table 2 lists a subset of these features that are essential to building a community and exploiting its services.

Our study was primarily qualitative and based on proposed design features that had not been prototyped but were described to the participants. In addition to claims analysis of the design features, we conducted an interview with the help of process scenarios. After analyzing the data and deriving propositions from each of the evaluation components, we looked for conflicts, tradeoffs, and agreements between them,

Table 2. ELENA-HCD Suite design features for community building

	Design Feature
D1	Employees skills assessment
D2	Motivation analysis
D3	Maintain a company profile
D4	Retrieving learning resource descriptions and services from a network of brokers and providers
D5	Personalization of user queries based on learner profile (e.g., topic, location)
D6	Strategic alignment analysis
D7	Notification service
D8	Recommender system
D9	Search heuristics
D15	Collecting learning service evaluation data

Copyright © 2007, Idea Group Inc. Copying or distributing in print or electronic forms without written permission of Idea Group Inc. is prohibited.

and the previously defined quality characteristics of open, intelligent, and effective of the ELENA-HCD Suite (see Figure 7). Hence, we aimed to discover whether the results of the claims analysis and interviews are in concordance with the quality characteristics and whether additional quality characteristics emerge.

As shown in Figure 8, requirements for two additional quality characteristics appeared: trust and security/privacy. Whereas there may be conflicts between some of the characteristics such as open and efficient, others support one another such as open and intelligent. An open system demonstrating the ability to retrieve information from different online repositories is the basis for intelligence. However, the user demands even more trust if the system is to provide intelligence. Trust is among other things achieved through reliable data from an adequate number of sources, the transparency of activities, and the behavior of the system of which the

Figure 7. Evaluation of the ELENA-HCD Suite

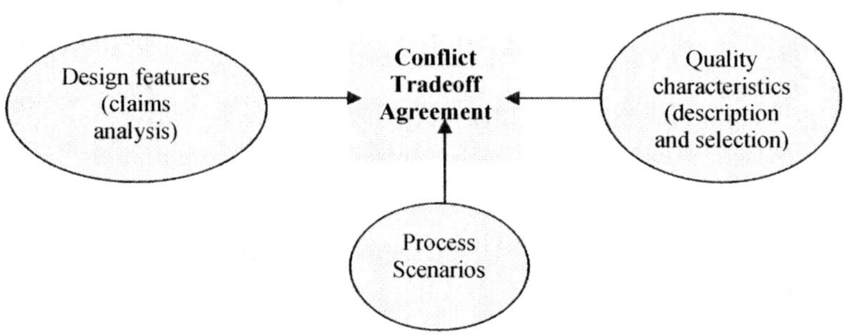

Figure 8. Results of the analysis on the ELENA-HCD Suite

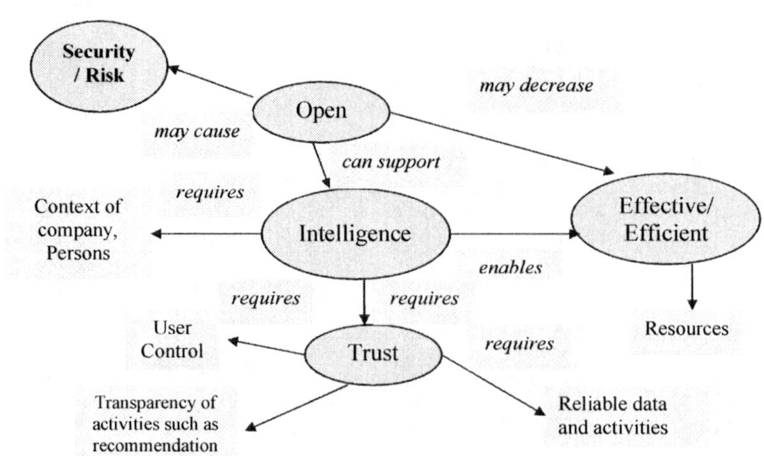

Copyright © 2007, Idea Group Inc. Copying or distributing in print or electronic forms without written permission of Idea Group Inc. is prohibited.

user is in control. Further, intelligence requires us to know about the context and state of the company, including organization, financial status and current products that are offered, and tasks that have to be carried out. Certainly, there may be other links between the quality characteristics, but we show the major ones that our data pointed to.

Feedback Loop Between Evaluation and Redesign of OLCS

Every IT system has its own characteristics that are influenced by its domain, its concepts and processes, and its environmental factors such as technology platform, and organizational and social characteristics. Online communities are no exception.

Evaluation

The specific characteristics of online communities and similar systems in an ambient environment where technologies are all encompassing, smart, and mobile, call for a different mode of evaluation. Recently, the notion of *experience and application research* (EAR) has emerged (Hvannberg, in press). It suggests that there are different phases of evaluation. At the conceptual stage in a so-called contextual laboratory, the feasibility and usability of new concepts can be evaluated in a laboratory that is built in a real context. A validation and demonstration phase allows the developer to present the system to the masses and get feedback. An assisted reality phase is where long-term studies can be carried out. In EAR, it is emphasized that the user can experience the technology (McCarthy & Wright, 2004) and use tangible artifacts; experiencing prototypes can make the interaction more realistic. There are numerous challenges for designing research methods that can be used in EAR.

Since the evaluation of an OLCS is so highly situational and the quality characteristics are difficult to translate into metrics that are numerical, a more desirable option may be to focus on qualitative studies. The current difficulty we have with qualitative studies is that the quality models all assume that the methods are quantitative, at least that the results are presented quantitatively. Here is an open research problem to allow the quality models to be built in such a way that they can be validated with qualitative data results, such as causal networks, matrices, hypotheses, and so forth. As qualitative methods work from the bottom up, the quality model should emerge from the data gathered; then we look for facts or indicators that tell us that the quality of the OLC is bad or good according to the quality model developed.

Copyright © 2007, Idea Group Inc. Copying or distributing in print or electronic forms without written permission of Idea Group Inc. is prohibited.

Redesign

Much more effort has been spent on user interface evaluation than on methods that can guide designers in correcting problematic situations discovered. To learn more about the problems discovered, different defect classification schemes have been devised (e.g., Andre, Hartson, Belz, & McCreary, 2001; Chillarege et al., 1992; Hvannberg & Law, 2003). They are meant to classify a defect further according to when it was discovered; what triggered it; its effect on the user in terms of how severe it was; point of origin of the defect, that is, during which development process it occurred; what caused it; and what can be done in the future to prevent such a defect from reoccurring.

Whereas these classification schemes have been successful in software development, it still needs to be validated how helpful they are for correcting human-computer interaction faults. One can speculate whether they are only good for micro-level inspections. Preliminary results of an empirical study indicate that once developers recognize the problems, general solutions aiming to correct a set of problems are designed. This is in contrast to taking each problem and trying to correct it. It may be an indication that problems need to be categorized further and linked better to main concepts (e.g., user cognitive models), and not just tasks. Thus if a problem originates at a presentation level, it is concrete. If it originates at the conceptual level, all problems that originate in the same concept should be considered as input into the redesign.

OLCs are characterized by their fluidity, large and heterogeneous user population, as well as wide geographical and temporal distribution; we may speculate that a problem-based redesign may be too fine grained. This can be mitigated by grouping the problems together. Another approach to re-design may be examining the constraints behind a design. If an evaluation shows that there are conflicts between constraints, either a trade-off has to be considered in the redesign or simply removal of the conflicting constraints.

Case Study: Evaluating and Redesigning the Owl System

The Owl (in Icelandic it is called "Ugla") system is a kind of learning management system (LMS) used in universities (see Figure 9). Owl's users are students and teachers. It enables students to see courses, syllabi, calendars, and various learning resources. The community part of Owl allows students to participate in discussions, be part of subgroups of a course, and store their files in a shareable folder in the subgroup. Each course forms the default community of students and teachers. Teachers can create a discussion thread, create a shareable folder, and send an announcement to students. Students can look up in a phonebook which other students are in the same

Copyright © 2007, Idea Group Inc. Copying or distributing in print or electronic forms without written permission of Idea Group Inc. is prohibited.

Figure 9. The community part of the Owl system

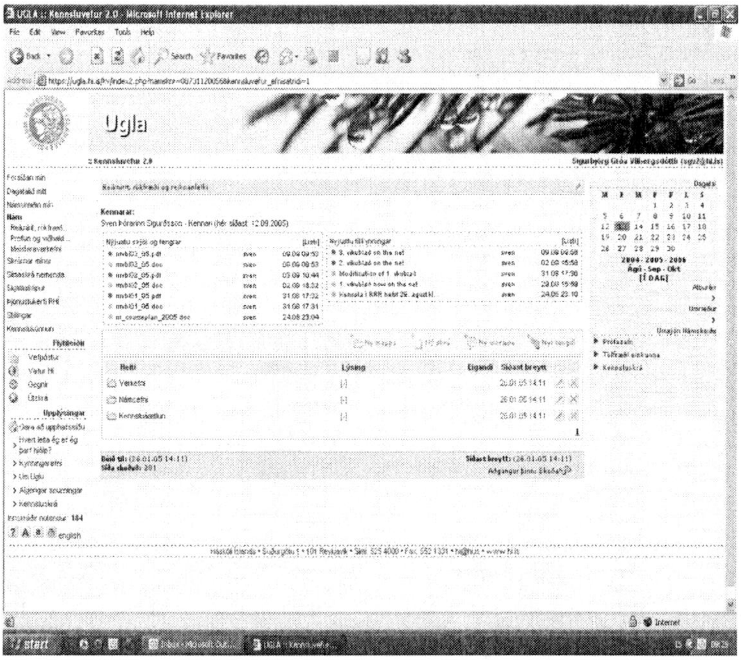

course. It is possible to see how many users are logged into Owl at any time. A log of all activities is kept so that a teacher can see the activity of the community.

We performed a usability evaluation of Owl by asking the users (teachers and students) to perform a set of community tasks (e.g., create a discussion thread). The usability problems and improvement requests thus identified (see Table 3) were

Table 3. Examples of usability problems and improvement requests for the Owl

(P)roblem or (R)equest	Rationale
P1—unable to reply to a particular posting in the discussion	Inflexibility
P2—detailed logs invade a user's privacy	Privacy threat
P3—unable to see the student's view	Lack of control
R1—Edit discussions, e.g., delete a message	Lack of trust
R2—More support for student teamwork, e.g., shareable folders and files, bulletin board, etc.	Increase collaboration and communication but limit the scope with targeted bonding
R3—It would be good to receive messages in the LMS and not in regular e-mail	Cognitive workload

Copyright © 2007, Idea Group Inc. Copying or distributing in print or electronic forms without written permission of Idea Group Inc. is prohibited.

communicated to the development team of the Owl system. They were convinced about the necessity to fix most of the problems and to build in the new features. Specifically, the Owl system has been undergoing the iterative cycle of evaluation and redesign with the deployment of the CUP (classification of usability problems) scheme (Hvannberg & Law, 2003).

A Generic Framework for User Interface Quality Models

Based on the reviews of the relevant quality models, standards, guidelines, and literature, we aim to derive a generic framework for user interface quality models for OLCSs. Specifically, we adapt Montero, González, Lozano, and Vanderdonckt's (2005) work and instantiate the fields of individual levels with examples being germane to OLCSs (see Figure 10). The framework consists of two tiers: the quality concept and evaluation scheme, with the former being subsumed by the latter. *Factors* and *criteria* constitute the core of the quality concept. *Factors* are important for determining the quality of a Web site, and *criteria* are specific descriptions providing evidence either for or against the existence of a specific quality factor. *Guidelines* are theory- as well as experience-based design and evaluation principles, and *metrics* are measurement methods to quantify *criteria,* rendering them objective and unambiguous, and to verify *guidelines,* either manually or through some means of automation. The four levels are integral parts of the *evaluation scheme.* Note that the *criteria* level differs from the *guidelines* level in the way that the former is at a more empirical level and the latter is at a more operational level (cf. the hierarchy of "operation," "action," and "activity" of the Activity Theory). In fact, real-life applications of *criteria* can lead to the creation of new *guidelines* and the enrichment of existing ones. In summary, this generic framework adopts a top-down approach with which quality is progressively refined into *factors, criteria, guidelines,* and *metrics.* Apparently, what we specify in Figure 10 is not exhaustive; we simply highlight those aspects that we have addressed, albeit to different depths, in the foregoing text. In fact, quality models need to be customized for each application domain and even individual applications.

Basically, a quality concept and an evaluation scheme, once defined, can facilitate the development team of an OLCS to monitor the quality level of the user interface and to diagnose problems bottlenecking user performance. The lack of well-defined quality models for software systems can be one of the significant reasons for their low quality. Quality models are difficult to define, especially when technical and financial problems constrain which measures to take. Presumably, research paradigms and international standards can guide the definition of a quality model. It

Copyright © 2007, Idea Group Inc. Copying or distributing in print or electronic forms without written permission of Idea Group Inc. is prohibited.

is realized by performing the following steps in an iterative, incremental, parallel, and time-boxed manner:

1. establish goals, target groups, and contexts of use of the system being developed via scenario-based strategy (Rosson & Carroll, 2002);
2. derive a list of quality factors and criteria from the data collected in (1), prioritize and quantify them right at the start of the system development;
3. identify what, how, and when to measure during design and implementation stages; such measures should be consistent with the quality factors and criteria identified in (2);
4. take measures at each phase of the software development lifecycle; such measures need to be done at both local and global levels, and within technical, financial, and organizational constraints (Olsina et al., 2001);
5. analyze measures and validate the quality model as well as the product prototype; and
6. feedback results of analysis and validation to stakeholders to identify improvement suggestions and implement them.

If possible, reuse an existing quality model (cf. corporate quality assurance scheme), and extend or tailor the quality model as required (Firesmith, 2003).

Conclusion

Traditionally, quality models focus on software qualities. We have seen through our studies that an *interaction quality model* depends on three major sub-quality models: *information quality, cognitive quality,* and *software quality.* The first one describes the quality of the data, content, and knowledge accessible in the information system. Cognitive quality describes how willing and able the human is in participating in the community. Finally, the software quality is the ability of the technology to provide certain guarantees. Ideally, the design of an OLCS can address all three aspects in a consistent and balanced manner.

Conventionally, general methods have been applied to evaluate quality metrics that determine quality factors. Clearly, better results could be obtained with targeted evaluation methods for individual application domains. When evaluating OLCs, the extent of the evaluation needs to be such that it covers a wide range of situations, including data, task scenarios, contexts, and participants. It is likely that for all these factors, we encounter high variability. Besides, the extended period of interaction

Copyright © 2007, Idea Group Inc. Copying or distributing in print or electronic forms without written permission of Idea Group Inc. is prohibited.

Figure 10. A generic framework for User Interface Quality Model for OLCSs (adapted from Montero et al., 2005). As the quality model of an OLC varies with the domain of the community, we address its unique characteristics and goals as depicted in Figure 1. Thus, for example, empathy may not be as important in online learning communities as it is in online health communities.

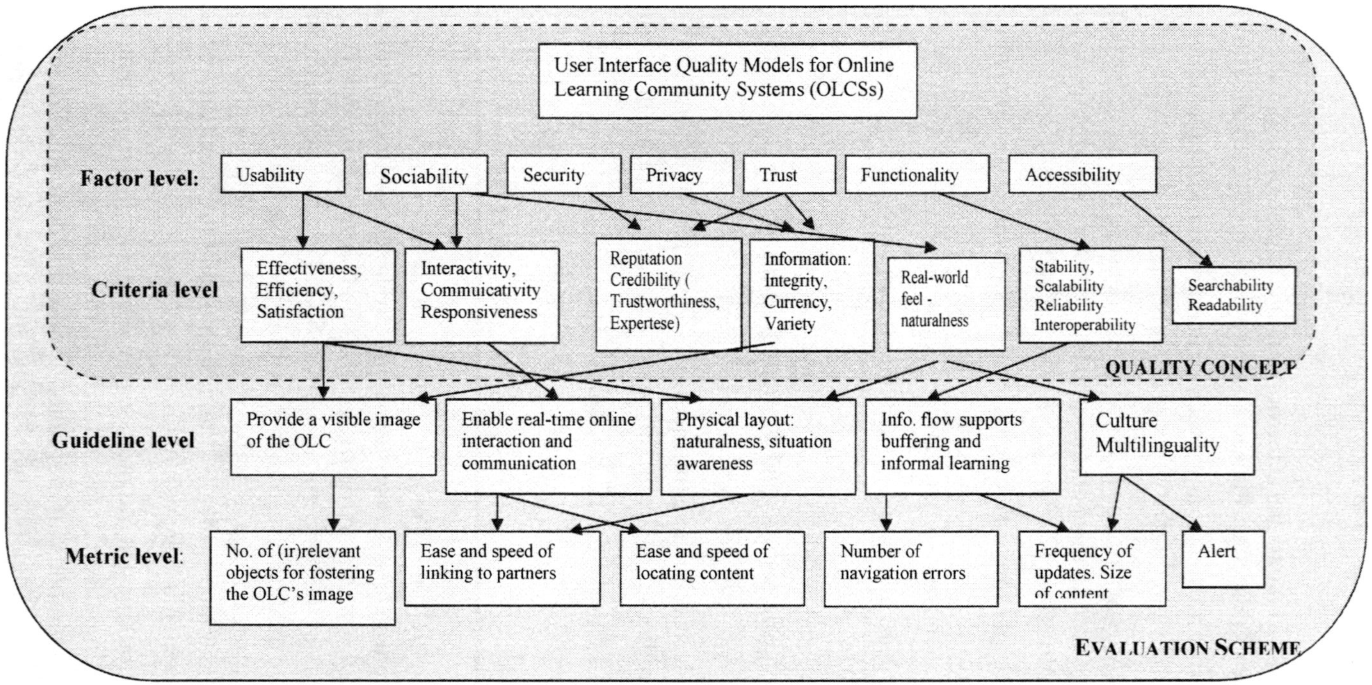

Copyright © 2007, Idea Group Inc. Copying or distributing in print or electronic forms without written permission of Idea Group Inc. is prohibited.

among multiple users may render the traditional, general evaluation methods inappropriate for OLCSs, especially when the reliability and validity of the evaluation are at issue. Consequently, remote field evaluations in addition to local laboratory-based evaluations are considered more appropriate.

Further, as shown in the earlier reviews, there are a number of drawbacks of existing standards, including the fuzzy notion of goal, the interdependence of quality factors, the almost exclusive emphasis on quantitative quality metrics, and the imprecise specifications of such metrics. Of particular concern is that the standards are not adequate to address the quality attributes that are essential for an OLCS, especially trust that is intricately correlated with security and privacy. Nevertheless, given the ever-increasing complexity of interactive systems, it is very difficult, if not impossible, to specify all quality attributes within one standard. Consequently, pluralistic compliance with multiple standards is deemed necessary so as to ensure the quality of such a complex application as an OLCS. Certainly, the well-designed infrastructure is a robust scaffold to enable the development of a successful online community. Analogously speaking, the quality of vehicle for transporting food cannot guarantee the quality of the food being transported. Hence, it is of utmost important that the food for thought in terms of formal as well as informal learning materials can stimulate and sustain the growth of an OLC.

References

Andre, T. S., Hartson, H. R., Belz, S. M., & McCreary, F. A. (2001). The user action framework. *International Journal of Human-Computer Studies, 54*, 107-136.

Arthur, W. B. (2005). The changing character of technology. In O. D. Jonsson & E. H. Huijens (Eds.), *Technology in society—Society in technology* (pp. 191-200). University of Iceland Press.

Bannon, L. J. (1997). Dwelling in the "great divide": The case of HCI and CSCW. In G. C. Bowker, S. L. Star, W. Turner, & L. Gasser (Eds.), *Social science, technical systems, and cooperative work: Beyond the great divide* (pp. 355-378). Mahwah, NJ: Lawrence Erlbaum.

Barab, S., Kling, R., & Gray, J. H. (2004). *Designing virtual communities in service of learning*. Cambridge: Cambridge University Press.

Bevan, N. (2001). International standards for HCI and usability. *International Journal of Human Computer Studies, 55*(4), 533-552.

Blandford, A., & Furniss, D. (2005). DiCoT: A methodology for applying distributed cognition to the design of team working systems. *Proceedings of DSVIS 2005* (LNCS).

Copyright © 2007, Idea Group Inc. Copying or distributing in print or electronic forms without written permission of Idea Group Inc. is prohibited.

Blythe, M., Hassenzahl, M., & Wright, P.C. (2004). More funology. *Interactions, 11*(1), 36-37.

Brajnik, G. (2001). Towards valid quality models for Web sites. *Proceedings of the 7th Conference on Human Factors and the Web,* Madison, WI.

Chillarege, R. et al. (1992). Orthogonal defect classification. *IEEE Transactions on Software Engineering, 18*(11).

Corritorea, C. L., Krachera, B., & Wiedenbeck, S. (2003). Online trust: Concepts, evolving themes, a model. *International Journal of Human-Computer Studies, 58,* 737-758.

Davis, F. D. (1989). Perceived usefulness, perceived ease of use, and user acceptance of information technology. *MIS Quarterly, 13*(3), 319-340.

Dewey, J. (1925/1981). Experience and nature. In J. A. Boydston (Ed.), *John Dewey: The later works, 1925-1953* (Vol.1, pp. 1-326). Carbondale/Edwardsville: Southern Illinois University Press.

Dewey, J. (1933/1986). How we think. In J. A. Boydston (Ed.), *John Dewey: The later works, 1925-1953* (Vol. 8, pp. 105-352). Carbondale/Edwardsville: Southern Illinois University Press.

Earthy, J., Jones, B. S., & Bevan, N. (2001). The improvement of human-centered processes—Facing the challenge and reaping the benefit of ISO 13407. *International Journal of Human-Computer Studies, 55,* 553-585.

Elliot, M., & Kling, R. (1997). Organizational usability of digital libraries. *Journal of the American Society for Information Science, 48*(11), 1023-1025.

Firesmith, D. (2003). Using quality models to engineer quality requirements. *Journal of Object Technology, 2*(5), 67-75.

Fogg, B. J. et al. (2001). What makes a Web site credible? A report on a large quantitative study. *Proceedings of CHI 2001* (pp. 61-68). New York: ACM Press.

Golbeck, J., & Hendler, J. (2004). Accuracy of metrics for inferring trust and reputation. *Proceedings of 14th International Conference on Knowledge Engineering and Knowledge Management,* Northamptonshire, UK.

Grudin, J. (2004). Crossing the divide. *ACM Transactions on Computer-Human Interaction, 11*(1), 1-25.

Kelly, D., & Cool, C. (2002). The effects of topic familiarity on information search behavior. *Proceedings of the Second JCDL* (pp. 74-75).

Hvannberg, E. T. (in press). Experience research. In E. Aarts & J. Encarnaçao (Eds.), *True visions: Tales on the realization of ambient intelligence.* Springer-Verlag.

Hvannberg, E. T., & Law, E. L.-C. (2003, September 5-9). The classification of usability problems (CUP) scheme. *Proceedings of INTERACT 2003,* Zurich, Switzerland.

Copyright © 2007, Idea Group Inc. Copying or distributing in print or electronic forms without written permission of Idea Group Inc. is prohibited.

Lave, J. (1988). *Cognition in practice: Mind, mathematics, and culture in everyday life.* Cambridge: Cambridge University Press.

Lewis, J. R. (1995). IBM computer usability satisfaction questionnaires: Psychometric evaluation and instructions for use. *International Journal of Human-Computer Interaction, 7*(1), 57-78.

McCall, J., Richards, P., & Walters, G. (1977). *Factors in software quality. Volumes 1, 2, & 3.* AD/A-049-015/055, National Technology Information Service, Springfield, VA.

McCarthy, J., & Wright, P. (2004). *Technology as experience.* Cambridge, MA: MIT Press.

McGrath, J. E., & Hollingshead, A. B. (1994). *Groups interacting with technology.* New York: Sage.

Montero, F., González, P., Lozano, M., & Vanderdonckt, J. (2005). Quality models for automated evaluation of Web site usability and accessibility. *Proceedings of the International COST294 Workshop on User Interface Quality Models* (pp.37-43), Rome, Italy.

Mumford, E., & Beekman, G.J. (1994). *Tools for change and progress: A socio-technical approach to business re-engineering process.* Leiden, The Netherlands: CSG Publications.

Nardi, B. A. (1994). Studying context: A comparison of activity theory, situated action models, and distributed cognition. In A. B. Nardi (Ed.), *Context and consciousness: Activity theory and human-computer interaction* (pp. 69-102). Cambridge, MA: MIT Press.

Olsina, L., Lafuente, G., & Rossi, G. (2001). Specifying quality characteristics and attributes for Web sites. *Proceedings of Web Engineering: Managing Diversity and Complexity of Web Application Development* (LNCS 2016, pp. 266-277). Berlin: Springer-Verlag.

Preece, J. (2000). *Online communities: Designing usability, supporting sociability.* Chichester, UK: John Wiley & Sons.

Rheingold, H. (1994). *The virtual community.* London: MIT Press.

Rosson, M. B., & Carroll, J. (2002). *Usability engineering: Scenario-based development of human-computer interaction.* San Francisco: Morgan-Kaufman.

Salomon, G. (Ed.). (1993). *Distributed cognitions: Psychological and educational considerations.* Cambridge: Cambridge University Press.

Schön, D. A. (1983). *The reflective practitioner.* New York: Basic Books.

Schulte, M., & Huber, O. (2003). Information search in the lab and on the Web. *Behavior Research Methods, Instruments & Computers, 35*(2), 227-235.

Simon, B. (2001). *E-learning an Hochschulen: Erfolgsfaktoren und Gestaltungsräume von Wissensmedien.* Lohmar/Köln: Eul-Verlag.

Copyright © 2007, Idea Group Inc. Copying or distributing in print or electronic forms without written permission of Idea Group Inc. is prohibited.

Suchman, L. (1987). *Plans and situated action: The problem of human-machine communication.* Cambridge: Cambridge University Press.

Svenonius, E. (2000). *Intellectual foundation of information organization.* Cambridge, MA: MIT Press.

Vanderdonckt, J., Law, E. L.-C., & Hvannberg, E. T. (2005, September 12-13). *Proceedings of the International COST294 Workshop on User Interface Quality Models,* Rome, Italy.

Vygotsky, L. S. (1978). *Mind in society: The development of higher psychological processes.* Cambridge, MA: Harvard University Press.

Wenger, E. (2001). *Supporting communities of practice: A survey of community-oriented technologies.* Retrieved from http://www.ewenger.tech/com

Copyright © 2007, Idea Group Inc. Copying or distributing in print or electronic forms without written permission of Idea Group Inc. is prohibited.

Section II:

Analysis and Design of Online Learning Communities

Chapter V

Designing Online Learning Communities to Encourage Cooperation

Miranda Mowbray, HP Laboratories Bristol, UK

Abstract

This chapter is concerned with how to design an online learning community in such a way as to encourage cooperation, and to discourage uncooperative or antisocial behavior. Rather than restricting design to visual and interface issues, I take a wide view, touching on aspects of the governance, social structure, moderation practices, and technical architecture of online learning communities. The first half of the chapter discusses why people behave antisocially in online learning communities, and ways to discourage this through design. The second half discusses why on the other hand people behave cooperatively in online learning communities, and ways to encourage this through user-centered design, applying some results of experiments in social psychology. The chapter is intended to be of practical use to designers of online learning communities.

Copyright © 2007, Idea Group Inc. Copying or distributing in print or electronic forms without written permission of Idea Group Inc. is prohibited.

Introduction

Human beings being what they are, any social venue is likely to experience some antisocial behavior. The kind of antisocial behavior that appears in a particular venue will depend on the characteristics and opportunities of the venue, and of the tenor of the social interaction that takes place; this applies to online venues as well as to off-line ones. In this section, I will give some examples of antisocial behavior in online learning communities. As will be seen, there are some differences in what is possible (and in what is common) online from off-line.

Flaming is disruptive emotional speech. It has been noted for a long time as a problem with online conversations. For instance, in an early experiment by Sproull and Kiesler (1991), a group solving a problem online threw more flames than a control group solving the same problem off-line (p.119). A flame by one annoyed, angry, or frustrated person can often bring another flame in response, leading to an escalation that disrupts the possibility of calm conversation.

Obscene or violent speech can be a problem in that it destabilizes the tone of communications in the learning community. Some online learning communities for teenagers, for example, have experienced students testing the boundaries of language permitted.

Harassment and bullying do occur in online learning environments, just as harassment and bullying by mobile text message, off-line written message, and the spoken word occur in off-line learning environments. In a survey of 770 UK youngsters aged 11 to 19 (NCH, 2005), 14% said they had been bullied by text message, 5% in Internet chat rooms, and 4% via e-mail. For the youngsters in formal education, half of the bullying messages happened at school or college, and 11% said that they had sent a bullying or threatening message using a digital medium.

Identity theft is easier to carry out online than off-line. I have been successfully impersonated in an online learning community, on several occasions, by a man; I doubt that he would have been successful face-to-face.

Malware can be spread via online communication and shows no signs of becoming less common. According to measurements by MessageLabs® (2005), about 1 in 28 e-mails sent in June 2005 contained computer viruses.

MessageLabs® also estimates that 2 out of every 3 e-mails sent in June 2005 were *spam*. Spam occurs not only via e-mail, but via other online media too. For example, open wikis and the comment pages of blogs have been invaded by spammers in the last few years. In addition to advertisers and fraudsters who try to reach as many people as possible over the public Internet, members of online learning communities can cause a problem if they decide to send many messages to a very large number of community members.

Copyright © 2007, Idea Group Inc. Copying or distributing in print or electronic forms without written permission of Idea Group Inc. is prohibited.

Privacy intrusion can be a problem in online learning communities, particularly if the norms of how information in the online environment may be used are not clear.

Online learning offers enhanced opportunities for *cheating* (Foster, 2003; Jones, 2003). The ease of cutting and pasting from Web pages, and the very wide variety of information available online, makes plagiarism easier than it was pre-Web. Ready-made essays on commonly set topics and illicitly obtained exam questions may be obtained from specialist Web sites or from other students. The ease of online impersonation may allow students to let a substitute sit their exam for them. Students have been known to change their marks by gaining entry to online databases containing their results.

Finally, online learning communities can suffer from a *low signal-to-noise ratio.* For instance one online learning community based at the University of Virginia, originally designed for serious discussions on postmodern literary theory, turned out to be very popular with members of the public who logged in from all over the world just to tell silly jokes. In general, the ease and convenience of online communication can lead to the practice of near-immediate responses in asynchronous media, allowing members little time to think about or edit their messages before sending them. Synchronous online media such as chat rooms allow little time for editing by their very nature.

Why do People Behave Badly in Online Learning Communities?

Possibly the main factor contributing to bad behavior in online learning is *disinhibition.* Contrary to early findings on computer-assisted communication by the RAND Corporation, modern online communication technology tends to have a disinhibiting effect. The Internet sage Esther Dyson has likened the Internet to a beer party. This disinhibition can lead to greater feelings of involvement and social warmth than might be expected, but also weakens internal censorship of antisocial behavior.

The disinhibition arises from several factors. Online communication offers some protection from adverse consequences of antisocial behavior. Speaking aggressively to someone face-to-face may lead to a punch in the nose. If you do so online, your nose is safe. Some members of online learning communities regard the online environment as not the "real" world, but as some sort of theater or playpen, where normal courtesies and rules need not apply. Weak feedback may limit the effectiveness of social restraints; if I say something to your face that you take the wrong way, I have the opportunity of noticing that I have upset you and explaining that I did not intend to do so, and apologizing. If I say it online, I may not even notice that I have upset you. Finally, online learning environments have different social rules (for technical reasons, among others) from that of face-to-face environments—and

Copyright © 2007, Idea Group Inc. Copying or distributing in print or electronic forms without written permission of Idea Group Inc. is prohibited.

indeed from other online environments that members are used to. Since the rules are different, it may not be clear to members what they are, or even if there are any rules at all, resulting in a loosening of inhibitions.

In addition to disinhibition, there are other factors contributing to bad behavior in online learning communities.

Disinhibition not only weakens self-censorship which otherwise would prevent a user from engaging in antisocial behavior, but it can also lead to *weakened defenses to emotional hurt* by the victims of such behavior. A student in a disinhibited state will be less shy about expressing her ideas and more open to positive social interaction, but will also be, for example, more vulnerable to harassment.

Several of the examples of antisocial behavior described previously would be more difficult or actually impossible off-line, because they are facilitated by *technical opportunities* for antisocial behavior. For instance, spam and computer viruses do not have precise off-line equivalents, because they are enabled by technical properties of the software and protocols used for online communication; and learning online may make it easier to cheat.

Some learning communities deliberately—and laudably—attempt to engage as diverse a studentship as possible, using the wide reach of the Internet as an enabler. Although the resulting *cultural diversity* can have strikingly positive outcomes, cultural differences can also compound the problem of unclear rules.

Some antisocial online behavior is partially motivated by the *opportunity to demonstrate technical and creative prowess.* An ingenious program that exploits a previously unknown flaw in the system to cause social disruption may be a source of pride to the programmer.

A final factor contributing to bad behavior is the extent to which online communication affects the environment, which Kollock (1999, p. 228) calls its *efficacy.* If you are in a very bad mood and are rude to everyone you meet for 10 minutes off-line, you may ruin the day of 20 or 30 people. If you broadcast an offensive message in an online learning community, you may be able to upset many more people than that. Online learning communities offer an efficient way of distributing communication, whether that communication is pleasant or unpleasant.

It is important to notice that most of these factors contributing to antisocial behavior have a positive side too. Eliminating these factors would reduce the capabilities of the community for socially positive behavior. We need ways to discourage antisocial behavior online without reducing the learning community's potential for good. Although many social, environmental, and technical factors influence the quality of interaction between the members of an online learning community, the design of the online community can have a significant effect. In the following sections I will discuss ways to design the online learning community to discourage antisocial or uncooperative behavior without reducing its positive capabilities.

Copyright © 2007, Idea Group Inc. Copying or distributing in print or electronic forms without written permission of Idea Group Inc. is prohibited.

Discouraging Antisocial Behavior

Lessig (1999) makes a useful classification of methods for discouraging antisocial behavior into *law, norms,* and *architecture. Law* consists of sets of rule systems and punishments for transgressions. It does not refer exclusively to national or international laws—for instance, the "law" that aims to limit where cars can be parked includes national and local laws, but also includes notices saying PARKING FOR CUSTOMERS ONLY, and the car park attendants who enforce them. Lessig points out that laws are a relatively expensive way of controlling behavior, and should be regarded as a backup for when other methods fail. *Norms* consist of social pressure and socialization. Social norms can be the most effective approach to controlling behavior. Most car owners do not park on their neighbors' lawns, not principally because they are afraid of punishments for doing so, but because they have been socialized into believing that it would not be a good thing to do. Finally, by *architecture* Lessig refers to aspects of the design of the environment that make unwanted behavior difficult to carry out. For instance, putting a fence around a lawn makes it more difficult for neighbors to park there. I will discuss each of these approaches in turn in the context of online learning communities.

Law

Many online learning communities do have the equivalent of laws: they are the terms of service documents, which specify behavior that is forbidden in the community and sometimes the sanctions for such behavior. Unfortunately, the terms of service for most online communities (with a few pleasant exceptions, such as those for the investment community The Motley Fool®) tend to be written in legal language and are heavy-going to read. The clearer your terms of service document is, the easier it will be to keep order. One student who admitted repeated online plagiarism threatened to sue his UK university for negligence, for allegedly not warning him that it was against their regulations (BBC, 2004). There are well-designed resources for teachers of pre-teens on the specific issue of cheating (online and off-line) at CastleWorks (2005).

Laws are of little use unless there are also means to enforce them, along with a procedure for resolving disputes about whether the laws have been infringed.

Reid (1994) has noted that online multi-player games have "mediaeval" punishment systems, with punishment as a public spectacle (Chapter II, p. i). More modern components of justice systems, including mediation, restoration, and rehabilitation, are worth incorporating in online learning communities. My own experience in the online community Little Italy was that some of the members who contributed

Copyright © 2007, Idea Group Inc. Copying or distributing in print or electronic forms without written permission of Idea Group Inc. is prohibited.

most to the community had initially been problem members displaying antisocial behavior; the process of rehabilitation had succeeded in redirecting their energy from disruptive activities to positive ones.

Norms

In addition to the terms of service page, which specifies behavior that is forbidden, it can be helpful to have a netiquette page for your community to describe norms of polite behavior.

If new members join the community over time, more experienced members can play a role in socializing them and clarifying the community norms to them. Several online communities have official helpers, who are experienced members who volunteer to assist novice users of the community (and not-so-novice users), solving their technical problems, helping them to navigate community information sources, and advising them on etiquette.

A related idea, although one that is only applicable to some limited types of online learning communities, is to require new members to have a sponsor. A sponsor is an existing member who vouches for the new member's good behavior. It is the sponsor's responsibility to communicate the community's norms to the new member. If the member misbehaves, the sponsor may be penalized, and the sponsor is expected to take part in rehabilitating the offender.

Since novice users may make mistakes while they are learning the norms, one technique used in some online learning communities is for there to be a learner-driver period for new members, during which their communications are marked with some sign indicating to other members that they are new and should therefore be treated with patience if they infringe social norms.

Online mediation can be a useful technique for managing conflict between online learning community members. A disagreement or argument can be taken out of the public forum into a semi-private space until it is resolved by the disagreeing parties working with the mediator, and can be pursued again in the public space without causing disruption. It can be useful to have a mediator who is neither the administrator, nor immediately involved in the dispute, but a volunteer from the community.

The commonest and most effective tools for socialization in learning communities are social ridicule of disruptive members and reinforcement of pleasant behavior, carried out by other members as part of online conversations. Administrators of learning communities can set an example by the tone of their online interactions. As a consequence of the weakened feedback in online communications, explicit acknowledgment of positive online behavior is especially important. For good advice on hosting online conversations, see Rheingold (1998).

Copyright © 2007, Idea Group Inc. Copying or distributing in print or electronic forms without written permission of Idea Group Inc. is prohibited.

An entertaining way of countering bad language through social ridicule, invented by Lawrence Ladomery, is for a community administrator to edit nastier messages, substituting offensive words by flower names. The effect of this can be an outburst of "flowers" from the author before he or she works out what is going on.

The economic success of the auction site eBay®, which has a reputation system for its buyers and sellers based on ratings of their behavior by other members, has led to reputation systems becoming *de rigueur* for some categories of commercial Web sites. Resnick, Zeckhauser, Swanson, and Lockwood (1992) found in a controlled experiment that an established seller with high reputation could sell items on eBay® at prices 7.6% higher than a newcomer could. Reputation systems may also provide an incentive for good behavior in learning communities where it does not confer any economic advantage, by decreasing the likelihood of reciprocation for members with low reputation (and increasing it for those with high reputation), and by validating the positive self-image of cooperative members.

Reputation systems may award positive points for good behavior, negative points for bad behavior, or both. However, systems that award negative points may be fooled by miscreants who leave the community and return as apparent newcomers, thus wiping out their negative points. This can be prevented in some cases by identity checks on newcomers; for instance, if the online community is associated with an off-line course, it may be straightforward to tie members' online identities to their off-line ones. However, if such access control is not feasible in your online community, then you should use reputation systems that award positive points. Experiments by Yamagishi and Matsuda (2002) demonstrate that introducing positive reputation to an auction market without access control can increase the quality of the goods offered for sale, and the honesty of the sellers about their goods.

Reputation can be calculated not only for members, but also (or alternatively) for individual messages, and this information can be used to decide the prominence with which messages will be displayed.

Architecture

A few antisocial behaviors can be completely prevented by architecture—that is, by the code of the online site. For example, censorware can automatically prevent certain words from being published on the site (although it may not be able to suppress variations of the words that are still comprehensible to members). In some cases an architectural component does not completely prevent a particular behavior, but limits the damage that it can cause; for instance, a filter that allows a member to choose not to see any more messages originated by another particular member will not prevent harassment, but may prevent repeated harassment by the same person. (Good practice in the implementation of such a filter is that both the member that is filtered and a mediator are automatically informed when it is applied.)

Copyright © 2007, Idea Group Inc. Copying or distributing in print or electronic forms without written permission of Idea Group Inc. is prohibited.

More commonly, architecture does not provide a solution in itself, but can support other solutions. Disputes about whether prohibited behavior took place can be more easily resolved if conversations are automatically logged. It is helpful to have a separate channel for mediation, so as to isolate mediation from public conversations. Collaborative technologies such as collaborative filtering software and reputation software can harness community input to increase the signal-to-noise ratio, by making posts more prominent if community members judge them to be good, and by deleting posts judged to be worthless.

Some antisocial behavior in online communities, especially by teenagers and pre-teens, is attention seeking. A problem member who is very active and who likes to provoke arguments is known as an "energy beast," after a Star Trek® episode about an alien that feeds on intense emotions. Paying attention to an energy beast just gives it more energy; the solution is to ignore it. One architectural approach to help achieve this is to give energy beasts their own space where they can post as many messages as they like, but where other members can choose not to go. Administrators should take care to avoid being provoked into disputes with energy beasts, and should answer any long messages from them with short but courteous replies.

Cooperative Behavior in Online Learning Communities

The problems described in the first half of this chapter tend to be minority phenomena. In general, online learning communities tend to have positive social atmospheres with remarkable amounts of cooperation. In this second half of the chapter, I will outline different types of cooperative behavior, reasons for such behavior, and ways of designing online learning communities to encourage it, applying some findings from social psychology.

Types of Cooperative Behavior

Perhaps the most obvious category of cooperative behavior in a learning community is the provision of useful information or interesting ideas related to the learning topic. There are however other kinds of cooperation and interpersonal support. One is to provide meta-level assistance, for instance helping other members to use the interface or underlying technology or to navigate the online space, or giving them information about social norms, or introducing them to others who might have interests in common, or giving input into the design of the learning community itself. Another is to stimulate and shape the online discussion, for instance asking

Copyright © 2007, Idea Group Inc. Copying or distributing in print or electronic forms without written permission of Idea Group Inc. is prohibited.

fruitful questions, seeking clarifications, summarizing previous discussions, or bringing back a conversation to the main topic after a digression. Another kind of cooperation that is sometimes ignored by the designers of learning communities, but which can be extremely important to members, is emotional support. This can be as minor an activity as thanking someone for a contribution, or as major as supporting another member through bereavement. Yet another form of cooperation is to take real-world action implementing online suggestions and discussions, and to report back on this to the online community.

Internet technology also can enable some types of cooperation that are difficult or impossible off-line. A striking example of this is the story of LEGO® MINDSTORMS™ and BrickOS™. LEGO® MINDSTORMS™ products, which were developed for educational purposes, are kits for building programmable robots that can interact with their environment. Several school projects use them to teach students math, science, computing, and design technology, by getting students to program the robots to carry out particular actions. Schools can (and do) share their ideas for projects involving these via a community Web site (LEGO® Group, 2005). The "brain" of the robot is a special programmable LEGO® brick. When it was first sold, this brick could only be programmed using a special-purpose programming language. Markus Noga and others reverse-engineered the programmable brick's operating system to create the open source operating system BrickOS™, available for free on the Web, which allows the robots to be programmed in C and C++, and has much more power and flexibility than the original. The free availability of this operating system contributed to a remarkable creative proliferation of ideas for these robots. Enthusiasts published descriptions and photos of many new robots, together with the code to run them, on public Web sites. Although the reverse engineering had been carried out without permission, the LEGO® Group decided not to sue, perhaps because they saw the potential of the new operating system for increasing sales; the download site for BrickOS™ is now linked from the official LEGO® MINDSTORMS™ site. The Hall of Fame page (LEGO® Group, 1999-2001) on the official site, which contains programs voted for by the site's online community, includes code for—among many other things—a pinball machine, 3D scanner, and stair climber all constructed using LEGO® MINDSTORMS™, and a robot for painting stripes on Easter eggs. Neither the open-source creation and wide distribution of BrickOS™, nor the wide publication of code for interesting robots and the resulting mutual inspiration and learning by their creators, would have been possible without Internet technology.

Why Do People Cooperate in Online Learning Communities?

Although people certainly do cooperate in online learning communities, it is not immediately obvious why. According to Volund (1993) and other sociobiologists,

Copyright © 2007, Idea Group Inc. Copying or distributing in print or electronic forms without written permission of Idea Group Inc. is prohibited.

cooperation between non-kin should only happen in very long-lived groups with very stable membership. Online learning communities rarely have these characteristics. Indeed, one advantage of online learning is precisely that its flexibility allows for cooperation among learning groups that are short-lived or have rapidly changing membership. Short-lived groups can easily interact online without having to arrange to be in the same location, and standard software for online archiving and retrieval can make it easy for messages from members of rapidly changing groups to continue to be used after the member has left the group.

Similarly, Tarlow (2003) asked about Markus Noga: "What's in it for him? He didn't get *anything* for doing this. Why would he spend a huge amount of talent and knowledge developing something for LEGO®? I'm not sure I would."

Kollock (1999) discusses several motivations for cooperation in online communities (pp. 227-229). These are anticipated reciprocation (that is, the expectation of later help or information in return) increased personal reputation, a sense of efficacy, benefit to oneself as a member of a group, and attachment to a group.

Two more reasons that people cooperate in online learning communities are disinhibition—which can make members more emotionally supportive, for instance—and a desire to display creative or technical prowess. As remarked earlier, these can also motivate antisocial behavior. Finally, although it is possible to explain much of the cooperation that can be seen in online learning communities without assuming that members are motivated by altruism, there is general agreement among people with long experience of such communities that altruism does play a role.

Encouraging Cooperative Behavior

Now that I have outlined reasons why people cooperate in online learning communities, I will discuss ways to encourage and enhance such cooperation through user-centered design, applying some results of experiments in social psychology.

Are Tangible Rewards Effective?

It appears to be common sense that people are more likely to contribute to a community if they are rewarded for doing so, and this has led to a variety of tangible rewards being offered for contribution to online communities, ranging from additional course credits to personalized ballpoint pens.

In their study of online forums used in universities in Hong Kong, McNaught, Cheng, and Lam (Chapter VIII, this volume) found that structured forums with course credits offered for particular levels of activity were generally more successful than "free"

Copyright © 2007, Idea Group Inc. Copying or distributing in print or electronic forms without written permission of Idea Group Inc. is prohibited.

forums, and that to make a free forum successful, it was necessary for the teacher to be particularly skilled at motivating students to participate. However, it is not clear how much of the success of the structured forums was due to the extrinsic rewards and how much to, for example, the specific goals and integration with classroom activity, which were features of these forums but not of the free forums. McNaught et al. remark that it is not easy to maintain a forum of consistently high quality, and if students have only extrinsic motivation.

Moreover, research by Fahey (2005, pp. 81-90) reveals that tangible rewards can have a deleterious effect. Members of a large multinational knowledge-sharing community were offered points for contributions in the community, which they could save up and exchange for rewards such as key rings, mugs, or laptop bags. Fahey discovered that when these rewards were introduced, the quantity of messages rose, but their quality significantly deteriorated. There was conflict among members concerning abuses of the reward system, and a loss of collective trust. Fahey attributes these phenomena to the change in members' motivation for contribution. Before the introduction of rewards, members were motivated to contribute by collective interest and moral obligation; afterward, many members were motivated primarily by economic self-interest.

Although additional points were given for messages rated as useful by other members of the knowledge-sharing community, it was possible to gain some points merely by posting a message. It is possible that a more carefully constructed reward scheme, in which only high-quality messages were rewarded, might have led to an increase rather than a decrease in quality. Fahey however discusses the possibility that introducing *any* reward scheme into a successful online community may lead to a deterioration of quality, one reason being that members may lose interest in doing more than the bare minimum necessary to gain the reward. If rewards are given at the discretion of an administrator rather than at the achievement of some published minimum criteria, then members may devote energy to buttering up the administrator rather than contributing to the community. Certainly, if you plan to offer tangible rewards for contributions in your learning community, you should design your reward system with care, bearing in mind that it will encourage members to seek the easiest way of earning the rewards.

Enhancers of Cooperative Behavior

Several social psychologists have run (off-line) experiments using social dilemmas to discover the factors in group interaction that encourage cooperation (Brewer & Kramer, 1986; Kerr, 1996). They found that the presence of norms of cooperation, communication to other members of cooperative actions, awareness by members

Copyright © 2007, Idea Group Inc. Copying or distributing in print or electronic forms without written permission of Idea Group Inc. is prohibited.

of the efficacy of their contribution, a strong group identity, and non-anonymity of group members all increase the amount of group cooperation. For each of these factors, I will now outline some ways that design of the online learning community can introduce or enhance the factor.

Cooperative Norms

In the first part of the chapter I described several ways to support norms that discourage antisocial behavior. These can also be used to support norms that encourage cooperative behavior. In addition there are a few design features that assist specifically with the development of norms of cooperation. A community structure that includes small teams of members who are expected to communicate more intensively with each other can allow for more repeat interactions among the same set of members, and hence increase opportunities both for more sophisticated cooperation and for the upholding of cooperation as a norm. Teams may be groups of members with particular interests, or groups of members who invite each other join their team, or failing that, teams may be arbitrarily assigned. "Buddy list" technology can be used so that members know when another member of their team is online. Interfaces can include prominent design features for responses to contributions from other members, and for meta-level suggestions. However, it is good design practice to have a separate communication channel for meta-level discussions, to avoid them from interrupting the conversational flow.

Following the principles of user-centered design, members should be encouraged to participate in decisions affecting the design of the community (where design is understood in its widest sense). This not only encourages one form of cooperation, but also can strengthen cooperative norms by giving members a sense of ownership and a desire to support the smooth running of the community.

Communication of Cooperation

As mentioned earlier, making reputations visible to other members is one way of communicating that a member has behaved in a cooperative fashion.

Information about ways in which a member has contributed may be added (automatically or manually) to their personal profiles. For instance, a profile might contain the number of messages posted by that member that were highly rated by other members, with links to them, a reputation rating for the member, and a star awarded to a group of members for an act of particularly impressive cooperation, linked to a featured members Web page describing this cooperative act. Some of this information might be visible in icon form on messages sent by that member.

Copyright © 2007, Idea Group Inc. Copying or distributing in print or electronic forms without written permission of Idea Group Inc. is prohibited.

A personal profile displays information about a single member. If the number of community members is not too large, then a visualization tool such as i-Bee (Mochizuki et al., Chapter XVI, this volume) could be used to display some information about all the members at once, thus giving a picture of the overall level of cooperation in the community as a whole, or of how cooperation varies between different parts of the community.

Some architectural features can be effective in encouraging the basic cooperative act, that of engaging in discussion with other community members. One of these is *answer notify*; when another member responds online to a message, the author of the original message is automatically notified by e-mail. The introduction of this simple mechanism can lead to a noticeable increase in the frequency of messages and the level of conversational engagement. A similar effect is achieved by the *trackback* functionality of blogs, which can be used to link a blog back to other blogs that comment on its content, thus encouraging cross-blog conversations.

Efficacy

In order for members to know the efficacy of their contributions, it is useful to have specific goals for users or groups of users, and information on current progress toward those goals. The goals should, of course, be related to user needs and user requirements—that is, to the members' own tasks and goals, which user-centered design methodology will aim to discover.

One aspect of a system with high efficacy is that the effort required for cooperation and collaboration is small. Designers of online learning environments should therefore aim to reduce the steps required, both in terms of physical activity (the number of mouse clicks, for instance) and in terms of conceptual difficulty. When possible, steps to cooperation should be automated. For example, for some types of goals, information on progress toward the goals can be obtained automatically. Reputation systems may incorporate measurements that can be carried out by software instrumentation of the online learning environment in addition to feedback by other members.

Instrumentation may also automatically identify features of the online environment that are being rarely used, or rarely used by particular types of members, and this information can be used to improve the environmental design. Software that identifies pairs of members with potentially matching interests can be a useful addition to personal recommendations.

Some experiments on ways to encourage contribution through increasing members' awareness of the efficacy of their contributions were carried out by the CommunityLab project (Ling et al., 2005) studying an online movie-rating community. They found that reminding individual members who rated rarely-rated types of movies of

Copyright © 2007, Idea Group Inc. Copying or distributing in print or electronic forms without written permission of Idea Group Inc. is prohibited.

their uniqueness had the effect of increasing contributions by these members, and that groups of members who were set challenging, specific goals (to rate a specific number of movies) produced more ratings than those given the vague goal to rate "as many as you can." Collective goals for groups of 10 members produced higher contributions than individual goals; this is contrary to predictions from off-line research that individual goals are more effective than goals for groups of more than five or six members. Interestingly, reminding members of either the individual or the collective benefits (but not both) of the act of rating movies had the effect of decreasing the number of movies rated. The researchers suggest that this last effect may be because the reminder of a benefit of contribution may undermine other motivations; if this is the case, it suggests a common mechanism underlying both this effect and the deleterious effects of introducing tangible rewards observed by Fahey (2005).

The efficacy of past messages depends on the ease of finding them again. Good search technology is essential for large communities, and processes for categorization and editing of material can greatly improve the signal-to-noise ratio.

The environment of an online learning community includes the online environment itself, as well as the off-line environment in which it is embedded. Effects of actions on the online environment may be more immediately noticeable for members than off-line effects. Therefore following user-centered design principles in which users' preferences, goals, and actions feed back into the design of the online environment can enhance users' awareness of the efficacy of their contributions.

Group Identity

A unified on-screen look for the online community, with consistent colors, fonts, icons, buttons, and screen layouts, can help to support a group identity, as well as contributing to usability. A logo for the community can provide a handy visual identifier that can be used to link to the community site from other Web pages, or on publications and t-shirts.

Induction courses for new members can serve to foster a group identity as well as to introduce social norms.

A simple tool for assisting group identity that was first developed on Usenet newsgroups is the FAQ, a public list of frequently asked questions and answers to those questions. The FAQ can greatly reduce time spent answering common queries, but also can enhance group identity by recording the most useful community knowledge, or community decisions, in a quickly accessible form. A vocabulary list that records and explains technical terms that are commonly used by the community, or words that are used by the community with specialized meanings, can also be

Copyright © 2007, Idea Group Inc. Copying or distributing in print or electronic forms without written permission of Idea Group Inc. is prohibited.

helpful. There needs, of course, to be a process by which the community can update the FAQ and the vocabulary list. Usenet FAQs typically had one volunteer editor who accepted suggestions from the community; wiki technology now allows the production of documents that any member can update at any time.

Online communities have one advantage over purely off-line ones when it comes to maintaining a group identity, in that online community software makes archiving very easy, and so it is relatively easy to have a group history available to current members. Techniques of editing, summarizing, and storytelling can help to produce a group history that is more conducive to the formation of a group identity than mere raw transcripts of past activity would be.

Non-Anonymity

In order to achieve non-anonymity, it is not necessary for members to be fully identified; it is enough for members to have persistent pseudonyms, which allow a history to be built up of a member's interactions with the community, and also allow the development of social reputation and nontrivial social relationships within the community. Personal profile pages can play a useful role in making individual members less anonymous. Some elements of the profile (for instance, numbers of postings and links to recent ones) may be automatically produced by the community software, while others (for instance, a list of interests) may be written or edited by the member herself. One effective way of reducing anonymity is to integrate online learning with activities where members meet each other face-to-face.

Integration with Off-Line Activities

My experience of several online learning communities suggests that cooperation is increased by integration of the online learning with face-to-face activities. Off-line activities may allow opportunities for extra communication of cooperation and for strengthening of group identity, enable additional forms of contribution, and decrease anonymity, so the apparent positive effect of this may be entirely explained by the factors discovered in the off-line social psychology experiments; however, it is also possible that such integration provides an extra boost to cooperation independent from these other factors.

Many online learning communities begin as extensions of off-line educational courses or have some other off-line interaction between their members right from the beginning. Although not all start this way, successful online learning communities develop new or strengthened off-line links: it is natural for people who have learned together online to wish to meet each other off-line as well.

Copyright © 2007, Idea Group Inc. Copying or distributing in print or electronic forms without written permission of Idea Group Inc. is prohibited.

Off-line interaction can significantly improve not only the amount of cooperation by community members, but also the quality of the online learning in general. This is understood, for instance, by the Open University, a UK university dedicated to distance education with around 150,000 undergraduates and 30,000 postgraduates, which has a policy of including residential or day schools as part of many of its courses. An assessment of teaching records in 2004 (Times Newspapers, 2004) put the Open University in the top five UK universities. In contrast, the educational model of several e-education companies that were started during the dot.com boom emphasized access to written course material over interaction (either on- or off-line) between teachers and students or between students, downplaying the social aspects of learning. The result was a reduction in learning quality.

If your community is associated with an off-line course, then it clearly makes sense to integrate the off-line and online learning, making the most of the different capabilities of off-line and online communication. For instance, threaded discussion boards, wikis, and Web sites can be used for students and teachers to hold non-real-time discussions and share information on course topics, set and deliver course assignments, suggest and discuss related reading, and communicate course logistics, without requiring the learning community members to be simultaneously present in the same physical space, and with easy archiving for later reference. Meanwhile, the greater capabilities of the off-line world for interaction with physical objects, for creating a sense of occasion, and for reaching group consensus on contentious issues can be exploited in the off-line meetings.

Online communities can also be used by students while they are actually present in an off-line class or meeting. For instance, law students can quickly find legal precedents online that are relevant to a legal question that comes up during an off-line discussion. One particularly interesting use of real-time online community support during lectures was initially tried out by a project at the University of California at San Diego (Ratto, Shapiro, Truong, & Griswold, 2003). The technology is now used by other universities as well. In this project, students used handheld wireless devices during lectures to suggest questions to be answered by the lecturer, to answer questions suggested by others if they had a good answer themselves, and to vote for which questions on the list of current suggested questions should be given priority by the lecturer. The identity of the student suggesting a question was not revealed to other students, although the lecturer could discover it later. Students' ability to ask questions without revealing their identity reduced their embarrassment about asking questions in class, and this produced questions of a high quality and broad range. The voting system allowed lecturers to know that a question was of interest to many students, rather than only to the questioner. A professor who used the system said (p. 7) that students asked questions that had not ever been asked in prior versions of the course, some of them especially insightful, with the result that all students were able to benefit.

Copyright © 2007, Idea Group Inc. Copying or distributing in print or electronic forms without written permission of Idea Group Inc. is prohibited.

If your community does not have an obvious off-line component, it makes sense to plan off-line meetings for community members. These should include both meetings for serious learning, and social meetings—or alternatively it is possible to combine the two, allotting time for socializing when planning the timetable for a study meeting. The technical and informational resources of the online learning community can be used to support off-line meetings. For instance, the agenda can be discussed in advance online, background material and introductions by speakers and delegates can be provided in advance, logistical and travel information can be circulated online, the venue and questions to put to speakers can be decided by online vote, and members unable to attend can use the online community to appoint delegates who will find out about a particular topic or make particular points on their behalf, reporting back to them. It can be possible for community members who are not physically present to take part in dialogs and question sessions during the meeting itself by, for instance, responding to live blogs written by members who are present.

After the meeting, edited write-ups of the meeting and summaries of any outcomes can be posted online, and follow-up discussions can take place there, taking advantage of the archiving capabilities of online communication as well as its capabilities for non-real-time, geographically distributed discussions. Write-ups and photos of social events can also be valuable for increasing social capital within the community.

Finally, it is a mistake to think of any online learning community as a completely self-contained entity. Its members will have links and affiliations with other organizations, both online and off-line, and these links can be exploited to enhance the community.

Future Trends and Conclusion

In the early days of online learning communities, students were likely to have Internet access only from a computer owned by their educational organization; now some have Internet access from their own mobile phone. Future technology trends are for personal Internet access to become increasingly available, mobile, and affordable. Simultaneously, there is a social trend (in Europe at least) toward lifelong learning, with learning taking place throughout a person's life, rather than being limited to formal education during a particular age span. The effect of this trend is that future learning management systems will need to be flexible, to allow remote personal access, and to be easily integrated into the everyday lives of learners, who will not necessarily be in formal education. Online learning communities will be a crucial part of this. Many of the mechanisms for social control and promotion of cooperation that are used in traditional education are difficult to apply in a distributed community

Copyright © 2007, Idea Group Inc. Copying or distributing in print or electronic forms without written permission of Idea Group Inc. is prohibited.

of learners outside formal education. Therefore it will be particularly important to design such online learning communities to encourage cooperation.

In this chapter I have given reasons for uncooperative and cooperative behavior in online learning, and suggested some ways to design online learning communities in order to encourage cooperation. However, the design of your community should be based on its specific purpose and the particular set of users that it is designed for. You will therefore need to adapt the recommendations to your particular circumstances, involving your users in the design from the beginning, and continuously feeding back users' tasks, goals, experiences, and ideas into potential design changes. For instance, if your community is designed for lifelong learning, and shared off-line activity is impractical, then you may find that users draw particular benefit from design features that foster a group identity and help to build cooperative social norms.

Finally, do not be afraid to experiment. Almost all the design suggestions that I have mentioned were developed through experimentation with the assistance and participation of users, and this is the best way to discover further design improvements that will be useful for your community's purpose. As Howard Rheingold's e-mail signature says, "What it is—is—up to us."

Acknowledgments

Thanks to the many people who contributed to the ideas in this chapter, including members of Little Italy, e-mint, the online communities seminar group at HP Labs, *Online Social Networks,* and the Interaction Design Institute, Ivrea.

References

BBC (British Broadcasting Corporation). (2004). "Plagiarist" to sue university. *BBC News World Edition,* (May 27). Retrieved December 5, 2005, from http://news.bbc.co.uk/2/hi/uk_news/education/3753065.stm

Brewer, M., & Kramer, R. (1986). Choice behavior in social dilemmas. *Journal of Personality and Social Psychology, 50,* 543-549.

CastleWorks. (2005). *Resources by topic: Cheating.* Retrieved December 5, 2005, from http://pbskids.org/itsmylife/parents/resources/cheating.html

Fahey, R. (2005). *Knowledge management. The impact of rewards within communities of practice. A case study.* Unpublished master's thesis, Sheffield Hallam University, UK.

Copyright © 2007, Idea Group Inc. Copying or distributing in print or electronic forms without written permission of Idea Group Inc. is prohibited.

Foster, D. (2003). Test piracy: The darker side of certification. *Certification Magazine,* (January). Retrieved December 5, 2005, from http://www.certmag.com/articles/templates/cmag_feature.asp?articleid=2

Jones, K. (a.k.a. "handy vandal"). (2003). Student logs teacher's keystrokes. *Slashdot,* (February 5). Retrieved December 5, 2005, from http://yro.slashdot.org/article.pl?sid=05/02/03/0156243

Kerr, N. L. (1996). Does my contribution really matter? *European Review of Social Psychology, 7,* 209-240.

Kollock, P. (1999). The economies of online cooperation: Gifts and public goods in cyberspace. In M.A. Smith & P. Kollock (Eds.), *Communities in cyberspace* (pp. 220-239). London/New York: Routledge.

LEGO Group. (1999-2001). *LEGO.com MINDSTORMS Hall of Fame.* Retrieved December 5, 2005, from http://mindstorms.lego.com/eng/community/halloffame/default.asp

LEGO Group. (2005). *LEGO.com Educational Division—MINDSTORMS for schools.* Retrieved December 5, 2005, from http://www.lego.com/eng/education/mindstorms/home.asp?menu=community&pagename=community

Lessig, L. (1999). *Code: And other laws of cyberspace.* New York: Basic Books.

Ling, K., Beenen, G., Ludford, P., Wang, X., Chang, K., Li, X., et al. (2005). Using social psychology to motivate contributions to online communities. *Journal of Computer-Mediated Communication, 10*(4).

MessageLabs. (2005). *Monthly report: June 2005.* Retrieved December 5, 2005, from http://www.messagelabs.com/publishedcontent/publish/threat_watch_dotcom_en/intelligence_reports/june_2005/DA_118149.chp.html

NCH. (2005). *Putting U in the picture—Mobile bullying survey 2005.* Retrieved December 5, 2005, from http://www.nch.org.uk/uploads/documents/Mobile_bullying_%20report.pdf

Ratto, M., Shapiro, R. B., Truong, T. M., & Griswold, W. G. (2003). The ActiveClass project: Experiments in encouraging classroom participation. In B. Wasson, S. Ludvigsen, & U. Hopper (Eds.), *Computer support for collaborative learning 2003* (pp. 477-486). Dordect: Kluwer.

Reid, E. (1994). *Cultural formations in text-based virtual realities.* Unpublished master's thesis, University of Melbourne, Australia.

Resnick, P., Zeckhauser, R., Swanson, J., & Lockwood, K. (2002). *The value of reputation on eBay: A controlled experiment.* Working Paper Series No. RWP03-007, John F. Kennedy School of Government, Harvard University, USA.

Rheingold, H. (1998). *The art of hosting good conversations online.* Retrieved December 5, 2005, from http://www.rheingold.com/texts/artonlinehost.html

Copyright © 2007, Idea Group Inc. Copying or distributing in print or electronic forms without written permission of Idea Group Inc. is prohibited.

Sproull, L., & Kiesler, S. (1991). Computers, networks and work. *Scientific American, 265,* 116-123.

Tarlow, M. (2003, January 30). Paper presented at HP Laboratories, Palo Alto, CA.

Times Newspapers. (2004). The Sunday Times university guide 2004. *Sunday Times* (London), (September 12), supplement.

Volund, E. (1993). *Grundriss der soziobiologie.* Stuttgart/Jena: G. Fischer Verlag.

Yamagishi, T., & Matsuda, M. (2002). *Improving the lemons market with a reputation system: An experimental study of Internet auctioning.* Retrieved December 5, 2005, from http://joi.ito.com/archives/papers/Yamagishi_ASQ1.pdf

Copyright © 2007, Idea Group Inc. Copying or distributing in print or electronic forms without written permission of Idea Group Inc. is prohibited.

Chapter VI

Videoconferencing Communities: Documenting Online User Interactions

Dianna L. Newman, University of Albany/SUNY, USA

Patricia Barbanell, Project VIEW, USA

John Falco, College of Saint Rose, USA

Abstract

Online communities have expanded to include a complex array of technologies that allow us to integrate multiple modes of interaction among participants. One such method of interaction is videoconferencing. As part of a multi-year national program, the authors developed and investigated multiple methods by which videoconferencing could be used to expand PK-12 educational communities such that students at geographically distanced sites have opportunities to interact with external resources. The authors identified four major types of videoconferencing communities and common patterns within each that help to support effective use of the process. The chapter examines the nature and structure of these videoconferencing communities, provides examples of successful use, summarizes key user variables

Copyright © 2007, Idea Group Inc. Copying or distributing in print or electronic forms without written permission of Idea Group Inc. is prohibited.

that impact the process, and makes recommendations for methods that should be used when studying videoconferencing communities.

"Education is longing for a deeper more connected, more inclusive and more aware way of knowing." (Kind, Irwin, Grauer, & DeCosson, 2005, p. 33)

Introduction

As the 21st-century online revolution gains momentum, there is growing understanding that new modes of education consist of intersecting communities of teachers, administrators, parents, students, and informal educators (e.g., museum educators, zoo educators, librarians, artists, scientists, etc.). While these communities have divergent missions and goals, they clearly unite in their common desire to provide resources that will result in higher levels of student achievement (Barbanell, Falco, & Newman, 2003). As a result, educators are creating new online structures using innovative tools to provide content that will enable students to reach higher standards while preparing for the interactive digital world of their future.

Online instructional environments encompass structures that facilitate access to Web-based learning resources and the learning tools embedded in those resources. Access to high-level learning resources is supported in online environments through both synchronous and asynchronous communications that use e-mail, digital bulletin boards and discussion groups, and, sometimes, videoconferencing. As noted by Rigou, Sirmakessis, Stravrinoudis, and Xenos (Chapter X, this volume) and Schwier and Daniel (Chapter II, this volume), these online communication modalities possess different characteristics and provide different levels of interaction, which include but are not limited to linear written response, asynchronous analytic discussion, and real-time interactive socialization. These differences in turn promote different types of communities.

Online learning, in its many manifestations, is emerging as a primary mode for transforming existing content and curriculum into a more cognitively engaging medium, and as a result is leading to a more efficient and productive education of the new era. Online learning has been shown to yield positive educational results in several areas. For example, several authors (e.g., Childers & Berner, 2000; Hardwick, 2000; Heragu, Graves, Malmbourg, Jennings, & Newman, 2003; Hull, 1999) have shown that Web-based (online) education can increase student motivation and participation in both class discussions and student projects. Lauzon (1992) indicated that online technologies provide an excellent medium for allowing learners to interact

Copyright © 2007, Idea Group Inc. Copying or distributing in print or electronic forms without written permission of Idea Group Inc. is prohibited.

in meaningful ways with both a distant instructor and other distant students. Online forums and bulletin boards also have been shown to provide platforms that support variations in interpretation and construction of meaning among students. Alexander (1995) noted that learners interpret reality individually as they engage in apprehending structure, integrating parts, and acting and reflecting on the world.

One of the most interactive modes of online learning is videoconferencing. This medium breaks down the barriers of communication among participants by providing online access to learning and information in a way that encourages the building of interactive communities. Videoconferencing has been defined as "a live connection between people in separate locations for the purpose of communication, usually involving audio and often text as well as video" (Tufts University: Educational Media Center, n.d.). Unlike many other forms of online communication, videoconferencing requires the participants' real-time physical presence to communicate with learners at distant sites. To take advantage of this modality, learning communities must adapt pedagogy and educational content to form a more dynamic mode of interaction. In the best of scenarios, students participate in classroom activities that include interactive questioning and discussion with presenters, thereby merging the local classroom community with others at geographically distanced sites.

Proponents of the medium believe that using videoconferencing in the classroom community has many advantages. One of the benefits of videoconferencing rests in its capacity to import external resources to the classroom via advanced technology (Motamedi, 2001). In addition, it is believed that videoconferencing can better accommodate communities of diverse learning styles than do other online tools in which instructional strategies may be asynchronously mismatched with learners' needs. In fact, many state that it is the interactive element of videoconferencing that is the real key to its success when combined with well-planned, student-centered instruction (Greenberg, 2004; Omatseye, 1996).

Project VIEW, a U.S. Department of Education-funded Technology Innovation Challenge Grant,[1] has developed a model for transforming 20th-century education structures into successful 21st-century education communities via videoconferencing. A key purpose of Project VIEW was to explore the possibilities of videoconferencing as a means of expanding the community of education in the PK-12 classroom; this was to be accomplished by enabling teachers, administrators, students, and external content providers to become immersed in the development and use of this interactive resource. As a result, Project VIEW has created a model of participant engagement involving the creation of learning communities through a combination of constructivist training and hands-on program development. This model fosters interactive cooperation among the collaborating communities, as well as the creation of formal and informal educational societies, by nurturing the collaborations that are founded on true partnerships and sharing of experiences and resources. As a result, new alignments of educational communities are developed to integrate interactive digital content into all levels of curriculum.

Copyright © 2007, Idea Group Inc. Copying or distributing in print or electronic forms without written permission of Idea Group Inc. is prohibited.

Over the five years of the grant, a core element in the creation of VIEW's interactive educational communities was the formative evaluation and research embedded within design and use. As part of this process, the research and evaluation team gathered data pertaining to implementation of more than 100 videoconferences in over 40 buildings and 70 classrooms that encompassed more than 2,000 children and 30 providers. Both quantitative and qualitative methodologies were used. Paper-pencil surveys, randomly selected classroom observations, and structured interviews were used to generate an overview of community building. In addition, case studies of selected teachers and buildings provided an in-depth look at supporting practices. This documentation has resulted in the identification of four major types of videoconferencing communities found in PK-12 educational settings: *provider-classroom videoconferencing, collaborative classroom videoconferencing, multi-point videoconferencing,* and *electronic field trip videoconferencing.* Each of these four types of communities has unique user characteristics and patterns of interaction that reflect variations in goals and member composition. The remainder of this chapter examines the nature and structure of these videoconferencing communities, provides examples of successful use, summarizes key user variables that impact the process, and makes recommendations for methods that should be used when designing and studying videoconferencing communities.

Provider-Classroom Videoconferencing

In *provider-classroom videoconferencing,* a classroom of students uses videoconferencing to communicate directly with a representative of an external expert provider organization. Provider organizations may consist of museums, zoos, historical sites, scientific organizations, and so forth.[2] The provider community representative may be a member of the educational staff, an expert in the field, a group of program sponsors, or others who have external information that can be shared with a group of students. The majority of providers utilize a series of replicable curriculum units based on their internal archives and gallery programs. In Project VIEW, these programs are co-developed with teams of teachers to ensure that the program and supporting materials align with content-based learning standards and are adaptable to differing classroom and student needs.

Classroom communities involved in provider-videoconferencing represent all grade levels (Pre-K through 12 as well as higher education) and include all ability levels of students. This method of videoconferencing is possible in schools with varying technological complexity; schools need only a modern computer, a communication connection, a video camera, and videoconferencing software (Penn, 1998). As a result, classrooms are able to become part of active online learning communities, allowing all students to benefit from a mutual learning context (Menlove, Hansford,

Copyright © 2007, Idea Group Inc. Copying or distributing in print or electronic forms without written permission of Idea Group Inc. is prohibited.

& Lignugaris-Kraft, 2000). Teachers may integrate these external provider-based videoconferences in many ways to support their traditional curriculum; videoconferencing may serve several purposes such as an advanced organizer, enrichment of regular instruction, exposure to primary resources, and summary overviews. In provider-classroom videoconferencing, teachers are no longer viewed as the primary experts, but rather as facilitators whose major task is to enable students to gain insight from these external experts, and to interact with artifacts and resources not usually available within the traditional boundaries of a local school community (Silverman & Silverman, 1999). A brief example of a provider-classroom scenario may be found in Vignette One.

Many school systems use provider-classroom videoconferencing to counteract issues of equity, student safety, and a decreasing economic base. Provider-classroom videoconferencing promotes equal access to resources and increases the quality of educational opportunity for learners in remote or economically disadvantaged schools; it provides access to subject matter experts and career role models for students across gender, ethnic, and racial divisions; it eliminates security issues related to travel; and it overcomes time and budgetary constraints typically associated with field trips.

In general, researchers have found that students who participate in videoconferencing are more motivated and interested in the topic at hand, and report high levels of achievement in problem-solving and critical thinking than before access (Gernstein, 2000; Silverman & Silverman, 1999). Studies conducted as part of Project VIEW indicate that, as a result of participation in provider-classroom videoconferencing, students are more interested in learning the topic, have a greater interest in continuing to learn more, want more access to similar resources, and perceive that they

Vignette One

Janet, a first-grade teacher, brought 5 one-hour videoconferences to her class from a variety of content providers including the Smithsonian Environmental Research Center and the Buffalo Zoo. She used pre-materials to prepare her students for the videoconference and asked them to write to providers asking questions. During the videoconferences, the providers showed students authentic objects, conducted simple experiments, and engaged students in lively discussions. Janet took the role of classroom manager during the videoconferences and, at the end of each, assigned students tasks that included writing about connections, drawing conclusions, and making predictions based on what they had learned. Janet noted that videoconferencing has great potential value as an educational tool and allows her to explore different topics much more in depth than she had in previous years. She reported that videoconferencing generates excitement among students and that lessons involving videoconferencing are much more likely to motivate students to learn. In Janet's words, students "are becoming responsible partners in their own learning."

Copyright © 2007, Idea Group Inc. Copying or distributing in print or electronic forms without written permission of Idea Group Inc. is prohibited.

have a better understanding of the material. Teachers report that students gain a wider perspective of the material, are more actively involved in learning, and work at higher levels of cognition than when exposed only to in-class teaching (Newman et al., 2004; Newman, 2005). Newman, Gligora, King, and Guckemus (2005) also found over a series of studies that students involved in provider-classroom videoconferencing tended to have greater gains in content-related academic outcomes than did students who received parallel traditional classroom instruction.

Several features of the videoconference session contribute to learning and gains in academic outcomes. One of the key characteristics studied, as part of Project VIEW, was the role of the external expert within the provider-classroom community. Abrahamson (1998) noted that the success or failure of the use of interactive television as a means of instruction depended largely on the effectiveness of the content provider and the amount of interaction between provider and students. As a result, Project VIEW research and evaluation of provider-classroom videoconferencing investigated the relationship between provider roles, provider-student interactions, and perceived outcomes of the videoconferencing experience.

A key study conducted by Newman and Goodwin-Segal (2003) investigated the outcomes of 32 videoconferences using 13 different providers, delivered to 550 students across 14 buildings. As part of delivery assessment, students were asked to indicate the activities in which they participated during videoconferencing with an external provider and the degree to which the program was interactive. All videoconferences were observed in the classroom setting by evaluators to validate student-provider interactions. Findings indicate that 95% of the students were actively engaged in watching the program, 59% asked and answered questions, and 52% participated in activities directed by the content provider. To determine if patterns of activities supportive of instructional styles could be documented, a cluster analysis of possible interaction variables was performed. Presented in Table 1 are the results of that analysis. Based on student reported and evaluator-validated activities, three distinct patterns of community interactions, each with distinct roles and relationships, were identified: *provider-centered, provider-guided inquiry,* and *student-centered.*

The first group, labeled *provider-centered,* was the largest, consisting of 250 students (45% of the respondents). The majority of the students in this scenario watched the program, but only a few were involved in asking and answering questions. The remainder of potential instructional activities was not part of these students' videoconference experience. In essence, the students were observers to the development of the community. The role of the teacher in this scenario was that of classroom management or technology monitor. Student and provider interactions in this type of community are similar to those of a teacher-centered classroom, in which an expert provides information to learners who are expected to acquire knowledge via a passive role.

Copyright © 2007, Idea Group Inc. Copying or distributing in print or electronic forms without written permission of Idea Group Inc. is prohibited.

The second group of students (n=196), representing 36% of the participants, was labeled *provider-guided inquiry.* Students in this type of community tended to passively receive information from a provider for the first part of the program and then participated in an activity led by the provider. During this later stage of the videoconference, the provider instructed the students in the steps they were to take as part of the activity, corrected their mistakes, and led them to the correct outcome. The students contributed to an emerging educational community, and were moderately active in asking and answering questions and discussing the topics with other students as they sought to follow directions and reach the correct outcome. In this type of community, the role of the teacher expanded to that of a facilitator: helping to identify students who had questions of the provider, indicating those who had achieved correct or incorrect outcomes, and managing the distribution of local archives. The provider-student relationship in this community was similar to that found in guided inquiry classrooms, but did allow for interaction with an external expert and use of materials that would not otherwise be available.

The final group of students (n=104; 19% of all students), representing participation in *student-centered* settings, tended to reflect the most hands-on interactive learning community. These students worked in groups, asking and answering questions with

Table 1. Instructional groups occurring in provider-classroom videoconferencing

Provider-Centered (n=250)		**Student-Centered (n=104)**		**Provider-Guided Inquiry (n=196)**	
Activity	**Weight**[a]	**Activity**	**Weight**	**Activity**	**Weight**
Watching the program	.93	Watching the program	.93	Watching the program	.93
Answering questions	.48	Answering questions	.87	Participating in an activity with the presenter	.74
Asking questions	.43	Working in a group	.85	Asking questions	.72
Talking with my friends	.21	Discussing the topic with others	.76	Participating in an activity with my teacher	.64
Discussing the topic with others	.18	Designing or making something	.76	Answering questions	.23
Working in a group	.12	Asking questions	.71	Discussing the topic with others	.10
		Participating in an activity with my teacher	.64		
		Taking with my friends	.54		
		Taking notes	.49		
		Solving a problem with the presenter	.43		

[a]*Weights represent relative contribution to the construct of activities.*

Copyright © 2007, Idea Group Inc. Copying or distributing in print or electronic forms without written permission of Idea Group Inc. is prohibited.

the provider, and discussing the topic with other students as well as the teacher. Additionally, these students tended to be involved actively in solving a problem with the presenter, designing or making something, writing or taking notes about the topic, or participating in a teacher-led activity. In this setting, both the teacher and the content provider were active in facilitating learning. The provider allowed students to make mistakes, responded to student-suggested solutions to problems, and encouraged all students to be active in developing scenarios, generating hypotheses, and solving problems. The role of the teacher was that of a co-instructor who helped encourage all students to question the provider, other students' work, and their own work. This provider-classroom community is similar to a constructivist classroom setting but has been enhanced to include an outside expert as well as hands-on problem solving.

Collaborative Classrooms Videoconferencing

The second type of videoconferencing community evidenced by Project VIEW incorporated the concept of *collaborative classrooms*. In this setting, two classrooms at geographically distanced sites use videoconferencing as a means of accessing, sharing, or transmitting information between each other (Newman, 2005). The overall goal of a collaborative classroom is to engage students in the process of instruction and assessment, thereby modeling and supporting higher-level thinking and problem solving (Jonassen, 2002). Instructional practices generally include students at various performance levels working together in small groups toward a common academic goal (Gokhale, 1995). Several researchers (e.g., Davis, 1993; Totten, Sills, Digby, & Russ, 1991; Woolfolk, 2004) have offered empirical evidence that students are more satisfied with learning, engage in higher levels of thought, have greater retention and improved oral skills, and take greater responsibility for their own learning when working in a collaborative setting within their own classroom. The use of collaboration, however, does not decrease the need for individual learning. According to Slavin (1989), effective collaboration settings incorporate the establishment of common group goals backed by individual accountability. This impetus for collaborative learning has been further strengthened by advances in technology and changes in the workplace that emphasize the need for collaborative skills (Beckman, 1990; Gokhale, 1995). When technology becomes part of this process, classroom collaboration can be expanded to include students in separate locations communicating via Web-cams, streaming audio, and the Internet. The use of videoconferencing adds to this process by making it possible for students to see and hear each other, in both small and large groupings. Collaboration is no longer just

Copyright © 2007, Idea Group Inc. Copying or distributing in print or electronic forms without written permission of Idea Group Inc. is prohibited.

within the classroom; it is now synchronous across two communities, and involves the sharing of instruction, resources, and assessment (Newman, 2005).

Educators are exploring four major types of collaborative classroom videoconferencing at the current time. Though similar in overall objective, each serves a distinct group of users, and has unique characteristics and special evaluation needs. The first of these, *student-to-student collaborative videoconferencing,* is utilized when two classrooms or groups of students geographically distanced from each other use videoconferencing as part of their regular instructional process. The goal of the videoconference is to share instructional and learning opportunities across classrooms studying similar content, usually with learners who are similar in ability level and grade placement. In this setting, an interactive community evolves as students work both with their classroom peers and with peers at an alternative site, under the guidance of teachers at both sites, to plan and implement projects, share and present information, and investigate or do research on common themes. Vignette Two provides a brief description of a collaborative classroom videoconferencing community.

The second type of collaborative classroom experience builds on the sharing of information across grade and ability barriers. In *tutoring collaborations,* students who are more advanced or at a higher ability level form online videoconferencing communities with students who are learning basic concepts. In this setting, ad-

Vignette Two

A collaborative classroom videoconferencing project was developed by two sixth-grade teachers who met at Project VIEW training. Teachers jointly created preparatory activities in which all students were paired with another student from the partner school. The pairs corresponded via e-mail for three months (at least one correspondence exchange per pair per month) and eventually met face-to face through a classroom-to-classroom videoconference. Both classes then participated in separate provider-classroom videoconferences with the Museum of Television and Radio (MTR) on the theme, "Not judging others by their outward appearance," in which the museum showed TV clips relating to stereotyping. During this videoconference, the presenter engaged the students in a discussion on stereotypes, and asked them to make predictions and draw conclusions based on the clips they had seen.

Following the MTR videoconferences, the students again held classroom-to-classroom videoconferences. The purpose of these exchanges was for students to make presentations on the books they had studied (students from one school had read Foxman; students from the other had read The Witch of Blackbird Pond). Student presentations reflected on similarities between the MTR videoconference resources and the books. Teachers helped students work collaboratively on their presentations via e-mail, and in some cases via videoconferencing.

Copyright © 2007, Idea Group Inc. Copying or distributing in print or electronic forms without written permission of Idea Group Inc. is prohibited.

vanced students work with teachers in both classrooms to determine basic concepts related to specific content, develop innovative ways of teaching and reinforcing these concepts, and serve as tutors or lay instructors to lower-level students in geographically distanced classrooms. For instance, students in an eighth-grade middle school American History class may teach components of the American Revolution to students in a fifth-grade class located in an elementary school. Without the use of videoconferencing, formation of these interactive communities would require transportation of one or both groups, thereby limiting involvement to classrooms within the same building or, at best, within the same district, and curtailing the frequency of community contact. The use of videoconferencing allows these communities to be formed without consideration of geographical distance or limitations of frequency. Tutorial videoconferencing communities provide tremendous advantages to both student groups; the advanced students have the opportunity to review, enlarge, and enhance their knowledge base as they select and develop methods of sharing knowledge; students who are gaining basic knowledge are, in turn, more motivated to learn the material and see it as more relevant because it is presented by other students.

The third type of collaborative classroom assists in serving the needs of *students with special needs*. This method combines the tutorial approach with student-to-student collaboration and allows for the formation of videoconferencing communities that support the academic, social, physical, and emotional needs of students who are in inclusion and self-contained classrooms. The communities may be composed of students, geographically distanced, who have similar or dissimilar needs and ability levels, and are working together to master skills and knowledge under the guidance of either teachers or advanced students. For example, students in an inclusion classroom may form, via videoconferencing, collaborative learning groups with students with similar needs in another geographically distanced inclusion classroom. Similarly, students in a self-contained classroom may, through the use of videoconferencing, become part of a collaborative group within a heterogeneous classroom. Through the use of videoconferencing, students with special needs have the opportunity to eliminate geographical and structural boundaries that have limited their interactions with other students and curtailed their learning opportunities.

After-school collaboration is the fourth type of collaborative online community being studied by those who are exploring the different uses of videoconferencing. As a result of social, economic, and educational requirements, almost all K-12 districts now have some form of a local after-school program housed within their buildings. These programs represent a sub-community of the larger educational domain, frequently reflecting those students and families most in need of additional academic support, social assistance, or who have limited access to cultural experiences. Multiple types of videoconferencing communities can be formed in these settings to meet these needs. *Student-to-student, tutorial, and special needs collaboration* models can be adapted in after-school settings to assist in meeting the academic needs of

Copyright © 2007, Idea Group Inc. Copying or distributing in print or electronic forms without written permission of Idea Group Inc. is prohibited.

students; geographically distanced study groups of students with equivalent needs in content and ability level can work in a more relaxed environment while obtaining extra help; expert tutors, both adult and peer, can become part of study teams, but still be geographically distanced from the learning site. The use of these active, synchronous, and highly involved online communities also fosters the development of social and emotional supports needed by many of these students.

Designing and evaluating collaborative videoconferencing communities requires additional input and resources to those involved in provider-to-classroom videoconferencing. Because two sub-communities representing the two classrooms are involved in the process, there is a need to delineate the unique characteristics of each and to determine their specific role in the relationship. This includes identifying the contextual, cultural, and technological variables located at each site, as well as the student and teacher variables. Variations in learner ability, access to technology, layout of the classroom, and local support for the process have all been shown to impact the process. As a result, while there is positive evidence supporting the impact of collaborative classroom videoconferencing on learning (e.g., Andrews & Marshall, 2000; Newman, 2005), the complex relationship of these contextual variables has only begun to be studied.

As part of Project VIEW's investigation of the variables involved in collaborative classroom videoconferencing, a major review of collaborative classroom videoconferencing was undertaken. This included selected observations of multiple short- and long-term collaborative communities, in-depth case study documentation of three communities, and an in-depth review of 68 collaborative classroom videoconferencing curriculum plans. In summarizing the findings of this work, Newman (2005) confirmed the diversity and adaptability of collaborative videoconferencing efforts, noting that they served multiple purposes including functioning as/or supporting advance organization efforts, sharing resources and research materials, practicing oral and visual reporting, assessing students, tutoring, and practicing direct remediation. Observations of these collaborative interactions indicated that students were more engaged in learning, tended to perceive more ownership of their work, accessed a broader array of resources (both paper and electronic), and participated in more complex problem solving than when working only within their classroom. In addition, the use of videoconferencing allowed the students to work with students of different ethnic, socio-cultural backgrounds and reinforced respect for multiple viewpoints.

These studies also supported the hypothesis that collaborative classroom videoconferencing is a complex, dynamic process that is actually made up of interdependent communities. The evolving collaborative roles of the teachers influenced the interactions of the students both within and across the communities. The evolution of the teachers' roles, however, was influenced in large part by the availability of technology and technology support during the planning stage as well as during the implementation stage. Teachers who used videoconferencing to develop their col-

Copyright © 2007, Idea Group Inc. Copying or distributing in print or electronic forms without written permission of Idea Group Inc. is prohibited.

Table 2. Collaborative classroom videoconferencing

Instructional Purpose	Communities Involved and Their Role	Instructional Placement
Advanced organizer	Older students introducing materials to younger students	At the beginning of a unit
Resource for research	Older students providing, assisting younger students with insights, resource clarification, assistance in finding information	Mid-unit, after the classroom teachers have covered materials with both groups
Sharing resources for research	Same aged and ability level of students, studying the same content **while** sharing insights, resources, and conclusions	Throughout the unit, with instruction from teachers interspersed with student work
Reporting and presenting	Same aged and ability level of students reinforcing and sharing learning; older students reporting to younger students	At the end of units; prior videoconferencing not required
Assessment	Older students observing and providing feedback to younger students or to students of equal ability without the pressure of friendship bias	Informal assessment midway through units and prior to summative assessments; summative assessment at the end of units
Tutoring	Older students to younger students; older students with special needs to younger students; peer-to-peer	Before and during instruction
Remediation	Older students to younger students; parents to students	During instruction and as part of after-school programs
Motivation	Older students to younger students or to students with special needs; parents or community adults with student groups to other student groups	Before, during, and after instruction; classroom and after-school programs

laborative classroom plans had greater access to technology and technical support, involved the students in videoconferencing more frequently and in a more independent manner, and also saw the need to develop means by which students used other modes of communication. Subsequently, teachers who were more comfortable with videoconferencing, and whose students where more involved in the process, also tended to arrange for telephone calls, letters, and, where possible, in-person visits after the videoconference. In these settings, the community developed by the collaborating classroom videoconference endured longer and allowed for more sharing of cultural and social knowledge.

Multi-Point Videoconferencing Communities

Multi-point videoconferencing is an expansion of classroom videoconferencing to involve three or more communities. These communities may be composed of all

Copyright © 2007, Idea Group Inc. Copying or distributing in print or electronic forms without written permission of Idea Group Inc. is prohibited.

students, or a combination of students and content providers. Variations in the types of communities and the timing, the placement, and the frequency of their involvement make almost every multi-point videoconference unique; however, there are some underlying similar characteristics that can be noted. The most common patterns are expansions of the provider-classroom videoconferencing and collaborative classroom videoconferencing approaches described earlier.

In *multi-point provider-classroom videoconferencing,* a provider simultaneously works with two or three classrooms, sharing not only his or her organization's resources, but also facilitating the sharing of resources among and across the communities of students in the distanced classrooms. This process is synchronous; representatives of all communities are videoconferencing at the same time. In these settings, the students are generally studying similar content and are typically of the same ability level. The role of the provider varies; in some situations, artifacts and discussions are used as advance organizers or for the generation of hypotheses, and students share their thoughts, theories, and hypotheses across classrooms as well as with the provider. In other settings, the provider may serve, along with students in a distant classroom, as an audience and respondent to student questions and presentations from one of the participating classrooms. In the most successful multi-point videoconferences, the provider members of the community begin with a provider-centered approach to learning, presenting facts, and leading a discussion, but then switch to a student-centered approach, acting as the facilitator and moderator between the classroom communities.

In *multi-point collaborative classroom* communities, three or more classrooms of students are simultaneously sharing information, resources, and student-generated products under the guidance of the teachers. Each classroom serves as a provider and an audience to the needs of the other classrooms. This model can be used successfully among students studying the same content. When the method is used for tutorial, research, or reporting purposes, usually at least two of the three classrooms should be at the same cognitive ability level. In situations when the goal of videoconferencing is related directly to the sharing of culture as well as academic information, it is beneficial to have frequent interactions among classrooms at similar ability levels learning similar content. This allows for more opportunity for discussions of different interpretations, and for more secondary questions and elaboration on about why different cultures might perceive information differently. The use of pre-planned or guided inquiry on the part of the collaborating teachers can facilitate this sharing of culture so that it happens in a non-threatening manner.

Copyright © 2007, Idea Group Inc. Copying or distributing in print or electronic forms without written permission of Idea Group Inc. is prohibited.

Electronic Field Trip Videoconferencing

The fourth type of videoconferencing community provides a unique opportunity for interaction between providers and educational communities, and represents an extreme variation of videoconferencing methodologies. In this scenario, a provider community simultaneously broadcasts to a large number of classroom communities, generally for a limited duration for a limited number of times. In this situation, because there are too many classroom communities for student-to-student interactions or for provider-to-student interactions, the predominant mode of communication is provider-centered. In most cases, the provider community has a pre-developed but informal script that is used to guide the presentation of pre-selected artifacts and resources, and the student communities primarily serve as recipients of information during the videoconference. In Project VIEW electronic field trips, teachers assisted in the development of the scripts, ensuring that they met national learning standards, and in many cases, students were included in the design and piloting of supporting instructional materials. Students also played a role in the delivery of the videoconferences, serving as aides in use of archives and in asking and responding to selected provider-generated questions. In some settings, students who were members of the geographically distanced communities played active roles by submitting real-time questions, hypotheses, and comments during the videoconference via e-mail or telephone.

Although electronic field trips are by necessity provider-centered and with limited student interactions, there are scenarios in which they may be the best method of forming a community of short duration that can share important information. Examples include electronic field trip videoconferences of the National Baseball Hall of Fame (e.g., "Untold Stories: Baseball & The Multi-Cultural Experience"), Space Center Houston and Johnson Space Center (e.g., "Journey to the International Space Station"), and the Whitney Museum of American Art (e.g., "Over the Line: The Art & Life of Jacob Lawrence"). Each of these settings involved a unique user characteristic that could not easily be replicated because of the nature of the provider-experts (e.g., membership in the Negro Baseball League or a retired astronaut), the cost of the enterprise, or security issues pertaining to archival access. As a result, a "one-time-only" scenario exists that makes it necessary to allow access to as many learner communities as possible. Most providers have some resources or archives that can only be accessed for a limited time period, and consequently, there is a need to increase access to as wide an audience as is possible. As a result, electronic field trips have a special place in education. Worthington and Ellefson (n.d.) found that a key benefit of electronic field trips was student exposure to "real" people and events that could not be accessed any other way, thereby giving classroom content more meaning by connecting facts to people and occurrences.

The unique characteristics of these communities necessitate a different form of evaluation that emphasizes group goals and socialization/culturalization instead of

Copyright © 2007, Idea Group Inc. Copying or distributing in print or electronic forms without written permission of Idea Group Inc. is prohibited.

individual changes. As noted in Newman (2003), students were less engaged and less motivated to continue learning the content when part of this videoconferencing community than in any of the other types; however, in settings where it was documented that teachers embedded the electronic field trip within their regular curriculum and made use of supporting materials before and after the presentation, students' motivation to learn increased on par with other types of videoconferencing, and teacher-assessed outcomes were achieved.

Conclusion

The role of online communities in the field of education is expanding in an exponential manner. Educators are developing and implementing, on a regular basis, online courses, online components of courses, and online supplements to courses. Studies of *human-computer interactions* that examine the relationships among individuals and computers have led to the identification of patterns of user interaction variables. Knowledge that relationships exist among users has challenged us to expand our research to study the community of the learner involved in the process, not just the individual learner. At the same time, we also have expanded the technologies being used to support learning so that it is no longer human-computer interactions that are important, but rather *community-technology interactions* that must be studied. The use of videoconferencing in the formation of technology-based communities, their interactions and outcomes, and the sustainability of these communities exemplify the need for inclusion of user characteristics when designing and supporting online communities.

Through its five-year program, Project VIEW designed, implemented, and studied four major types of online videoconferencing communities: *provider-classroom, collaborative classroom, multi-point,* and *electronic field trip.* Within each type, common roles and characteristics of the participants were noted that set that community type apart from the others and which yielded explicit implications for user-centered design.

- Provider-classroom communities had as their major objective the expansion of resources to include distant expert participants. Within this goal, varying patterns of interaction were noted that allowed for the formation of different types of relationships with the provider.
- Collaborative classroom communities had as their major objective the expansion of opportunities for collaborative learning such that students could engage with those who were outside their own building's culture. Again, variations in user characteristics played an important role. Teacher, student, building, and

Copyright © 2007, Idea Group Inc. Copying or distributing in print or electronic forms without written permission of Idea Group Inc. is prohibited.

culture interacted to yield variations in the process of reaching the overall goal of collaborative learning.

- Multi-point videoconferencing communities combined the complexities of these two approaches and revealed the importance of flexibility, creativity, and organization in identifying the roles of the participants, and the frequency and depth of the interactions among the key users.
- Studies of electronic field trip videoconferencing also highlighted their unique place in videoconferencing; when providers represent, or only allow access, to a limited resource, tradeoffs of some community members' status may be needed to allow for more equitable access to more members.

Each of these unique settings calls for identification and acknowledgement of different types of planning, implementation, and assessment. As the role of the provider shifts from that of an expert to a peer, from that of a one-time interaction to a series of ongoing, developing conversations, the variables in planning will shift, the types of resources needed for implementation will change, and the outcomes identified as primary to assessment will be altered. In addition, as the size of the community and the sub-communities change, the complexities of the interactions and relationships supporting the community will change and will require different forms of documentation and different variables.

Videoconferencing as a form of online community building is only beginning to be explored. Many school and provider organizations are only now seeing the potential of this method of sharing information. As the technology improves, as more schools and providers are trained and acquire equipment, as more consumers become accustomed to and expect to have this means available to them, the role of videoconferencing will change. Within the next few years, this "innovative" mode of forming communities across geographic boundaries will become common. As this evolution occurs, there is a need to continue to study the characteristics of the members of the communities, and to determine the methods and resources that best meet those members.

References

Abrahamson, C. (1998). Issues in interactive communications in distance education. *College Student Journal, 32*(1), 33-43.

Alexander, S. (1995). *Teaching and learning on the World Wide Web.* Retrieved September 15, 2005, from http://ausweb.scu.edu.au/aw95/education2/alexander/index.html

Copyright © 2007, Idea Group Inc. Copying or distributing in print or electronic forms without written permission of Idea Group Inc. is prohibited.

Andrews, K., & Marshall, K. (2000). Making learning connections through tele-learning. *Educational Leadership,* 53-56.

Barbanell, P., Falco, J., & Newman, D. (2003). Accessing museums through the Web: A model for evaluating the impact of museum and school partnerships In J. Trant & D. Bearman (Eds.), *Museums and the Web 2005.* Toronto: Archives & Museum Informatics. Retrieved September 15, 2005, from http://www.archimuse.com/mw2003/abstracts/prg_200000770.html

Beckman, M. (1990). Collaborative learning: Preparation for the workplace and democracy. *College Teaching, 38,* 128-133.

Childers, J. L., & Berner, R. T. (2000). General education issues, distance education practices: Building community and classroom interaction through the integration of curriculum, instructional design, and technology. *Journal of General Education, 49*(1), 53-65.

Davis, B. G. (1993). *Tools for teaching.* San Francisco: Jossey-Bass.

Gernstein, R. B. (2000). Videoconferencing in the classroom: Special projects toward cultural understanding. *Integration of Technology in the Classroom, 16,* 177-186.

Gokhale, A. A. (1995). Collaborative learning enhances critical thinking. *Journal of Technology Education, 7,* 1045-1064.

Greenberg, A. (2004, February). *Navigating the sea of research on videoconferencing-based distance education: A platform for understanding research into the technology's effectiveness and value.* Retrieved September 9, 2005, from http://www.wainhouse.com/files/papers/wr-navseadistedu.pdf

Hardwick, S. W. (2000). Humanizing the technology landscape through collaborative pedagogy. *Journal of Geography in Higher Education, 24,* 123-130.

Heragu, S. S., Graves, R. J., Malmbourg, C. J., Jennings, S., & Newman, D. L. (2003). Multimedia tools for use in materials handling classes. *European Journal of Engineering Education, 28*(3), 375-393.

Hull, D. (1999). The power and peril in technology. *Community College Journal, 70*(1), 38-44.

Jonassen, D. H. (2002). Engaging and supporting problem solving in online learning. *The Quarterly Review of Distance Education, 3,* 1-13.

Kind, S., Irwin, R. L., Grauer, K., & DeCosson, A. (2005). Medicine wheel inag(in)ings: Exploring holistic curriculum perspectives. *Art Education, 58,* 33-38.

Lauzon, A. (1992). Integrating computer-based instruction with computer conferencing: An evaluation of a model for designing online education. *American Journal of Distance Education, 6,* 32-46.

Copyright © 2007, Idea Group Inc. Copying or distributing in print or electronic forms without written permission of Idea Group Inc. is prohibited.

Menlove, R., Hansford, D., & Lignugaris-Kraft, B. (2000). *Creating a community of distance learners: Putting technology to work.* Proceedings of the American Council on Rural Special Education on Capitalizing on Leadership in Rural Special Education: Making a Difference for Children and Families, Alexandria, VA.

Motamedi, V. (2001). *A critical look at the use of videoconferencing in United States distance education.* Retrieved September 15, 2005, from http://www.highbeam.com

Newman, D. L. (2003). *The virtual information education Web project: Formative evaluation of the Schenectady City School District Technology Innovation Challenge Grant, Schenectady Component, Year Three 2002-2003 Report.* Albany, NY: SUNY Albany Evaluation Consortium.

Newman, D. L. (2005, March). *Beyond the barriers: Benefits of K-12 teacher participation in collaborative classroom videoconferencing training.* Proceedings of the Annual Meeting of SITE Conference, Phoenix, AZ.

Newman, D. L., Gligora, M. A., King, J., & Guckemus, S. (2005, April). *Breaking down the classroom walls: The impact of external videoconferencing on children's cognition.* Proceedings of the Annual Meeting of the American Educational Research Association, Montreal, Canada.

Newman, D. L., & Goodwin-Segal, T. (2003, November). *Evaluation of a technology integration challenge grant program: Using technology to connect museums and classrooms.* Proceedings of the Annual Meeting of the American Educational Research Association, Chicago.

Newman, D. L., King, J. A., Gligora, M. A., Guckemus, S. M., & Pruden, J. M. (2004, November). *Evaluating the impact of videoconferencing: Documenting teacher outcomes and changes in instructional strategies.* Proceedings of the Annual Meeting of the American Evaluation Association, Atlanta, GA.

Newman, D. L., Nolan, A., & Quinlan, B. (2004, April). *Views from opposite sides of the camera: Teachers' perceptions of videoconferencing.* Proceedings of the Annual Meeting of the American Educational Research Association, San Diego, CA.

Omatseye, J. N. (1999). Teaching through tele-conferencing: Some curriculum challenges. *College Student Journal, 33*(3), 346-353.

Penn, M. (1998). Videoconferencing one-to-one but far from home. *Technology Connections, 5*(2), 22-23.

Silverman, S., & Silverman, G. (1999). The educational enterprise zone: Where knowledge comes from. *T H E Journal, 26.*

Slavin, R. E. (1989). Research on cooperative learning: An international perspective. *Scandinavian Journal of Educational Research, 33,* 231-243.

Copyright © 2007, Idea Group Inc. Copying or distributing in print or electronic forms without written permission of Idea Group Inc. is prohibited.

Special Education Programs. (1990). The use of technology with special needs students. *Research Progress, 8,* 1-5.

Totten, S., Sills, T., Digby, A., & Russ, P. (1991). *Cooperative learning: A guide to research.* New York: Garland.

Tufts University Educational Media Center (n.d.). *Glossary*. Retrieved September 15, 2005, from http://www.tufts.edu/orgs/edmedia/gloss.shtml

Woolfolk, A. (2004). *Educational psychology* (9th ed.). Boston: Pearson Education.

Worthington, V., & Ellefson, N. (n.d.). *Electronic field trips; theoretical rational.* Retrieved September 15, 2005, from http://commtechlab.msu.edu/sites/letsnet/noframes/bigideas/b1/b1thor.html

Endnotes

1 U.S. Department of Education Award Number R303A000002.

2 A list of potential providers may be found at www.projectview.org.

Copyright © 2007, Idea Group Inc. Copying or distributing in print or electronic forms without written permission of Idea Group Inc. is prohibited.

Chapter VII

Online Communities of Practice as a Possible Model to Support the Development of a Portal for Science Teachers

Anne Jelfs, Open University, UK

Jen Harvey, Dublin Institute of Technology, Ireland

Ann Jones, Open University, UK

Abstract

This chapter looks at how the ideas discussed in the literature on online communities and communities of practice have been applied to the development of two European "blended" communities: communities with both online and face-to-face components. The chapter discusses the development and support of two communities of science teachers located in Ireland and Bulgaria as a way to support the development of an online portal. We discuss the communities in relation to recognized criteria and features that may be conducive to the success of small communities, and

Copyright © 2007, Idea Group Inc. Copying or distributing in print or electronic forms without written permission of Idea Group Inc. is prohibited.

specifically online communities and how these relate to the different stages of resource development. Sociotechnical findings indicate the need to blend the face-to-face meetings with electronic communications. The role of a key respected teacher/educator was also a pivotal feature in gaining the trust and respect of other participants at an initial stage.

Introduction

This chapter discusses how two communities of science teachers located in Ireland and Bulgaria were established as a way to support the creation of a shared online teaching resource that would subsequently be made more widely available within a broader teaching community. In the last decade, communities have become a hot topic in educational settings, and the number of *online communities* has increased rapidly. One reason for the popularity of communities among educationalists is the features that make them potentially powerful structures for supporting learning and professional development. This is particularly relevant given that the current dominant theoretical approaches to teaching and learning (e.g., the social constructivist approach) view learning as a *social* activity and emphasize the importance of the *social context* of learning, as do contemporary theoretical approaches to adult learning (e.g., Lea & Nicoll, 2002). This emphasis on social activity and the importance of locating learning within such contexts that we see in the field of education is also echoed by contemporary concerns in the fields of computing and HCI, for example in investigating how mobile devices can support learning (Taylor, Sharples, O'Malley, Vavoula, & Waycott, in press), or increasing our understanding of participation in technologically mediated communication (Nonnecke, Andrews, & Preece, 2005).

In discussions of communities, Wenger's (1998) concept of communities of practice (COPs) has been particularly influential. It has been identified as a group of people that are tied together by their engagement in a joint enterprise, by a shared understanding of its purpose, and by the corresponding codes of conduct (Brown & Gray, 1995), all frequently dispersed over a wide geographical distance (Putz & Arnold, 2001).

This chapter looks at how the ideas discussed in the literature on *online* communities and communities of practice have been applied to the development of two European "blended" communities: communities with both online and face-to-face components as a way to support the creation of the new resource. These communities were developed as part of an EU-funded project with the formal title: "PDCDScience: Developing a Periphery-Driven Curriculum Development Model for School Science." For the public access portal for the project, the title has been changed to the rather more manageable STAR Science (STAR). This project was part of the Socrates

Copyright © 2007, Idea Group Inc. Copying or distributing in print or electronic forms without written permission of Idea Group Inc. is prohibited.

EU program, Minerva, the aim of which is the promotion of ODL-ICT in the field of education across the European Union. STAR's main aim was to produce a Web portal in physics and chemistry for secondary-level school teachers. An important feature of the portal development was creating associated *communities of practice* of science teachers who would be actively involved in all stages of the resource development in each country in order to ensure the portal's relevance to the teachers' needs. This user-centered and action research approach aimed to encourage the longer-term potential usability and usage by the wider teacher population.

Preece, Rogers, and Sharp (2002) propose various milestones within such an interaction design process: firstly, there is a need to identify needs and establish user requirements in order to develop alternative designs and build interactive prototypes before undertaking a final evaluation. Preece et al. (2002) also suggest a need for users to be involved the design process immediately after an idea for community groupware is created and before an online community is developed. Schwier and Daniel's chapter (Chapter II) in this volume also identifies virtual communities and perceptions of community building.

A user design collaborative model should follow the natural process of producing any social systems architecture: market research, expert opinions, users' needs, production, and a continuous evaluation process. While national teacher communities—the potential end users of the portal—were already in existence within each country, it was important for this project that the new community established to support the creation of this new resource would both be representative and be able to further develop the appropriate skills as necessary. It was anticipated that all those involved within this new community would bring different levels of skills, whether technical, subject based, or organizational, and that by the coordination of appropriately structured and evaluated activities, these skills would be incorporated and further developed as part of the portal evolution process. It was planned that, after some initial face-to-face planning meetings, the evolving project communities would primarily work online, and so the shared online group spaces would also need to support the associated collaborative activities in parallel to the new resource development.

The chapter outlines the user-centered formative evaluation of the STAR project and considers the extent to which the case study communities meet criteria for virtual communities that are described in the literature (Whittaker, Isaacs, & O'Day, 1997). These case study communities serve to illustrate some important issues in the literature, to discuss the extent to which ideas about virtual communities and communities of practice apply in particular contexts, and to relate this to key debates in the field.

Virtual learning communities have been described as having cycles of development, and with these, differing individual roles, levels of involvement, and therefore group productivity (Paloff & Pratt, 1999; Wenger, 1999). Some of Wenger's later work (2002) describes a process from potential to coalescing, maturing, active through to dispersing. As members of these communities are essentially self-selecting, and

Copyright © 2007, Idea Group Inc. Copying or distributing in print or electronic forms without written permission of Idea Group Inc. is prohibited.

community boundaries are perceived as fuzzy or fluid (Paloff & Pratt, 1999), some of those recognized stages of group development such as the storming, norming stages (Tuckman & Jensen, 1977) are not considered to be so relevant. The social dimension of learning communities, the relevance of the tasks involved (Wegerif, 1998), as well as an early establishment of mutual trust (Kimble et al., 2001; Fukuyama, 1995) have been shown to be important in affecting the quality of subsequent group interactions. Timely, appropriate, and structured activities are important to maximize engagement of members (Fischer, 1998; Bonk & Cunningham, 1998) as well as try to alleviate dropout or communities fading back. Hawthornthwaite et al. (2000) and Ricketts et al. (2000) describe a method of scaffolding to support online learning community-based activities, and Oliver and Herrington (2000) emphasize the importance of training and guidelines in order to try to maximize and increase the quality of online engagement.

The chapter is structured as follows. First we briefly review relevant literature on online communities and communities of practice. We then describe the case study communities and the STAR project within which these virtual communities are being developed. Five characteristics of online interaction that contribute to the phenomenon of "community" were used as criteria for evaluating the two communities (Whittaker et al., 1997). We discuss the communities in relation to these criteria, and then we discuss similarities between the communities—features that may be conducive to the success of small communities. We identify seven such common features, and in the final section draw some conclusions about supporting such blended communities and how they might relate to much larger online communities while retaining their local connections. The second section describes the processes involved during the different stages of community development and the role of various formative evaluation activities within the portal development process—in particular, those activities involved in the process of establishing user requirements and evaluation criteria, recommendations for community, ways of working, the final development of the portal structure, and the subsequent re-evaluation of process by the user group.

Online Communities

Many virtual communities discussed in the educational literature are *communities of learners* rather than communities of practice. Goodfellow (2003) offers the following distinction:

'Communities of practice' differ from 'communities of learners' in that the latter are reflexively concerned with learning whereas the former are concerned with practice, of which learning is a corollary. (p. 3)

Copyright © 2007, Idea Group Inc. Copying or distributing in print or electronic forms without written permission of Idea Group Inc. is prohibited.

So learning outcomes of some kind are the main focus for virtual learning communities, and much of the educational literature, until relatively recently, has been concerned with such communities, which have often been designed by course developers around "virtual" courses. Investigations into particular aspects of online learning have tried to understand when and why online learning becomes productive and what makes online communities work. Examples of such work include the impact of online learning on the role of teaching staff (Jelfs & Colbourn, 2002; Light, Nesbitt, Light, & White, 2000).

In their review of the factors influencing the success of online learning environments in university teaching, Tolmie and Boyle (2000) include group size, knowledge of other participants, experience, ownership of task, and the need for/function of online learning environments. Too large a group may make it difficult for learners to get to know each other sufficiently to develop trust: a crucial component of a successful community (e.g., Wegerif, 1998; Fukuyama, 1995). Knowledge of other participants is also very important, as is the credibility of the participants and key individuals (Harvey, 2003). While these studies are concerned with virtual educational communities, findings about group size and trust are also likely to apply to online communities more generally.

Preece (2000) discusses the phenomenal growth of online communities more generally—their nature and how best to support them—and pays considerable attention to social and affective aspects. She argues for the importance of sociability in communities, which depends on trust, collaboration, and appropriate styles of communication. In contrast, Mowbray's chapter (Chapter V) in this volume considers anti-social behavior in online communities. It has been considered that for online communities to be successful, developers and designers need to pay attention to social as well as technical issues, and Preece describes five stages of community development. Goodfellow (2005) considers shared community membership to be characterized by shared stories, jokes, jargon, and shortcuts to communication, which are used not only to negotiate meaning but also to signify membership.

As noted earlier, Wenger's ideas about communities of practice (Wenger, 2002) have been taken up enthusiastically by many educationalists. It has also been suggested that new technologies can support "virtual" communities of practice, which can allow more contextualized teaching, where students can access communities of experts who are operating in real-world contexts. In science teaching for example, students might communicate with practicing scientists or school pupils with meteorologists, and post questions to them or discuss their projects with them. However, Barab and Duffy (2000) argue that such virtual environments are *practice fields* rather than authentic communities of practice. The aims of such environments are educational: students may be talking to real scientists, but the tasks they are engaged with are educational, not part of the science community's working life. Wenger also argues that communities of practice cannot be created:

Copyright © 2007, Idea Group Inc. Copying or distributing in print or electronic forms without written permission of Idea Group Inc. is prohibited.

Communities of practice are about content...not about form. In this sense, they cannot be legislated into existence or defined by decree. They can be recognized, supported, encouraged, and nurtured, but they are not reified, designable units.

However, there have been attempts to develop communities, or using Wenger's words, "to support, encourage, and nurture communities." Such attempts present a real challenge, and the difficulties should not be underestimated. Nevertheless, there are some successful examples such as the Tapped-In Project—which also aimed to develop a teacher professional development community. The virtual environment "Tapped In" (Schlager, Fusco, & Schank, 2002) aimed to support the online activities of a large diverse community of educational professionals. It appears to have been successful in bringing together and forging new worldwide relationships among education practitioners, providers, and researchers, and is used by thousands of different people each month. Activities include courses, workshops sessions, public discussions, and group meetings across a range of school topics. However, there is a question about whether it is a *community of practice* in the sense that Wenger uses the term, in that the activities online are not related to the members' professional practice (for example, in the teachers' own school districts).

We would suggest that there is a very real tension here which is an issue for many online communities with a global reach. The global nature of such communities removes them from local activities and thus weakens this aspect of practice. It is very difficult to achieve both at once. This issue of tension between success on a very large scale—as evidenced by a large active community—and relating back to the local community of practice, is one that will be returned to.

Some criteria were needed to evaluate the two case study communities in the STAR project. Five characteristics of online interaction have been identified as contributing to the phenomenon of "community" (Whittaker et al., 1997). They are:

1. A sense of community among the participants
2. Social networking, which may include, for example, an economy of public goods in the form of exchanges of information
3. Shared discourse
4. Social control (for example, control over undesirable behavior)
5. Membership trajectories—involving patterns of participation and non-participation

In evaluating the two communities in Ireland and in Bulgaria, we were interested in whether these five characteristics could be met and how they work and apply in practice. We wanted to explore whether, if these communities were successful,

Copyright © 2007, Idea Group Inc. Copying or distributing in print or electronic forms without written permission of Idea Group Inc. is prohibited.

there were common features that might contribute to that success and whether the tools designed to support these communities were successful. The two communities are similar in type (experienced science teachers) but located in very different contexts.

The evaluation process also explored the way in which the communities worked to produce the portal during the different stages of the portal development.

The Case Studies and the STAR Project

The case studies discussed here were developed as part of the STAR project. A major aim of this project was to produce a Web portal in physics and chemistry for secondary-level school teachers to provide resources for students aged between 14 and 16 years. The portal was intended to be developed through a user-centered design process of establishing teacher action-research groups and other representatives of the teachers' community to play an active role in designing the portal for subsequent use by a wider science teacher community. The project had partners in England—the London Metropolitan University UK (LondonMet); Bulgaria—the National Center of Distance Education, University of Sofia; and Ireland—the Dublin Institute of Technology, (DIT).

DIT and the University of Sofia have both produced a tailor-made online resource for physics and chemistry respectively. Initially, for DIT, this involved creating a portal, which integrated existing publicly available online resources with relevant pedagogical content. Although many Internet resources are available, they are not always appropriate for the Irish or Bulgarian curriculum. Furthermore, teachers do not always have time to access, select, and update suitable resources. It was therefore decided to develop a portal to provide quick and easy access to peer-reviewed resources linked to subjects within the school physics curriculum, and to work with teachers in developing it. Third-level teaching staff here would be consulted as part of the process. The development of the resource portal has involved four main stages so far: undertaking a needs analysis and development of the prototype portal, establishing the community, creating the portal content, and subsequent community maintenance. Evaluative activities were embedded at all stages of this process.

The educational and technological contexts are quite different for the two case study countries. The Irish Government Taskforce recently made a series of recommendations including creating a "virtual learning environment [to] include a system populated by e-learning content for science, particularly the physical sciences …" and also for a "framework allowing teachers…to structure and manage learning resources, curriculum content, student access, collaboration and assessment" (*http://www.education.ie/servlet/blobservlet/physical_sciences_report.pdf*). One goal of the STAR

Copyright © 2007, Idea Group Inc. Copying or distributing in print or electronic forms without written permission of Idea Group Inc. is prohibited.

project—to explore and develop a transferable and sustainable process in which a community group could negotiate the structure and outline of an online resource to support individual teaching practice—addresses both these recommendations.

The context in Bulgaria is rather different, with access rates to personal computers and the Internet significantly lower than in Ireland, although telecommunications access is relatively high and Internet access is increasing rapidly. Here it was decided that the portal would also include curriculum materials for parts of the secondary school chemistry curriculum—and the advice of a team of very experienced chemistry teachers was sought in developing these materials. The teachers were particularly interested in the Internet resources, which were new to many of them as their Internet access is rather limited. Based on the distinction drawn earlier, the teacher communities are much more like communities of practice than communities of learners, although we should note that they have been "created" by the project, rather than having evolved "naturally". So far, the resources have been created or located by the teachers, but students have also become very involved, and there are plans to include resources developed by students of some of the teachers in the Bulgarian community. Another advantage of using a WebCT environment has been that associated resources can be used to support ongoing community activities and as a method of capturing the group process.

Community Development in Association with Resource Development

Preece et al. (2002) describe various stages within an interaction design process: firstly, there is a need to identify needs and establish user requirements in order to develop alternative designs. During the initial stages of this project, all partners assembled key stakeholder groups as a way of establishing user needs. On the basis of these structured discussions, a further needs analysis survey tool was created to gauge user skill levels and requirements, and also as a means of inviting teachers to become members of the new resource development community. In this way, it was anticipated that a self-selecting group of interested teachers would become involved. The majority (63%) of Irish questionnaire returns (41 from 200 circulated) were from those with between 5 and 30 years teaching experience; all except four accessed the Internet at least weekly, and the same number also indicated that they would find it easy to use a computer with their classes. Out of a broad selection of potential portal resources offered, online simulations and online laboratory activities were considered by respondees to be the most useful for this community. Continual updating of resources, a forum for sharing ideas, and the ability for teachers to upload and share reviewed resources were felt to be the key features to elicit their usage of such a resource. Based on this feedback, a prototype portal was developed by the project team. This was then evaluated during the first face-to-face session of

Copyright © 2007, Idea Group Inc. Copying or distributing in print or electronic forms without written permission of Idea Group Inc. is prohibited.

the teacher groups. Preece et al. (2002) emphasize the need for users to be involved the design process during the initial stages of groupware development. During the structured evaluation session with the teacher group, the structure, a proposed way of working, and the evaluation criteria for the resources were then developed.

Although fairly broad evaluation criteria for the resources were collaboratively developed during the first face-to-face session—an activity led by the initial project team—these have subsequently been changed to link more directly to the course syllabus. At this stage, the community has decided to move from a categorization of resources as being *core*, *added value*, or *no good* to a five-star rating. Review comments and any additional materials will be available from associated links beside the resource URL. In addition, there has been a gradual change in the way in which the reviews are carried out. From the range experienced during the first six months, including evaluation seminars, structured online discussions, chat sessions, online forms, group review teams, and e-mail, the group has decided that they prefer to evaluate resources as small review teams using personal e-mail accounts, and then report back to the group using the online WWW discussion area. Strategies for re-reviewing resources, and archiving reviewed but not appropriate resources and associated materials, have also been negotiated by the group during the face-to-face sessions. Each face-to-face session is currently being used as a deadline for reviews and to reflect upon and explore the next group task.

Face-to-face sessions were organized in consultation with the teacher groups; these sessions along with the various associated online activities occurred during times when other work commitments were less onerous. "Reviewing resources" and "keeping in touch with what is going on" were the main reasons cited at that stage for accessing the portal. The Physics topics area was most frequently used, as might have been predicted by the original needs analysis. The teaching physics and equipment areas were used least often. Interestingly, these had been added primarily on the instigation of the project team; while the teachers felt it was important to include these for the wider community group, they did not feel any personal need to make use of them. All respondents indicated that they felt that the resultant portal structure developed as part of the project eased access to appropriate resources and that the rating system they developed worked well. This could however be a result of group members becoming more familiar with the content so issues of retrieval are lessened.

The teachers also felt that they would be more likely to use a star rated resource, as it had been reviewed by one member of their community. The ways of working as a group were felt to be effective as: "Communications worked well and suited everyone," "The format meant that it didn't matter when I found time to work, could have been midnight." However, they did feel that "it was easier to motivate yourself when you are working in groups face to face" and "I would be happy to meet more regularly." They also appeared to appreciate that they were in control of the portal design and development: "Sometimes the group seems a little all over

Copyright © 2007, Idea Group Inc. Copying or distributing in print or electronic forms without written permission of Idea Group Inc. is prohibited.

the place and are not moving so fast, yet the site has greatly improved and is getting there," and "Improvements were clear by the end of the year." They felt that being part of the community "has had sharing and motivational outcomes" and "I would be interested in keeping in touch with the group over the next year" and also "being actively involved in reviewing the resources" and "letting other people know about the site/recommend to others." This, after the project funding had ceased.

Both groups have had face-to-face meetings in addition to their use of virtual spaces. This was not the original intention but evolved as the community developed. This issue will be discussed along with the activities and achievements of the groups. Examination of these two groups allows us to consider communities of practice in two very different contexts: both in terms of learning—but also more widely in terms of technology access and use, an important contextual issue. While Ireland has a technology "history" and access similar to many other European countries, Bulgaria has little history of Internet use, but is developing this history rapidly. These case studies are therefore of particular interest, given this book's emphasis on the role of contexts in building environments for e-learning and in understanding the influences of contextual issues on learning.

Applying the Characteristics of Virtual Communities

The five characteristics of virtual communities listed earlier were starting points for considering the success of the STAR project communities in Dublin and Sofia. We explored the first characteristic, the participants' sense of community and their commitment to it, in interviews conducted in Dublin. Goodfellow (2003) expands on this idea of sense of community as follows:

"Sense of community... 'of belonging, that members matter to one another and to the group—and a shared faith that members needs will be met through their commitment to be together'" [Wilson, quoted in Goodfellow]. "It is characterized by belonging, trust, expected learning and obligation."

The second characteristic is a social network, derived from social network theory. This is the idea of an economy of public goods in the form of exchanges of information. Community members benefit from the exchange of goods—that is, information including resources, software tools, commentary, and advice. The third characteristic explored was that of shared discourse—the shared stories/jokes, jargon, and shortcuts to communication and styles of speaking that indicate community membership. The fourth characteristic was forms of social control, although we had some doubts about

Copyright © 2007, Idea Group Inc. Copying or distributing in print or electronic forms without written permission of Idea Group Inc. is prohibited.

its relevance as the groups are well moderated, small, and not open to outsiders, so there may be no need for such control. The final characteristic is that of differing membership trajectories involving patterns of participation and non-participation.

A further issue in the literature is that of the *leadership roles* that are needed for supporting online communities which include: defining codes of conduct and cyclical events, providing a range of roles, facilitating member created subgroups, and so on.

Discussion of the Case Studies

The Teacher Groups as a Learning Community

The first part of this section is based on face-to-face interviews with the Dublin teacher community, conducted at a regular STAR group meeting, where teachers took part in evaluating and discussing Web materials. This account is both of the process of developing a community of practice and of that community's perceptions of its success.

A sense of community can be found when individuals join together in common interest groups, with shared goals and aims. The Dublin teacher community shared a number of aims: one of these was improving student understanding of physics from a theoretical and a practical standing, and in particular everyday situations. This community was established from teachers who responded to a survey circulated to 200 local schools. The Dublin project team was fortunate to obtain the assistance of a local education officer for physics, who was a consultant to the project from the initial stages of the prototype development. She was well known to the teachers as a respected member of her field, had taught physics for over 20 years, and from her role within the Education Department was well informed of recent and planned curriculum developments, and of the issues facing physics teachers in Ireland. This was important in the initial stages of the project as the community was being established. She acted as a bridge between the teachers' group and the project team, and due to her unique position as a member of both groups, perceived herself as interpreter between them. In fact, the Education Department had made previous unsuccessful attempts to get regional clusters of teachers to work together. Both teachers and the consultant felt that these groups broke down because of the teachers' lack of motivation and commitment. They felt the STAR group worked, however, because they were a committed, hard-working group, as exemplified by their willingness to give up their weekend time to work on the project.

Initially, only one face-to-face meeting was planned for the beginning of the project. However, after a few months, partly through pressures of work, the online activities started to fade, and telephone interviews with the teachers revealed that they preferred to combine meetings on and offline. Many of the teachers interviewed

Copyright © 2007, Idea Group Inc. Copying or distributing in print or electronic forms without written permission of Idea Group Inc. is prohibited.

commented positively on the opportunity to meet and talk about school issues. It relieved the feelings of professional isolation, as often the individual teacher was the only physics teacher in the school.

The physics teachers did have particular styles of discourse (third characteristic), and most of them felt able to share their comments on the Web sites and to justify their ratings of the materials. The site has a discussion Web-board, but none of the messages on the Web-board were extensive and very few were chatty. However, this should be viewed in the context of the face-to-face discussions that they enjoyed and valued at their meetings.

When the teachers were questioned about the need to restrict other members of the group—the need for social control—they unanimously said "no." This is confirmed when reading the bulletin board messages. The final element of a virtual community, that of differing trajectories, is where different members are involved in different but complementary activities that support the group as a whole. The Dublin teachers have different skills ranging from IT skills to extensive and varied teaching experience, and so the group is able to benefit accordingly. Different members appear to take on more active roles as they lead on different aspects of the portal development. For example, one member provided a CD copy of resources that he had collated and distributed to all the other teachers. Many of these were then reviewed for inclusion within the portal. Another teacher provided his own digitized images for use by others in developing worksheets. Therefore, while the portal aimed to provide quick access to existing Internet resources, it has evolved into a way of sharing and developing community knowledge.

So the Dublin teacher group does appear to have all the characteristics of a virtual community, even though it is, of course, a mix of on and off-line activity. In the next section, we consider the Sofia teachers.

The Sofia teachers all teach chemistry, although some also teach environmental protection and physics. Their average teaching experience is 11 years. Like the Dublin teachers, they are a very experienced group of teachers who use a wide range of teaching methods.

On the face of it, the Sofia teachers had reasonable access to computers: all had *some* access, with just over a third having access at home and nearly all at school. Most used computers fairly infrequently though—with seven reporting monthly use and four reporting weekly use. Their access is often not suitable for classroom use: for example, Internet access in schools is very difficult for science teachers, as it is in the information and communication laboratories and heavily used for teaching information technology (also see Wood, Mueller, Willoughby, Specht, & Deyoung, 2005).

The teacher community in Sofia (i.e., the community of practice) remains at 13 at the time of writing. Impressively, no teachers have dropped out of the project. Like the Dublin teachers, the group has been meeting face-to-face, and at the time of the interview with the project leader, they had just had a seminar.

Copyright © 2007, Idea Group Inc. Copying or distributing in print or electronic forms without written permission of Idea Group Inc. is prohibited.

E-mail discussion in the group was still sparse (and new), but increased after the seminars and mostly concerns technical matters. A particular issue at the time of the interview was finding ways to improve the dialog box through which the discussions take place in the resource. Note that these teachers are very recent e-mail users; however, although they had received training, the teachers wanted a simpler discussion box. The seminars had covered some of the same issues as in Dublin, for example, conducting evaluations of the sites on the resource.

Sofia had taken a rather different approach to Dublin in that it had developed *content* for the resource: they developed what we might call online textbooks for a number of reasons. Firstly, the teachers recruited to the action research team include several experienced textbook authors—hence this reflects their experience and strength. Secondly, much existing Web material is in English rather than Cyrillic and hence not accessible. Finally, given that there is a "gap" here, there was the opportunity to produce demonstration sites, where the teaching could make good use of the interactive qualities of computers. The teachers were therefore very motivated in this direction.

Further issues concern the differences in the curricula in Ireland and Bulgaria, and language. The Bulgarian teachers' English was not good enough for them to be able to use English Web sites in their teaching—yet it is difficult to find good Cyrillic sites, although they have found Russian sites, in Cyrillic, for chemistry teaching. However, although the sites are relevant, they do not have the simulations that they would like to use or that are visually unappealing. The sites they have found are not always satisfactory sites for chemistry: often they do not have the simulations and visualization that the teachers would like. The students' English is better than the teachers, so English sites are less of a problem for the students than for the teachers.

Discussion of the Dublin and Sofia Communities: Issues for the Communities

As noted earlier we were interested in the similarities between the Dublin and Sofia communities, as they may suggest common features that are conducive to the success of such small communities. We identified seven common features, which are first listed and then elaborated:

1. experienced teachers,
2. blended face-to-face and online activities,
3. strongly connected to local context and community,

Copyright © 2007, Idea Group Inc. Copying or distributing in print or electronic forms without written permission of Idea Group Inc. is prohibited.

4. strong and active leadership that was flexible and listened to the group's wishes,
5. strong "core" members who legitimized the group and added value,
6. small groups, and
7. shared purpose/motivation to be involved.

Experience

Both groups are extremely experienced teachers. Such teachers are likely to be very confident and will certainly be experienced in using different methods. Their length of service (and therefore age) might suggest that they are less likely to have ICT experience; however, this is not the case, as many are also IT specialists.

Blended Communities

It was clear in both countries that an online-only community would not have worked. Both groups valued the opportunities to meet up: indeed the Dublin grouped pressed for Saturday morning meetings followed by an informal lunch in the pub, as this worked well for them. They found it motivating; it paced them and also helped to overcome or at least mitigate the access problems that both groups had. The Dublin project manager had to be flexible and change previous plans to accommodate the group's wishes. Without such flexibility, the group may well not have survived.

Strongly Connected to Local Context and Community

The groups were concerned with issues relevant to their local curriculum and were strongly connected to these. In Dublin, for example, the teachers became particularly interested in how the resource could support their teaching of applied science—one part of the curriculum that had recently had much emphasis—while in Sofia the concern was to develop curriculum content, for reasons outlined previously.

Leadership

Both groups required considerable input from the project site leaders. For example, the site leader in Dublin organized regular Saturday workshops and within these curriculum and Web site-related activities (e.g., the software evaluation activities). The pattern in Sofia was similar. The groups also needed administrative support to remind them that they were meeting or that they had deadlines due.

Copyright © 2007, Idea Group Inc. Copying or distributing in print or electronic forms without written permission of Idea Group Inc. is prohibited.

Strong Core Members

Each group contained strong *core* members who added legitimacy and value to the group. As we mentioned earlier, the Dublin team included a local education officer for physics, who was well known to the teachers and who had been associated with the government task force. The Sofia team included a teaching inspector. This was particularly important during the community establishment phase; but as the groups started to work together, once trust was established in the community, other key members started to emerge.

Manageable Size

The small size of the groups meant that members could easily get to know everyone else in the group. There were core members that were noticeably more active than others. Some attended all the meetings, while others came along only once or twice.

Shared Purpose

Having a shared purpose was also an important factor for the Dublin teachers. Although they enjoyed meeting other physics teachers, this on its own would not have been enough. There was the benefit of sharing out and collaborating on work, as well as access to a range of resources and knowledge that members would not have the time or skills to develop individually.

Sociotechnical Aspects

Language was an issue for the Sofia group. The language of the Internet is overwhelmingly English, but many of the teachers did not have a strong command of English, although their students were often better placed. The teachers in Sofia were also much closer to the beginning of the ICT adoption curve. For instance, unlike professional groups in many European countries, they were not accustomed to communicating via e-mail. At the time of evaluation, there had been little online communication for these reasons. Project members at the two sites worked with the strengths and preferences of the groups. The Sofia teachers were experienced textbook writers and wanted to write resources that could act as demonstration examples for how science could be supported and taught through ICT. Thus Sofia produced resources, while Dublin worked with existing resources.

Copyright © 2007, Idea Group Inc. Copying or distributing in print or electronic forms without written permission of Idea Group Inc. is prohibited.

Despite the first two differences—language and ICT adoption/access—a similar model was successful in both contexts. Neither community looks much like the virtual communities discussed in the literature for the main reason that their online presence is currently too sparse. However, they meet the five characteristics of virtual communities: they have shared interests and goals, very much rooted in their professional practice—and if access were easier for them, more of this might well be manifested online. So there is certainly evidence of successful communities here, and this suggests that in certain contexts, with much hard work, such communities can indeed be created.

Although in part the groups wanted face-to-face meetings because of access difficulties, this was not the whole story. The Dublin group in particular enjoyed the social cohesion of their Saturday morning meetings and the pub lunches that followed, as well as the pacing it imposed. With better access, great care would still need to be taken to build-in online activities, and ways of expressing identity and feeling safe that would be as enjoyable and motivating and thus keep the group on board.

Implications on the Design Process

Involvement of the potential user group was important from the initial stage in the portal development rather than the design and way of working being imposed upon the group. Although changes to the final portal structure were not substantial as a result of the ongoing evaluation activities, this is perhaps more a reflection of the appropriateness of the original design developed by the key-stakeholder group during the pre-prototype development phase. Key changes were made to the associated discussion fora supporting the collaborative activities of the community as a way to compensate for the limited online engagement by the teachers. This was perhaps due to their unfamiliarity in the use of asynchronous discussion boards. Although training was provided, any messages posted during those stages were brief, and little social engagement was observed.

Structured evaluation activities including online forms, paper-based questionnaires, and focus group discussion were integral to the whole process, but only because the portal designers and the associated project team were responsive to their comments, making changes, however minimal, as required upon agreement with the group. Thus, perhaps avoiding what has been described as the autistic social software, outcomes derived as a result of little user design involvement (Boyd, 2005). The identified need for the face-to-face sessions to complement online activities were felt to be useful as the group had a definite purpose; rather than just meeting to talk about the science curriculum, they had an outcome from their meetings. This is the second characteristic of a virtual community—social networking—and here there is the exchange of public goods and information, and the development of resources.

Copyright © 2007, Idea Group Inc. Copying or distributing in print or electronic forms without written permission of Idea Group Inc. is prohibited.

Conclusion: Supporting Blended Communities of Practice

There appears to be a number of factors that have influenced the development of the communities of practice and the associated resource development, such as the need to blend the face-to-face meetings with electronic communications. The teachers in both Dublin and Sophia have appreciated the opportunity to meet and discuss site content and future work, while continuing between meetings to send resources, evaluate them, and return comments electronically.

One of the crucial questions facing the project was: Could a community of practice be successfully created? From the case studies presented here, it appears that it can, but in the contexts studied, there were certain requirements, such as the face-to-face meetings. The need for such meetings has been noted in some communities of learners too, such as in some of the professional development courses at the Open University which have also evolved to be a blended mix of online and face-to-face communication. The role of the key respected teacher/educator was also a pivotal feature of gaining the respect of the other participants, and this is recognized in the research literature as one of the factors in a successful community of practice. Having a common goal and achievable outcomes was also clearly important.

The other factors common to both groups included strong *core* members who legitimized the group and added value, a strong link to the local context (in this case the curriculum was very important), good leadership, and small groups. The fact that both groups were very experienced was important in the type of community that developed and the activities that the groups engaged in. While one can imagine the value that a similar community could have for new or trainee teachers, they would clearly not have the experience to share and so would have different goals.

The two communities are relatively small and locally relevant; there is less known about how large-scale communities continue to successfully interact as they grow and can still have members rooted in their local communities. It is unlikely that these models as such can "scale up"; their strength is in being small, close groups, and these groups are closely connected to the local community and to the members' own practice. However, the two communities can be viewed as models for a number of smaller groups that could be linked together—a kind of federal approach. We would suggest that in building a larger community, links could still be made to smaller groups such as this who are rooted in their community. There needs to be a role for such groups in order to keep the larger community in touch with the needs and issues of practitioners.

The STAR Science project has, in fact, built a prototype overall portal to help establish and then support a wider national and international community. This portal offers descriptions of the project, opportunity to join, discussion support, and some

Copyright © 2007, Idea Group Inc. Copying or distributing in print or electronic forms without written permission of Idea Group Inc. is prohibited.

access through to selected content links. There is a facility for users to suggest further links and provided review comments. This portal site also provides an umbrella for the DIT and Sofia sites that operate with the small directly supported communities in Ireland and Bulgaria. At a recent conference (September 2005), physics teachers in Ireland commented on how they continued to make use of simulations, although with the proviso that access to broadband and projectors in the laboratory were of paramount importance to enable the use of simulations.

In continuing its support for a national and international community through the overall portal, the project will need to investigate ways of supporting a global community while remaining locally "rooted": the tension we have referred to earlier. One starting point might be for the overall portal to essentially provide an information service where contributors are subject-based teachers, and within this to have core users. These might, for example, be existing local groups (such as the ones in Dublin and Sofia) who already have shared goals and activities, but for whom the portal would provide further resources and allow them to share experiences of groups elsewhere. Further funding is being sought to support the continued professional development for science teachers and particularly for physics teachers. In order to make best use of the Internet and other digital resources, while also supporting communities of learners that are strongly based in local practice, it will be important to continue to investigate, through this and other projects, ways in which a large-scale community can remain locally relevant by connecting itself to genuine communities of practice.

References

Barab, S. A., & Duffy, T. (2000). From practice fields to communities of practice. In D. J. Jonasson & S. M. Land (Eds.), *Theoretical frameworks of learning environments.* Hillsdale, NJ: Lawrence Erlbaum.

Bonk, C. J., & Cunningham, D. J. (1998). Searching for learner-centred, constructivist and sociocultural components of collaborative educational learning tools. In C. J. Bonk & K. S. King (Eds.), *Electronic collaborators: Learner-centered technologies for literacy, apprenticeship, and discourse* (pp. 25-50). Mahwah, NJ: Lawrence Erlbaum.

Boyd, D. (2005). Autistic social software. In J. Spolsky (Ed.), *Best software writing.* Berkeley, CA: Apress.

Brown, J. S., & Gray, E. S. (1995). The people are the company. *Fast Company, 1,* 78. Retrieved September 15, 2005, from http://pf.fastcompany.com/magazine/01.people.html

Copyright © 2007, Idea Group Inc. Copying or distributing in print or electronic forms without written permission of Idea Group Inc. is prohibited.

Fischer, M. (1998). Using lotus learning space for staff development in public schools. *Journal of Management Inquiry, 9*, 221-234.

Fukuyama, F. (1995). *Trust.* New York: The Free Press.

Goodfellow, R. (2005). Virtuality and the shaping of educational communities. *Education, Communication & Information, 5,* 113-129.

Goodfellow, R. (2003). *Communities of practice and other frameworks for conceptualizing developing and evaluating NCSL's initiatives in linking staff and school communities.* Internal Report, Institute of Educational Technology, Open University, UK.

Harvey, J. (2003, September 8-10). Supporting communities in practice: An exploration of two case studies. In J. Cook & D. McConnell (Eds.), *Communities of Practice. Research Proceedings of the 10th Association for Learning Technology Conference* (ALT-C), University of Sheffield & Sheffield Hallem University, UK.

Haythornthwaite, C., Kazmer, M., & Robins, J. (2000). Community development among distance learners: Temporal and technological dimensions. *Journal of Computer Mediated Communication, 6,* 1. Retrieved February 8, 2006, from http://jcmc.indiana.edu/vol6/issue1/haythornthwaite.html

Jelfs, A., & Colbourn, C. (2002). Virtual seminars and their impact on the role of the teaching staff. *Computers and Education, 38,* 127-136.

Lea, M., & Nicoll, K. (Eds.). (2002). *Distributed learning: Social and cultural approaches to practice.* London: Routledge.

Light, P., Nesbitt, E., Light, V., & White, S. (2000). Variety is the spice of life: Student use of CMC in the context of campus based study. *Computers and Education, 34,* 257-267.

Nonnecke, B., Andrews, D., & Preece, J. (2005). Non-public and public online community participation: Needs, attitudes and behavior. *Electronic Commerce Research Journal.*

Oliver, R., Omari, A., & Herrington, J. (1998). Exploring student interactions in collaborative WWW computer based learning environments. *Journal of Educational Multimedia and Hypermedia, 7*(2/3), 263-287.

Palloff, R., & Pratt, K. (1999). *Building learning communities in cyberspace: Effective strategies for the online classroom.* San Francisco: Jossey-Boss.

Preece, J. (2000). *Online communities: Designing usability, supporting sociability.* New York: John Wiley & Sons.

Preece, J., Rogers, Y., & Sharp, H. (2002). *Interaction design: Beyond human-computer interaction.* New York: John Wiley & Sons.

Putz, P., & Arnold, P. (2001). Communities of practice: Guidelines for the design of online seminars in higher education. *Education, Communication & Infor-*

Copyright © 2007, Idea Group Inc. Copying or distributing in print or electronic forms without written permission of Idea Group Inc. is prohibited.

mation, 1, 181-195.

Ricketts, J., Wolfe, F., Norvelle, E., & Carpenter, E. (2000). Multimedia: Asynchronous distributed education – A review and case study. *Social Science Computer Review, 18*(2), 132-146.

Schlager, M., Fusco, J., & Schank, P. (2002). Evolution of an online education community of education professionals. In K.A. Renninger & W. Shumar (Eds.), *Building virtual communities: Learning and change in cyberspace.* New York: Cambridge University Press.

Taylor, J., Sharples, M., O'Malley, C., Vavoula, G., & Waycott, J. (in press). Towards a task model for mobile learning: A dialectical approach. *International Journal of Learning Technology, Special Issue on Interactions, Objects, and Outcomes in Learning, 2*(2/3), 138-158.

Taskforce on the Physical Sciences. (2002). *Report and recommendations.* Retrieved September 2005 from http://www.education.ie/servlet/blobservlet/physical_sciences_report.pdf

Tolmie, A., & Boyle, J. (2000). Factors influencing the success of computer mediated communication (CMC) environments in university teaching: A review and case study. *Computers and Education, 34,* 119-140.

Tuckman, B. W., & Jensen, M. A. C. (1977). Stages of small group development revisited. *Group and Organisational Studies, 2,* 419-427.

Wegerif, R. (1998). The social dimensions of asynchronous learning. *The Journal of Asynchronous Learning Networks, 2*(1). Retrieved from http://www.aln.org/alnweb/journal/vol2_issue1/Wegerif.pdf

Wenger, E. (1998). *Communities of practice: Learning, meaning, and identity.* New York: Cambridge University Press.

Wenger, E., McDermott, R., & Snyder, W. (2002). *Cultivating communities of practice: A guide to managing knowledge.* Cambridge, MA: Harvard Business School Press.

Whittaker, S., Isaac E., & O'Day, V. (1997). Widening the Net: Workshop report on the theory and practice of physical and network communities. *SIGCHI Bulletin, 29*(3).

Wood, E., Mueller, J., Willoughby, T., Specht, J., & Deyoung, T. (2005). Teachers' perceptions: Barriers and supports to using technology in the classroom. *Education, Communication & Information, 5,* 183-206.

Copyright © 2007, Idea Group Inc. Copying or distributing in print or electronic forms without written permission of Idea Group Inc. is prohibited.

Chapter VIII

Developing Evidence-Based Criteria for the Design and Use of Online Forums in Higher Education in Hong Kong

Carmel McNaught, The Chinese University of Hong Kong, Hong Kong

Kin Fai Cheng, The Chinese University of Hong Kong, Hong Kong

Paul Lam, The Chinese University of Hong Kong, Hong Kong

Abstract

This chapter describes the evaluation of 13 educational online forums. The forums were classified into structured or free, and teacher-centered or student-centered forums according to the learning designs used to prepare the tasks and the style of online interactions. The study provides empirical data across multiple online forum experiences to better inform the pedagogy of using online forums. Findings are that structured forums generally have a higher quantity and quality of postings than free forums, and that student-centered ones also tend to be more effective than teacher-centered ones in encouraging quality online discussion. Further, through

Copyright © 2007, Idea Group Inc. Copying or distributing in print or electronic forms without written permission of Idea Group Inc. is prohibited.

analyzing the evaluation feedback from students and teachers in these cases, the study has identified three key factors that tend to affect forum success—ease of use, clear facilitation, and motivation to engage. The centrality of the role of the teacher was confirmed.

Forums in Online Learning Communities

Online community broadly refers to a community that has some kind of online presence (Preece, Abras, & Maloney-Krichmar, 2004). In general, online communities have characteristics that include:

- a defined community membership, as members usually demonstrate some legitimate interest before participating (Lave & Wenger, 1991);
- the asynchronous nature of computer-mediated communications (CMC) (Daft & Lengel, 1986; Hiltz & Turoff, 1978);
- an extension of community membership, as members can be physically distant and geographically dispersed in an online community (Zhang & Storck, 2002);
- a capacity for rapid dissemination of ideas (Markus, 1994); and
- the possibility of revealing a more holistic picture of the topics under discussion through the cumulative contributions of each member (Zhang & Storck, 2002).

A closer look, however, reveals that online communities are indeed very varied, especially in the purposes for which the communities have been established and the technology used. One of the main purposes of online communities is related to communication between members of a similar profession (often called communities of practice) (e.g., Zhang & Bascelli, 2005), while another main purpose is for the maintenance of communities "that support interest groups such as dog-owners, gardening, football, bridge, and book" (Preece et al., 2004, p. 4); these are known as communities of interest.

The focus of this chapter is the use of online communities for learning purposes (learning communities) (Bielaczyc & Collins, 1999). Online learning communities often claim to be aligned with a social constructivist perspective of learning (Farmer, 2004) in which learners use the contributions of other members to construct for themselves an understanding of a given topic (Zhang & Storck, 2002). It is claimed that the unique features of online communities bring in new qualities that are fun-

Copyright © 2007, Idea Group Inc. Copying or distributing in print or electronic forms without written permission of Idea Group Inc. is prohibited.

damentally different from traditional classroom settings. Ashcroft and McAlpine (2004) envisaged that this new use of technology should "enable students to learn in more active ways, leading to a deeper understanding of the course materials" (p. 1). Salmon (1998) also suggested that the online learning environment can support the development of cognitive processes such as skills in asking questions and reflecting on personal positions. However, as will be discussed next, the evidence about claims such as these is patchy and context-bound.

The technology used in online communities can vary. For example, Ma (2005) reported the use of e-mail to assist collaborative activities, Luca and Cowan (2005) and Farmer (2004) investigated online discussion with blogs or Weblogs, and Xiao (2005) mentioned videoconferencing. All these reports indicate a mix of positive outcomes and some challenges.

Nevertheless, the use of the forum is regarded as one of the most common and important strategies to help build online learning communities. Online forums serve as virtual environments in which students and teachers can interact. Intuitively, it is thought that this mode of communication should assist in the creation of a sense of community within the course. Forums can also be a supplementary source of course-related information for students. Kirk and Orr (2003) claimed that "discussion forums are the enabling tools for those teaching in the e-learning area to build greater student learning outcomes by engaging students in productive discourse" (p. 2). Online forums do allow students to discuss and exchange ideas in flexible times and locations, and considerably extend teaching and learning outside the normal contact hours of the classroom. This chapter focuses on online communities of a very specific type—course-based learning communities using online forums for communication.

There is literature that records serious problems in realizing the potential of online learning communities. For example, Mohan and Lam (2005) outlined problems such as increased workload and group conflicts. Farmer (2004) mentioned the weakness of the forum in maintaining social presence—the ability of the users to project themselves and appear as real persons can be severely limited (p. 4). Cuthell (2005) described the difficulty in achieving active learning among all students: "A common observation is that one-third of online community members are active, one-third read postings and only occasionally contribute, and the final third are inactive" (p. 323). Wozniak and Silveira (2004) remarked that "studies … have concluded that students do not take full advantage of the opportunities available to them, and the e-moderator needs to devote considerable time overseeing the process" (p. 1).

There are several examples of guidelines and strategies that can provide practitioners with tactics to use in online communities so as to achieve better outcomes. In this vein, Preece et al. (2004), for example, advocated that online communities should be constructed with attention paid to their "usability" and "sociability." Salmon (2000) developed a five-stage model for designing activities in online forums, so as

Copyright © 2007, Idea Group Inc. Copying or distributing in print or electronic forms without written permission of Idea Group Inc. is prohibited.

to progressively induct learners into the community. For example, critical thinking and knowledge construction will only occur after online socialization and information exchange have taken place.

As the use of online forums is now more common, it is timely to examine a number of cases to see if there are any overarching success factors that operate in varied contexts. We thus decided to do a meta-analysis looking at the empirical evaluation data of multiple cases. The study investigated how forum designs relate to student learning outcomes, and the general factors that tend to positively and/or negatively influence the success of online forums.

We are particularly interested in a smaller size online community—that developed within a relatively short period of time, usually a semester, with the definite purpose of students supporting and enabling each other to understand some defined academic concepts and skills with the aid of a teacher facilitator.

Methodology

The Nature of the Data in this Study

We have as our data set a rich collection of cases which have come from a project across three universities in Hong Kong. The forums we have investigated were all in course Web sites built by the e3Learning (Enrich, Extend, Evaluate Learning; e3L) project, designed to support teachers in three universities to supplement classroom teaching with e-learning. Details of this project are in James, McNaught, Csete, Hodgson, and Vogel (2003) and at the project Web site. The e3L project operates across three universities: the Hong Kong Polytechnic University, the City University of Hong Kong, and The Chinese University of Hong Kong. Over a three-year period, the e3L project has supported the Web development of nearly 140 sub-projects, and the outcomes of 70 of them have been evaluated. By the end of the 2004-2005 academic year, a total of 4,951 students have used these 70 Web sites and the number of accesses to these Web sites was over 67,000.

All e3L evaluations began at the very beginning of the design process. Discussion about how to evaluate the experience occurred alongside design and development decisions. For each evaluation, after a number of discussions (online and face-to-face), our evaluation team suggested evaluation questions based on the nature of the Web site. Together with the teacher, we decided the types of data to collect and the instruments to use, taking into consideration limitations such as the availability of the students and the teachers. We also set the time schedule for the use of each of the selected instruments. Decisions concerning evaluation questions, data types, evaluation instruments, and the evaluation schedule were put into a formal evalu-

Copyright © 2007, Idea Group Inc. Copying or distributing in print or electronic forms without written permission of Idea Group Inc. is prohibited.

ation plan. The evaluation was conducted in one semester of teaching, and after the data had been analyzed, a full report was returned to the teacher and further discussion offered.

Thirteen of the 70 evaluated course sites had active online forums; 10,713 messages were recorded in these 13 forums which involved 1,280 students. We defined an active forum as one where:

- the teacher saw the forum as a key component of the course,
- there was a plan of using the forum at the start of the course, and
- the teachers introduced and/or demonstrated the forum to the class.

Further, all these 13 teachers were willing to allow project staff to conduct a detailed evaluation of the forum data. The forums were situated in courses in a variety of disciplines and year levels of university education, and the forum profiles are summarized in Table 1. By examining the forums and course documentation, it is possible to classify the forums. Forums 1 to 9 are structured, student-centered forums; Forums 10 and 11 are free, student-centered forums; and Forums 12 and 13 are free, teacher-centered forums.

Table 1. General profiles of the 13 cases

Forum Number	Forum Type		Class Size	Discipline	Year Level
	Activity	Major Role			
1	Structured	Student	229	Nursing	Undergraduate
2	Structured	Student	200	English	Undergraduate
3	Structured	Student	149	Nursing	Undergraduate
4	Structured	Student	84	English	Undergraduate
5	Structured	Student	84	Finance	Undergraduate
6	Structured	Student	82	Nursing	Undergraduate
7	Structured	Student	41	Textile & Clothing	Undergraduate
8	Structured	Student	26	Nursing	Postgraduate
9	Structured	Student	12	Food & Nutritional Science	Undergraduate
10	Free	Student	129	Nursing	Undergraduate
11	Free	Student	89	Nursing	Undergraduate
12	Free	Teacher	108	Nursing	Undergraduate
13	Free	Teacher	47	Biology	Undergraduate

Copyright © 2007, Idea Group Inc. Copying or distributing in print or electronic forms without written permission of Idea Group Inc. is prohibited.

Forums varied in the degrees of flexibility available in the structure of the discussions and the directionality of the communication. There are nine structured forums and four free forums. The nine *structured* forums all have the following characteristics:

- There were pre-assigned topics/ problems in projects to be discussed which were set at the beginning of the course. The assignments could be in the form of peer review, within-student-group discussions, or between-student-group critique.
- Some course grade was allocated to the participation in the online forum, either on a group or an individual basis.
- The forum was designed to be a supplement to the traditional classroom teaching and learning.
- Contributions by students or student groups were mandatory.
- The online forum was introduced to the students at the beginning of the course.
- Students needed to visit the forum from time to time to read the postings by classmates in order to get involved in the discussions.

The *free* forums have the following features:

- There were no pre-set topics to be discussed and activities to be carried out in the forum.

Figure 1. Nature of online forums in this study

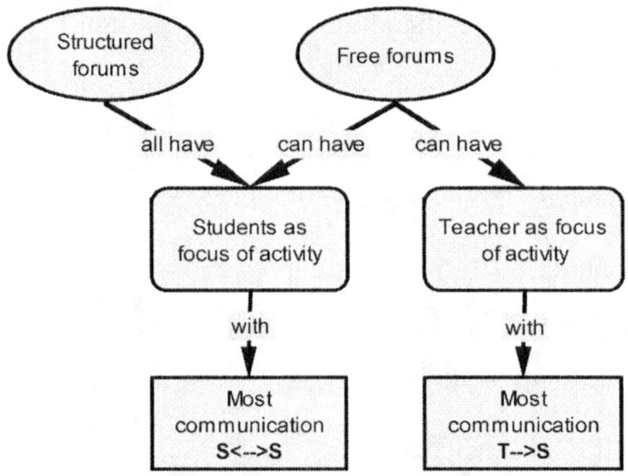

Copyright © 2007, Idea Group Inc. Copying or distributing in print or electronic forms without written permission of Idea Group Inc. is prohibited.

- Students' participation in the forum would not be counted as a part of the course assessment.
- The forum was designed to be an extra component in the course and act as a platform for students to have free discussion on course-related topics.

The directionality of the communication ranges from *teacher-centered* designs (where the communication direction is mostly from teacher to student) to *student-centered* designs (involving much more student-student communication). The nature of the forums is illustrated in Figure 1.

As shown in Table 1, most of the 13 active forums were student-centered. The main reason for the small number of teacher-centered forums is that the teacher-centered forums are less likely to be active ones and thus were not included in our study. Most teacher-centered forums were free forums with no pre-assigned discussion topics and little incentive for students to contribute; the forums were thus mainly used as a place for course announcements. As teacher-centered forums seem to be less successful in general, this type of forum does not have a strong focus in our analysis.

There is also an imbalance in the number of cases between the two categories (nine structured forums vs. four free forums). However, there is a great deal of data—more than in most studies—covering various disciplines and year levels, and so we believe there is value in this approach.

Evaluation Strategies

The evaluation data set for each of these 13 cases included: the quantity of messages posted, the quality of the discussion, and the students' and teachers' comments about what made or could have made the forums successful.

Figure 2. Evaluation data types

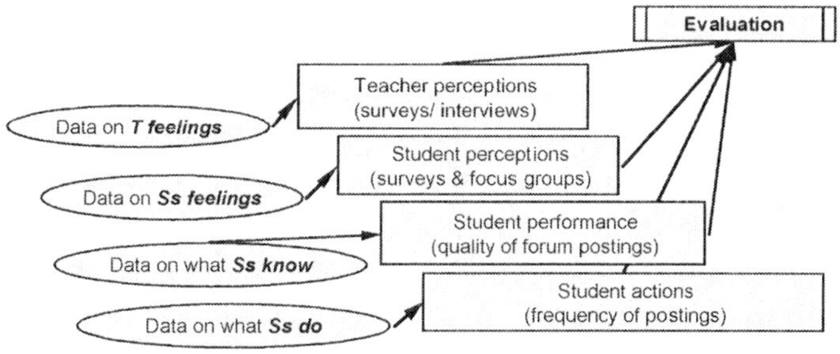

Copyright © 2007, Idea Group Inc. Copying or distributing in print or electronic forms without written permission of Idea Group Inc. is prohibited.

The evaluation strategies employed have allowed us to collect evaluation data from various sources. Put simply, there is perception data from both teachers and students (what we term *feel* data). We also have data on what students *do* through a study of the forum logs. A content analysis of the forum discussions provides some information about what students *know*. This is summarized in Figure 2.

The evaluation strategies used in each of the 13 cases are summarized in Table 2.

Opinions of students and teachers were all recorded in the evaluation reports. Evaluation strategies included student surveys, teacher surveys, focus-group meetings, forum log data records, and forum postings analyses.

1. *Student surveys* were made up of two sections: "closed" force-choice questions on a range of matters about the course, and "open-ended" type questions which were designed to collect students' free opinions on the use of the Web, including the forums.
2. *Teacher survey* was a standardized six-item, open-ended survey which asked about the teachers' feelings on the design and implementation of the course Web site.
3. *Focus-group meetings* were carried out at the very end of the courses. The main aim was to elicit more details concerning students' feelings about the

Table 2. The evaluation data for the 13 cases

Forum	Class Size	Source of Data				
		feel			*know*	*do*
		Student Survey	*Teacher Survey*	*Focus Group*	*Postings Analysis*	*Forum Log Data*
1	229	√	√	√	√	√
2	200		√	√	√	√
3	149	√	√		√	√
4	84			√	√	√
5	84	√		√		√
6	82	√	√		√	√
7	41	√	√		√	√
8	26	√	√		√	√
9	12	√	√			√
10	129	√	√	√		√
11	89	√	√	√	√	√
12	108	√	√	√	√	√
13	47			√	√	√
Total	*1,280*	*10*	*10*	*8*	*10*	*13*

Copyright © 2007, Idea Group Inc. Copying or distributing in print or electronic forms without written permission of Idea Group Inc. is prohibited.

usefulness of the Web sites and Web components. All the expressed opinions by the participants were recorded in focus group reports written by the evaluators within two days of the meetings.

4. The *postings analysis* looked at the content of the postings and classified them into non-substantive (usually social, though we do recognize the value of social interaction in community-building online; in this case the public forum was the social arena), substantive (related to the topic), and elaborated substantive. These classifications are related to the Structural Observation of Learning Outcomes (SOLO) classification (Biggs & Collis, 1982; Biggs, 1999), as shown in Table 3. The SOLO classification or taxonomy has also been used by Hatzipanagos (2005) and seems more manageable than using a tool such as NVivo on all the full text messages, such as discussed by Stacey and Gerbic (2003).
5. The *forum log data* recorded the number of postings contributed by students and teachers in the forums.

The student questionnaires used in these 13 evaluations covered a range of aspects of the whole course, and the closed items did not specifically relate to the forums. For this reason, the data for the analysis focused on the open-ended comments.

Table 3. Forum postings classification categories related to the SOLO taxonomy

SOLO Taxonomy Categories	**Explanation of SOLO Categories**	**Postings Classification Categories**	**Type of Posting**
Pre-Structural	Misses the point	Non-substantive	• Social
Uni-Structural	Single point	Substantive	• Adding new points • Enhancement and clarification of points
Multi-Structural	Multiple unrelated points		
Relational	Logically related answer	Elaborated substantive	• Making clear contrary statements • Developing complex arguments
Extended Abstract	Unanticipated extension		

Copyright © 2007, Idea Group Inc. Copying or distributing in print or electronic forms without written permission of Idea Group Inc. is prohibited.

All of the *feel* data from surveys and focus groups were manually processed by the second author with the help of QSR NVivo (2005). NVivo allows flexible coding and processing of large amounts of data (in this case the forum-related data situated in large evaluation reports). A NVivo project was created to hold the data for the current study. Rich text records of the 13 evaluation reports were imported into the project database for processing. Every comment concerning the use of the forums in the surveys and focus group meeting reports was identified and coded. Three types of coding were adopted in this study:

- *positive data* (the things teachers and students liked or appreciated about the online discussion experience);
- *negative data* (the weaknesses of the forums); and
- *suggested improvements* (suggestions of improvement that will make the online discussion a better experience).

After making codings on all the 13 reports, NVivo was used to generate separate reports for each of the codings. These new groupings of comments were then re-interpreted, compared, and contrasted, revealing a set of factors that appear to influence forum uses. The analysis was cross-checked and validated by the first and the third authors.

Findings

Ranking the Forums through Analyzing the Postings

As shown in Tables 4 and 5, the quality and quantity of the postings of the 13 cases were varied. The number of postings per student ranged from 0.1 (Forum 12) to 22.2 (Forum 4), while the number of postings by teacher fell between 0 (Forum 4) and 154 (Forum 10). For the quality of postings, which was indicated by the percentage of substantive postings under the simplified SOLO classification, the range was wide also—from 34.0% (Forum 7) to 98.9% (Forum 8). No SOLO analyses were carried out on Forums 5, 9, and 10; Forum 9 was small, and the teachers in Forums 5 and 10 did not wish a SOLO analysis done at this time as they wanted to gain more experience of teaching online first.

A rough ranking on quantity and quality for all the cases were carried out. On each aspect we classified the forums into three categories: High (H), Medium (M), and Low (L). For the quantity ranking, Forums 2, 3, 4, 6, and 7 were graded as H because they received large total numbers of postings and also many postings by

Copyright © 2007, Idea Group Inc. Copying or distributing in print or electronic forms without written permission of Idea Group Inc. is prohibited.

Table 4. Quantity of the forum postings in each forum

Forum	Class Size	Number of Postings				
		Total	By Students	Per Student	By Teacher
1	229	167	104	5.0 *	63
2	200	3443	3431	17.2	12
3	149	1793	1709	11.5	84
4	84	1862	1862	22.2	0
5	84	462	390	4.6	72
6	82	1127	1064	13.0	63
7	41	782	774	18.9	8
8	26	91	88	3.4	3
9	12	94	82	6.8	12
10	129	411	357	2.8	154
11	89	449	370	4.2	79
12	108	22	10	0.1	12
13	47	10	5	0.1	5

* *number of postings per group instead of per student was noted here*

Table 5. Quality of the forum postings in each forum

Forum	Class Size	SOLO Analysis Statistics (% of messages in forum)		
		Non-Substantive	Simple	Elaborated
1	229	34.1	65.3	0.6
2	200	4.78	91.8	3.4
3	149	13.8	72.3	13.8
4	84	45.0	47.2	3.3
5	84	/	/	/
6	82	19.1	53.5	27.4
7	41	66.0	19.7	14.3
8	26	1.1	94.5	4.4
9	12	/	/	/
10	129	/	/	/
11	89	8.8	30.4	60.8
12	108	30	70	0
13	47	20	80	0

students. In contrast, Forums 8, 10, 12, and 13 were ranked L because their average numbers of postings by students were relatively lower. The rest of the forums fell in between and were ranked as M. Similarly, for the quality ranking, Forums 2, 6, 8, and 11 received H ranking because they contained few non-substantive postings and a relatively high proportion of elaborated postings. Forums 1, 4, and 7 comprised a high proportion of non-substantive postings and thus were ranked L. With these rough rankings, the 13 forums can be compared on both quantity and quality; the result is listed in Table 6.

Copyright © 2007, Idea Group Inc. Copying or distributing in print or electronic forms without written permission of Idea Group Inc. is prohibited.

Table 6. Forums' rankings based on both quantity and quality

Forum	Activity Type	Major Role	Quantity Ranking	Quality Ranking
6	Structured	Student	H	H
2	Structured	Student	H	H
11	Free	Student	M	H
3	Structured	Student	H	M
4	Structured	Student	H	L
7	Structured	Student	H	L
8	Structured	Student	L	H
9	Structured	Student	M	/
5	Structured	Student	M	/
1	Structured	Student	M	L
10	Free	Student	L	/
13	Free	Teacher	L	M
12	Free	Teacher	L	M

Only Forums 6 and 2 were ranked high on both quality and quantity. In both cases, peer review was central to the activity in the forums. Forum 11, which is a free forum, was ranked the third. The remaining three free forums were ranked the lowest among the 13 forums. It is of note that teacher-centered forums tend to have lower quality and quantity than student-centered forums.

Analysis of the Open-Ended Data

The *feel* data from each case were extracted from teacher and student surveys, and focus group meeting with students. A meta-analysis of the 13 sets of qualitative data was conducted to generate a list of factors related to forum use and forum success. In the data set of comments, there were 36 different positive comments (26 from structured forums and 10 from free forums); 13 negative comments (9 and 4 from structured and free forums, respectively); and 29 suggestions for improvements (18 and 11 from structured and free forums, respectively).

A grounded approach (Strauss & Corbin, 1990), with iterative cycles of refinement, was taken in order to identify the categories which best described the open-ended *feel* data. There were three key clusters of comments, and these are summarized in Table 7. Note that our categorization is not unique but has been arrived at as a "best fit" decision.

While we have classified most of our forums as student-centered in that the students are the focus of the activity and that most of the communication is between students, the evaluation data point out unequivocally that the teacher has a vital central role.

Copyright © 2007, Idea Group Inc. Copying or distributing in print or electronic forms without written permission of Idea Group Inc. is prohibited.

The three main factors we have described as:

- **Ease of Use:** teacher as organizer and planner

Table 7. Major factors contributing to success of online forums as gauged from teachers' and students' comments

Main Factors	Specific Exemplification	Where Mentioned	Examples of the Nature of the Comments
Ease of Use: Teacher as Organizer & Planner	Making it easy to enter and quickly understand the environment	In nine evaluation reports; both free & structured	• Giving the forum good organization • Providing good technical support • Preventing technical problems
	Clear structure and procedures	In two evaluation reports; both structured	• Teacher planning well at the beginning • Arranging students in functional groups
Clear Facilitation: Teacher as Learning Guide	Good teacher participation	In nine evaluation reports; both free & structured	• Teacher participating actively, giving feedback frequently, and replying promptly
	Timely teacher guidance and monitoring	In six evaluation reports; both free & structured	• Teacher giving background knowledge to help students perform online tasks • Teacher following up on students' discussions
	Building group dynamics	In one evaluation report; structured	• Facilitating online group-working effectiveness (by close monitoring, teaching of workgroup skills, etc.)
Motivation to Engage: Teacher as Community Builder	Active encouragement of individual students	In two evaluation reports; both structured	• Maintaining high student participation
	Active encouragement of whole class	In two evaluation reports; both free	• Teacher encouraging the use of the forum in class • Giving marks to online tasks (particularly at the beginning) so that students get used to contributing to the forum later on
	High perception of usefulness by students	In four evaluation reports; both free & structured	• Making students aware of the benefits • Making the forum suit students' own learning styles
	High perception of usefulness by teachers	In two evaluation reports; both free & structured	• Teachers realizing the learning benefits that the forum activities can bring

Copyright © 2007, Idea Group Inc. Copying or distributing in print or electronic forms without written permission of Idea Group Inc. is prohibited.

- **Clear Facilitation:** teacher as learning guide
- **Motivation to Engage:** teacher as community builder

The numbers in the third column of Table 7 relate to the number of forums being referred to. In most cases there are many more than one comment relating to the factor or one of its exemplifications. What we have recorded here are the "clusters" of comments.

Discussion of the Three Success Factors

Ease of Use: Teacher as Organizer and Planner

Careful planning beforehand is important to achieve a good outcome in any learning environment—building an online learning community is no exception. Teachers need to design and give an organization to the forum. Such organization usually relates to the nature of the course, grouping of students, and the activities to be carried out in the forum. Students also commented that the teachers should tackle all IT-related problems before the forum is in use. There were forums in our dataset where the forum use was delayed due to the existence of technical problems; students had difficulty attaching files in the forums, and this problem effectively halted activities.

Figure 3. Forum structure of Forum 3

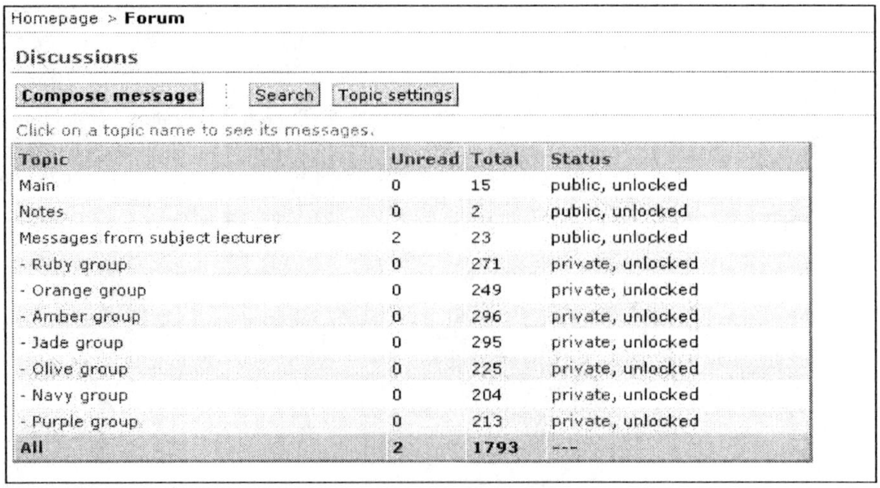

Topic	Unread	Total	Status
Main	0	15	public, unlocked
Notes	0	2	public, unlocked
Messages from subject lecturer	2	23	public, unlocked
- Ruby group	0	271	private, unlocked
- Orange group	0	249	private, unlocked
- Amber group	0	296	private, unlocked
- Jade group	0	295	private, unlocked
- Olive group	0	225	private, unlocked
- Navy group	0	204	private, unlocked
- Purple group	0	213	private, unlocked
All	**2**	**1793**	---

Copyright © 2007, Idea Group Inc. Copying or distributing in print or electronic forms without written permission of Idea Group Inc. is prohibited.

Forum 3 (ranked 4 in the postings analysis) is an example of a well-organized forum. The course was a large class, with a class size of 149. The teacher divided the students into seven groups of group size of around 20 and carried out within-group "Web-based tutorials" on a weekly basis (see Figure 3 which is a capture of the main page of the forum). The sub-forums were private forums in which access from non-members were blocked. This feature gave students a sense of security so that they would not be intimidated in posting their work. After the course was finished and with the consent of the students obtained, the course teacher made all the sub-forums public so that other students could gain access to others' ideas.

Thus, making use of useful forum functions, keeping the forums error-free, and also briefing the students on the use of the functions in the forum at the beginning of the course help create a better discussion environment. Existence of technical problems, lack of technical support, and poor forum organization are clearly disadvantageous (cf. Preece et al.'s (2004) criteria of "usability").

This is true for both structured and free forums. For example, teachers in Forums 6 (structured) and 11 (free)—ranked 1 and 3 in the postings analysis—were especially aware of the importance of their involvement in the forums. So, while the purposes of the forums varied, both teachers introduced the online forum in the first class, made the first contribution in the forum to initiate the use, gave clear instructions, and answered students' queries with great conscientiousness at the beginning of the semester.

Clear requirements about the online assessments were also welcomed by the students. They wanted clarity in setting the scene. Information such as the minimum number of postings required, number of tasks, and the description of each task are seen to be helpful. It was observed that teachers of good forums set discussion topics, gave clear instructions, and grouped students in an appropriate way at the beginning of the semester.

Clear Facilitation: Teacher as Learning Guide

As in a traditional classroom, teachers are responsible for planning and facilitating in order to establish a useful learning environment. Feedback from students showed that they like their teachers to give comments frequently, to give encouraging feedback, to follow up students' discussions, to reply promptly in the forum, to raise questions in the forum, and to inspire their thoughts. For example, although Forum 12 received the least number of postings per student, the students expressed in the focus-group meeting that they regarded the forum as a useful tool in the course, partly because the course teacher always made timely announcements in the forum and gave prompt replies to students' questions during the whole semester. It reveals that even though students did not explicitly participate by making contributions to

Copyright © 2007, Idea Group Inc. Copying or distributing in print or electronic forms without written permission of Idea Group Inc. is prohibited.

the forum (which is perhaps related to their preferred learning style), they would still check the forum for any updates by the teacher.

Teachers also need to monitor the forum use throughout the whole semester in order to keep students on task. One main reason for the lower-than-expected participation of Forum 9 (ranked 8 in the postings analysis) was that the teacher did not regularly remind her students to make contributions. The teacher remarked:

"It was a course requirement that each student must submit at least three postings each to the [two sub-forums]. Unfortunately I did not stress this throughout the term, nor did I provide a frequency or schedule to be followed for their submissions, and only a few contributed early on. As a result, the interaction I had hoped for never flourished. Next year I will require each student [to] post 3 contributions per term, but at a rate of one a month, e.g. one in January, one in March, and one in April. Hopefully, this will encourage more and earlier interactions and postings and learning."

There is a tension here in that an overly protective and directive approach by teachers can hinder the development of students' independence in learning and sense of initiative. There is a delicate balance to be maintained here so that a sense of community is nurtured and not just a culture of compliance. It may be that Hong Kong students expect more guidance than students elsewhere in the world would welcome. Certainly the Hong Kong school education system is remarkably highly structured. With the growing number of Chinese students studying in the West and the growth of transnational programs, this is certainly a factor worthy of further investigation (McNaught, 2004).

Students also needed guidance throughout the process in order to perform well in the graded activities in the online forums. Clear guidelines given as early as possible were commented as being useful by students in several cases. For example, in Forum 4, students did not feel they had enough background knowledge to review peers' work. So, they found it hard to give feedback during the process. Teachers need to be aware of students' needs and provide timely support throughout their learning.

Forum 2 (one of the two highest ranked forums) is especially interesting in that the forum had a much more central role than in most of the other cases. Traditional lectures were replaced with students' online study. Teachers and students met in the one-hour seminar each week. Students produced a number of assignments in a portfolio format. Students discussed their assignments online in small groups and revised them based on the peer reviews before the final submission. Students were also asked to evaluate online the quality of help their group members had given them throughout the online discussion at the end of the course. This learning design was quite a change for many students, and the success of the forum seems to be related

Copyright © 2007, Idea Group Inc. Copying or distributing in print or electronic forms without written permission of Idea Group Inc. is prohibited.

to the ongoing support of the teachers. The weekly seminar was integrated with the online activities to provide continuous support and encouragement for students.

Facilitating group dynamics is a key role for teachers. The teacher of Forum 7 designed an interesting ice-breaking activity for her students to get to know each other at the beginning of the course. First she divided the students into groups. Then she required each student to participate in their belonged sub-forum and give three descriptions about themselves, one of which had to be a false statement. Students were then asked to chat freely and try to find out other group members' lies. The quantity of postings of this forum was boosted up to quite a high number (18.9 postings per student) due to this activity. A sense of community was built among group members, and a high student involvement was recorded.

One more example is Forum 5. Student groups were formed and each group took either the role of researchers or editors. Once each group's members finished their own tasks, they would pass the tasks to the corresponding group for checking or amendments. With this design setup, there were both within-group and between-group discussions. Different kinds of interactions among students were thus created, which in turn created a good learning and discussion environment.

Of course, not all successful uses of forums result in high activity statistics. This happened in Forum 1 (ranked 10 on the postings analysis). Again, students were formed in groups to produce projects for peer review. Within-group discussions were carried out off-line (not using the online forum). Project productions were uploaded to the forum for peer review, and reviewers made the comments in the forum as well. It turned out that there were only 150 postings by students (0.66 per student), which would apparently be regarded as an unsuccessful forum. Yet, the reason behind this low number of postings was that student groups did the peer review together, and then made only one summarized comment in the forum for each production. Thus, the forum log data could not reveal the hidden dynamics among the students. Nonetheless, the students did collaborate, discuss, and make decisions.

Motivation to Engage: Teacher as Community Builder

Feedback also suggested that teachers need to motivate their students to participate in the forum by encouraging, questioning, responding, and commenting there. It is just like the teacher asking questions and encouraging student discussion in traditional classroom learning. Also, it is the teacher's role to foster group dynamics among the students. Teachers need to guide students to make substantive discussions.

Even in structured forums where students obtained extrinsic motivation (participation marks), students should explore the intrinsic potential that might arise from the forum use. For the one successful case of a free forum investigated (Forum 11), the teacher did much to encourage the students to participate in the no-marks-allocated

Copyright © 2007, Idea Group Inc. Copying or distributing in print or electronic forms without written permission of Idea Group Inc. is prohibited.

discussions and let the students know the benefits of the extra learning arena. The outcome of the forum was obvious.

Being the participants of the forums, the students themselves influence the forum use. Regardless of all the *manipulations* by the teachers of the learning environment during the whole process, students' perceptions on the usefulness of the forum are of vital importance. Data revealed that students in successful forums perceived the forums to be a good tool in their learning process. They were aware of the advantages brought about by the forum use, such as the flexibility, the rich content, and the value of articulating ideas.

For example, in Forum 2 and Forum 4 (structured forums), students were required to work on exercises and discuss the answers with group members in the online forum. The students realized that this was a good channel for them to learn the subject matter better. Also, they could gain marks for online participation. With both the intrinsic and extrinsic motivations, students participated actively in the forums and posted messages with high quality. As the students in these two courses possessed a positive attitude towards the online communities, the outcomes of the two forums were high among all the 13 cases (rankings of 2 and 5 in the postings analysis).

The successful free forum (Forum 11) was similar. Though extrinsic motivation did not exist (students' postings were just for sharing purposes), students recognized the benefits and still contributed well to the forums.

When students perceive the forum as useless or they prefer other means of communication, their involvements in the forum drop. For example, for Forum 13 (ranking 12), apart from the online forum, there were several other means for the students and the teacher to communicate with each other. Students preferred other means of communication to the forum. Together with the low participation of the teacher, the forum was used just as an announcement corner.

It is also important that teachers believe in the learning effects that online discussion can bring. It was observed that if the online forum was not valued by the teachers, the students would also not initiate or take part in the discussion. For example, the teacher of Forum 13 used the forum together with other means to make announcements. The value of the forum was recognized but yet not fully utilized. There was only low activity in the online forum. Students knew that the forum could be a place for better information exchange among the members of the course (e.g., one could know what others did not understand if there were questions posted in the forum), but they preferred to ask the teacher questions directly by stopping by the teacher's office or sending an e-mail to him or her. One student commented that if there was someone (the teacher, the tutor, or some active students) to initiate discussions in the forum, he would definitely participate in the online forum discussions. Another student suggested that after personal discussions with students, the teachers could post those inspiring and interesting questions to the discussions for student reference. All in all, teachers' initiation of the utilization of the forum seems to be crucial to a positive outcome with online forums.

Copyright © 2007, Idea Group Inc. Copying or distributing in print or electronic forms without written permission of Idea Group Inc. is prohibited.

Due to the fact that participation in the structured online forums is mandatory, a guaranteed quantity of postings can be obtained in this kind of forum design. The students are motivated extrinsically to contribute to the online community, as marks are allocated to forum participation. Students may post some postings with quality so as to get the marks. Yet, once the requirements are fulfilled, the motivation drops and students may quit the online discussion. Also, when quality of postings is not set as the criterion for assessment, students may post messages with vague content. As a result, without intrinsic valuing of the forum, it is not an easy task to maintain a structured forum with consistently high quantity and quality of postings.

It is therefore natural to find that users of this type of forum are concerned with the clarity of the descriptions, and instructions of the required and pre-assigned activities. Also, they are particularly concerned about the smooth operations of the online discussion process. As the smoothness of this type of forum depends as much on students' contributions as the teachers', structured forums need to focus on the organizational, facilitative, and motivational aspects we have discussed. These ideas are echoed by Hatzipanagos' (2005) finding that forums need to have interfaces that emphasize both the cognitive and the affective aspects of learning, and also Preece et al.'s (2004) second principle of "sociability."

Structured or Free Forums?

As mentioned, three of the four free forums were ranked the lowest among all the investigated forums on both quantity and quality. This illustrates the difficulty in planning and carrying out successful free forums. The one successful free forum (Forum 11) was moderated by a teacher whose skills of induction (Salmon, 2000) were strong enough to build an online community without the *coercion* of marks.

In the structured forums, pre-assigned course-related discussion topics were set. Students usually discussed in a serious manner and provided substantive ideas with a focus on solving the problems. There were follow-up postings which were also content-rich. For many teachers in a semester university course, structured forums may be better than free forums in achieving teaching and learning outcomes.

Challenges that seem to be particular to the structured forums as revealed in this study seem to focus on the provision of clear instructions and guidelines for the required online activities, and the ability of the forums to continually involve the students and maintain group dynamics.

There are, of course, other important considerations that have to be taken account of when designing Web-supplemented teaching and learning. For example, the nature of the course, the teachers' educational beliefs, and the type of non-Web activities obviously influence forum use. For example, in a postgraduate course that

Copyright © 2007, Idea Group Inc. Copying or distributing in print or electronic forms without written permission of Idea Group Inc. is prohibited.

emphasizes research or professional training, it may not be appropriate to impose a significant mandatory online participation. Forum 8, which was from a postgraduate course, is an example. The average number of postings per student was 3.4 and per teacher was 3. However, the quality of postings was very good with serious and apt discussions.

Conclusion

This chapter studied 13 online forums. Two kinds of forum designs were observed, structured and free. Structured forums generally performed better than free forums. In addition, forums where the communication was largely between students seem to be more effective than teacher-directed forums. However, the centrality of the role of the teacher is confirmed. The evidence from the 13 evaluation studies is that the teacher's capacity to plan activities and continually support learners is crucial. The skilled teacher remains as a strong key to effective learning in a university course; teacher skills in the online world are just as important as in the classroom.

The results of this study indicate that successful forums in the Hong Kong context are ones where:

- it is easy for students to enter and quickly understand the environment;
- the teacher provides a clear structure to the task and suggests procedures for students to consider using in tackling the task;
- the teacher actively participates in the discussion;
- the role of the teacher is recognized as not being the same as a student, and is more about timely guidance and monitoring;
- the teacher seeks to build group dynamics;
- there is active encouragement of individual students, initially at least by the teacher;
- there is active encouragement of the whole class, initially at least by the teacher;
- the students rate the forum as being of real value for their learning; and
- the teacher rates the forum as being of real value for students' learning.

It is hoped that the findings of the study will assist teachers in planning teaching and learning experiences using forums that genuinely build an online learning community.

Copyright © 2007, Idea Group Inc. Copying or distributing in print or electronic forms without written permission of Idea Group Inc. is prohibited.

Acknowledgments

Funding support from the University Grants Committee in Hong Kong and the Hong Kong Polytechnic University is gratefully acknowledged, as is the collaborative support of many colleagues in the three universities associated with the e3Learning Project. Teachers willingly gave permission for the use of the data described in this chapter.

References

Ashcroft, B., & McAlpine, I. (2004, December 5-8). Student moderators in online discussions. In R. Atkinson, C. McBeath, D. Jonas-Dwyer, & R. Phillips (Eds.), *Beyond the Comfort Zone, Proceedings of the 21st Annual Australian Society for Computers in Learning in Tertiary Education 2004 Conference* (pp. 88-94), University of Western Australia. Retrieved November 27, 2005, from http://www.ascilite.org.au/conferences/perth04/procs/ashcroft.html

Bielaczyc, K., & Collins, A. (1999). Learning communities in classroom: Advancing knowledge for a lifetime. *National Association of Secondary School Principals (NASSP) Bulletin,* (February), 4-10. Retrieved November 27, 2005, from http://www.findarticles.com/p/articles/mi_qa3696/is_199902/ai_n8847685

Biggs, J. (1999). What the student does: Teaching for enhanced learning. *Higher Education Research & Development, 18*(1), 57-75.

Biggs, J. B., & Collis, K. F. (1982). *Evaluating the quality of learning: The SOLO taxonomy (Structure of the Observed Learning Outcome)*. New York: Academic Press.

Cuthell, J. P. (2005). What does it take to be active? Teacher participation in online communities. *International Journal of Web-Based Communities, 1*(3), 320-332.

Daft, R. L., & Lengel, R. H. (1986). Organizational information requirements, media richness and structural design. *Management Science, 32*(5), 554-571.

e3Learning. (n.d.). *Enrich, Extend, Evaluate Learning.* Retrieved November 27, 2005, from http://e3learning.edc.polyu.edu.hk/

Farmer, J. (2004, December 5-8). Communication dynamics: Discussion boards, Weblogs and the development of communities of inquiry in online learning environments. In R. Atkinson, C. McBeath, D. Jonas-Dwyer, & R. Phillips (Eds.), *Beyond the Comfort Zone, Proceedings of the 21st Annual Australian Society for Computers in Learning in Tertiary Education 2004 Conference*

Copyright © 2007, Idea Group Inc. Copying or distributing in print or electronic forms without written permission of Idea Group Inc. is prohibited.

(pp. 274-283), University of Western Australia. Retrieved November 27, 2005, from http://www.ascilite.org.au/conferences/perth04/procs/farmer.html

Hatzipanagos, S. (2005, June 27-July 2). Empathic interfaces and communication protocols: Groupwork and dialogues in discussion forums. In G. Richards & P. Kommers (Eds.), *Proceedings of the 17th Annual World Conference on Educational Multimedia, Hypermedia & Telecommunications* (pp. 2004-2011), Montreal, Canada. Norfolk VA: Association for the Advancement of Computers in Education.

Hiltz, S. R., & Turoff, M. (1978). *The network nation: Human communication via computer*. Reading, MA: Addison-Wesley.

James, J., McNaught, C., Csete, J., Hodgson, P., & Vogel, D. (2003, June 23-28). From MegaWeb to e^{3}Learning: A model of support for university academics to effectively use the Web for teaching and learning. In D. Lassner & C. McNaught (Eds.), *Proceedings of the 15th Annual World Conference on Educational Multimedia, Hypermedia & Telecommunications*, Honolulu, Hawaii (pp. 3303-3310). Norfolk VA: Association for the Advancement of Computers in Education.

Kirk, J. J., & Orr, R. L. (2003). *A primer on the effective use of threaded discussion forums*. Retrieved November 27, 2005, from http://www.eric.ed.gov/ERICDocs/data/ericdocs2/content_storage_01/0000000b/80/28/24/10.pdf

Lave, J., & Wenger, E. (1991). *Situated learning: Legitimate peripheral participation*. Cambridge: Cambridge University Press.

Luca, J., & Cowan, E. (2005, June 27-July 2). Supporting collaborative learning with blogs. In G. Richards & P. Kommers (Eds.), *Proceedings of the 17th Annual World Conference on Educational Multimedia, Hypermedia & Telecommunications* (pp. 3711-3714), Montreal, Canada. Norfolk VA: Association for the Advancement of Computers in Education.

Ma, J. (2005, June 27-July 2). What e-mail can do for foreign language writing. In G. Richards & P. Kommers (Eds.), *Proceedings of the 17th Annual World Conference on Educational Multimedia, Hypermedia & Telecommunications* (pp. 748-753), Montreal, Canada. Norfolk VA: Association for the Advancement of Computers in Education.

Markus, M. L. (1994). Electronic mail as the medium of managerial choice. *Organization Science, 5*(4), 502-527.

McNaught, C. (2004). Bridging two worlds: Viewing Australian universities from an Asian location. *Malaysian Journal of Distance Education, 6*(1), 111-127.

Mohan, J., & Lam, P. (2005, June 27-July 2). Learning for understanding: A Web-based model for inquisitive peer-review learning activities. In G. Richards

Copyright © 2007, Idea Group Inc. Copying or distributing in print or electronic forms without written permission of Idea Group Inc. is prohibited.

& P. Kommers (Eds.), *Proceedings of the 17th Annual World Conference on Educational Multimedia, Hypermedia & Telecommunications* (pp. 2083-2090), Montreal, Canada. Norfolk VA: Association for the Advancement of Computers in Education.

Preece, J., Abras, C., & Maloney-Krichmar, D. (2004). Designing and evaluating online communities: Research speaks to emerging practice. *International Journal of Web-Based Communities, 1*(1), 2-18.

QSR NVivo. (2005). Retrieved November 27, 2005, from http://www.qsrinternational.com/products/productoverview/NVivo.htm

Salmon, G. (1998). Developing learning through effective online moderation. *Active Learning, 9*(December), 3-8.

Salmon, G. (2000). *E-moderation: The key to teaching and learning online.* London: Kogan Page.

Stacey, E., & Gerbic, P. (2003, December 7-10). Investigating the impact of computer conferencing: Content analysis as a manageable research tool. In G. Crisp, D. Thiele, I. Scholten, S. Barker, & J. Baron (Eds.), *Interact, Integrate, Impact, Proceedings of the 20th Annual Conference of the Australasian Society for Computers in Learning in Tertiary Education* (pp. 495-504). Adelaide, Australia. Retrieved November 27, 2005, from http://www.ascilite.org.au/conferences/adelaide03/docs/pdf/495.pdf

Strauss, A., & Corbin, J. (1990). *Basics of qualitative research: Grounded theory procedures and techniques.* Newbury Park: Sage.

Wozniak, H., & Silveira, S. (2004, December 5-8). Online discussions: Promoting effective student to student interaction. In R. Atkinson, C. McBeath, D. Jonas-Dwyer, & R. Phillips (Eds.), *Beyond the Comfort Zone, Proceedings of the 21st Annual Australian Society for Computers in Learning in Tertiary Education 2004 Conference* (pp. 956-960), University of Western Australia. Retrieved November 27, 2005, from http://www.ascilite.org.au/conferences/perth04/procs/wozniak.html

Xiao, M. (2005, June 27-July 2). The effects of Internet-based desktop videoconference on EFL students' oral skills in terms of linguistic accuracy, fluency and complexity. In G. Richards & P. Kommers (Eds.), *Proceedings of the 17th Annual World Conference on Educational Multimedia, Hypermedia & Telecommunications* (pp. 882-884), Montreal, Canada. Norfolk VA: Association for the Advancement of Computers in Education.

Zhang, W., & Bascelli, D. (2005, June 27-July 2). Making work real: Building virtual learning communities. In G. Richards & P. Kommers (Eds.), *Proceedings of the 17th Annual World Conference on Educational Multimedia, Hypermedia & Telecommunications* (pp. 1827-1830), Montreal, Canada. Norfolk VA: Association for the Advancement of Computers in Education.

Copyright © 2007, Idea Group Inc. Copying or distributing in print or electronic forms without written permission of Idea Group Inc. is prohibited.

Zhang, W., & Storck, J. (2002). *Peripheral members in online communities.* Retrieved November 27, 2005, from http://opensource.mit.edu/papers/zhang.pdf

Copyright © 2007, Idea Group Inc. Copying or distributing in print or electronic forms without written permission of Idea Group Inc. is prohibited.

Section III:

Evaluation and Case Studies

Chapter IX

Evaluation: A Link in the Chain of Sustainability

Frances Bell, University of Salford, UK

Elena Zaitseva, University of Salford, UK

Danuta Zakrzewska, Technical University of Lodz, Poland

Abstract

Our emphasis in this chapter is on the sustainability of online educational communities, particularly the role that evaluation has to play in promoting sustainability. From the literature on online communities and evaluation of technology, we select and extend models of online community and technology acceptance that inform and enable the design and evaluation of sustainable online educational communities. Sustainability is a key issue that highlights the sociotechnical nature of these communities. Collaboration Across Borders is an online learning community that has received EU Socrates-Minerva funding to establish international collaboration between tutors and students, and investigate sustainability of online learning communities. We present a case study of the development of the CAB community and its associated portal http://www.cabweb.net as a chronology of significant events. We then chart the evaluation process, using examples of tools and data to highlight the role of evaluation in the development of CABWEB and the sustainability of the CAB community. Finally, we offer practical advice to those who wish to develop online learning communities, either small-scale collaborations between two groups of students or international networks of students and tutors.

Copyright © 2007, Idea Group Inc. Copying or distributing in print or electronic forms without written permission of Idea Group Inc. is prohibited.

Introduction

Despite the hyperbole that has surrounded the growth and spread of the Internet, we can see that, year by year, more people—young and old—in countries across the Americas, Europe, and the rest of the world are using the Internet in their everyday lives for work, play, and education. It is easy to imagine the educational opportunities presented by cheap and easy communication between people in different countries. More challenging questions are:

How can we turn those opportunities into viable and satisfying educational experiences?

How can we manage the social, technical, linguistic, and pedagogical challenges in realising these opportunities?

Evaluation makes an important contribution to understanding learners' and tutors' experiences in online learning communities, which can help to improve the social and technical aspects of those communities. In this chapter, we link theory with practice by exploring the relationship between evaluation and sustainability in a case study on the process of development of an online community over the period of a two-year funded project. Of particular interest is the use of an open source software (OSS)[1] package in the development of an online educational community. We extend two existing models of online community sustainability, both firmly grounded in the literature, to explore the sociability and usability aspects of online learning communities in an educational setting.

The Role of Evaluation in the Sustainability of Online Learning Communities

What is an Online Learning Community?

Goodyear (2001) defines *networked learning* as:

"...learning in which information and communications technology (ICT) is used to promote connections: between one learner and other learners, between learners and tutors; between a learning community and its learning resources."

Copyright © 2007, Idea Group Inc. Copying or distributing in print or electronic forms without written permission of Idea Group Inc. is prohibited.

Based on these ideas of connections and the conceptions of community developed later in the section on "Planning for Sociability in an Online Learning Community,' we define an online learning community as:

"A group of people who join together, usually at an identifiable online space, to engage in networked learning, guided by policies that are developed by the community. Sociability and usability are key factors in the sustainability of the online learning community."

In the recent past, online communities used discrete software tools, sometimes linked through a Web site, to share resources and communicate online. Increasingly, package software is used instead where the implementation involves configuration and possible customisation[2] of packages, rather than creating bespoke software or Web sites. This puts the initial emphasis on requirements for choice of package rather than on requirements for software development.

Evaluation of Software

Evaluation of processes and products is undertaken to maximise learning from experience and to support decision making in many fields, including the implementation of online learning communities. Generic software evaluation can be published as reviews in magazines or online by relevant organisations, a good example in the education domain being the comparison of course management systems offered by Edutools as a decision-making tool (see http://www.edutools.info/course/compare/index.jsp). Specific evaluations are undertaken for particular implementations that use such generic evaluations and previous experience to decide on the best fit between requirements, constraints (such as time and cost), and the attributes of the software package.

Ongoing Evaluation in Online Learning Communities

Online learning communities exhibit two key features: they are sociotechnical, and they are organic in nature. An online learning community is sociotechnical, not only because its development involves both technical artefacts *and* social processes and policies, but also because these are intertwined and should be understood holistically. Evolutionary design, participatory design, and member involvement in the community evolution are seen as key design principles for community design. Preece recommends *adaptive structuration* with a reflexive relationship between design (*designing usability* and *planning for sociability*) and use (Preece, 2000), as

Copyright © 2007, Idea Group Inc. Copying or distributing in print or electronic forms without written permission of Idea Group Inc. is prohibited.

illustrated in Figure 1. Preece highlights evaluation as the assessment (and re-assessment) of community needs.

A range of evaluation approaches that identify the "fit" of the software implementation and the social plans with community needs can be used to generate quantitative and qualitative data to inform community design decisions at various points in its evolution. Evaluation can inform the choice of software package, the initial and ongoing configuration/customisation of the software package, the resources provided, and the social activities offered, all with the goal of ensuring the sustainability of the community. When a software package for an online community is chosen and implemented, the decision on whether and when to customise the software is an important one for the developers and community owners, since changes to the software (as occurs in customisation) have to be re-applied when the package is upgraded.

Planning for sociability is also an ongoing process. Kim (2000) elaborates a clear *etiquette cycle* of "create, enforce, evolve" for social policies and procedures. Wenger, McDermott, and Snyder (2002), though generally favouring a top-down approach to community building aligned with pre-existing strategy, recognises that the approach to community development should reflect the degree of definition of the domain and the professional culture, and may therefore be bottom-up (for example for poorly defined domains) or a hybrid of the two approaches.

Figure 1. Usability and sociability based on a diagram by Preece (2000, p. 27). Copyright John Wiley & Sons Limited. Reproduced with permission.

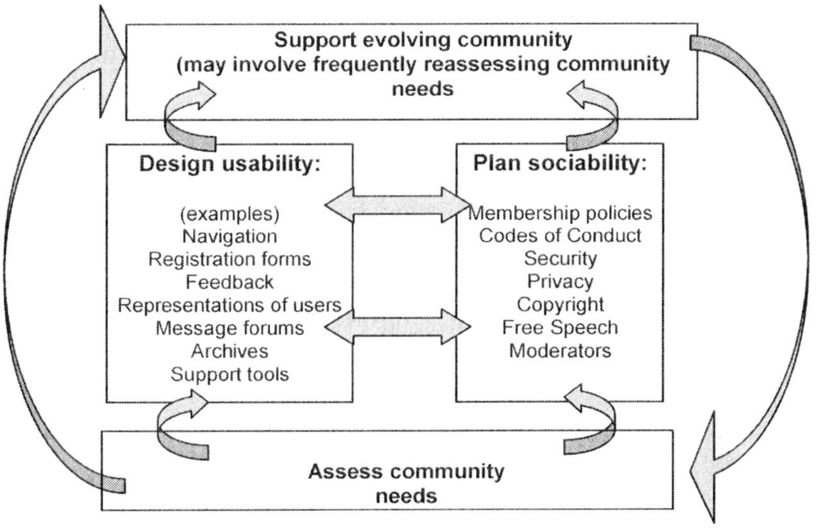

Copyright © 2007, Idea Group Inc. Copying or distributing in print or electronic forms without written permission of Idea Group Inc. is prohibited.

Planning for Sociability in an Online Learning Community

Understanding Online Community

Tonnies (1957) identified community in two ways—family or neighbourhood where community members have strong ties, and society or state where community members have weaker ties but may be united by shared purpose or national identity. Originally intended to aid understanding of 19th century social change during the Industrial Revolution, Tonnies' concepts have been re-interpreted in the context of the Internet where millions of people have formed themselves into groups online, some of which perceive themselves as *online communities*. Rather than agreeing on a definition of community, commentators agree on the uncertainty of the meaning of community (Cherny, 1999).

Our literature review has revealed a broad agreement on the factors important in the sociability of online communities, namely *membership*—which people join and which participate, *purposes*—why they join, and *policies*—the explicit and implicit norms (see Kim, 2000; Preece, 2000; Steinmueller, 2002). Preece also includes usability factors, building on previous work in human-computer interaction and Web site design. We prefer to include these factors within the broader concept of sustainability. Of the many online communities that have been launched, a significant proportion are ghost towns, with few or no recent postings. We have adapted Steinmueller's economic model of *virtual (online) community* to use in network development within the CAB project, since it resists a normative view and allows us to examine online communities empirically.

Membership

Boundaries are defined by who is a member of that community and who is not. This may be realised concretely with user ids and passwords, and also symbolically with boundaries existing in the minds of members (and non-members). Community members may include moderators who help to modify behaviour and guide activity within the group, active participants who post and reply to messages, and lurkers—the silent observers in online communities.

Purpose

In online learning communities the purpose is related to learning, directly in communities where students learn, or indirectly where teachers share their experiences

Copyright © 2007, Idea Group Inc. Copying or distributing in print or electronic forms without written permission of Idea Group Inc. is prohibited.

in creating and sustaining online learning communities (and thereby learn). Tradition and Practice definitions stress the importance of *purpose* (Kim, 2000; Lipnack & Stamps, 2000; Preece, 2000; Wenger et al., 2002). The concept of situated action emerges from a strong body of ethnographic research into organisational life (Suchman, 2000), and the cognitive and learning aspects of this have been further developed (Brown & Duguid, 1998).

The concept of community of practice (CoP) was developed initially in the analysis of learning within a variety of social and work settings (Lave & Wenger, 1991), and has recently been defined as "... group(s) of people who share a concern, a set of problems, or a passion about a topic, and who deepen their knowledge and expertise in this area by interacting on an ongoing basis" (Wenger et al., 2002). Shared interest or workgroups, such as virtual teams, can also unite around a common purpose. Shared purpose can lead to stability and a reduction in hostile postings (Preece, 2000).

Policies

Policies express expected behaviours within a community, ultimately how the community chooses to define and enforce its boundaries. When it is perceived that current or potential members devalue the collective by their behaviours, the collective can take action to deter or modify unacceptable behaviours, formally by enforcing known sanctions, or informally by example or group pressure. Governance is the processes and systems by which a community operates, and the governance of educational communities that are organised by a college or university should be understood in the institutional setting (Bell & Heinze, 2004).

Sustainability

When a social group is voluntary, its persistence relies on the perceived value it offers to its members, and there are many examples of deserted online "communities" (Steinmueller, 2002). Steinmueller focuses on the issue of *sustainability* by characterising it as something that can be lost either when there is a coordination failure or when, for enough individuals, the costs of participation exceed the perceived benefits. Costs of participation include membership fees, costs of computer hardware and software, Internet connection charges, and time spent in communicating. Benefits can be seen as *social* where participants enjoy discussion and forming relationships online; *functional* related to information seeking and gathering; *psychological* where participants can develop and express their identity, and experience a sense of belonging and affiliation; and *hedonic* where they enjoy

Copyright © 2007, Idea Group Inc. Copying or distributing in print or electronic forms without written permission of Idea Group Inc. is prohibited.

themselves (Wang & Fesenmaier, 2004). In the case of educational communities, functional benefits extend beyond information gathering to learning.

Evaluation for Designing Usability: The Role of the TAM Model

Defining Usability

Usability was defined in an ISO standard as follows:

"Usability is the effectiveness, efficiency and satisfaction with which specified users can achieve specified goals in particular environments." (ISO CD 9241-11.3, version 8.8, May 1993)

We can think of usability as the feature that decides how the specified goals are achieved, and it may be defined as " the capacity of an object to be easy to use by a given person to carry out the task for which it has been designed" (Nogier, 2005). For software and Web sites, usability seems to be one of the most significant factors influencing their success. There exist many elements that affect the usability of Web sites like front page layout, navigation, supporting tools, and so forth, but the user's experience is the indicator of usability. Marsico and Levialdi (2004) presented Web site design issues with all the factors that influence Web site usability. They describe user satisfaction as a measure of perceived quality of the interface and the most significant issue for system usability. The most important design categories and ones that should be evaluated by users are: information representation and appearance; access, navigation, and orientation; and the informative content architecture of Web sites. Especially the last one of these categories means that usability may be measured by users' satisfaction with content and amount of information, access policies, and type of communication channels, which significantly depend on the type and amount of information, and the cohesiveness of information organisation assigned to participants—the features that Teo, Chan, Wei, and Zhang (2003), in their model for online learning community sustainability, defined as information accessibility.

Copyright © 2007, Idea Group Inc. Copying or distributing in print or electronic forms without written permission of Idea Group Inc. is prohibited.

Technology Acceptance Model (TAM)

The technology acceptance model was introduced by Davis (1989) to explain the intention of usage of an information system and has been used widely since 1989, more recently developed into a Web site acceptance model by Lin and Lu (2000), and extended by Teo et al. (2003) for the sustainability of online learning communities. Davis (1989) presented two main factors influencing the intention of usage of the information system—perceived usefulness (PU) and perceived ease of use (PEU)—as strongly dependent on the external variables that may differ in different circumstances. Lin and Lu (2000) concluded that a user's perceived usefulness of a Web site is significantly affected by the quality of information provided by the Web site, the response time, and system accessibility. Though usefulness is seen as more important than ease of use, the latter can have an indirect effect on the former.

Figure 2. The role of usability evaluation in achieving PEU

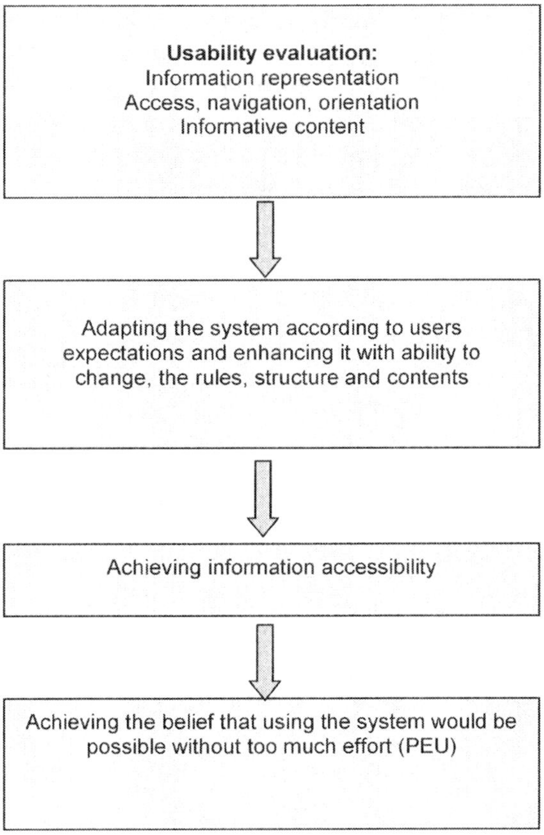

Copyright © 2007, Idea Group Inc. Copying or distributing in print or electronic forms without written permission of Idea Group Inc. is prohibited.

These usability features may be considered as elements of information accessibility, which together with community adaptivity affect PU and PEU in this extended TAM. Teo et al. (2003) indicated that information content, access policies, communication channels, and information organisation, all influence the sustainability of online learning communities. They also emphasised the significance of users' ability to adapt the system according to their expectations. One way of achieving this is by usability evaluation, which supports the process of designing the system; another is by enhancing the system with the ability to change the rules, structure, and content, and thus obtaining information accessibility and PEU, as presented in Figure 2.

What is more, information accessibility together with social and pedagogical benefits may increase PU feature, which in the case of online learning communities signifies the belief that portal could enhance the teaching and learning process.

CAB Community Case Study

The origins of the Collaboration Across Borders (CAB) community can be traced back to 2001 when a small network of tutors from three European countries organised student collaborations. In 2003, a two-year project funded by the Socrates-Minerva program started whose particular focus was on practicing and researching the educational benefits of international collaboration between staff and students. The extended project partnership comprised lecturers and researchers from higher education institutions in Poland, The Netherlands, Spain, Germany, and the United Kingdom. Project partners were able to collaborate online and meet face to face, but they realised that if the benefits to tutors and students were to extend beyond the partnership, then an online educational community, comprising different sub-communities, would have to be developed.

In order to provide readers with better understanding of the evaluation process that took place, we shall describe the chronological process and milestones of the community development in three phases. Phase One was where the technology was evaluated, piloted, selected, and configured; here, a strong conceptual view of the portal and the community in general took shape. Phase Two was where the CABWEB portal was launched and used by users beyond the project partnership. Phase Three is where the lessons learned are being incorporated into the sociotechnical enterprise that is the CAB community.

Copyright © 2007, Idea Group Inc. Copying or distributing in print or electronic forms without written permission of Idea Group Inc. is prohibited.

Phase One: Community Building (December 2003-October 2004)

The project plan anticipated a choice of tools and platform to be made within the first three months, but this choice took much longer. The first seven months of Phase One (December 2003-June 2004) was a period of experimentation, with student collaborations taking place on a variety of discussion boards, before the requirements were elaborated and a clear vision of the collaboration platform was shared across the project partnership. This experience of collaborations within project partnership demonstrated that separate discussion tools and information resources were not suitable for the purposes of the project because of their limited educational and user management functionality, and that we should consider an integrated platform as an alternative. In June 2004 we proceeded to a pilot implementation and test of the Microsoft Sharepoint portal, recommended by one of the project partners.

By April 2004, although a firm decision on the tools and platform for CAB collaborations had not yet been made, a clear conceptual model of the portal had emerged (see Figure 3 and Table 1). The CABWEB portal was envisaged as a place that would host the student collaborations, the tutor network called HELP (Higher Education Learning Professionals), and a fledgling Student Network. *Networks* and *Collaboration Spaces* are the two main metaphors for the organisation of collaborative learning on the portal. The HELP and Student Networks are voluntary associations

Figure 3. Conceptual model of CABWEB portal

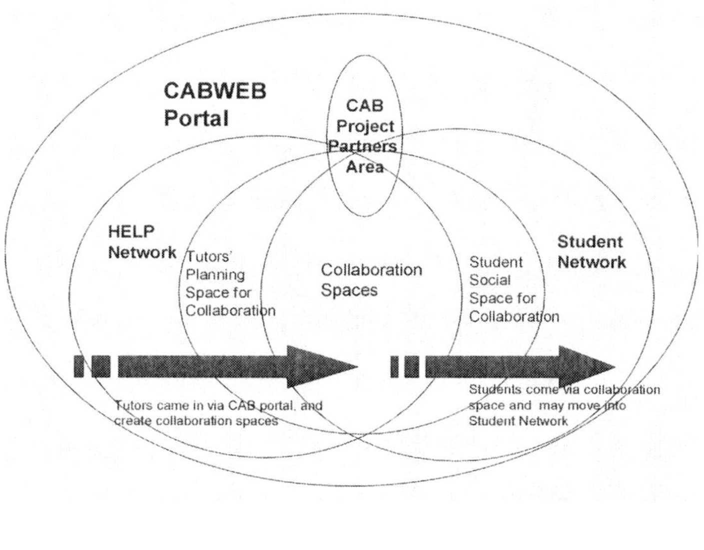

Copyright © 2007, Idea Group Inc. Copying or distributing in print or electronic forms without written permission of Idea Group Inc. is prohibited.

where members are free to join or leave, whereas the collaboration spaces are usually prescribed by the tutors as part of the course of study, and participation may be further influenced by assessment of student interactions. HELP corresponds to a community of practice.

As shown in Figure 3, tutors are expected to enter the portal via the HELP network, possibly going on to ask for a collaboration space, configure it together with partner tutor(s), and carry out the activity. The collaboration tools include asynchronous discussion forums, synchronous chat, collaborative building of Web pages (WIKI),

Table 1. CABWEB sub-communities

Community	Membership	Purpose (stated in portal)	Policies	Sustainability
HELP Network	Open to guests; users must self-enrol before joining discussions; overtly aimed at tutors in higher education	For tutors to share experiences and resources for planning and running collaborative activities for students, and to meet other tutors with whom they can organise a collaborative activity	CAB policies developed iteratively with user feedback, and customs based on interests of sub-community	Mutually dependent on sustainability of CAB community
Student Network	Open to guests, but students must self-enrol before joining discussions	For students to meet and socialise in the CAB Cafe, to find out about collaborative activities, and how to get the most from them	CAB policies developed iteratively with user feedback, and customs based on interests of sub-community	Problematic because of short-term collaborations, high expectations of students
Collaboration Spaces	Private spaces (usually) open only to students doing the short-term collaborative activity as part of a course of study	To host collaborative activities and social interaction between students taking part in the collaborative activity	Although subject to CAB policies, guided by tutors who organise collaboration space	Depends on HELP network or existing tutor contacts to come into being; focus on tutor-assigned tasks and activity, good pedagogy makes for successful collaborative activity
Project Partners Area	Private to project partners	Shared workspace and communication focus for project partners	Primary source of CAB policies developed iteratively with user feedback	Lasts for duration of project, driven by project milestones and deliverables; core group will migrate to HELP network and undertake community leadership

Copyright © 2007, Idea Group Inc. Copying or distributing in print or electronic forms without written permission of Idea Group Inc. is prohibited.

and glossaries. Students will be directed to a collaboration space by their tutors, and may venture out into the Student Network.

The basic concepts of Membership, Purpose, and Policies for each sub-community, as shown in Table 1, were agreed in April 2004, based on the literature and evaluation conducted between December 2003 and April 2004. An understanding of sustainability for each sub-community and the CAB community as a whole has developed over time.

The realisation that license costs could prove a hurdle to long-term sustainability prompted the project partnership to question the adoption of the commercial product, Microsoft Sharepoint. The limited evaluation possible before the evaluation license expired also revealed the community's dependence on the Dutch students who had been tasked to configure the portal and were available for only a limited period. Since open source software (OSS), with no license costs and with support available from a community of users and developers, was an attractive solution, supplementary software evaluation focused on a range of OSS community software. Moodle (an open source course management system) emerged as the clear leader, mainly because of its range of tools for collaboration and multi-lingual user interface. In July 2004 Moodle was configured on a free test server using requirements already identified from the work done over the preceding six months. The configuration and initial testing showed that it was possible to have the CABWEB portal ready for use in the academic year, commencing September 2004.

During the period August-October 2004, detailed evaluations of the test installation were done by tutors and students (mainly from partners' institutions). Positive user feedback and better understanding of necessary improvements in usability, sociability, and educational settings strengthened partners' decision to stay with Moodle, but to move to a permanent hosting and launch the CAB network more widely in Europe and beyond.

Phase Two: Beyond the Partnership (November 2004-June 2005)

The rapid growth in the number of collaboration spaces and registered users from October 2004 meant that migration to a properly resourced and supported server became a matter of urgency. The portal was moved to a hosting service used by one of the partner institutions. Migration whilst collaborative activities were taking place caused some problems, but these were resolved during November 2004. We became aware that different groups of portal users were experiencing the CABWEB portal in different ways, depending on many factors including technical environment, level of IT literacy, language skills, and most importantly, the activity and support established by their tutors. As the CAB community started to grow rapidly,

Copyright © 2007, Idea Group Inc. Copying or distributing in print or electronic forms without written permission of Idea Group Inc. is prohibited.

exceeding 1000 users early in 2005 (the majority of which were students participating in collaborations), the importance of ongoing evaluation done by different groups became obvious. During the period December 2004 to August 2005, evaluation improved understanding of the needs of the different sub-communities, informed the realisation that the growing CABWEB portal required a new hosting service experienced in Moodle, and confirmed the importance of securing the technical sustainability of CAB community after the end of the project.

Phase Three: Beyond the Project (July 2005 onwards)

This consolidation phase, in progress at the time of writing, is aimed at maximising the benefit obtained from the partnership and project funding in order to leave the CAB community and its online presence (the CABWEB portal) in as robust a state as possible to optimise its sustainability. The evaluation undertaken throughout Phase Two has generated valuable data, not all of which could be acted on during the academic year. Our experience has shown that the summer period, when no collaborative activities occur, is a good time to make changes to the information representation, access, navigation, orientation, and informative content, identified by usability and other evaluations. Hosting is secured until July 2006, and funding is being sought for the extension of CABWEB and continuity of service beyond that date. Sustainability is a sociotechnical issue for the CAB community, which seeks to avoid coordination failure and to increase portal usability for community members.

Evaluation Process

Evaluation Tools

During all phases of the CABWEB development, a broad range of evaluation tools was used. These tools provide data and user feedback on different aspects of pedagogy, sociability, and usability, however they are often specific to one sub-community (e.g., different questionnaires for students and tutors). Qualitative and quantitative data generated by the tools supported decisions on improvements to the portal, its interface, and organisation. The detailed roles of the tools in the evaluation process and their distinctive features are reflected in Table 2.

CAB community research has generated an extensive volume of data that has been and is being analysed by partners and other community members in several research

Copyright © 2007, Idea Group Inc. Copying or distributing in print or electronic forms without written permission of Idea Group Inc. is prohibited.

Table 2. Evaluation tool roles and features

N	Type of Tools	Role	Special Features
1	Student Online Post Collaborative Questionnaire **(SQ)**	Distributed to all students and covers all main aspects of evaluation (educational, social, and usability) (see Appendix 1)	Generates qualitative and quantitative data across specific and general collaborative activities during lifetime of the project
2	Tutor Post Collaborative Questionnaire (**TQ**)	Distributed to all tutors who completed collaborative activity (provides complementary data to SQ)	Qualitative data on collaboration efficiency in a particular educational context (course, module)
3	Focus Group (students) (**FG**)	Allows in-depth exploration of issues raised during collaboration activity	Needs local facilitator (not tutor) Effective for getting less formal feedback and students' personal feelings about experience gained
4	Usability Evaluation (all groups of users, including partners) (**UE**)	Evaluation of user interface, information representation access, navigation, and informative content	Needs resources to undertake and report this evaluation (some groups might be "external"—not taking part in the collaborations)
5	Reflective Discussion Threads (all groups of users, including partners) (**RT**)	Encourage reflective dialogue that may generate new ideas	Give valuable insights into user experiences Can change what CABWEB offers, and what teachers and students do in collaborative activities
Other methods: accessibility evaluation, marketing workshops, peer review, polls, face-to-face meetings, feedback via helpdesk (emergency), "hands-on" evaluation			

papers. In this section we present a selection of results to highlight the roles and outcomes of the different types of evaluations at different phases in the development of the CAB community

Evaluation in Phase One

Student and Tutor questionnaires (SQs, TQs) were the first tools created for evaluation purposes. Since collaborations took place on the different institutional discussion boards during first few months (December 2003-April 2004), users' feedback was the most important source of evaluation data. These detailed evaluations of discussion tools in use complemented the software evaluation of alternative platforms done

Copyright © 2007, Idea Group Inc. Copying or distributing in print or electronic forms without written permission of Idea Group Inc. is prohibited.

Table 3. Access problems in collaboration hosted by a UK institution (SQs)

Access Problems	Country					Total
	Australia	Germany	The Netherlands	Spain	United Kingdom	
yes	0%	**36.4%**	**20.0%**	**53.1%**	9.5%	35.1%
no	100.0%	63.6%	80.0%	46.9%	90.5%	64.9%

by one of the partners (Shaylor & Cookson, 2004). This evaluation data clarified understanding of the functional requirements for the collaborative platform software as well as generating research findings.

Each discussion tool trialled for evaluation was hosted on a different partner institution's server. Results of SQs demonstrated that there was a discrepancy in PEU between students in the host institution and those from other institutions. Usually (generally) students from the host institutions had fewer problems with access, registration, and stability of the server work than "external" participants (Table 3).

While reflecting on the usability and sociability of their institutions' discussions boards (RT), tutors from partner institutions identified the needs for: a general social area where students can communicate off-topic, and a resources area for students to use during collaboration. The importance of trying other collaboration tools, for example WIKI and videoconferences, as a valuable addition to the discussion forum was also reflected in tutors' evaluation on this stage. The emphasis moved away from the *choice* of discussion board to the consideration of a common integrated platform for the development of the CABWEB portal.

Though a "neutral" CAB discussion forum was developed as a temporary solution, and several collaborations took place there, this was not without its problems. The subsequent experimental configuration of the MS Sharepoint portal was subject only to limited evaluation for technology acceptance factors PEU and PU, and was rejected on the grounds of sustainability, because of license and support cost issues, by means of online and face-to-face discussion by project partners.

Evaluation of Test Moodle Installation

As described in the case study, the decision to adopt Moodle rather than MS Sharepoint did not follow the planned evaluation process, but was in response to what was learned about online community sustainability requirements through a combination of literature review and experience. Usability evaluation (UE) done by partners contributed to that decision, and informed both the configuration and choice of resources.

Copyright © 2007, Idea Group Inc. Copying or distributing in print or electronic forms without written permission of Idea Group Inc. is prohibited.

Table 4. Usability evaluation: Comparative data across collaboration platforms (SQs)

Question	An institution's discussion board (01.2004)		CAB temporary discussion board (06.2004)		Moodle test installation (10.2004)	
	yes	no	Yes	no	yes	no
Did you have any technical problems accessing the Web site/ discussion board/portal on which collaboration took place?	33.0%	61.0%*	6.5%	93.5%	5.0%	95.0%
Did the functionality and practical use of the platform motivate you to use it?	57.0%	37.0%	60.9%	39.1%	70.0%	30.0%
Did the interface design of the platform motivate you to use it?	59.0%	35.0%	63.0%	37.0%	56.3%	43.8%

* *There were a few missing cases.*

SQs also allowed us to compare users' perceptions of ease of use (PEU) across platforms. Table 4 compares students' responses to Moodle and two of the discussion tools previously used, showing that many aspects of usability were improved in the test installation, as well as there being a reduction in reports of problems with portal access.

Even though users perceived Moodle to be generally easier to use in terms of technical problems functionality, the interface design was rated slightly lower than on two other discussion boards used (see Table 4). Despite the reduction in technical problems with Moodle, some problems were reported, in particular "the problem with the speed of access to the Web page (dial-up connection)." This data was influential in the consideration of moving the server to a permanent hosting, closer to the Internet backbone.

Partners' usability evaluation examined information representation and access, navigation, orientation, and informative content as indicated in the TAM. Partners have paid special attention to organisation of the portal front page, the HELP Network, and the Students Network; clarity of the portal and the networks' purpose/mission; quality and accessibility of users' guidance and information resources; and performance of available collaborative tools. As a result, the portal configuration and front page content were changed to improve usability and appearance. For example: instructions for the first-time users were improved and made more accessible, and the number of information blocks on the front page was reduced and they were rearranged to make users' orientation easier. Text of the introductory message on the

Copyright © 2007, Idea Group Inc. Copying or distributing in print or electronic forms without written permission of Idea Group Inc. is prohibited.

front page was shortened, since it slowed down uploading. In case of informative content, purpose of the Tutor (HELP) Network was clarified and new resources were added: tutors' checklist, tutor guide, and links to external resources.

TQ revealed that while tutors welcomed the more sophisticated functionality of collaboration spaces compared with the earlier simple discussion tools, they needed additional support in organising and optimal use of these spaces. As well as the data from planned evaluation tools such as TQs and SQs, evaluation data can be obtained from unsolicited user responses that can require immediate response. An example of this was overloading and blocking of students' university mailboxes, caused by automatic subscription, which means that every student was getting copies of forum postings not only from his/her own thread, but also from other threads. The response was to include recommended forum settings for tutors and to alert students to the possibility to unsubscribe from forums.

Evaluation in Phase Two

As described in the case study, the beginning of the second phase was marked by the migration of the portal to a permanent server. At the same time, the launch of CAB community more widely in Europe and beyond brought in new users with even more diverse language and cultural backgrounds and experiences in IT. Using SQs established at the start of the project, we were able to enrich the longitudinal data by virtue of a broader user base alone. We still use focus groups for collaborative activities involving partners, but we could not extend these across the breadth of the new user base, for practical and resource reasons.

Discussion of the CAB Ethos statement (ethical/moral foundations of online discussion and social interaction on the portal) on HELP and Student Networks via reflective discussions was an important part of sociability evaluation. One of the interesting results of a multi-cultural discussion, for example, was the realisation that attitude to privacy and confidentiality differs in different cultural groups. Some users were reluctant to have their personal information available via Google search; there were also preferences to communicate in a "closed for guests" environment expressed by certain cultural groups. Based on users' feedback, CABWEB Discussion Guidelines were reviewed, and a template of an Informed Consent Form for obtaining users' permission to use data from discussion transcripts for research purposes was created.

In the situation of having a great number of non-native-English speakers on the portal, language emerged as an important issue during the evaluation process. Focus groups (FGs) showed that students would like to have online translation tools in their collaboration spaces, and prefer collaboration instructions written also in their native languages. Students' feedback also demonstrated that the Moodle HTML editor has a number of bugs and cannot reproduce some language-specific symbols.

Copyright © 2007, Idea Group Inc. Copying or distributing in print or electronic forms without written permission of Idea Group Inc. is prohibited.

To help tutors/teachers less experienced in IT with the organisation of collaboration spaces and selection of the tools, two templates of collaboration spaces, including instructions on how to edit the templates, were developed. Tutors' feedback has shown that this was helpful and saved time in the preparatory stage.

FGs also demonstrated that students from a non-IT background are reluctant to explore a collaboration environment and tools functionality on their own initiative, and therefore need more time to get used to the interface, and to try out the platform and its tools under their tutor's supervision. Recommendations on this were included in the tutors' instructions.

SQs and FGs also provided us with feedback on the educational efficiency and organisational aspects of collaborations. For example, students pointed out that responding as a group in a peer evaluation activity is not the best way to collaborate, since it made the collaboration less personal and seemed to stress the negative points. Mismatch in level of technical ability was also stressed by students as a negative factor: "I … want to make collaboration more equal—with mutual interest, and similar level of technical ability, even better if the exercise can be reciprocal."

Students' feedback helped to reconsider collaboration instructions, and tutors were advised about better matching of authors and evaluators in peer evaluation activities, writing clearer collaboration instructions/guidelines and evaluation criteria. The role and reciprocity of assessment, timing, and other organisational issues raised by students became the subject of additional research.

Phase Three: Reflection and Redesign for the Future

A community will survive only if new members, which mean tutors as well as students, will join it. As the portal stabilises, it is time for reflection on which features of the portal attract and which may repel users, from data gathered in Phase Two. In contrast to incremental small changes made to the portal in Phase Two, Phase Three is an opportunity to make more radical changes based on outstanding issues and problems from previous evaluation, using the summer, a dormant period for collaborative activities.

In this phase, the evaluation process is concentrated on:

- consolidation and efficient use of available resources to conduct further evaluation and research;
- prioritising important implementation tasks, based on evaluation results, that will improve the portal operation after the end of the project; and
- making best use of the evaluations done in Phase Two.

Copyright © 2007, Idea Group Inc. Copying or distributing in print or electronic forms without written permission of Idea Group Inc. is prohibited.

Two of these evaluations gave findings very relevant for Phase Three: the first was a usability evaluation done by Polish students who were not involved in a collaborative activity, and the second was a portal design exercise by a different group of Polish students. These forms of evaluations have the advantage of combining an educational opportunity for students with the generation of useful evaluation data for the CABWEB leaders and facilitators.

The usability evaluation was a detailed non-participant observation based on criteria provided by their tutor. This evaluation exercise gave a valuable perspective from a set of surrogate "guest" or first-time users. Table 5 presents results from selected questions aimed at usability evaluation (done by non-participant Polish students.)

This UE identified specific elements that can be improved like interface and navigation changes, adding more interactive elements and enhancing the graphics. The results in Table 5 show that although most of them (81.25%) found it to be user friendly, the non-participant evaluators expressed significant dissatisfaction with the appearance, usability, and navigation of the portal. Evaluators made a number of useful suggestions such as introducing a "search" function to be able to find information on the forum, as it is difficult "to find something at the moment." Other suggestions included creation of an interactive map of the portal, more access to data for people with "guest" login, improvement of graphics, and so forth. These suggestions are currently being considered with respect to other classes of users, and some of them will be incorporated into the next version of the portal, currently under development.

Specific improvements identified to improve perceived usefulness included:

1. *make the portal more educationally valuable* (where to find the answer to difficult questions, materials which can be helpful to learn something, links to good courses, especially to courses that described techniques that are used while making projects);
2. *enlarge variety of the collaborations, including collaborations in languages other than English;*

Table 5. Usability evaluation by external students

Question	Yes	No	Not Sure
Do you find the CABWEB portal user friendly?	81.25%	8.33%	10.42%
Do you like the portal outlook?	20.83%	56.25%	22.92%
Do you think the portal is usable?	41.67%	20.83%	37.50%
Do you find the navigation easy?	54.17%	43.75%	2.08%
Do you find the graphics attractive?	52.08%	10.42%	37.50%

Copyright © 2007, Idea Group Inc. Copying or distributing in print or electronic forms without written permission of Idea Group Inc. is prohibited.

3. *provide more information about participants of the forums;* and
4. *introduce elements of competition, "... for example the ranking of people who take part in collaboration, the points for everyone who give comments on the forum," and others.*

These suggestions were thought provoking, and even though not all were within the scope of CABWEB (for example, course materials may be better hosted on institutional spaces), they enriched the reflection and redesign activities. Not only did this evaluation identify areas for improvement, it also highlighted benefits, educational and social, that should be retained. They emphasised the portal role in improving assessing skills, exchanging knowledge and opinions, as well as making progress in language skills for non-native-English speakers.

Moodle's open source code made it possible to implement another evaluation strategy—student portal design projects. Using a test Moodle installation on their institutional server, students were able to develop their own portal graphic themes and front page layout, taking into account usability (see Figures 4 and 5). Although the designs will not be used as they stand, the best ideas from them will be combined into a design that can be established and maintained within available resources.

From these and other user evaluation data, CABWEB leaders and facilitators have been able to identify a set of improvements for usability, sociability, and educational effectiveness, including:

Figure 4. Sample Moodle front page and theme design 1

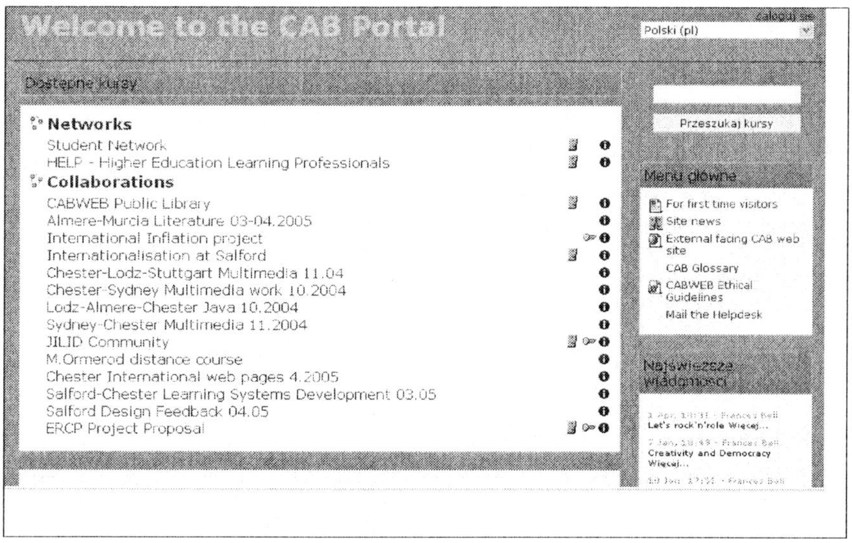

Copyright © 2007, Idea Group Inc. Copying or distributing in print or electronic forms without written permission of Idea Group Inc. is prohibited.

Figure 5. Sample Moodle theme and front page design 2

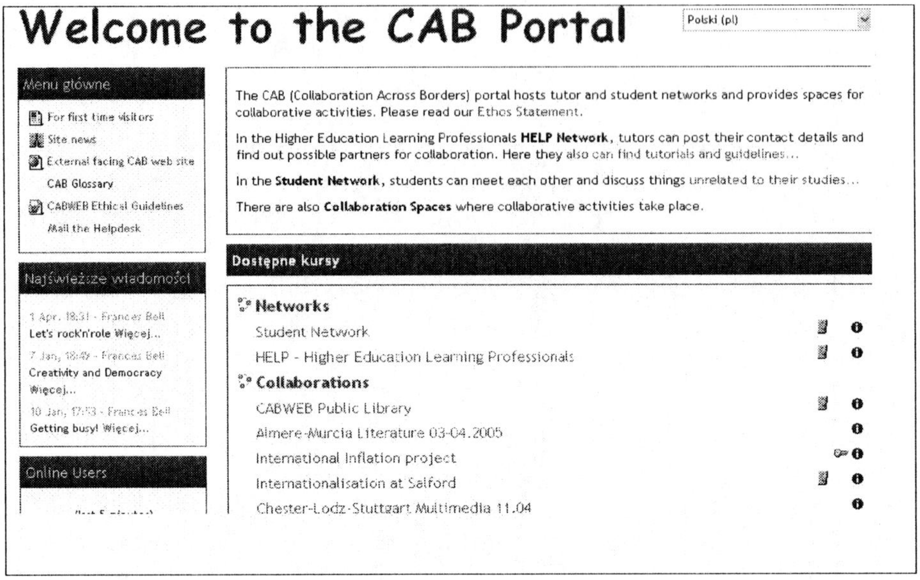

- *Enhanced Language Support:* Implement spell checkers for different languages, make HTML editor more suitable/stable for different languages.
- *Improve Usability:* Change the forum settings (possibility to see all the postings in the thread when you reply).
- *Incorporate New Tools:* Possibility to create a built-in questionnaire for tutors (for educational and evaluation purposes).

The Results of Evaluation: Practical Advice

Evaluation and Change

The sustainability of an online learning community depends not only on the attractiveness of the initial concept, but also on how successfully the community can negotiate change. Through its leaders and facilitators, the community should identify the important socio-cultural, educational, and usability issues that need to be addressed in the process of community building and development. How effectively can the community negotiate and implement the procedures of community operation? The

Copyright © 2007, Idea Group Inc. Copying or distributing in print or electronic forms without written permission of Idea Group Inc. is prohibited.

community, composed of individuals, needs "... a strong sense of open-mindedness, and a willingness to listen to ideas and respond to change" (Smith, 2000).

We agree with de Souza and Preece (2004) that policies and software supporting a new community may need to be changed as the community becomes established. In case of CAB, which is relatively new but has undergone different phases of development, we regard evaluation as a *phase-based, multidimensional process,* where a wide range of methodologies and tools could be applied. Our experience shows that the organisation of evaluation process of such a complex community is a challenge; its results can contain quite discrepant points of view that cannot all be satisfied. Hence, although the software package offers some opportunity for users to personalise their view of the portal, not all sub-groups of users will be satisfied with how their requirements were interpreted. Balanced responses to interpretive evaluations, aimed at incorporating appropriate changes informed by different users' feedback, is what we are trying to achieve.

Though vital to online community growth, evaluation and development consume community and individual resources, the supply of which resources may vary at different stages of the community's lifecycle. CAB project funding provided researcher effort to construct research and evaluation instruments; to conduct detailed evaluations such as student focus groups, interviews; to analyse data generated by these and from system logs and other data; and to implement changes to the portal and community based on these evaluations. CAB project partners were also able to combine evaluation with meaningful educational activities as a source of data and new ideas. These intensive evaluations have informed both the recent re-development of the portal from a usability perspective and the planning of HELP network events and CABWEB participation guidelines from a sociability perspective. Figure 6 is an adaptation of Preece's model (see Figure 1) that maps features of Moodle and our configuration of it onto Preece's examples for usability, and social roles and events on to sociability. Informational resources such as statements of purpose and ethos, discussion guidelines, tutor guidelines, and collaboration space templates impact on usability, sociability, and pedagogic aspects, and thus are open to change by and for users.

Sustainability

The future challenge is to achieve a balance between evaluation and development on the one hand, and on the other hand the resources available for these activities in the longer term, when evaluation and development may be done by community members. During the lifetime of the project, we have discovered repeatedly that improvements we desired would become available in forthcoming versions of Moodle. This is a great benefit of widely adopted OSS—the user-developer com-

Copyright © 2007, Idea Group Inc. Copying or distributing in print or electronic forms without written permission of Idea Group Inc. is prohibited.

munity both generates and satisfies software requirements and shares knowledge of the software in use.

Sustainability is clearly a challenge for online learning communities, and CAB is no exception. However, community can be sustained in different ways: CAB may survive through a combination of institutional support, external funding, and the enthusiasm of members; student collaborative activities may move to another online space; or CAB may become unsustainable if groups of members or whole sub-communities such as HELP or JILID moved on to other online communities. Staying and moving on are both normal responses by individuals in an evolving community. An ongoing cycle of evaluation that informs redesign for usability and re-planning for sociability can improve the technology and social practices, and thereby improve members' experiences within the community. The experienced-based learning that was situated within one online community—how to *do* online community—belongs to the individual as well as to the community, and thus goes with members who move between online communities over time. Such learning is promoted by reflection and dialogue about the process of community interactions, such as sharing resources and discussion.

Figure 6. Usability and sociability adapted from Preece (2001, p. 27) for CAB community. Copyright John Wiley & Sons Limited. Reproduced with permission.

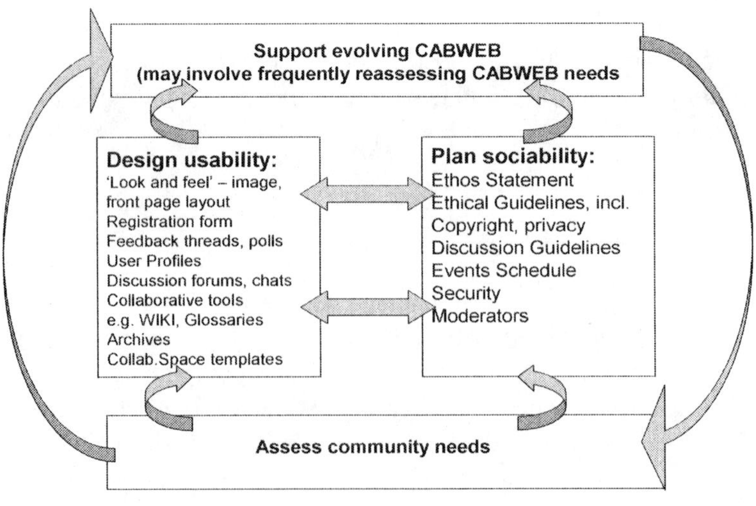

Copyright © 2007, Idea Group Inc. Copying or distributing in print or electronic forms without written permission of Idea Group Inc. is prohibited.

Advice to Online Learning Community Developers

- Time spent on evaluating community software packages is a good investment if it finds one that satisfies the functional requirements, facilitates adaptation of community support, supplies usage data, and satisfies sustainability criteria.
- Social, educational, and usability aspects are all important, and evaluation should take all of these into consideration. Questions raised about any of these aspects by questionnaire responses may be explored via other evaluation tools, such as focus groups or dialogic approaches.
- Evaluation associated with software package choice may be relatively rare within a community lifecycle, happening when the community is established or when it has "outgrown" the software package in use. In contrast, evaluation that identifies changes to information content, social roles, events, and pedagogical aspects will proceed in parallel with the development of the portal and the collaborative activities. Such evaluation can be embedded into community activities, particularly if a culture of open and reflective communication is established. If community leaders and developers are flexible and responsive, and are able to make manageable changes, this can contribute to the sustainability of the community.
- The Using Moodle community at http://moodle.org demonstrates the use of Moodle for community as well as course management. One year's use of Moodle on CAB has not given us any regrets about our choice to date. An advantage of OS Software is that there is usually an associated user/developer community (albeit enthusiasts) who can provide rich examples of the software in use and answer technical queries without charge. We have benefited from this on CAB. Whilst the freedom from license costs has been welcome, we have come to realise the importance of a stable and experienced hosting service that can offer data backup, recovery, and security. Using Open Source is not *free*; it is a different distribution of resources. In our case, with limited resources for development, our focus is on configuring, rather than customising (that has to be re-done when software upgrades are applied) with effort applied to effective use of existing functionality, feeding requirements into the OSS community, and publishing support resources for tutors and students.

Conclusion

In this section, we explore what differentiates CAB from other online learning communities and summarise what we have contributed to knowledge of the role of evaluation in achieving sustainability.

Copyright © 2007, Idea Group Inc. Copying or distributing in print or electronic forms without written permission of Idea Group Inc. is prohibited.

What is special about the CAB community?

- The first item is the explicit *interdependence* of the CAB sub-communities, where the healthy functioning of the HELP network is a basis for stable/steady functioning of the collaboration spaces. A vibrant, active HELP network leads to a growth in the number of collaborative spaces, with new tutors learning from the student activities who will then be able to contribute to the HELP network.
- It is a *heterogeneous* community, where different users (teachers, students, researchers) work together towards a common goal, improving the quality of student learning. These users nevertheless have their own interests in and expectations of the collaborative environment.
- It is an *international* community, whose members came from different educational traditions, possess different levels of shared language proficiency (usually English), and have various communication styles.
- It is *developing* from a formal partnership of several institutions pursuing project-determined goals to an informal community with voluntary involvement, based on intrinsic motivation (at least for the tutors).

Evaluation and Sustainability

Evaluation and sustainability are inextricably linked. Whilst good evaluation and effective action on the results of that evaluation cannot guarantee that an online learning community will survive, previous research on online communities reveals the importance of a learning and adaptation cycle. Our experience in CAB confirms this, and further, we have shown the variety of ways in which evaluation can be designed, resourced, and used in order to inform the ongoing community development of an international community of tutors and students. Evaluation and concomitant changes improve usability (perceived ease of use) and perceived usefulness. Perceptions of usefulness vary across different groups of users.

We used two metaphors for community on CAB, networks and collaborations. The network of tutors that is HELP corresponds to a community of practice whose members share an interest in international student collaboration online. There is no clear focus for the Student Network on CABWEB, and not surprisingly there has been limited activity to date. Collaboration spaces are cross-institutional in that they involve students from more than one institution, yet they tend to be strongly linked to the modules within the institutions to which the groups of students belong. Modules last for an academic year at most, and it seems unlikely that students or tutors would wish an online learning community associated with collaborative activities within modules to persist beyond the lifetime of a particular cohort of students for

Copyright © 2007, Idea Group Inc. Copying or distributing in print or electronic forms without written permission of Idea Group Inc. is prohibited.

those modules, though student connections may persist through shared interest or experiences.

Evaluation is resource-intensive yet vital to the promotion of the sustainability, or the sensible decision to abandon, an online learning community. We learn and sometimes move on.

Acknowledgments

We wish to acknowledge the contributions of all students and tutors who have been involved in the CAB community; the funding provided by Socrates- Minerva for the CAB project (110681-CP-1-2003-1-UK-MINERVA-M); and the time and commitment given by all CAB project partners, their colleagues, and students who so enriched the evaluations.

References

Bell, F., & Heinze, A. (2004). With regard to respect—A framework for the governance of educational virtual communities. *International Journal of Web-Based Communities, 1*(1), 19-33.

Brown, J. S., & Duguid, P. (1998). Organizing knowledge. *California Management Review, 40*(3), 90+.

Cherny, L. (1999). *Conversation and community: Chat in a virtual world.* CA: CSLI Publications.

Davis, F. D. (1989). Perceived usefulness, perceived ease of use, and user acceptance of information technology. *MIS Quarterly, 13*(3), 319-340.

De Marsico, M., & Levialdi, S. (2004). Evaluating Web sites: Exploiting users' expectations. *International Journal of Human-Computer Studies, 60*(3), 381-416.

de Souza, C. S., & Preece, J. (2004). A framework for analyzing and understanding online communities. *Interacting with Computers, 16*(3), 579-610.

Goodyear, P. (2001). *Effective networked learning in higher education: Notes and guidelines.* Centre for Studies in Advanced Learning Technology, Lancaster University, UK.

Kim, A. J. (2000). *Community building on the Web*. Berkeley, CA: Peachpit Press (Addison-Wesley Longman).

Copyright © 2007, Idea Group Inc. Copying or distributing in print or electronic forms without written permission of Idea Group Inc. is prohibited.

Lave, J., & Wenger, E. (1991). *Situated learning: Legitimate peripheral participation*. Cambridge, UK: Cambridge University Press.

Lin, J. C., & Lu, H. (2000). Towards an understanding of the behavioural intention to use a Web site. *International Journal of Information Management, 20,* 197-208.

Lipnack, J., & Stamps, J. (2000). *Virtual teams: Reaching across space, time, and organizations with technology* (2nd ed.). New York: John Wiley & Sons.

Nogier, J.-F. (2005). *What is usability?* Retrieved August 18, 2005, from the World Wide Web.

Preece, J. (2000). *Online communities: Designing usability, supporting sociability.* New York: John Wiley & Sons.

Shaylor, J., & Cookson, G. (2004). *Establishing process and evaluating tools: Report on stage 3 of the CAB project.* Retrieved from the World Wide Web.

Smith, A. (2000, September 11-13). Collaboration between educational institutions: Can various individual successes translate into a broad range of sustained partnerships? *Proceedings of the "Distance Education: An Open Question?" Conference,* Adelaide, Australia.

Steinmueller, W.E. (2002). Virtual communities and the new economy. In R. Mansell (Ed.), *Inside the communication revolution: Evolving patterns of social and technical interaction* (pp. 21-54). Oxford: Oxford University Press.

Suchman, L. (2000). Organizing alignment: A case of bridge-building. *Organization Science, 7*(2).

Teo, H.-H., Chan, H.-C., Wei, K.-K., & Zhang, Z. (2003). Evaluating information accessibility and community adaptivity features for sustaining virtual learning communities. *International Journal of Human-Computer Studies, 59*(5), 671-697.

Tonnies, F. (1957). *Community and society: Gemeinschaft und Gesellschaft.* Michigan State University Press.

Wang, Y., & Fesenmaier, D. R. (2004). Towards understanding members' general participation in and active contribution to an online travel community. *Tourism Management, 25*(6), 709-722.

Wenger, E., McDermott, R., & Snyder, W. (2002). *Cultivating communities of practice.* Boston: Harvard Business School Press.

Copyright © 2007, Idea Group Inc. Copying or distributing in print or electronic forms without written permission of Idea Group Inc. is prohibited.

Appendix 1. Examples of Questions from Student Questionnaire and Purposeful Evaluations

Educational

I consider the opportunity to participate in a collaborative activity as beneficial. (strongly agree-strongly disagree)

The collaborative activity was actively discussed in my group. (strongly agree-strongly disagree)

Did the collaboration increase/strengthen your interest in the topic of your project/assignment? (yes, no)

Social

Were your messages answered in reasonable time? (yes, no)

Please give up to three reasons why you did or did not communicate on different topics. (open)

Did you use any non-verbal symbols, for example "emoticons" (winks, smiley faces, and others), during the communication process? (yes, no)

Accessibility/Usability

Did you have any technical problems accessing the Web site/portal? (yes, no)

If yes, please say what kind of problems. (open)

Did you communicate with your partner by any (other) means that the Web site/platform does not provide? Please choose one or more from the list. (no, e-mail, chat/other IMT, phone, other)

Did the functionality and practical use of the platform motivate you to use it? (yes, no)

What is your opinion of the registration procedure?

Do you like the interface of CABWEB/What would you change in the interface and in the navigation?

What language tools would you like to have for supporting your communication?

What kind of information do you find necessary, not useful, and missing?

Copyright © 2007, Idea Group Inc. Copying or distributing in print or electronic forms without written permission of Idea Group Inc. is prohibited.

General

What were the three best/worst things about being involved in the collaboration? (open)

What things could be changed to improve future peer-evaluation exercises? (open)

Do you find Student Network useful?

Endnotes

1. Open source software is written so that programmers can read, redistribute, and modify the source code for a piece of software, with the result that the software evolves rapidly, usually within a community (see http://www.opensource.org/docs/definition.php).

2. In this chapter, configuration refers to the "switching on and off" of functionality that comes with the software, and customisation is meant to describe changes or additions to the functionality available in the standard software package by software modification. In general, configuration is preserved when a software package is upgraded to a new version, unlike customisation where software modifications have to be re-applied, incurring a significant maintenance overhead.

Copyright © 2007, Idea Group Inc. Copying or distributing in print or electronic forms without written permission of Idea Group Inc. is prohibited.

Chapter X

Tools and Methods for Supporting Online Learning Communities and Their Evaluation

Maria Rigou, University of Patras &
Research Academic Computer Technology Institute, Greece

Spiros Sirmakessis, Research Academic Computer Technology Institute
& Technological Educational Institution of Messolongi, Greece

Dimitris Stavrinoudis, University of Patras &
Hellenic Open University, Greece

Michalis Xenos, Research Academic Computer Technology Institute
& Hellenic Open University, Greece

Abstract

Scientific observation during the last few years has indicated that learning on the Web in many cases is accompanied and promoted by the creation and maintenance of an online learning community. The goal of this chapter is to define and describe the notion of online communities, describe their types and core functionalities, and focus on the specific domain of online learning communities. More specifically, the chapter presents an overall categorization of the technological tools used for supporting online learning communities and suggests a set of general-purpose evalu-

Copyright © 2007, Idea Group Inc. Copying or distributing in print or electronic forms without written permission of Idea Group Inc. is prohibited.

ation methods suitable for assessing quality aspects of these tools, along with a method for the statistical analysis of the derived data. The chapter concludes with a discussion on foreseen future trends concerning ways to enhance the everyday life of online learning community inhabitants and upgrade the effect of online teaching and learning.

Introduction

Online communities have been studied by a number of scientific domains including communication studies, sociology, psychology, information systems, business studies, computing, information science, and newly formed departments of cyber or Internet studies (Preece, Maloney-Krichmar, & Abras, 2003). Their evolution depended primarily on the evolution of the supportive technology that provided the communicational infrastructure for bringing community members together. The first medium deployed for community support was e-mail, which was developed in 1972 and, in its primitive form, allowed only point-to-point communication. One-to-many postings were enabled by listserv technology, which became available after 1975. Their basic form has not changed much until today, and they are still used by some online communities. In the 1980s bulletin boards appeared and allowed the threading of postings on a topic-by-topic basis. Similar functionalities were also provided by Usenet News, which along with the rest of the technologies mentioned so far, comprise the set of asynchronous communication technologies deployed by online communities. Chat systems on the other hand (IRC, AOL Instant Messenger, etc.) belong to the set of synchronous communication technologies used for supporting online communities.

The advent of the World Wide Web in 1992 led to the widespread use of Web sites and the formation of online community groups supported by integrated communication infrastructures and graphical environments in 2 or 3 dimensions (e.g., Palace—www.palace.com and Activeworlds—www.activeworlds.com). The next step was to move to more sophisticated interfaces and interaction modes like the ones used in gaming worlds (Doom, Quake, etc.), where users are represented as avatars and interact through text, sound, and streaming video. In recent years, there have been strong and highly populated communities gathered around a certain technology, such as MP3, or open source. Today, with the wide availability of Internet telephone, streaming video, photographs, sound, voice Web cams, blogs, and wikis, the technological alternatives for setting up and maintaining an online community are numerous (Preece et al., 2003).

The notion of setting up user communities is of vital importance in the framework of e-learning. Learning is a process closely connected to social interaction (Hiltz,

Copyright © 2007, Idea Group Inc. Copying or distributing in print or electronic forms without written permission of Idea Group Inc. is prohibited.

1998; Vygotsky, 1986) and sociability (Preece, 2000). Scientific observation during the last few years has indicated that learning on the Web in many cases is accompanied and promoted by the creation and maintenance of online learning communities (OLCs). In fact, research provides evidence that:

...strong feelings of community may not only increase persistence in courses but may also increase the commitment to group goals, cooperation among members, satisfaction with group efforts, and motivation to learn. (Rovai, 2002)

Thus, given that the strong sense of community is related to increased persistence and learning, it can be the basis for designing and facilitating online teaching and learning. And though in real life most communities are formed through geographical proximity, OLCs are mostly formed around a shared interest or need, and are a powerful tool for building trust and relationships, for acquiring and exchanging knowledge, leading to more *human* Web environments.

This chapter begins with defining online communities, describes their types and core functionalities, and then focuses on the specific domain of OLCs. Next, it provides an overview of IT tools and methods used for supporting OLCs, proposes an overall categorization of these tools, and suggests a set of evaluation methods suitable for applying in the domain of OLC support systems. The chapter concludes with a discussion on foreseen future directions concerning ways to enhance the everyday life of OLC inhabitants and upgrade the effect of online teaching and learning.

Online Learning Communities: A Field Background

Defining online communities is not a trivial task. A search in the related bibliography (in both the sociology and the IT domains) results in a variety of definitions with different focus and prerequisites as to what constitutes an online community. Probably the best known definition of online communities comes from Rheingold (1994), who described them as "cultural aggregations that emerge when enough people bump into each other often enough in cyberspace" (p. 57). Schmid (2000) proposed a more agent-based approach (that does not solely take into account real people), in which communities are put together through agents—human or software—that are linked by a common language and set of values, and pursue common interests. These agents are tied together through a medium in which their roles interact with each other accordingly. Another approach from the IT domain came from Preece (2000), who identified four ingredients in online communities (p.10):

Copyright © 2007, Idea Group Inc. Copying or distributing in print or electronic forms without written permission of Idea Group Inc. is prohibited.

1. *People,* who interact socially as they strive to satisfy their own needs or perform special roles (such as leading or moderating).
2. A *shared purpose,* such as an interest, need, information exchange, or service that provides a reason for the community.
3. *Policies,* in the form of tacit assumptions, rituals, protocols, rules, and laws that guide people's interactions.
4. *Computer systems,* to support and mediate social interaction and facilitate a sense of togetherness.

Core attributes of an online community (in the sense that communities with more such attributes are clearer examples of communities than those that have fewer) comprise (Whittaker, Isaacs, & O'Day, 1997, p. 137):

- a shared goal, interest, need, or activity;
- repeated, active participation, with intense interactions and strong emotional ties between participants;
- access to shared resources with policies to determine access;
- reciprocity of information, support, and services between members; and
- shared context (social conventions, language, protocols).

According to the same source, less central attributes of online communities comprise: (1) differentiated roles and reputations, (2) awareness of membership boundaries and group identity, (3) initiation criteria, (4) history and long duration, (5) events or rituals, (6) shared physical environment, and (7) voluntary membership.

The relevant literature offers a multitude of categorizations for online communities, which is indicative of their many facets. Based on the purpose and the shared characteristics of their members, online communities can be categorized as *communities of practice* (where individuals share the same profession), *communities of circumstance* (where individuals share a personal situation), *communities of purpose* (where individuals share a common objective or purpose), and *communities of interest* (where individuals share an interest). In some cases, a community may fall into more than one definition, and over time a community may develop sub-communities formed around special interest groups.

Another interesting categorization distinguishes online communities by the technological platforms they deploy as:

Copyright © 2007, Idea Group Inc. Copying or distributing in print or electronic forms without written permission of Idea Group Inc. is prohibited.

- *Web-based communities* based on Internet or intranet technologies;
- *peer communities,* which are based on peer-to-peer technologies and involve network structures where each connected computer offers its resources to be used by other computers;
- communities that use *mobile technologies* and also provide new forms of media-supported learning (mobile learning); and
- communities that occur in *virtual worlds* (such as Multi-User Dungeons), used mainly in the field of edutainment.

Regardless of the specific platform, the list of typical functionalities that should be supported for maintaining an online community comprises (Seufert, 2002):

- mailing lists;
- e-polls for the collection of community members' opinions;
- Web blackboards;
- visualization of sub-groups;
- community chronicle;
- expert index (who's who, yellow pages, etc.);
- document management;
- photo album and member guestbook;
- audio and video conferences, chat and discussion forums, buddy lists;
- team workspaces, group calendar, work-flow based task administration; and
- feedback mechanisms (rating functionalities, scoring models for the grading of content, discussion contributions, etc.).

Table 1 lists a number of widely used platforms for building and supporting electronic communities.

Moving to the e-learning domain, a real-world OLC is a group of people who are dedicated to learning together in a safe environment that encourages dialogue, feedback, reflection, and empowerment. Members of an OLC may be students, lecturers, tutors, researchers, practitioners, and domain experts who: (1) work in teams; (2) have agreed upon aspirations that develop personal goals; (3) create a learning community vision for what is possible; (4) engage in meaningful conversations; and (5) are respectful, encouraging, and forgiving. Technology can be used to create learning (or educational) communities that foster collaborative learning so that students can learn together and benefit from sharing ideas and resources with the support of skillful moderators and mentors (Hiltz, 1998; Salmon, 2000). According

Copyright © 2007, Idea Group Inc. Copying or distributing in print or electronic forms without written permission of Idea Group Inc. is prohibited.

Table 1. Platforms for building and maintaining online communities (Seufert, 2002)

Platform	Description/Features	Application Domain
Cassiopeia www.cassiopeia.com	*Community platform with personalization, functionalities for the organization of teams, integrated incentive system for active participation in the community*	*Knowledge communities, communities of practice (on an intranet), B2B communities (Internet)*
Vignette www.vignette.com	*Community platform for the support of customer relations, personalized information for customers, analysis of customer profile (e.g., visitor activities, activities regarding campaigns, through content, advice, feedback).*	*Specialization in customer-related communities (Internet)*
WebFair www.webfair.com	*Community platform with personalization, integrated feedback mechanism with feedback recorded in a database, integrated scoring model as the basis of an incentive system*	*Knowledge communities in the broader sense, business communities*
Arsdigida www.arsdigida.com	*Community platform with personalization, functionalities for the organization of teams; open source methodology: developers can develop the tool further according to their own needs*	*Knowledge communities in the broadest sense, business communities (Internet/intranet)*
e-groups groups.yahoo.com	*Communities can be set up on the prevailing server, simple functionalities such as synchronous or asynchronous communication, group calendar functionalities for peer-facilitated communities*	*Interest/free time communities (Internet), more for private use*
Groove www.grovenetworks.com	*Community platform with personalization, functionalities for the organization of teams, document and workflow management functionalities for peer-facilitated communities*	*Peer-to-peer knowledge communities (Internet, peer-to-peer technology)*

to Reinmann-Rothmeier, Mandl, and Prenzel (2000), a learning community is a community where people are joined together by a mutual interest to intensively examine a particular theme, and are able to learn together, exchange existing knowledge, and jointly work on aspects of problem solving. Ideally, within the context of a learning community, knowledge and meaning are actively constructed, and the community

Copyright © 2007, Idea Group Inc. Copying or distributing in print or electronic forms without written permission of Idea Group Inc. is prohibited.

enhances the acquisition of knowledge and understanding, and satisfies the learning needs of its members. The introduction of OLCs to the typical Web-based learning scenario has proved to be a quite promising concept, allowing the improvement of both the quality of online courses and the objective satisfaction of users in Web-based learning environments by offering a way to counteract the isolation of the independent learner and the associated dropout quota (Seufert, 2002).

Table 2 presents indicative examples of some widely used tools for supporting OLCs. These tools provide more sophisticated and integrated solutions, and are classified as either learning management systems (VCampus, Centra, and iCohere) or collaborative annotation systems (Case and Mole). More details on tools and methods used for supporting OLCs can be found in the third section of this chapter.

OLCs (just like online communities in general) are not defined (nor discerned) in a straight-forward manner. An interesting discussion on the matter is available by

Table 2. Tools supporting OLCs

Tool	Description/Features
VCampus Corporation www.vcampus.com	*Utilizes the "PowerBlend Blended Learning" concept, which provides various communication and collaboration options to its users (discussion boards, live chat, and shared whiteboards)*
Centra www.centra.com	*Enables online business collaboration, communication, and learning; provides support for synchronous Web conferencing, including chats, whiteboards, and video teleconferencing*
iCohere www.icohere.com	*Supports relationship building and collaboration, and allows easy integration of existing learning content; provides streaming presentations, custom e-learning modules, and other content, as well as online meetings and discussion areas with group process tools, fostering collaboration in service of learning*
Case *(Glover, Hardaker, & Xu, 2004)*	*Allows users to add an additional layer of information to the Web learning content in the form of collaborative annotations; developers of this system expect that by allowing the community members to collaborate on the learning material, the quality of learners' online discussion will be improved through the integration of the learning context directly into the content design*
Mole *(Whittington, 1996)*	*Combines exploratory learning with hypertext-based material and collaborative learning through the use of annotations; designed to enable learners to take an active role in their learning by facilitating the online annotation of hypertext notes*

Copyright © 2007, Idea Group Inc. Copying or distributing in print or electronic forms without written permission of Idea Group Inc. is prohibited.

Schwier and Daniel (see Chapter II, this volume). Despite the increasing interest in OLC design and the increasing number of newly built communities, the issue of identifying criteria for evaluating their success remains open. Designing and implementing an online environment for supporting a community requires much more that merely providing for the communication and resource sharing capabilities. OLC designers are people who must combine *"... the world of technology and the world of people, and try to bring the two together"* (Kapor, 1996). In attempting to set up a successful learning community on the Web, many things can go wrong, and the road from assuring all technical prerequisites to having people participating and keeping the community alive is long and winding.

Since the domain of OLCs is multidisciplinary, the evaluation of what constitutes a successful OLC should be based on more than one parameter. Most scientists measure success in terms of *sociability* (i.e., the social interactions between community members and the policies that guide them) and *usability* within the virtual community boundaries. Potential indicators of success in OLCs in terms of sociability are the number of participants in the community, the number of lurkers (Nonnecke, 2000; Nonnecke & Preece, 2000), the number of posted messages, the number of messages per participant, the degree of reciprocity (as indicated by, e.g., the number of responses per participant), the amount of on-topic discussion, the degree of empathy in interactions, the level of trust, the frequency of uncivil behavior incidences, the average duration of membership, and the percentage of people that are still members after a certain period of time (Preece, 2001). On the usability dimension, potential determinants of success may include speed of getting to know how to use the interface, productivity (how long it takes to perform trivial tasks in the community), frequency of errors in using the community infrastructure, and subjective satisfaction of community members (Preece, 2001).

OLCs (which are typically categorized as communities of purpose) should also be evaluated based on the degree they support learning and teaching in a remote collaborative scenario, and the degree they satisfy the needs of all community members (i.e., students, lecturers, tutors, researchers, domain experts moderators, etc.). These factors though depend on the specific domain each OLC is gathered around, as well as the learning scenarios employed. Lambropoulos (Chapter I, this volume) proposes a set of seven guidelines for OLCs that comply with the UCD approach, namely intention, information, interactivity, real-time evaluation, visibility, control, and support. Another consideration is whether the community is a closed, formal learning, class-based community or an open one supporting informal learning modes. The evaluation criteria must conform to the different objectives and priorities of each community type. In this chapter, we focus on general-purpose evaluation methods that assess more intrinsic features and quality characteristics of tools supporting OLCs: support for communication, access to resources and collaborative work, as well as sufficient moderation in order to protect learners against inappropriate behavior and guide interactions.

Copyright © 2007, Idea Group Inc. Copying or distributing in print or electronic forms without written permission of Idea Group Inc. is prohibited.

Tools and Methods Supporting Online Learning Communities

This section discusses the particular characteristics of the tools and methods used for supporting OLCs starting with an overall twofold categorization based on one hand the learner and the learning process, and on the other the technological complexity of the solutions offered.

In terms of technological complexity, both *basic* and *advanced* tools and methods are included in this presentation, enriched with practical experiences from their use. It must be noted that most of the presented technologies were not initially developed for OLCs; consequently their scope and users are quite broader. However, once introduced to the OLC environments, they have been easily adopted, since it was obvious that they would drastically improve the educational procedure.

As regards the learner-based classification, it must be noted that the related bibliography includes numerous studies classifying Web-based education systems that support OLCs. For example, Oliver, Omari, and Herrington (1998) are using the place and time parameters to classify learning communities into traditional vs. distance and synchronous vs. asynchronous. Most related studies (e.g., Crossman, 1997; Stenerson, 1998; McCormack & Jones, 1998) are focusing on the use of the World Wide Web as a combining medium that facilitates the work of OLCs. This chapter classifies the systems that support OLCs as: *synchronous* or *asynchronous* and *single-user* or *collaborative* ones. *Synchronous* refers to systems enabling more than one OLC member to work simultaneously and *asynchronous* to systems that

Figure 1. Discussion among the members of an OLC at the Hellenic Open University

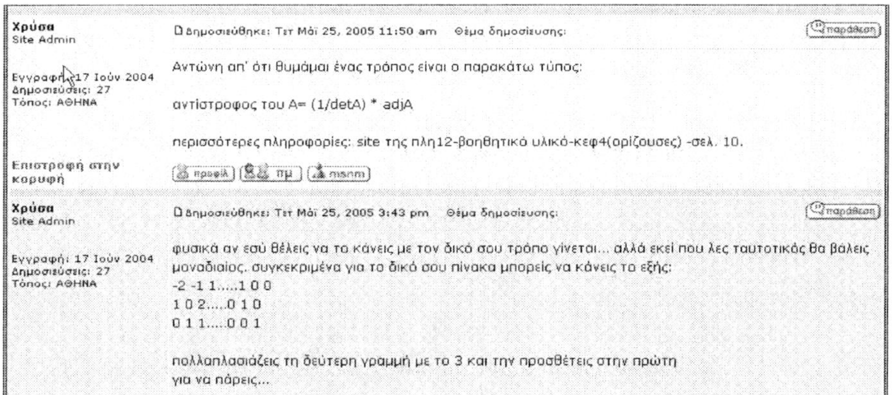

Copyright © 2007, Idea Group Inc. Copying or distributing in print or electronic forms without written permission of Idea Group Inc. is prohibited.

do not provide this possibility. *Collaborative* refers to systems enabling the collaboration of many learners within an OLC in order to complete a task that cannot be accomplished by a single learner.

Based on the earlier-mentioned twofold classification (learner and technology based), the following sections present some of the most widely used tools and methods. The order in which the tools and methods are discussed next does not imply any type of further classification, although it is partially based on their technological complexity.

Basic Communication Tools

Current basic communication tools that support OLCs are e-mail, fora, and discussion lists. All these tools are text based, as implied by the characterization *basic*. Namely, the use of these tools requires the members of the OLC to type a message that the other members will read. One of the main communication instruments in today's distance education is e-mail. Besides e-mail, the use of fora is also quite common in OLCs, since fora are mainly used for communication and publication. Figure 1 presents part of a learners-tutor discussion related to the *Introduction to Computer Science* module of the Hellenic Open University. Finally, discussion lists are quite similar to e-mail and fora, and are used by OLCs in a similar manner.

All the aforementioned tools are mainly used for asynchronous communication. Since their purpose is communication, they could also be considered collaborative tools, although they are mainly used to facilitate non-collaborative learner-tutor communication.

Advanced Communication Tools

Chat (realized in most cases with instance messengers) is a well-known communication means for OLCs, and it is text based also. The main difference between chat tools and the aforementioned text-based tools is that chat is synchronous. Furthermore, most instance messengers incorporate additional net-phone and net-meeting facilities, allowing faster and technologically advanced communication, and can therefore be used for lecturing purposes as well.

An example of a chat tool is Buddy Space (see Eisenstadt, Komzak, & Dzbor, 2003), used in the British Open University (found at http://kmi.open.ac.uk/projects/buddyspace/), which allows optional maps for geographical and office-plan visualizations, as well as build-in tools for Web casts and video communication (see Figure 2). Advanced communication tools are used for the collaboration of the members of an OLC in a synchronous manner.

Copyright © 2007, Idea Group Inc. Copying or distributing in print or electronic forms without written permission of Idea Group Inc. is prohibited.

Figure 2. Buddy Space allows advanced communication among members of an OLC

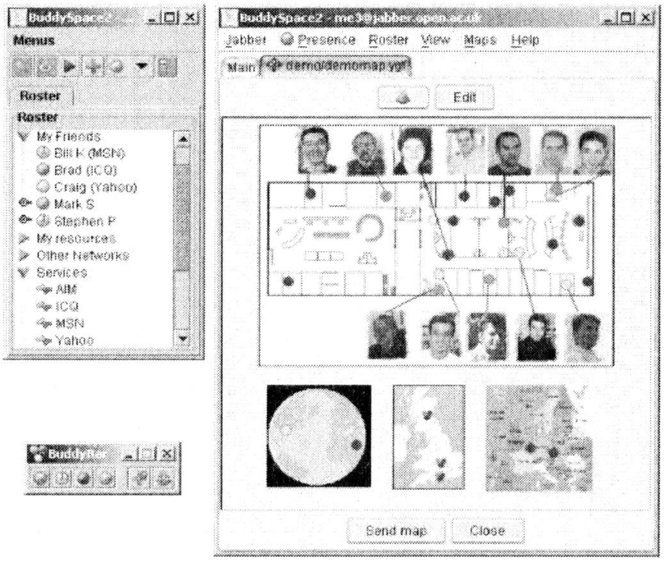

Tutor Lectures

Some universities offer their OLC members online course lectures. An example is shown in Figure 3 illustrating a screenshot from a lecture at Harvard University.

Figure 3. Lecture in Harvard DCE distance education platform

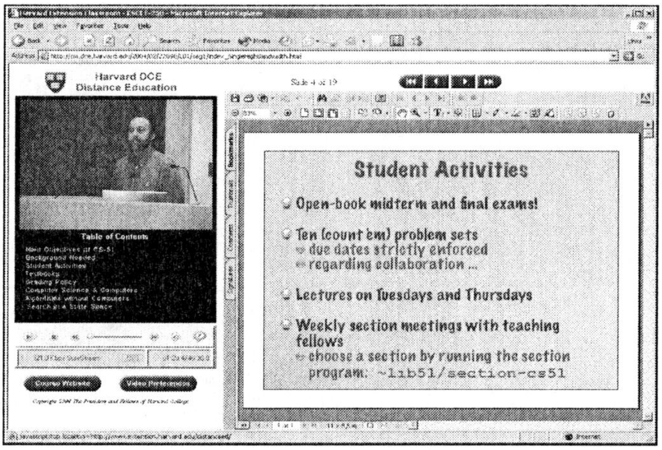

Copyright © 2007, Idea Group Inc. Copying or distributing in print or electronic forms without written permission of Idea Group Inc. is prohibited.

Online lectures resemble traditional university course classes and are usually stored for later review by the members of the OLC.

Depending on the system that supports this process, the members of the OLC may be able to either simply attend the lecture remotely or participate actively in it (i.e., ask or answer questions). A well-known system supporting online lectures for OLCs is eClass (http://www.cc.gatech.edu/fce/eclass). Online lectures are of course synchronous, but their storage and future viewing allows an asynchronous viewing mode as well. They are usually not collaborative, but in some cases collaboration among the members of the community is possible, provided that active participation of community members is allowed.

Remote and Virtual Laboratories

Remote laboratories are laboratories that allow the members of an OLC to participate remotely in a real experiment (an experiment that takes place in an actual laboratory in real time). In this case, the members' participation varies from defining a set of parameters and receiving the results to actually remotely controlling the experiment. Remote laboratories are synchronous, and in some cases collaborative, allowing the collaboration and communication among the members of the OLC.

Unlike remote laboratories, virtual ones do not require actual establishments. They simulate laboratories providing practice to OLC members. In most cases, these members act individually and are able to simulate (using a range of items from simple graphics to virtual reality tools) a real experiment by interacting with the system. In some cases, these experiments are collaborative and can be either synchronous or asynchronous, with the latter being the most common practice. It should be noted that the laboratories category may also includes simple tools (such as programming tools, compilers, etc.) that allow OLC members to work remotely in a laboratory-like manner.

Another tool of this category that is currently used for learning purposes in OLCs is collaboration games. In such games, members of the community are assigned roles and take part remotely. Such games are highly collaborative and in most cases synchronous.

Tools Allowing Synchronous Collaboration

A number of tools have been developed to enable synchronous collaboration of the members of OLCs. Among them are shared blackboards, virtual working spaces, and virtual classrooms. Most of these tools are enhanced with many communication tools such as the ones previously presented.

Copyright © 2007, Idea Group Inc. Copying or distributing in print or electronic forms without written permission of Idea Group Inc. is prohibited.

Shared blackboards, for example, have similar functionality to classroom blackboards and enable two or more OLC members to write on a common blackboard either by exchanging a key, or simultaneously. Such blackboards are integrated in most learning management systems (LMSs) and constitute a means of written expression that also allows collaboration among the members of the OLC.

A more complex form of blackboard is the virtual space, a system that enables a number of OLC members to share a common virtual space, while providing at the same time other communication tools as well. Virtual spaces are usually organized for a specific learning purpose (i.e., collaborative design). A representative example of such a system is Synergo (see Xenos, Avouris, Komis, Stavrinoudis, & Margaritis, 2004), a peer-to-peer application that allows members of OLCs of the Hellenic Open University to manipulate a number of developed diagrams in a shared activity space and to communicate directly through a chat tool, while offering measurements related to the degree of collaboration (for the tutor or the researcher). Figure 4 illustrates the result of the collaboration between two distant partners using Synergo. These two OLC members have completed the design of a flowchart. Synergo enables the distinguishing of each contribution (different colors) and the exchange of chat messages (frame in the right part of the screen). In most cases, the use of similar tools is synchronous and of course collaborative.

Figure 4. A common design space shared by two members of an OLC

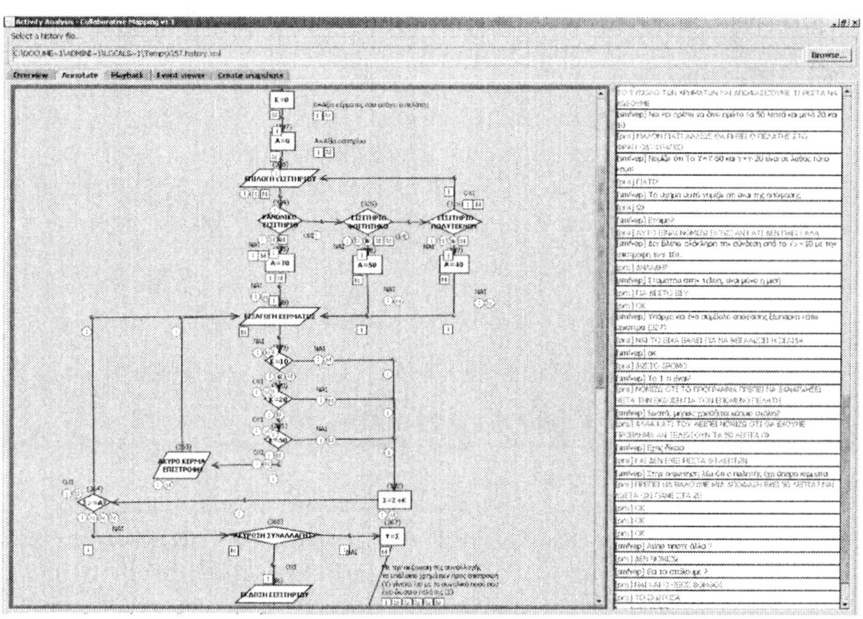

Copyright © 2007, Idea Group Inc. Copying or distributing in print or electronic forms without written permission of Idea Group Inc. is prohibited.

Figure 5. A virtual classroom instance

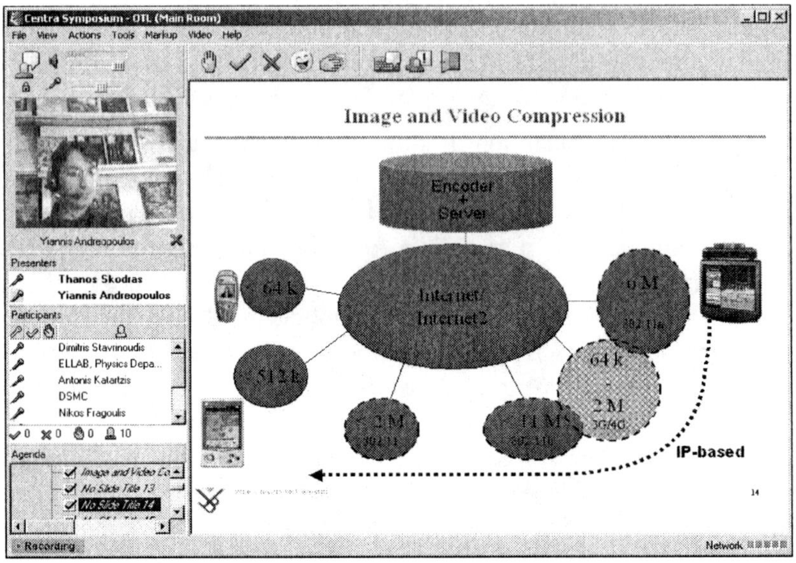

Virtual classrooms are currently used in distance education to emulate real classroom lectures. In virtual classrooms the members of an OLC log on to the system and attend a lecture, while interacting with the tutor and with each other. Virtual classrooms allow community members to interact with the object used (i.e., to write on the slides, to share their computer desktop or view, etc.) and therefore constitute a highly collaborative tool. Virtual classroom courses may be recorded and stored for later review, therefore their use is not only synchronous but could also be asynchronous. An example from a virtual classroom lecture in the Hellenic Open University is depicted in Figure 5, where a tutor is giving a lecture to 10 OLC members.

Evaluation Methods for Online Learning Communities

This section presents a set of general-purpose evaluation methods suitable for evaluating systems of OLCs and provides an overall classification. Discussion begins with a categorization of these methods according to the models they are based on and the way they can be applied. Typical examples are given for each case and a statistical method for the analysis of the results of these evaluation methods is described.

Copyright © 2007, Idea Group Inc. Copying or distributing in print or electronic forms without written permission of Idea Group Inc. is prohibited.

As in the beginning of the previous section, it must also be noted that most of the presented methods were not specifically developed for evaluating OLCs. In fact, they can be applied to any software product (for example, they can be used in surveys measuring user opinion of software quality in general). However, when these methods are applied in the case of software applications supporting OLCs, they allow us to reach specific conclusions regarding their evaluation.

Classification of Evaluation Methods

The evaluation methods for OLCs, just like evaluation methods in general, can be firstly divided into *analytic* and *empiric* ones (Nielsen, 1993), as presented in Figure 6. The analytic methods are theoretical models, rules, or standards that simulate the behavior of the user. They are mainly used during the requirements analysis phase and usually even before the development of the prototypes of a product. As a result, these methods do not require the participation of the user. On the contrary, the empiric methods depend on the implementation, the valuation and the rating of a software prototype or product. In this rating it is necessary to have the participation of a representative sample of the end users and/or a number of experienced valuators of the quality of a software product. The empiric methods can be divided into *experimental* and *inquiry* ones.

The experimental methods require the participation of the end users in a laboratory environment. The most widely known experimental methods comprise:

- **Performance measurement:** Performance measurement is a classical method of software evaluation that provides quantitative performance measurements

Figure 6. Classification of evaluation methods

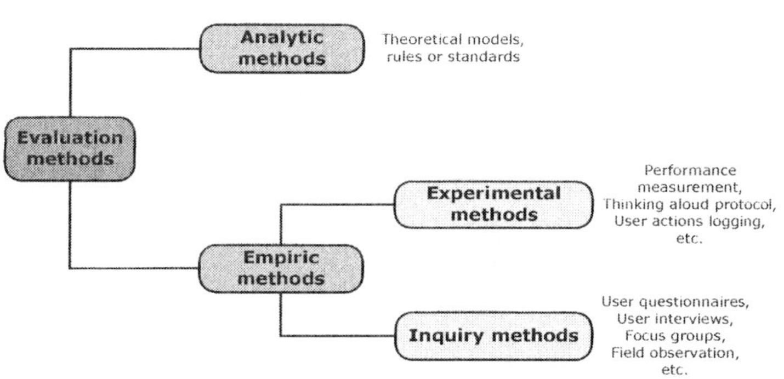

Copyright © 2007, Idea Group Inc. Copying or distributing in print or electronic forms without written permission of Idea Group Inc. is prohibited.

of a software product when users execute predefined actions or even complete operations. The users are left to perform these actions having only a narrow guidance at the beginning, so that the interaction between them and the person responsible for the survey will be restricted to a minimum.

- **Thinking aloud protocol:** The thinking aloud protocol method focuses on the measurement of the effectiveness of a system and the satisfaction of the user. According to this method, a small number of users, usually 3 to 4, interact with the system, while they state aloud their thoughts, opinions, emotions, and sentiments about the system. All the previously-mentioned are recorded, in order to be analyzed in combination with user actions, which are also recorded.
- **User actions logging:** There are many techniques for recording the actions executed by users while they interact with a software product. The most common comprise notes taken by the researcher, voice and/or video recording of users, computer logging and user logging. The researcher may use one or more of the earlier-mentioned techniques simultaneously.

The inquiry methods concern the examination of the quality characteristics of a software product by measuring users' opinion. According to these methods, the survey is generally conducted at the physical working place of the users, who evaluate either a forward prototype of a product or its final version. Inquiry methods require a large number of users and among the most popular are the following:

- **User questionnaires:** In this method, users are asked to express their opinions about the quality of a software product by completing a structured questionnaire, which consists of questions usually in a multiple-choice format. These questionnaires are sent to users, who answer them unaffectedly, i.e., without any possible influence (bias) by the person who conducts the survey. Each question addresses a specific quality characteristic, such as the quality characteristics of ISO9126 (ISO/IEC 9126, 2001) and has its own weight to the whole questionnaire evaluation. These weights are either equal for all characteristics or may vary in order to allow emphasis on one or more specific characteristics. In the former case, the questionnaire designer aims at the assessment of the quality of an OLC as equally affected by all quality characteristics. In the latter case, emphasis is placed on some specific OLC quality characteristics.
- **User interviews:** This is a structured method of evaluating a software product where the researcher is in direct contact with the user. The questions of the interview follow a hierarchical structure, through which the general opinion of the product is captured first, followed by more specific aspects of the quality characteristics considered.

Copyright © 2007, Idea Group Inc. Copying or distributing in print or electronic forms without written permission of Idea Group Inc. is prohibited.

- **Focus groups:** This method is a variation of user interviews, where a group of 5 to 10 users is formed under the supervision of a coordinator, who is responsible for the preparation of the topics of conversation in the focus group. At the end of this conversation, the coordinator will gather conclusions on the quality of the software product.
- **Field Observation:** With this method, the researcher observes the users at their workplace, while they are using and interacting with the software product in real-life conditions.

Examples of Evaluation Methods

The most commonly used methods for the evaluation of OLCs are user questionnaires and user interviews. Both methods are based on a questionnaire about the quality characteristics of an OLC system. In the first method the questionnaire is filled in directly by the user, without any further contact with the researcher. On the contrary, in the second one the researcher fills in the questionnaire while interviewing the user. In both cases, the responses of the user during the survey must be judged against the following criteria (Javeau, 1992):

- **The Capability of the User:** Does the user know the real subject of the questions? Is it a knowledge understandable to the user or not, deep or surface, present or past?
- **The Understandability of the User:** Does the user understand the content of all the questions of the questionnaire? Does the user meet any problems with the glossary or the terms used in it? Is there any external condition or personal situation of the user that disallows him/her to participate in the survey appropriately?
- **The Honesty of the User:** Does the user respond while participating in the survey according to his/her conscience or does he/she lie either knowingly or even unknowingly?
- **The Reliability of the User:** Does the user express himself/herself with the appropriate words or expressions? Does the user's memory fail him/her?

Furthermore, the various cultural traits that are mainly related to the individual behavior and the customs of the user may also be included in the criteria mentioned earlier.

Another common method for the evaluation of OLCs is the direct observation of users while they participate in an OLC and interact with OLC members. The researcher observes the users either at their workplace or in a usability laboratory.

Copyright © 2007, Idea Group Inc. Copying or distributing in print or electronic forms without written permission of Idea Group Inc. is prohibited.

Figure 7. Usability laboratory layout

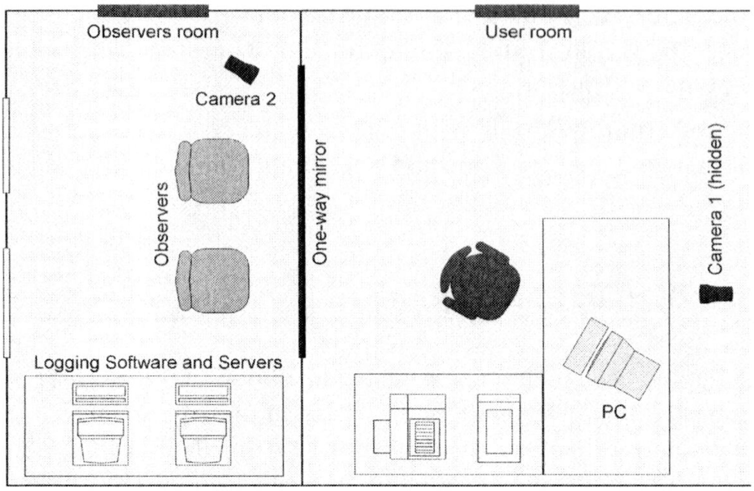

Figure 7 presents a typical example of such a laboratory, where the researchers are able to see the user working through a one-way mirror, whereas the user cannot see the researchers. Moreover, by the means of cameras, logging software and servers, all user actions can be recorded for later reproduction and analysis.

Figure 8. A software logging tool

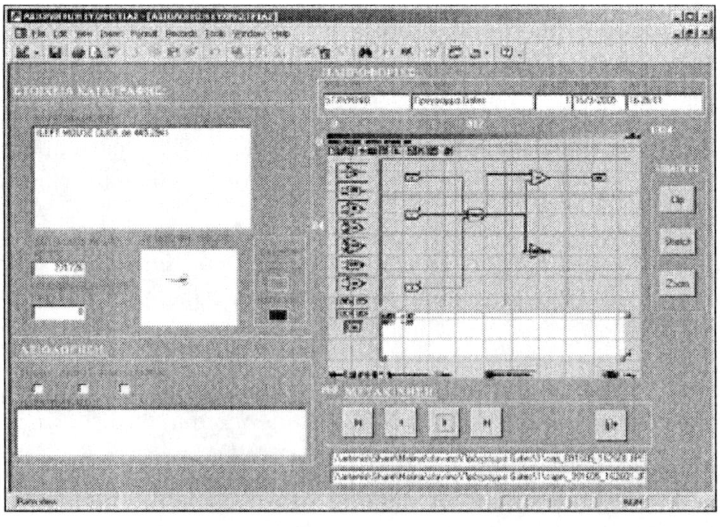

Copyright © 2007, Idea Group Inc. Copying or distributing in print or electronic forms without written permission of Idea Group Inc. is prohibited.

As far as user action logging is concerned, the researcher may also use appropriate software tools to record the actions of users while they interact with an OLC system. By means of these tools, the actions of every user (such as mouse movements and clicks, keyboard keystrokes, display on the user's screen, etc.) are stored into a database and are available for retrieval. Figure 8 presents an example of a software logging tool.

Statistical Analysis Method

In order to statistically analyze the data derived from the evaluation methods, this section describes an appropriate statistical method (Stavrinoudis, Xenos, Peppas, & Christodoulakis, 2005). This analysis focuses mainly on questionnaire-based surveys. However, it can be easily generalized so that it can be applied to any of the aforementioned methods of evaluating OLCs. First of all it is assumed that all the questions of the questionnaire have a multiple-choice format and users select predefined responses. Users are given specific clarifications that all available answers are of equal gravity, so responses are considered on an interval scale instead of an ordinal scale. Determining the opinion of a user regarding an OLC requires retrieving his/her responses to the survey already conducted. In the case of a structured questionnaire, the questions are clustered into groups, according to the quality characteristic they address.

Formula C_jO_i measures the opinion of a single user "i" about the quality of the OLC concerning a quality characteristic "j". In equation (E.1), "m" is the number of questions in the questionnaire referring to this characteristic, "Q_k" is the weight allocated to question "k", and "V_k" is the value of the response the user selected.

$$C_jO_i = \frac{\sum_{k=1}^{m}(Q_k \cdot V_k)}{\sum_{k=1}^{m} Q_k} \qquad \text{(E.1)}$$

Formula O_i measures the opinion of a single user "i" about the quality of the OLC concerning all quality characteristics referenced by the questionnaire. In equation (E.2), "n" is the number of the different quality characteristics, "C_j" is the weight associated with quality characteristic "j" (by the questionnaire designer), and "C_jO_i" is the opinion of the user for this quality characteristic.

Copyright © 2007, Idea Group Inc. Copying or distributing in print or electronic forms without written permission of Idea Group Inc. is prohibited.

$$O_i = \frac{\sum_{j=1}^{n} \left(C_j \cdot C_j O_i \right)}{\sum_{j=1}^{m} C_j} \qquad \text{(E.2)}$$

Finally, in order to measure the average user opinion regarding the quality of an OLC, either the QWCO (qualifications weighed customer opinion) technique, which is measured using the formula in equation (E.3), or the $QWCO_{DS}$ (qualifications weighed customer opinion with double safeguards) technique, which is measured using the formula in equation (E.4), can be deployed.

$$QWCO = \frac{\sum_{i=1}^{x} \left(O_i \cdot E_i \right)}{\sum_{i=1}^{x} E_i} \qquad \text{(E.3)}$$

$$QWCO_{DS} = \frac{\sum_{i=1}^{x} \left(O_i \cdot E_i \cdot \frac{S_i}{S_T} \cdot P_i \right)}{\sum_{i=1}^{x} \left(E_i \cdot \frac{S_i}{S_T} \cdot P_i \right)} \qquad \text{(E.4)}$$

The aim of these techniques is to weigh user opinions according to their qualifications. In order to achieve this, "O_i" measures the normalized score of the user's "i" opinion, as shown in equation (E.2), "E_i" measures the qualifications of user "i", while "x" is the number of users who participated in the survey. In order to detect errors, we use a number of *safeguards* embedded in the questionnaires. A safeguard is defined as a question placed inside the questionnaire in order to measure the correctness of responses.

In equation (E.4), "S_i" is the number of safeguards user "i" has replied to correctly, "S_T" is the total number of safeguards, and "P_i" is a Boolean variable which is set to zero in the case that one or more errors were detected by the safeguard when assessing the qualifications of user "i".

Copyright © 2007, Idea Group Inc. Copying or distributing in print or electronic forms without written permission of Idea Group Inc. is prohibited.

Conclusion

This chapter defined and described the notion of online communities in general and OLCs more specifically, and presented some of the most popular platforms and tools for building and maintaining such communities. It provided a twofold classification (learner and technology based) of tools and methods that support OLCs, and suggested a number of evaluation methods for OLC systems, along with a method for the statistical analysis of the derived data.

As regards the foreseen future trends in the field, OLCs may greatly benefit from incorporating personalization. More specifically, Rigou and Sirmakessis (2005) examine the integration of personalized functionalities in the framework of OLCs and study the advantages derived from generating dynamic adaptations on the layout, the content, as well as the learning scenarios delivered to each community member based on personal data, needs, and preferences. The proposed personalization functions are based on: (a) the user role in the community, (b) the level of user activity, (c) the discovery of association rules in the personal progress files of community members, and (d) the predefined content correlations among learning topics. Moreover, the introduction of the Semantic Web combined with the peer-to-peer technology give OLCs new potential for expanding to much wider scales, allowing for personalized access to distributed learning repositories and platform-independent learner profiles (Dolog, Henze, Nejdl, & Sintek, 2004; Dolog & Schaefer, 2005).

Currently prevailing open issues that are expected to become even more important in the near future come from the user-centered design and comprise assuring privacy, security, and universal access to all community members. In the case of more sophisticated community platforms that offer personalized features to community members, designers should also consider issues regarding speed of interaction (keep system response times at a minimum), accuracy of produced adaptations (avoid confusing users with recommendations that do not meet personal interests, preferences of needs), as well as locus of control (avoid loss of user control, as well as user intrusion by generating automatic adaptations that disrupt the learning process) (Rigou, 2004).

References

Crossman, D. M. (1997). The evolution of the World Wide Web as an emerging instructional technology tool. In B. H. Khan (Ed.), *Web-based instruction.* Englewood Cliffs, NJ: Educational Technology Publications.

Dolog, P., & Schaefer, M. (2005). A framework for browsing, manipulating and maintaining interoperable learner profiles. *Proceedings of the 10th Interna-*

Copyright © 2007, Idea Group Inc. Copying or distributing in print or electronic forms without written permission of Idea Group Inc. is prohibited.

tional Conference on User Modeling, Edinburgh, Scotland. Berlin: Springer-Verlag.

Dolog, P., Henze, N., Nejdl, W., & Sintek, M. (2004). Personalization in distributed e-learning environments. *Proceedings of the 13th International World Wide Web Conference.* New York: ACM Press.

Eisenstadt, M., Komzak, J., & Dzbor, M. (2003, May 19-21). Instant messaging + maps = powerful collaboration tools for distance learning. *Proceedings of TelEduc03,* Havana, Cuba.

Glover, I., Hardaker, G., & Xu, Z. (2004). Collaborative Annotation System Environment (Case) for online learning. *Campus-Wide Information Systems, 21*(2), 72-80.

Hiltz, S. R. (1998). Collective learning in asynchronous learning networks: Building learning communities. *Proceedings of WEB98,* Orlando, FL.

ISO/IEC 9126. (2001). *Software product evaluation—Quality characteristics and guidelines for the user.* Geneva: International Organization for Standardization.

Javeau C. (1992). *L'enquête par questionnaire, manuel à l'usage du praticien.* Brussels: University of Brussels.

Kapor, M. (1996). A software design manifesto. In T. Winograd (Ed.), *Bringing design to software.* Reading, MA: Addison-Wesley.

McCormack, C., & Jones, D. (1998). *Building a Web-based education system.* New York: John Wiley & Sons.

Nielsen, J. (1993). *Usability engineering.* San Diego: Academic Press.

Oliver, R., Omari, A., & Herrington J. (1998). Investigating implementation strategies for WWW-based learning environments. *International Journal of Instructional Media, 25*(2), 121-128.

Preece, J. (2000). *Online communities: Designing usability, supporting sociability.* New York: John Wiley & Sons.

Preece, J., Maloney-Krichmar, D., & Abras, C. (2003). History of emergence of online communities. In B. Wellman (Ed.), *Encyclopedia of community.* Sage/Berkshire.

Reinmann-Rothmeier, G., Mandl, H., & Prenzel, M. (2000). *Computer-supported learning environments. Planning, formation and assessment.* Munich: Wiley-VCH.

Rheingold, H. (1994). A slice of life in my virtual community. In L. M. Harasin (Ed.), *Global networks: Computers and international communication* (pp. 57-80). Cambridge, MA: MIT Press.

Copyright © 2007, Idea Group Inc. Copying or distributing in print or electronic forms without written permission of Idea Group Inc. is prohibited.

Rigou, M. (2004). On the development of adaptive Web-based learning communities. In V. Uskov (Ed.), *Proceedings of the IASTED International Conference on Web-Based Education* (WBE 2004) (pp. 625-630). Innsbruck, Austria: IASTED/ACTA Press.

Rigou, M., & Sirmakessis, S. (2005). Bringing personalization to online learning communities. *World Scientific and Engineering Academy and Society Transactions on Information Science and Applications, 12*(2), 2160-2167.

Rovai, A. P. (2002). Sense of community, perceived cognitive learning and persistence in asynchronous learning networks. *Internet and Higher Education, 5*(4), 319-332.

Salmon, G. (2000). *E-moderating: The key to teaching and learning online.* London: Kogan-Page.

Schmidt, M. P. (2000). *Using knowledge in a business effectively with virtual knowledge markets.* Munich: Addison-Wesley.

Stavrinoudis, D., Xenos, M., Peppas, P., & Christodoulakis, D. (2005). Early estimation of users' perception of software quality. *Software Quality Journal, 13,* 155-175.

Stenerson, J. F. (1998). Systems analysis and design for a successful distance education program implementation. *Online Journal of Distance Learning Administration, 1*(2).

Vygotsky, L. (1986). *Thought and language.* Cambridge, MA: MIT Press.

Whittaker, S., Isaacs, E., & O'Day, V. (1997). Widening the Net:Workshop. Report on the theory and practice of physical and network communities. *SIGCHI Bulletin, 29*(3).

Whittington, C. D. (1996). Mole: Computer-supported collaborative learning. *Computers & Education, 26*(1-3), 153-161.

Xenos, M., Avouris, N., Komis, V., Stavrinoudis, D., & Margaritis, M. (2004, August). Synchronous collaboration in distance education: A case study in a computer science course. *Proceedings of the 4th IEEE International Conference on Advance Learning Technologies*, Joensuu, Finland (pp. 500-504).

Copyright © 2007, Idea Group Inc. Copying or distributing in print or electronic forms without written permission of Idea Group Inc. is prohibited.

Chapter XI

Evaluation of Attitudes Towards Thinking and Learning in a CALL Web Site Through CMC Participation

Andrew Laghos, City University, London, UK

Panayiotis Zaphiris, City University, London, UK

Abstract

Computer-mediated-communication (CMC) is fast becoming a big part of our daily lives. More and more people are increasingly using the computer to communicate and interact with each other. The Internet and its advantages of connectivity enable CMC to be used from a plethora of applications. The most common uses of CMC include e-mail communication, discussion forums, as well as real-time chat rooms and audio/videoconferencing. By communicating through computers and over the Internet, online communities emerge. Discussion boards and other CMC applications offer a huge amount of information, and the analysis of this data assists in understanding these online communities and the social networks that form around them. There have been various frameworks by different researchers aimed at ana-

Copyright © 2007, Idea Group Inc. Copying or distributing in print or electronic forms without written permission of Idea Group Inc. is prohibited.

lyzing CMC. This chapter's main objective is to provide an overview of the models and frameworks available that are being used for analyzing CMC in e-learning environments. The significance of the proposed presentation is that it aims to provide the reader with up-to-date information regarding these methods. Advantages and disadvantages of each of the CMC analysis methods are presented, and suggestions for future research directions are made. Finally, these suggestions are applied to a characteristic scenario in e-learning.

Introduction

The focus of this study is to introduce the reader to the concept of computer-mediated communication (CMC) and online communities. Furthermore, we discuss the various types of CMC analysis that can take place. The purpose of each framework is described along with its strengths and weaknesses. The chapter begins with a literature review of CMC and online communities, and continues with the evaluation of the existing frameworks where we draw conclusions based on the advent of new technologies and platforms that are available, as to whether or not these frameworks are up-to-date in analyzing CMC as it exists today. Furthermore, we used a selection of the methods on a case study. More specifically the Attitudes Towards Thinking and Learning Survey (ATTLS) was used in conjunction with a technique called Social Network Analysis (SNA) to analyze the students' CMC in an e-learning courses. The chapter describes the methodology of the study, the results are presented, and the outcomes discussed, and ends with recommendations for future research.

Computer-Mediated Communication

It is by now no secret how vital the Internet was, is, and will continue to be in our lives. One of the most important characteristics of this medium is the opportunities it offers for human-human communication through computers and networks. As Metcalfe (1992) points out, communication is the Internet's most important asset and e-mail is the most influential aspect. E-mail is just one of the many modes of communication that can occur through the use of computers. Jones (1995) points out that through communication services like the Internet, Usenet and bulletin board communication has for many people supplanted the postal service, telephone, and even fax machine. All these applications where the computer is used to mediate communication are called computer-mediated communication or CMC.

Copyright © 2007, Idea Group Inc. Copying or distributing in print or electronic forms without written permission of Idea Group Inc. is prohibited.

"Computer-mediated communication (CMC) is the process by which people create, exchange, and perceive information using networked telecommunications systems (or non-networked computers) that facilitate encoding, transmitting, and decoding messages. Studies of CMC can view this process from a variety of interdisciplinary theoretical perspectives by focusing on some combination of people, technology, processes, or effects. Some of these perspectives include the social, cognitive/psychological, linguistic, cultural, technical, or political aspects; and/or draw on fields such as human communication, rhetoric and composition, media studies, human-computer interaction, journalism, telecommunications, computer science, technical communication or information studies." (December, 1997, p. 1)

Examples of CMC include asynchronous communication like e-mail and bulletin boards; synchronous communication includes chatting, and information manipulation, retrieval, and storage through computers and electronic databases (Ferris, 1997). Table 1 shows the main types of CMC, their mode (synchronous or asynchronous), and the type of media they support (text, graphics, audio, video).

CMC has its benefits as well as it limitations. For instance, a benefit of CMC is that the discussions are potentially richer than in face-to-face classrooms, but on the other hand, users with poor writing skills may be at a disadvantage when using text-based CMC (SCOTCIT, 2003).

Table 1. CMC systems, their mode, and the types of media that they support

Type of CMC	Communication Mode	Supports			
		Text	Graphics	Audio	Video
Audio Conferencing	Synchronous	Some applications	No	Yes	No
Video Conferencing	Synchronous	Yes	Yes	Yes	Yes
IRC	Synchronous	Yes	As attachments	As attachments	As attachments
MUD	Synchronous	Yes	No	No	No
WWW	Synchronous & Asynchronous	Yes	Yes	Yes	Yes
E-Mail	Asynchronous	Yes	As attachments	As attachments	As attachments
Newsgroups/BBS	Asynchronous	Yes	No	No	No
Discussion Boards	Asynchronous	Yes	As attachments	As attachments	As attachments
Voicemail	Asynchronous	Some applications	No	Yes	No

Copyright © 2007, Idea Group Inc. Copying or distributing in print or electronic forms without written permission of Idea Group Inc. is prohibited.

Advantages of CMC include (SCOTCIT, 2003):

- Time and place independence.
- No need to travel to the place of learning.
- Time lapse between messages allows for reflection.
- Speakers of other languages have added time to read and compose answers.
- Questions can be asked without waiting for a "turn".
- Allows all students to have a voice without the need to fight for "airtime", as in a face-to-face situation.
- Lack of visual cues provides participants with a more equal footing.
- Many–to-many interaction may enhance peer learning.
- Answers to questions can be seen by all□and argued.
- Discussion is potentially richer than in a face-to-face classroom.
- Messages are archived centrally, providing a database of interactions which can be revisited.
- The process of learning becomes more visible to learners and tutors.

Disadvantages of CMC include (SCOTCIT, 2003):

- Communication takes place via written messages, so learners with poor writing skills may be at a disadvantage.
- Paralinguistic cues (facial expression, intonation, gesture, body orientation) as to a speakers' intention are not available, except through combinations of keystrokes (emoticons) or the use of typeface emphasis (italics, bold, capital letters).
- Time gaps within exchanges may affect the pace and rhythm of communications leading to a possible loss in textual coherence.
- The medium is socially opaque; participants may not know who or how many people they may be addressing.
- The normal repair strategies of face-to-face communication are not available, and misunderstandings may be harder to overcome.
- Context and reference of messages may be unclear and misunderstandings may occur.

Copyright © 2007, Idea Group Inc. Copying or distributing in print or electronic forms without written permission of Idea Group Inc. is prohibited.

Online Communities

Through the use of CMC applications, online communities emerge. As Korzeny pointed out even as early as 1978, the new social communities that are built from CMC are formed around interests and not physical proximity (Korzeny, 1978). Another point to note is that CMC and the Internet give people around the world the opportunity to communicate with others who share their interests, as unpopular as these interests may be, which does not happen in the *real* world where the smaller a particular scene is, the less likely it will exist. This is due mainly to the Internet's connectivity and plethora of information available and posted by anyone anywhere in the world.

The term online community is multidisciplinary in its nature, means different things to different people, and is slippery to define (Preece, 2000). The relevance of certain attributes in the descriptions of online communities, like the need to respect the feelings and property of others, is debated (Preece, 2000). Online communities are also referred to as cyber societies, cyber communities, Web groups, virtual communities, Web communities, virtual social networks, and e-communities among several others.

For purposes of a general understanding of what virtual communities are, we present Rheingold's definition. "Virtual communities are social aggregations that emerge from the Net when enough people carry on those public discussions long enough, with sufficient human feeling, to form webs of personal relationships in cyberspace" (Rheingold, 1993, p. 5).

There are many reasons that bring people together in online groups. These include hobbies, ethnicity, education, beliefs, and just about any other topic or area of interest. Wallace (1999) points out that meeting in online communities eliminates prejudging based on someone's appearance, and thus people with similar attitudes and ideas are attracted to each other. People are using the Internet to make friends, colleagues, lovers, as well as enemies (Suler, 2004).

Preece, Rogers, and Sharp (2002) state that an online community consists of people, a shared purpose, policies, and computer systems while identifying the following member roles: moderators and mediators: who guide discussions/serve as arbiters; professional commentators: who give opinions/guide discussions; provocateurs: who provoke; general participants: who contribute to discussions; and lurkers: who silently observe.

Copyright © 2007, Idea Group Inc. Copying or distributing in print or electronic forms without written permission of Idea Group Inc. is prohibited.

CMC Analysis Frameworks

As mentioned earlier, the Internet plays a vital role in socially connecting people worldwide. The virtual communities that emerge have complex structures, social dynamics, and patterns of interaction that must be better understood. Through the use of CMC, we are provided with a richness of information and pools of valuable data ready to be analyzed.

There are various aspects and attributes of CMC that can be studied. Three important and widely used types of CMC analysis are content analysis, human-human interaction analysis, and human-computer interaction analysis.

Content Analysis

Content analysis is an approach to understanding the processes that participants engage in as they post messages (McLoughlin, 1996). There have been several frameworks created for studying the content of messages exchanged in CMC. Examples include work from Archer, Garrison, Anderson, and Rourke (2001), and McCreary's (1990) behavioral model which identifies different roles and uses these roles as the units of analysis. Furthermore, in Gunawardena, Lowe, and Anderson's (1997) model for examining the social construction of knowledge in computer conferencing, five phases of interaction analysis are identified: (1) sharing/comparing of information; (2) the discovery and exploration of dissonance or inconsistency among ideas, concepts, or statements; (3) negotiation of meaning/co-construction of knowledge; (4) testing and modification of proposed synthesis or co-construction; and (5) agreement statement(s)/applications of newly constructed meaning. Henri (1992) has also developed a content analysis model for cognitive skills used to analyze the process of learning within the student's messages. Mason's work (1991) provides descriptive methodologies using both quantitative and qualitative analysis.

In the case of e-learning for example, a useful framework is the Transcript Analysis Tool (TAT) (Fahy, 2003) as it:

- offers a student-centered approach,
- works with Gunawardena's model,
- was built on weaknesses of other models, and
- uses the sentence as the unit of analysis.

Copyright © 2007, Idea Group Inc. Copying or distributing in print or electronic forms without written permission of Idea Group Inc. is prohibited.

The TAT focuses on the content and interaction patterns at the component level of the transcript (Fahy, Crawford, & Ally 2001). Based on Fahy et al's experience with other transcript tools and reviews of previous studies, they chose to adapt Zhu's (1996) analytical model for the TAT. Zhu's (1996) assumption that electronic conferencing promoted student-centered learning led her to examine the forms of electronic interaction and discourse, the forms of student participation, and the direction of participant interaction in computer conferences. The TAT also contains echoes of Vygotskian theory (Vygotsky, 1978), primarily those dealing with collaborative sense making, social negotiation, and proximal development (Cook & Ralston, 2003). The TAT developers have come up with the following strategic decisions (Fahy et al., 2001):

- The sentence is the unit of analysis.
- The TAT is the method of analysis.
- Interaction is the criterion for judging conference success.
- Topical progression (types and patterns) is the focus of analysis.

Purpose and Advantages of the TAT

The TAT was designed to permit transcript content to be coded reliably and efficiently (Fahy et al., 2001), while the advantages of TAT are (Fahy, 2003; Cook & Ralston, 2003; Fahy et al., 2001; Fahy, 2002):

- It reveals interaction patterns useful in assessing different communication styles and online behavioral preferences among participants.
- It recognizes the complexity of e-conferences and measures the intensity of interaction.
- It enables the processes occurring within the conferences to be noted and recorded.
- It probes beyond superficial systems data, which mask the actual patterns of discussion.
- It relates usefully to other work in the area.
- It discriminates among the types of sentences within the transcript.
- It reflects the importance of both social and task-related content and outcomes in transcript analysis research.

Copyright © 2007, Idea Group Inc. Copying or distributing in print or electronic forms without written permission of Idea Group Inc. is prohibited.

Limitations of the TAT

After applying the TAT on several case studies, Fahy et al. (2001) found that a weakness of the TAT is the level of inter-rater agreement demonstrated to date. They conclude that further trials need to be conducted to determine how reliable the TAT is under conditions of greater practice (Fahy et al., 2001).

Units of Analysis

The unit of analysis of the TAT is the sentence. In the case of highly elaborated sentences, the units of analysis can be independent clauses which, punctuated differently, could be sentences (Fahy et al., 2001). Fahy et al. (2002) have concluded that the selection of message-level units of analysis might partially explain problematic results that numerous researchers have had with previous transcript analysis work. They also believe that the finer granularity of sentence-level analysis results in several advantages (Fahy et al., 2001; Ridley & Avery, 1979):

- reliability;
- ability to detect and describe the nature of the widely varying social interaction, and differences in networking pattern, in the interactive behavior of an online community, including measures of social network density and intensity; and
- confirmation of gender associations in epistolary/expository interaction patterns, and in the use of linguistic qualifiers and intensifiers.

TAT Categories

The TAT consists of the following categories (Fahy et al., 2001; Fahy, 2002; Fahy, 2003):

Category 1: Questioning

The questioning category is further broken down into two types of questions:

1A Vertical Questions

These are questions which assume a "correct" answer exists, and that they can be answered if the right authority to supply it can be found. An example of such a question is: "Does anybody know what time the library opens on Saturdays?"

Copyright © 2007, Idea Group Inc. Copying or distributing in print or electronic forms without written permission of Idea Group Inc. is prohibited.

1B Horizontal Questions

For these questions, there may not be only one right answer. They are questions that invite help and the provision of plausible or alternate answers, or information that would help shed light on the question. These questions invite negotiation, and an example is: "Do you really think mp3 files should become illegal, or you don't see any harm by them?"

Category 2: Statements

This category consists of two sub-categories:

2A Non-Referential Statements

These statements contain little self-revelation and usually do not invite response or dialogue, and their main intent is to impart facts or information. The speaker may take a didactic or pedantic stance, providing information or correction to an audience which he/she appears to assume is uninformed or in error, but curious and interested, or otherwise open to information or correction. Such statements may contain implicit values or beliefs, but usually these are inferred and are not as explicit as they are in reflections. For example: "We found that keeping content up-to-date, distribution and PC compatibility issues were causing a huge draw on Ed. Center time."

2B Referential Statements

Referential statements are direct answers to questions. They can include comments referring to specific preceding statements. An example of a referential statement is: "That's right, it's the 1997 issue that you want."

Category 3: Reflections

Reflections are significant personal revelations, where the speaker expresses personal or private thoughts, judgments, opinions, or information. He/she could also reveal personal values, beliefs, doubts, convictions, and ideas acknowledged. The reader is assumed to be interested and empathetic, and is expected to respond with acceptance and understanding. He/she receives both opinions as well as insights into the speaker and may reply with questions, support, and self-revelations in turn. An example of a reflection is: "My personal opinion is that it shouldn't have been a penalty kick."

Copyright © 2007, Idea Group Inc. Copying or distributing in print or electronic forms without written permission of Idea Group Inc. is prohibited.

Category 4: Scaffolding and Engaging

Scaffolding and engaging initiate, continue, or acknowledge interpersonal interaction. They personalize the discussion and can agree with, thank, or otherwise recognize someone for their helpfulness and comments. They also include comments without real substantive meaning, rhetorical questions, and emoticons. For example, "Thanks Dave, I've been trying to figure that out for ages ☺"

Category 5: References/Authorities

Category 5 comprises two types:

5A: Quotations, References to, Paraphrases of Other Sources: For example, "You said, 'I'll be out of the city that day'."

5B: Citations, Attributions of Quotations and Paraphrases: For instance, "Mathew, P. (2001). A beginners guide to mountain climbing."

Human-Human Interaction Analysis

Over the years there have been several models by different researchers for analyzing interaction. It is important to note that the type of interaction studied in this case is interpersonal interaction, more specifically the human-human interaction that takes place through the use of CMC. Examples of interaction analysis models include but are not limited to Bales' Interaction Process analysis (Bales, 1950; Bales & Strodbeck, 1951), the SIDE model (Spears & Lea, 1992), a four-part model of cyber-interactivity (McMillan, 2002), and Vrasidas's (2001) framework for studying human-human interaction in computer-mediated online environments and social network analysis (Krebs, 2004). We have found the technique called SNA to be more suitable for analyzing CMC in e-learning and explain it in more detail here.

Social Network Analysis

"Social Network Analysis (SNA) is the mapping and measuring of relationships and flows between people, groups, organizations, computers or other information/knowledge processing entities. Network analysis is concerned about dyadic attributes between pairs of actors (like kinship, roles, and actions), while social science

Copyright © 2007, Idea Group Inc. Copying or distributing in print or electronic forms without written permission of Idea Group Inc. is prohibited.

is concerned with monadic attributes of the actor (like age, sex, and income). The nodes in the network are the people and groups while the links show relationships or flows between the nodes. SNA provides both a visual and a mathematical analysis of human relationships." (Krebs, 2004, p. 1)

Preece (2000) adds that it provides a philosophy and set of techniques for understanding how people and groups relate to each other, and has been used extensively by sociologists (Wellman, 1982, 1992), communication researchers (Rice, 1994; Rice, Grant, Schmitz, & Torobin, 1990), and others. Analysts use SNA to determine if a network is tightly bounded, diversified, or constricted, to find its density and clustering and to study how the behavior of network members is affected by their positions and connections (Garton, Haythornhwaite, & Wellman, 1997; Wellman, 1997; Hanneman, 2001; Scott, 2000; Knoke & Kuklinski, 1982). Network researchers have developed a set of theoretical perspectives of network analysis. Some of these are (Bargotti, 2002):

- Focus on relationships between actors rather than the attributes of actors.
- Sense of interdependence: a molecular rather atomistic view.
- Structure affects substantive outcomes.
- Emergent effects.

Goals of SNA

The goals of SNA are (Dekker, 2002):

- to visualize relationships/communication between people and/or groups using diagrams;
- to study the factors which influence relationships and the correlations between them;
- to draw out implications of the relational data, including bottlenecks; and
- to make recommendations to improve communication and workflow in an organization.

Copyright © 2007, Idea Group Inc. Copying or distributing in print or electronic forms without written permission of Idea Group Inc. is prohibited.

SNA Approaches

Ego-Centered Analysis

This focuses on the individual as opposed to the whole network, and only a random sample of network population is normally involved (Zaphiris, Zacharia, & Rajasekaran, 2003). The data collected can be analyzed using standard computer packages for statistical analysis like SAS and SPSS (Garton et al., 1997).

Whole Network Analysis

The whole population of the network is surveyed, and this facilitates conceptualization of the complete network (Zaphiris et al., 2003). The data collected can be analyzed using microcomputer programs like UCINET and Krackplot (Garton et al., 1997). SNA data is represented using matrices, graphs, and sociograms.

Units of Analysis and Network Characteristics

The following are important units of analysis and concepts (Garton et al., 1997; Wellman, 1982; Hanneman, 2001; Zaphiris et al., 2003; Wellman, 1992):

- **Nodes:** The actors or subjects of study.
- **Relations:** The strands between actors. They are characterized by content, direction, and strength.
- **Ties:** Connect a pair of actors by one or more relations.
- **Multiplexity:** The more relations in a tie, the more multiplex the tie is.
- **Composition:** This is derived from the social attributes of both participants.
- **Range:** The size and heterogeneity of the social networks.
- **Centrality:** Measures who is central (powerful) or isolated in networks.
- **Roles:** Network roles are suggested by similarities in network members' behavior.
- **Density:** The number of actual ties in a network compared to the total amount of ties that the network can theoretically support.
- **Reachability:** In order to be reachable, connections that can be traced from the source to the required actor must exit.

Copyright © 2007, Idea Group Inc. Copying or distributing in print or electronic forms without written permission of Idea Group Inc. is prohibited.

- **Distance:** The number of actors that information has to pass through to connect the one actor with another in the network.
- **Cliques:** Sub-sets of actors in a network who are more closely tied to each other than to the other actors who are not part of the subset.

Limitations of SNA

Preece et al. (2002) and Beidernikl and Paier (2003) list the following as the limitations of SNA:

- More theory that speaks directly to developers of online communities is needed.
- The data collected may be personal or private.

As SNA is useful in collecting important actor relationship data, HCI techniques can be used to supplement some of its limitations.

Human-Computer Interaction Analysis

"Human-computer interaction is a discipline concerned with the design, evaluation and implementation of interactive computing systems for human use and with the study of major phenomena surrounding them." (ACM SIGCHI, 2002)

The focus is on the interaction between one or more humans and one or more computational machines. HCI is a multidisciplinary subject which draws on areas such as computer science, sociology, cognitive psychology, and others (Schneiderman, 1998). The concept of HCI consists of many tools and techniques that are used for information gathering and evaluation. The data collected in conjunction with data collected from other frameworks assists in assessing the online communities of courses and learning more about the users while collecting their feedback. Methods for CMC data analysis include: questionnaires, interviews, personas, and log analysis.

Copyright © 2007, Idea Group Inc. Copying or distributing in print or electronic forms without written permission of Idea Group Inc. is prohibited.

Interviews

An interview can be defined as a type of conversation that is initiated by the interviewer in order to obtain research-relevant information (Preece et al., 2002). The interview reports have to be carefully targeted and analyzed to make their impact. Interviews are usually done on a one-to-one basis where the interviewer collects information from the interviewee. Interviews can take place by telephone and face-to-face (Burge & Roberts, 1993). They can also take place via non-real-time methods like fax and e-mail, although in these cases they function like questionnaires. Interviews are useful for obtaining information that is difficult to elicit through approaches such as background knowledge and general principles. There are three types of interviews (Preece et al., 1994):

- **Structured:** Consist of pre-determined questions; asked in fixed order; like a questionnaire.
- **Semi-Structured:** Questions determined in advance; questions may be reordered, reworded, omitted, and elaborated.
- **Unstructured:** No pre-determined questions; interview has a general area of interest; conversation may develop freely.

The advantages of interviews are:

- What is talked about can directly address the informant's individual concerns.
- Mistakes and misunderstandings can be quickly identified and cleared up.
- More flexible than a questionnaire.
- Can cover low probability events.

The disadvantages of interviews are:

- Danger of analyst bias towards own knowledge and beliefs.
- Accuracy and honesty of responses.
- For validity, must be used with other data-collection techniques.

Copyright © 2007, Idea Group Inc. Copying or distributing in print or electronic forms without written permission of Idea Group Inc. is prohibited.

Personas

A persona is a precise description of the user of a system, and of what he/she wishes to accomplish. (Cooper, 1999). The specific purpose of a persona is to serve as a tool for software and product design, and although personas are not real people, they represent them throughout the design stage (Blomkvist, 2002). Personas are rich in details; include name, social history, and goals; and are synthesized from interviews with real people (Cooper, 1999). The technique takes user characteristics into account and creates a concrete profile of the typical user (Cooper, 1999).

The advantages of personas are:

- Can be used to create user scenarios.
- Can be anonymous, protecting user privacy.
- Represent the user stereotypes and characteristics.

The disadvantages of personas include:

- If not enough personas are used, users are forced to fall into a certain persona type which might now accurately represent them.
- Time-consuming.

Log Analysis

A log—also referred to as Weblog, server log, or log file—is usually in the form of a text file and is used to track the users' interactions with the computer system they are using. The types of interaction recorded include key presses, device movements, and other information about the users activities. The data is collected and analyzed using specialist software tools, and the range of data collected depends on the log settings. Logs are also time stamped and can be used to calculate how long a user spends on a particular task or how long a user lingers in a certain part of the Web site (Preece et al., 2002). Examples of what information can be collected include: when people visited a site, the areas they navigated, the length of the visit, frequency of visits, patterns of navigation, where they are connected from, and details of the computer they are using.

By carrying out log analysis, questions like student attendance can be answered more accurately. For instance, the log files will show which students were active in the CMC postings even if they were not active participants (few postings themselves), but just observing the conversations.

Copyright © 2007, Idea Group Inc. Copying or distributing in print or electronic forms without written permission of Idea Group Inc. is prohibited.

The advantages of logs, according to Preece et al. (2002) are:

- Help evaluators analyze users' behavior.
- Helps evaluators understand how users worked on specific tasks.
- It is unobtrusive.
- Large volumes of data can be logged automatically.

Disadvantages, also according to Preece et al. (2002), include:

- Powerful tools are needed to explore and analyze the data quantitatively and qualitatively.
- User privacy issues.

Questionnaires

A questionnaire is a self-reporting technique whereby subjects fill in the answers to questions themselves (Nielsen, 1993). Questionnaires were typically produced on printed paper, but due to recent technology and in particular the Internet, many researchers engage in the use of online questionnaires, thus saving time, money, and eliminating the problem of a subject's distance. There are three of questions that can be used with questionnaires. Open questions, where the participants are free to respond however they like; closed questions, which provide the participants with several choices for the answer; and scales, where the respondents must answer on a pre-determined scale. The purpose of a questionnaire is to elicit facts about the respondents, their behavior, and their beliefs/attitudes (Nielsen, 1993). The data is first recorded and then analyzed.

The main advantages of questionnaires are:

- Faster to carry out than observational techniques.
- Can cover low probability events.

Disadvantages are:

- Information is an idealized version of what should happen rather than what does happen.
- Responses may lack accuracy or honesty.

Copyright © 2007, Idea Group Inc. Copying or distributing in print or electronic forms without written permission of Idea Group Inc. is prohibited.

- Danger of researcher bias towards subset of knowledge he/she possesses.
- Must be used in conjunction with other techniques for validity.

ATTLS

The Attitudes towards Thinking and Learning Survey (ATTLS) is used to measure the quality of discourse within the course. It measures the extent to which a person is a "connected knower" (CK) or a "separate knower" (SK). People with higher CK scores tend to find learning more enjoyable and are often more cooperative, more congenial, and more willing to build on the ideas of others, while those with higher SK scores tend to take a more critical and argumentative stance to learning (Galotti, Clinchy, Ainsworth, Lavin, & Mansfield, 1999).

The two different types of procedural knowledge (separate and connected knowing) were identified by Belenky, Clinchy, Goldberger, and Tarule (1986). Separate knowing involves objective, analytical, and detached evaluation of an argument or piece of work, and takes on an adversarial tone which involves argument, debate, or critical thinking (Galotti et al., 1999). "Separate knowers attempt to 'rigorously exclude' their own feelings and beliefs when evaluating a proposal or idea" (Belenky et al., 1986, p. 111; Galotti et al., 1999). Separate knowers look for what is wrong with other people's ideas, whereas connected knowers look for why other people's ideas make sense or how they might be right, since they try to look at things from the other person's point of view and try to understand it rather than evaluate it (Clinchy 1989, Galotti et al., 1999). These two learning modes are not mutually exclusive and may "coexist within the same individual" (Clinchy, 1996, p. 207).

Initially the ATTLS consisted of 25 questions each for separate and connected knowing, and contained quotations from original papers on the "Ways of Knowing" framework (Belenky et al., 1986; Clinchy, 1990; Galotti et al., 1999). However it took a long time to administer, and thus a shorter version consisting of 20 self-report Likert-scaled items was developed. This shortened version is highly correlated with the longer version, nearly as reliable, and the authors propose that this shorter version be used in future research (Galotti et al., 1999). Based on their findings, the authors argue that difference in SK and CK scores "produce different behaviors during an actual episode of learning, and do result in different descriptions of, and reactions to, that session" (Galotti, Reimer, & Drebus, 2001, p. 435).

In the sections that follow we describe a case study where different techniques are applied to the analysis of an e-learning course.

Copyright © 2007, Idea Group Inc. Copying or distributing in print or electronic forms without written permission of Idea Group Inc. is prohibited.

Methodology

For our case study we used a synthesis of quantitative (SNA) and qualitative (ATTLS questionnaires) methods, and applied them to a computer-aided language learning (CALL) course. Data was collected directly from the discussion board of a student-centered e-learning course for learning Modern Greek called "Learn Greek Online" (LGO).

LGO was built through participatory design and distributed constructionism (Zaphiris & Zacharia, 2001). The course is hosted on Kypros-Net (2005), a non-profit organization for the promotion of the culture and language of Cyprus. It uses the Moodle (Dougiamas, 2001) open source course management system. LGO is not a required course. The students enroll on their own will, and their CMC participation is completely voluntary. Unlike other courses where the students are required to participate in the discussions allowing for experimental bias, LGO students contribute to the discussions because they want to and not because they have to. The students of the course include people with no knowledge of Greek language, bilingual members of the Greek Diaspora, as well as high-school teachers and higher education professors of non-Greek language teaching.

These students created an open online community whose collaboration has boosted the learning experience of the whole community. The Web-based discussion board has proven to be the most constructive tool for the students' learning experience and the main source of feedback for the maintainers of the project. The experiences shared on the discussion board included tricks and tips on how to record the audio files, installation of Greek fonts, learning methodologies, and questions about the Greek language itself that arise from the lessons. The experienced users had taken a lead role in the vast majority of the threads on the discussion board, answering most of the questions and encouraging the beginners to study the lessons further (Zaphiris & Zacharia, 2001). They have also become the communication interface between the maintainers of the project and the community's needs and requests.

In an ego-centered approach to SNA, we have carried out analysis on the first 50 actors (in this case the students of the course) of the discussion forum for Lesson 1 in the Greek 101 (Elementary) course of LGO and tabulated these interactions in the form of a network matrix.

To carry out the social network analysis, we used an SNA tool called "NetMiner for Windows" (Cyram, 2004) which enabled us to obtain centrality measures for our actors. The "in and out degree centrality" was measured by counting the number of interaction partners per each individual in the form of discussion threads (for example if an individual posts a message to three other actors, then his/her out-degree centrality is 3, whereas if an individual receives posts from five other actors then his/her in-degree is 5).

Copyright © 2007, Idea Group Inc. Copying or distributing in print or electronic forms without written permission of Idea Group Inc. is prohibited.

Due to the complexity of the interactions in the LGO discussion, we had to make several assumptions in our analysis:

- Posts that received 0 replies were excluded from the analysis. This was necessary in order to obtain meaningful visualizations of interaction.
- Open posts were assumed to be directed to everyone who replied.
- Replies were directed to all the existing actors of the specific discussion thread unless the reply or post was specifically directed to a particular actor.

In addition to the analysis of the discussion board interactions, we also collected subjective data through the form of a survey. More specifically, the students were asked to complete an ATTLS to measure the extent to which a person is a connected knower (CK) or a separate knower (SK).

Results

The out-degree results of the social network analysis are depicted in Figure 2 in the form of a sociogram. Each node represents one student (to protect the privacy and

Figure 1. Out-degree analysis sociogram

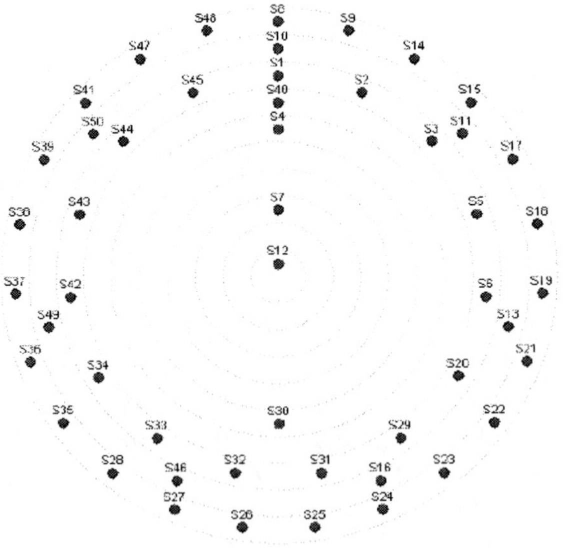

Copyright © 2007, Idea Group Inc. Copying or distributing in print or electronic forms without written permission of Idea Group Inc. is prohibited.

anonymity of our students, their names have been replaced by a student number). The position of a node in the sociogram is representative of the centrality of that actor (the more central the actor, the more active). As can be seen from Figure 1, students S12, S7, S4, and S30 (with out-degree scores ranging from 0.571 to 0.265) are at the centre of the sociogram, and possess the highest outdegree and in-degree scores. This is an indication that these students are also the most active members of this discussion board posting and receiving the largest number of postings. In contrast, participants in the outer circle (e.g., S8, S9, S14, etc.) are the least active with the smallest out-degree and in-degree scores (all with 0.02 out-degree scores).

In addition, a clique analysis was done (Figure 2) showing that 15 different cliques (the majority of which are overlapping) composed of at least three actors each have emerged in this discussion board. As part of this study, we look in more detail at the results from two of our actors. S12, who is the most central actor in our SNA analysis—that is, with the highest out-degree score—and S9, an actor with the smallest out-degree score. It is worth noting that both members joined the discussion board at around the same time. First, through a close look at the clique data (Table 2), we can see that S12 is a member of 10 out of the 15 cliques, whereas S9 is not a member of any—an indication of the high interactivity of S12 vs. the low interactivity of S9.

In an attempt to correlate the actors' position in the SNA sociogram with their stated attitudes towards teaching and learning, we looked more closely at the answers these two actors (S12, S9) provided to the ATTLS. Actor S12 answered all 20 questions of the ATTLS with a score of at least 3 (on a 1-5 Likert scale), whereas S9 had answers ranging from 1 to 5. The overall score of S12 is 86, whereas that of S9 is 60. A clear dichotomy of opinions occurred on five of the 20 questions of the ATTLS. S12 answered all five with a score of 5 (strongly agree), whereas S9 answered them with a score of 1 (strongly disagree): S12 strongly agrees that:

1. She/he is more likely to try to understand someone else's opinion than to try to evaluate it.
2. She/he often find herself/himself arguing with the authors of books read, trying to logically figure out why they're wrong.
3. She/he finds that s/he can strengthen her/his own position through arguing with someone who disagrees with them.
4. She/he feels that the best way achieve her/his own identity is to interact with a variety of other people.
5. She/he likes playing devil's advocate—arguing the opposite of what someone is saying.

Copyright © 2007, Idea Group Inc. Copying or distributing in print or electronic forms without written permission of Idea Group Inc. is prohibited.

Figure 2. Clique analysis sociogram

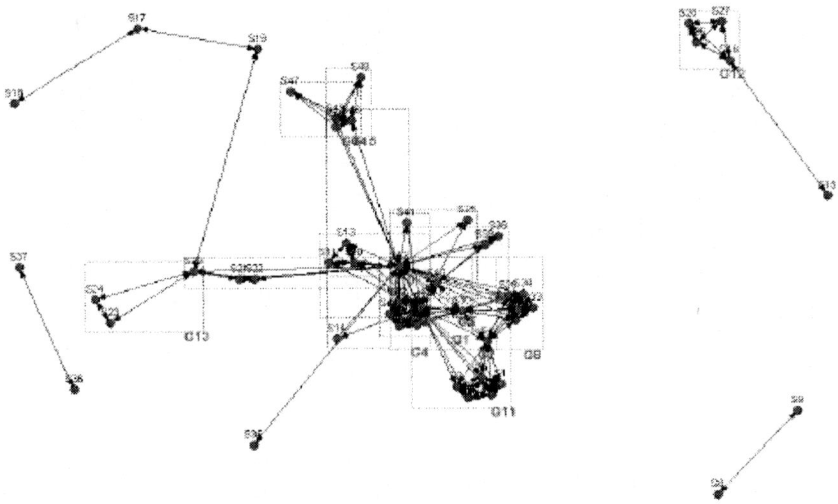

Table 2. Clique analysis of the LGO discussions

Cliques	Actors
K1	S12,S7,S30,S40,S42,S43,S44,S45
K2	S12,S7,S30,S4
K3	S12,S7,S10,S11,S13
K4	S12,S7,S14
K5	S12,S7,S25
K6	S12,S7,S41
K7	S12,S20,S21,S22
K8	S12,S29,S4,S30,S31,S32,S33,S34
K9	S12,S38,S39,S40
K10	S12,S46,S49,S50
K11	S2,S3,S4,S5,S6,S7,S1
K12	S16,S26,S27,S28
K13	S23,S20,S24
K14	S47,S46,S49,S50
K15	S48,S46,S49,S50

These are all indications that s/he is a "connected knower" (CK), whereas S9 is a "separate knower" (SK).

Copyright © 2007, Idea Group Inc. Copying or distributing in print or electronic forms without written permission of Idea Group Inc. is prohibited.

Conclusion

In this chapter we defined the concepts of online communities and computer-mediated communication. We discussed the different types of CMC analysis and evaluated the purpose of each of these frameworks. Following the literature review, we carried out a case study using the ATTLS and SNA.

It is apparent from our research that most existing frameworks make either a qualitative or quantitative analysis of CMC, but rarely do we see a mixture of these techniques or a comparison/correlation of their results. Also, some models can only be used on only synchronous or asynchronous communication, but not both. Our opinion is that it is important that a unified framework is developed, for the complete evaluation of all aspects of online communication. As new teaching methods and different learning activities emerge, new types of interaction and evaluation are necessary. The analysis of CMC should take all these updates into consideration and incorporate them into future CMC analysis models.

This chapter has demonstrated the application of social network analysis (SNA) in a computer-aided language learning course of Modern Greek. Furthermore, an Attitudes Towards Thinking and Learning Survey (ATTLS) was carried out. Both of the methods used had the same results. More specifically, the results of the SNA showed certain students to be more central in the discussions; these findings were matched by the results of the ATTLS, which identified the same individuals as the *connected knowers*. There are large amounts of data online, and it is becoming harder to monitor interaction. SNA was helpful in visualizing the network and in providing a mathematical analysis. It would be interesting to compare the SNA results with the ATTLS replies of more students, however at the time this was not possible since not everyone had answered the questionnaire. In the future we plan to extend this study with incorporations of more methods towards a unified framework.

Suggestions to Researchers

This study showed the use of SNA as a mechanism for better exploring the dynamics of online learning communities. Future research directions could include a more detailed comparison of the ATTLS questionnaire with SNA results, plus the comparison of the SNA results with other forms of standardized questionnaires (e.g., the Constructivist Online Learning Environment Survey—COLLES).

Copyright © 2007, Idea Group Inc. Copying or distributing in print or electronic forms without written permission of Idea Group Inc. is prohibited.

Suggestions to Practitioners

The approach provided in this chapter can be a useful methodology for developers and maintainers of online communities as it can provide insights about the dynamics of their community and will enable them to develop strategies for strengthening the centrality of students with low ATTLS scores, especially since ATTLS surveys could be administered prior to any online interaction of the actors.

References

ACM SIGCHI. (1992). *Curricula for human-computer interaction.* New York: Association for Computing Machinery.

Archer, W., Garrison, R. D., Anderson, T., & Rourke, L. (2001). A framework for analyzing critical thinking in computer conferences. *Proceedings of the European Conference on Computer-Supported Collaborative Learning,* Maastricht, The Netherlands.

Bales, R. F. (1950). A set of categories for the analysis of small group interaction. *American Sociological Review, 15,* 257-263.

Bales, R. F., & Strodbeck, F. L. (1951). Phases in group problem-solving. *Journal of Abnormal and Social Psychology, 46,* 485-495.

Beidernikl, G., & Paier, D. (2003, July). Network analysis as a tool for assessing employment policy. *Proceedings of the Evidence-Based Policies and Indicator Systems Conference 2003,* London.

Belenky, M. F., Clinchy, B. M., Goldberger, N. R., & Tarule, J. M. (1986/1997). *Women's ways of knowing: The development of self, voice, and mind* (2nd ed.). New York: Basic Books.

Blomkvist, S. (2002). *Persona—an overview.* Retrieved November 22, 2004, from http://www.it.uu.se/edu/course/homepage/hcinet/ht04/library/docs/Persona-overview.pdf

Borgatti, S. (2000). *What is Social Network Analysis.* Retrieved November 9, 2004, from http://www.analytictech.com/networks/whatis.htm

Burge, E. L., & Roberts, J. M. (1993). *Classrooms with a difference: A practical guide to the use of conferencing technologies.* Ontario: University of Toronto Press.

Clinchy, B. M. (1989). The development of thoughtfulness in college women: Integrating reason and care. *American Behavioral Scientist, 32,* 647-657.

Copyright © 2007, Idea Group Inc. Copying or distributing in print or electronic forms without written permission of Idea Group Inc. is prohibited.

Clinchy, B. M. (1996). Connected and separate knowing: Toward a marriage of two minds. In N. Goldberger, J. Tarule, B. Clinchy, & M. Belenky (Eds.), *Knowledge, difference, and power: Essays inspired by Women's ways of knowing.* New York: Basic Books.

Clinchy, B. M. (1990). Issues of gender in teaching and learning. *Journal on Excellence in College Teaching, 1,* 52-67.

Cook, D., & Ralston, J. (2003). Sharpening the focus: Methodological issues in analyzing online conferences. *Technology, Pedagogy and Education, 12*(3), 361-376.

Cooper, A. (1999). *The inmates are running the asylum.* Indianapolis: SAMS/Macmillan.

Cyram. (2004). *Netminer for Windows.* Retrieved from http://netminer.com

December, J. (1997). Notes on defining of computer-mediated communication. *Computer-Mediated Communication Magazine, 3*(1).

Dekker, A. H. (2002, January 28-February 1). A category-theoretic approach to Social Network Analysis. *Proceedings of Computing: The Australasian Theory Symposium* (CATS), Melbourne, Australia.

Dougiamas, M. (2001). *Moodle: Open-source software for producing Internet-based courses.* Retrieved from http://moodle.com

Fahy, P. J. (2003). Indicators of support in online interaction. *International Review of Research in Open and Distance Learning, 4*(1).

Fahy, P. J., Crawford, G., & Ally, M. (2001). Patterns of interaction in a computer conference transcript. *International Review of Research in Open and Distance Learning, 2*(1).

Ferris, P. (1997). What is CMC? An overview of scholarly definitions. *Computer-Mediated Communication Magazine, 4(1).*

Galotti, K. M., Clinchy, B. M., Ainsworth, K., Lavin, B., & Mansfield, A. F. (1999). A new way of assessing ways of knowing: The Attitudes Towards Thinking and Learning Survey (ATTLS). *Sex Roles, 40*(9/10), 745-766.

Galotti, K. M., Reimer, R. L., & Drebus, D. W. (2001). Ways of knowing as learning styles: Learning MAGIC with a partner. *Sex Roles, 44*(7/8), 419-436.

Garton, L., Haythorthwaite, C., & Wellman, B. (1997). Studying online social networks. In S. Jones (Ed.), *Doing Internet research.* Thousand Oaks, CA: Sage.

Gunawardena, C., Lowe, C., & Anderson, T. (1997). Analysis of a global online debate and the development of an interaction analysis model for examining social construction of knowledge in computer conferencing. *Journal of Educational Computing Research, 17*(4), 397-431.

Copyright © 2007, Idea Group Inc. Copying or distributing in print or electronic forms without written permission of Idea Group Inc. is prohibited.

Hanneman, R. A. (2001). *Introduction to social network methods*. Retrieved November 9, 2004, from http://faculty.ucr.edu/~hanneman/SOC157/TEXT/TextIndex.html

Henri, F. (1992). Computer conferencing and content analysis. In A.R. Kaye (Ed.), *Collaborative learning through computer conferencing: The Najaden papers* (pp. 117-136). Berlin: Springer-Verlag.

Jones, S. (1995). Computer-mediated communication and community: Introduction. *Computer-Mediated Communication Magazine, 2*(3), 38.

Knoke, D., & Kuklinski, J. H. (1982). *Network analysis*. Sage University Paper Series on Quantitative Applications in Social Sciences, Series No. 07-001. Beverly Hills/London: Sage.

Krebs, V. (2004). *An introduction to Social Network Analysis*. Retrieved November 9, 2004, from http://www.orgnet.com/sna.html

Korzenny, F. (1978). A theory of electronic propinquity: Mediated communication in organizations. *Communication Research, 5,* 3-23.

Kypros-Net. (2005). *The world of Cyprus*. Retrieved from http://kypros.org

Mason, R. (1991) Analyzing computer conferencing interactions. *Computers in Adult Education and Training, 2*(3), 161-173.

McCreary, E. (1990) Three behavioral models for computer-mediated communication. In L. Harasim (Ed.), *Online education: Perspectives on a new environment.* New York: Praeger.

McLoughlin, C. (1996, January 21-25). A learning conversation: Dynamics, collaboration and learning in computer mediated communication. In C. McBeath & R. Atkinson (Eds.), *Proceedings of the 3rd International Interactive Multimedia Symposium*, Perth, Western Australia (pp. 267-273).

McMillan, S. J. (2002). A four-part model of cyber-interactivity: Some cyber-places are more interactive than others. *New Media and Society, 4*(2), 271-291.

Metcalfe, B. (1992). Internet fogies to reminisce and argue at Interop Conference. *InfoWorld.*

Nielsen, J. (1993). *Usability engineering.* London: Academic Press.

Preece, J. (2000). *Online communities: Designing usability, supporting sociability.* Chichester, UK: John Wiley & Sons.

Preece, J., Rogers, Y., & Sharp, H. (2002). *Interaction design: Beyond human-computer interaction.* New York: John Wiley & Sons.

Preece, J., Rogers, Y., Sharp, H., Benyon, D., Holland, S., & Carey, T. (1994). *Human-computer interaction.* Wokingham, UK: Addison-Wesley.

Rheingold, H. (1993). *The virtual community: Homesteading on the electronic frontier.* Reading, MA: Addison-Wesley.

Copyright © 2007, Idea Group Inc. Copying or distributing in print or electronic forms without written permission of Idea Group Inc. is prohibited.

Rice, R. (1994). Network analysis and computer-mediated communication systems. In S. W. J. Galaskiewkz (Ed.), *Advances in Social Network Analysis.* Newbury Park, CA: Sage.

Rice, R. E., Grant, A. E., Schmitz, J., & Torobin, J. (1990). Individual and network influences on the adoption and perceived outcomes of electronic messaging. *Social Networks, 12,* 17-55.

Ridley, C., & Avery, A. (1979). Social network influence on the dyadic relationship. In R. Burgess, & T. Huston, (Eds.), *Social exchange in developing relationships* (pp. 223-246). New York: Academic Press.

Schneiderman, B. (1998). *Designing the user interface: Strategies for effective human-computer interaction.* Reading, MA: Addison-Wesley Longman.

SCOTCIT. (2003). *Enabling large-scale institutional implementation of communications and information technology (ELICIT). Using computer-mediated conferencing.* Retrieved November 2, 2004, from http://www.elicit.scotcit.ac.uk/modules/cmc1/welcome.htm

Scott, J. (2000). *Social Network Analysis: A handbook* (2nd ed.). London: Sage.

Spears, R., & Lea, M. (1992). Social influence and the influence of the social in computer-mediated communication. In M. Lea (Ed.), *Contexts of computer-mediated communication* (pp. 30-65). London: Harvester Wheatsheaf.

Suler, J. (2004). *The final showdown between in-person and cyberspace relationships.* Retrieved November 3, 2004, from http://www1.rider.edu/~suler/psycyber/showdown.html

Vrasidas, C. (2001). Studying human-human interaction in computer-mediated online environments (pp. 118-127). In Y. Manolopoulos & S. Evripidou (Eds.), *Proceedings of the 8th Panhellenic Conference on Informatics,* Nicosia, Cyprus.

Vygotsky, L. S. (1978). *Mind and society: The development of higher mental processes.* Cambridge, MA: Harvard University Press.

Wallace, P. (1999). *The psychology of the Internet.* Cambridge, MA: Cambridge University Press.

Wellman, B. (1982). Studying personal communities. In P. M. N Lin (Ed.), *Social structure and network analysis.* Beverly Hills: Sage.

Wellman, B. (1992). Which types of ties and networks give what kinds of social support? *Advances in Group Processes, 9,* 207-235.

Wellman, B. (1997). An electronic group is virtually a social network. In S. Kiesler (Ed.), *Culture of the Internet* (pp. 179-205). Hillside, NJ: Lawrence Erlbaum.

Zaphiris, P., & Zacharia, G. (2001). Design methodology of an online Greek language course. *Ext. Abstracts of CHI 2001.* ACM Press.

Copyright © 2007, Idea Group Inc. Copying or distributing in print or electronic forms without written permission of Idea Group Inc. is prohibited.

Zaphiris, P., Zacharia, G., & Rajasekaran, M. (2003). Distributed constructionism through participatory design. In C. Ghaoui (Ed.), *E-education applications: Human factors and innovative approaches.* London: Idea Group Reference.

Zhu, E. (1996). Meaning negotiation, knowledge construction, and mentoring in a distance learning course. *Proceedings of Selected Research and Development Presentations at the 1996 National Convention of the Association for Educational Communications and Technology,* Indianapolis, IN.

Copyright © 2007, Idea Group Inc. Copying or distributing in print or electronic forms without written permission of Idea Group Inc. is prohibited.

Chapter XII

Evaluation of an Online Community: Australia's National Quality Schooling Framework

Elizabeth Hartnell-Young, The University of Melbourne, Australia, & University of Nottingham, UK

Keryn McGuinness, Research Australia Development and Innovation Institute, Australia

Peter Cuttance, Research Australia Development and Innovation Institute, Australia

Abstract

This chapter considers the development and implementation of Australia's National Quality Schooling Framework (NQSF), created particularly for teachers and others involved in improving school education. This large-scale, highly structured, and outcome-focused community space, funded by the Australian government, was developed as a means of building and testing knowledge. Using Wenger's infrastructure for communities of practice, the chapter evaluates the NQSF in light of its capacity for engagement, imagination, and alignment. Although these three are often intertwined, we conclude that firstly, users value the space for engagement and that this needs to be supported by a national telecommunications infrastructure. Secondly, in terms

Copyright © 2007, Idea Group Inc. Copying or distributing in print or electronic forms without written permission of Idea Group Inc. is prohibited.

of imagination, a community of this scope and purpose benefits from management that shares the same purpose in order to develop the profession. Finally, alignment is achieved through visionary leadership and a rigorous process to maintain the quality of the resources introduced to and generated within the community.

Introduction

The National Quality Schooling Framework (www.nqsf.edu.au) is an online environment established by the Australian government to encourage knowledge building, particularly among school educators. The NQSF is managed by the Center for Applied Educational Research (CAER) at the University of Melbourne. In this chapter we describe the main features of the developing community and propose Wenger's (1998) model of community of practice as a framework for evaluating its capacity to build knowledge over the period from its inception in 2001 until 2005.

The use of *community* to describe certain online interactions raises expectations of a positive experience. Preece (2001) uses the term online community to mean any virtual social space where people come together to get and give information or support, to learn, or to find company. Rheingold (2000) calls these virtual communities: cultural aggregations that emerge when enough people bump into each other often enough in cyberspace. A virtual community is a group of people who may or may not meet one another face-to-face, and who exchange words and ideas through the mediation of computer bulletin boards and networks. These definitions do sound like the equivalent of the communities that develop in and around schools, where people bump into each other. Place has been important in such conceptions of community (Sergiovanni, 1999), among teachers and students in a school, parents in a local community, even students in a class group. However, like Wellman (2001), we see that this is changing, and that through online environments, those involved in schooling can constitute a new type of community, with both a focus on educational outcomes and a supportive role for individuals and families. We see this very purposeful community could be a community of practice.

Community of practice is a term grounded in a social constructivist approach to learning and frequently applied to the management of organizational knowledge. A community of practice is a group of people who share a concern, a set of problems, or a passion about a topic, and who deepen their knowledge and expertise in this area by interacting on an ongoing basis (Wenger, McDermott, & Snyder, 2002). The definition in itself is not new or startling, but, Wenger et al. argue, a focus on intentional and systematic knowledge management has become increasingly important in the knowledge economy, and communities of practice are seen to be a necessary structure for organizations.

Copyright © 2007, Idea Group Inc. Copying or distributing in print or electronic forms without written permission of Idea Group Inc. is prohibited.

We extend the scale of our consideration to the whole country. According to the definition earlier, a national community where the practice is improving school education could consist of teachers in schools and universities, academic researchers, funding agencies, local communities, education bureaucrats and ministers, and other specialists who share concerns, problems, or passions. This broad community would naturally be made up of smaller, more focused communities of practice on specific topics of interest. We posit that their purpose is to create knowledge by revealing, accessing, and sharing current practice and expert knowledge in order to build new solutions to both large-scale and local educational problems.

In his earlier work, Wenger (1998) established a detailed model for the community of practice and made a strong argument for its role in promoting learning. He argued that education is not limited to schooling, but is a mutual development process between communities and individuals, forming new identities. Designing education means creating an architecture that allows the formation of identities. Continuing the metaphor, Wenger suggested three infrastructures to achieve this: the first, places of *engagement* for people; the second, materials and experiences with which to build an image of the world and themselves *(imagination)*; and the third, ways of having an effect on the world and making their actions matter (*alignment*). We suggest that this model is useful in evaluating the NQSF: a national framework developed by educational experts which provides users with space in which they can operate in a range of ways.

Within each infrastructure, according to Wenger, there are specific areas to develop. Firstly, opportunities for engagement arise through mutual and shared activities, through challenges and responsibilities that call upon learners' knowledgeability and encourage them to explore new territories, and through continuity to develop shared practice and a long-term commitment. It appears that facilities of engagement can assist knowledge building, particularly by bringing people together, encouraging shared discourse, and recording information. Secondly, Wenger suggests, the three aspects of imagination are: *orientation*—locating self and learning about a wider world; *reflection*—looking at our situations with new eyes; and *exploration*—reinventing the self and in the process reinventing the world. He argues that imagination is the way a learning community can expand the definition of its enterprise. This is where knowledge building can be enhanced by time off for reflection and conversation, exploration and play. The third aspect of Wenger's learning architecture is alignment, which encompasses larger-scale understanding of power relations and how to have an effect on the world. Therefore, he suggests that any learning community must push its boundaries and interact with other communities of practice in a purposeful way; it must link participation inside with that outside the community (e.g., through multi-membership of its members in other communities); it must use the styles and discourses of the areas it wants to affect, and it must become involved in the organizational arrangements of its own institution. It is therefore deep and wide, able to know what it knows and use this in a range of arenas. For

Copyright © 2007, Idea Group Inc. Copying or distributing in print or electronic forms without written permission of Idea Group Inc. is prohibited.

those involved in school education, this demands that the knowledge thus created is available to make a difference in society. The community of practice model described here is intended to apply equally to co-located workers in an organization and professionals working in different organizations, and should therefore hold in situations of face-to-face and tele-communication.

Among those who have specifically considered online communities, Schlager, Fusco, and Schank (1999) argue that online communities of educators should exist within the context of daily practice and represent a variety of perspectives. A well-defined domain that underpins purpose (Wenger et al., 2002) and a commitment to meeting the needs of others are also criteria for judging success (Brook & Oliver, 2003). Kovaric and Bott (2000) suggest too that effective online communities should provide operational support through assistance with strategies, intellectual support through new ideas, and affective support, although the last is less likely to be provided online. Reporting on a specific community, Harasim (2002) notes the importance of the coordinator's role in creating and maintaining the social climate and professional relevance of the community. She also suggests indicators to measure success in two dimensions: contextual indicators such as user reports, active participation, and longevity; and substantive indicators including social discourse and intellectual progress.

Preece (2001) considers both social and technical aspects of interaction in evaluating the performance of an online community, labeling them sociability and usability. Sociability—human interaction supported by computers—is concerned with three key components: shared purpose, people and their roles, and policies (Preece, 2000). Usability, on the other hand, is concerned with how users interact with technology, and includes dialogue and social interaction support, information design, navigation, and access. Preece's quantitative determinants of sociability include the number of participants in a community, the number of messages per unit of time, members' satisfaction, the amount of reciprocity, the number of on-topic messages, and overall quality. For usability, she includes measures such as numbers of errors, productivity, and user satisfaction. We agree that evaluation of an educational community using online communication, such as the National Quality Schooling Framework, needs to consider critical sociability aspects such as purpose and content, roles of the various stakeholders, and policies to do with membership, discourse styles, and ownership of ideas. Similarly, usability issues include design and navigation, and larger-scale considerations such as national access to the Internet, state and institution policies, and individual access to resources for information and communication technology.

Any evaluation must take into account the culture of users. Like other professionals, teachers learn through their daily practice (Day, 1999), but this often flows from planning for and teaching their students rather than in dedicated sessions for their own development. While teachers focus on action (experiencing and implementing) in their practice, they have been less frequently involved in researching (reflecting

Copyright © 2007, Idea Group Inc. Copying or distributing in print or electronic forms without written permission of Idea Group Inc. is prohibited.

on and theorizing) this practice. Piaget (1969) expressed surprise that the large number of teachers did not produce a group of researchers among their ranks who focused on pedagogy as a discipline from the practitioner's point of view. Carr and Kemmis (1986; Kemmis, 1999) took up the challenge in their work in action research, arguing that it is conducted by those involved in a social practice—which it takes as its subject matter—and from a critical stance, proceeding through a spiral of cycles of planning, acting, observing, and reflecting, to achieve improvement and social change. In this case, the university-based managers of the NQSF should also be considered as users, as they share the purpose of school improvement and actively participate with teacher-users in the community. A national connection between action researchers in schools and university-based researchers has the potential to provide a critical mass for improvement and innovation that has broad impact. However, we need to be mindful of the cultural impact of teachers working in isolation in place-based communities, a rhetoric of reflection not yet matched by extensive practice, and the many boundaries between practice and research that could work against the development of communities of practice.

In the following sections we describe the development of the National Quality Schooling Framework and consider it in light of the three infrastructures comprising Wenger's framework (engagement, imagination, and alignment) in order to draw some conclusions about its development and sustainability as a community of practice.

Method

Our approach to the task was interpretive and drew on historical methods of document analysis, on social surveys and quantitative data. As managers of the community in question (through the Center for Applied Educational Research at the University of Melbourne—CAER), we brought a personal perspective to judging the value of the project, which gave us privileged access to information as well as a client relationship with other users and our funding body. To assess the development and the current strengths of the NQSF in terms of Wenger's three facilities, we drew on archival material such as minutes of meetings prior to the original proposal, correspondence with other developers of online communities, the original proposal, and annual contracts. We also used data from the user-centered trial phase with 46 schools. The range of data included school project reports, structured interviews with six trial schools in three states, surveys of information and communications technology environments in trial schools, skills surveys of teachers and school leaders, e-mail polling of participants, and transcripts of teletutorials and teleconferences. The quantitative usage data collected by the CAER, over two-and-a-half years since the completion of the pilot, included registrations by type of user and

Copyright © 2007, Idea Group Inc. Copying or distributing in print or electronic forms without written permission of Idea Group Inc. is prohibited.

date, site and page hits and downloads, and most popular pages on a monthly basis. Further, we had access to anecdotal comments made by current participants in the process of completing project reports, in telephone calls, face-to-face workshops, or in response to e-mails or newsletter items. Finally, we drew on the master's thesis of Capponi (2004), a member of the NQSF pilot team, which focused on interviews with a sample of 13 participants and other data from the pilot. All items were sorted into one or more of Wenger's categories.

The data are therefore in different forms from a range of sources and reflect the various stakeholders in the community—the Australian government, the users, and managers—in a form of triangulation that, we believe, helps to verify the story told in this chapter.

NQSF: Context and Structure

The National Quality Schooling Framework (NQSF) is a highly structured interactive Web environment designed to support Australian school leaders and teachers develop, implement, and research innovative and evidence-based projects to improve student learning outcomes. To move from locale-based concepts of educational community normally found in schools, to an ambitious national reach in a geographically large country with widely dispersed populations, is a challenge. In addition, while the Australian Commonwealth Government's education department holds some control, particularly through its funding programs, school education in Australia is in the jurisdiction of the eight states and territories, which tend to guard their separate identities. A national school education system comprising 34 different educational systems—including a relatively large independent schools sector—results in different curricula, term dates, employment practices, and even school entry ages and transition levels across Australia. On the other hand, all systems use a common language (English) and are bound together by the shared multicultural identity of being Australian. Several attempts have been made to draw together these fragmented systems, including a set of National Goals for Schooling in the Twenty-First Century (Ministerial Council on Education Employment Training and Youth Affairs, 1999) drawn up by a committee representing all states.

The developers of the NQSF, under the leadership of the project director, Professor Peter Cuttance, were contracted by the Australian government to develop a framework of quality schooling to support the national goals, and to add value to the range of school innovations and initiatives being undertaken in government and non-government schools, through disseminating information more widely across boundaries than in the past. This need had been identified by schools in a previous project (Cuttance & Innovation and Best Practice Consortium, 2001).

Copyright © 2007, Idea Group Inc. Copying or distributing in print or electronic forms without written permission of Idea Group Inc. is prohibited.

The developers' specific objectives for the NQSF were addressed both to schools and individuals in the broad education community, with the intention of valuing teachers' professional practice and evidence-based research, and to support their professional development.

The key project stages were development (July 2001-April 2002), pilot (April 2002-September 2002), and redevelopment (September 2002-March 2003), leading up to the launch in April 2003.The project outcome was originally conceived to be a publication for distribution to all schools in Australia that would include a framework of quality schooling, and examples of *best practice* and resources to support school improvement. However, during the development stage the project director initiated the notion of a Web-based platform to create a national online community. Informed by the work of UK projects at Ultralab (www.ultralab.net) and NCSL's Talk2Learn (https://www.ncsl.org.uk/UAAlogon_t2l.cfm?service=9)—a Web-based portal to support school leadership and professional learning—Cuttance proposed an online environment to support quality schooling in Australia. The move from paper to the Web was motivated by the desire to create an interactive community of practice, rather than a static resource, to provide up-to-date quality support for Australian schools, and in particular to better meet the needs of schools in rural and remote areas.

Underpinning the proposal was Fullan's (1993) concept of pressure and support, whereby high expectations for school improvement and innovation would be supported by user-friendly tools and resources. A specific new role had also been identified for educational bureaucracies and policymakers in supporting schools and teachers to undertake new tasks (Darling-Hammond, 1998). Among other goals, the NQSF aimed to build a shared understanding of how student learning outcomes could be improved by quality assurance processes grounded in professional practice and evidence-based research, to develop and support whole-school approaches to school improvement, and to develop a framework for the lateral transmission of best practice knowledge across schools. These are congruent with a communities of practice model that includes space for engagement, creating knowledge through imagination, and affecting the world by alignment (Wenger, 1998). The purpose is clear, as is the potential identity of the community, and as we shall see later, the policies and procedures for involvement.

The NQSF includes 10 key dimensions of quality schooling; a dynamic repository of quality-assured resources in the form of literature, tools, and strategies; and a Web platform to engage and support teachers and professional educators in interactive professional e-learning activities and communities.

The key dimensions were developed from the findings of a review of literature in the fields of school and teacher effectiveness, school improvement and innovation, and educational change. They were based on an Australian model of literacy learning in the early years of schooling (Hill & Crévola, 1997) which, when reviewed, was

Copyright © 2007, Idea Group Inc. Copying or distributing in print or electronic forms without written permission of Idea Group Inc. is prohibited.

found robust as a framework for school improvement in the early years. Additional depth and scope in the individual dimensions and the inclusion of the nature of student learning and leadership and management were required, however, to guide improvement in secondary schools and to address the complexities of large schools. The NQSF Ten Key Dimensions comprise: beliefs and understandings, curriculum, standards and targets, monitoring, assessment and reporting, learning, teaching, professional learning, school and class organization, intervention and special assistance, home, school and community partnerships, and leadership and management. These are areas that schools and teachers are expected to consider when working on improvement projects, and each is fleshed out by explanatory statements based on the available evidence. They form one of the facilities of alignment.

The searchable *resources* repository is populated in two main ways. First, existing resources in the form of research papers, reports, and tools are scrutinized for relevance to school improvement or innovation, trustworthiness, and clarity of expression for the school-based audience, and then linked through the NQSF portal. Members can "request a resource" if none are found online, and these requests are dealt with by CAER staff. Secondly, school members are encouraged to submit project reports with a strong evidence base that provides provenance for the effectiveness of their strategies within an action research framework. This "Your School and Your Cluster Project" (YSP/YCP) framework uses the 10 dimensions of quality schooling. By providing such a framework, the NQSF aims to create a space and tools for shared discourse between practitioners, as participating schools work within the same broad structure to develop projects that address local needs. The four YSP/YCP documents are:

1. **Project plan:** Context, evidence of need, project overview, and resources required.
2. **Evaluation plan:** Baseline data, goals, targets, and milestones across key dimensions.
3. **Development strategies:** The wider research and practitioner knowledge base for the strategies and their implementation.
4. **Evidence, analysis, and impact:** Data and evidence of impact on the intended outcomes, other impacts, reflections on the project and on the support used to achieve the results, and lessons and advice to other schools planning a similar project.

These documents combine pressure and support, as they prove quite difficult for schools, but show well how improvement projects can be planned and documented. They are another facility of alignment. Once completed and quality-assured, the documents are published to the Web site, providing rich data for meta-analysis by

Copyright © 2007, Idea Group Inc. Copying or distributing in print or electronic forms without written permission of Idea Group Inc. is prohibited.

community members who are interested in both interpretive and quantitative methods of research. This resource can inform several constituencies including teachers, policymakers, and the public, thus enhancing engagement.

All schools in Australia, throughout the various jurisdictions, were invited to join the NQSF at no cost. The school is the primary unit of registration, with an unlimited number of teachers able to register and receive individual passwords. Thus the connections are formally between schools, with only the contact details of school principals available on the Web site. In addition to collecting participation data, this provides a level of security that was deemed necessary to protect against misuse and guarantee the integrity of data.

The Web site was developed from the view that users need assistance to benefit from an online community, so in addition to online and telephone support, called teletutorials, the NQSF facilitates external links to Web-based collaborative tools designed to foster a true community of practice looking outward. One of these tools is Think.com, a site that enables students and teachers to publish and interact with others in a protected community space. Here too, teachers and researchers can present professional development activities by teleconference and synchronous and asynchronous text-based communication, called teletopics. To enhance usability and thereby increase sociability for school personnel, a brief handbook was developed by CAER, and regular tutorials covering various aspects of using both Web sites are offered by teleconference. However, this chapter refers to Think.com only in passing, as it is a discrete site, owned by the Oracle Education Foundation, and global in intent and reach.

Measures of Participation

In March 2005, the number of schools registered in the NQSF represented 28% of all schools in the nation (2,801 of 9,877) and, by sector, represented 25% of government schools, 25% of Catholic schools, and 29% of independent schools. Registrations by stage of schooling indicated a higher proportion of secondary schools (42%) than primary schools (20%). Table 1 shows the proportion of schools registered in all states and territories.

The table shows a wide range of uptake. The proportion of registered schools in the government sector by state/territory differs greatly: the highest proportion (56%) in the Australian Capital Territory (the smallest and least populous) and the lowest (17%) in New South Wales (the most populous). The Catholic sector ranges from a low of 14% in Western Australia to a high of 42% in the Australian Capital Territory (ACT), while registrations of other schools are lowest in Tasmania (19%) and highest in South Australia (39%). Within states, the proportions in each sector are

Copyright © 2007, Idea Group Inc. Copying or distributing in print or electronic forms without written permission of Idea Group Inc. is prohibited.

Table 1. NQSF-registered schools as percentage of all schools, and by sector, in Australian states and territories, March 2005

State/Territory	Total %	% Govt	% Cath	% Other
ACT	63	56	42	24
SA	40	36	34	39
NT	37	27	35	33
QLD	32	27	40	36
TAS	32	27	35	19
VIC	30	29	23	29
WA	25	24	14	29
NSW	20	17	21	27
Average	35	30	31	30

relatively similar in Victoria and the Northern Territory, and greatly divergent in Western Australia and Tasmania. The reasons for these variations have not yet been examined in detail, but could include sociability aspects such as openness to new ideas, time available in the working day, and ease of face-to-face links with other schools, as well as national and state-influenced usability aspects such as access to reliable Internet connections and teachers' access to computers.

As noted earlier, the school is the primary unit of registration. During the pilot stage with 46 schools, all users had a common temporary password, but subsequently, registration processes for individuals were developed. In March 2005, the second year of full operation, individual registrations in the NQSF community stood at 5,877 school users from 2,801 schools, and an additional 705 non-school users. In over 1,000 schools, only one staff member is registered, which has the effect of funneling all communication through one username and password. In addition to teachers and school leaders, users include university academics, researchers, and a sprinkling of education bureaucrats in state, federal, and non-government jurisdictions; education consultants; members of parent associations; education unions; professional associations; and community representatives.

In terms of access to the site, the figures from the first two years of operation showed that the level of access increased between April 2004 and March 2005. The daily average number of hits increased from 2,456 to 10,550 (more than a three-fold increase), and the average number of actual pages accessed daily increased from 1,047 to 6,682 (more than a five-fold increase). Site usage rates were highest on all measures in March 2005. As time has passed, schools have accessed resources, and in a reciprocal fashion, submitted almost 400 reports, of which 350 have also been quality assured and published on the Web site. Users have also participated in teletutorials, teleconferences, and teletopics. In the early teletutorials, most conver-

Copyright © 2007, Idea Group Inc. Copying or distributing in print or electronic forms without written permission of Idea Group Inc. is prohibited.

sations focused on instruction for users in the various features of the NQSF online environment and conveying information about the NQSF project itself. Participation rates during the pilot ranged from a consistent 80-100% of schools in Queensland, Western Australia, and South Australia, to 50% or fewer of Victorian and New South-Wales/ACT project schools. Participation was higher among non-metropolitan than metropolitan schools. Over time, users have shown reduced interest in instruction and more in professional learning on substantive topics. From 2005, some teachers have also hosted teletopics to share their quality school improvement projects. Some of this reciprocity, which Preece (2001) considers to be an important measure of the success of an online community, is not just the result of teacher interest, but is the result of a requirement of another national project that populates the NQSF site: the Boys' Education Lighthouse Schools Project. This gives a particular focus and purpose for many community members.

Facilitation of online communities can involve a *push* factor, and for this, since May 2003, the NQSF has used e-mail to alert registered users to the publication of the regular online newsletter. This promotes resources and sites available through the NQSF. The site usage statistics appear to show a newsletter effect: an increase in visits to the site following each newsletter, and an increase in hits on resources highlighted in and linked to the newsletter. However, in those schools where there is only one registration, this means the newsletter reaches only one person in the first instance.

Evaluating the NQSF as a Community of Practice

In this section we consider the three broad areas suggested by Wenger—engagement, imagination, and alignment—and make some judgments on the development and strengths of the NQSF based on the quantitative and qualitative data. We posited earlier that its purpose is to build knowledge by revealing, accessing, and sharing current practice in order to create new solutions to educational problems identified by the users.

Engagement

The facility of engagement—the Web site—provides the space to reveal, access, and share current practice. First, however, people must engage through registration. We argue that the figure of one-third of the potential schools is indicative of a successful community, but that for an ambitious nationwide project, quality is a better

Copyright © 2007, Idea Group Inc. Copying or distributing in print or electronic forms without written permission of Idea Group Inc. is prohibited.

measure. The quantitative measures noted previously came from the perspective of the Web site managers and are likely to be of little concern to the users. Quality, rather than quantity, can be judged by the users themselves.

The rate of participation in teletutorials, teleconferences, and teletopics is higher for members in rural and remote areas and less populous states in Australia than in more urban areas. This may indicate that the NQSF provides new and acceptable ways for teachers in these locations to foster mutual and shared activities that are not place-based. Urban teachers are much closer to each other than those in the vast rural areas of states such as Western Australia, South Australia, and Queensland, and they can often meet in face-to-face settings. One rural teacher stated:

The opportunity to work with a team outside the school environment brings in fresh ideas and approaches. The overall package offered by the NQSF has given us the opportunity to really assess the structures currently in place and to fine-tune them further.

The action research framework of the Your School and Your Cluster Project documents provides a common discourse, and tools for evaluation, accountability, and engagement through documentation that enhances continuity or corporate memory (Wenger, 1998). One member commented:

I like the idea of planning and evaluation frameworks and found this information particularly useful. I will use the NQSF framework for the development of future projects. It provides...reference points to define the scope of the project and also the source of indicators to measure the success of the project.

To share knowledge and increase competence, users engaged with professional educators who have undertaken research or developed a high level of expertise and knowledge in priority improvement areas. Many teachers valued access to resources from other researchers and practitioners, as in this case:

Research information...has been current and relevant and at my fingertips when I needed it for my project, wanted an issue clarified or just sought up-to-date findings on educational topics that interested me.

In 2002 and 2003, one section of the NQSF Web site was the Forum, intended to foster mutual and shared activities, and to encourage users to explore new territories via asynchronous communication. In the Forum, facilitated discussions were

Copyright © 2007, Idea Group Inc. Copying or distributing in print or electronic forms without written permission of Idea Group Inc. is prohibited.

established on topics considered to be of interest to members such as thinking skills, information and communication technologies in the curriculum, literacy assessment, and parent involvement. As a result, one teacher asked:

Does anyone use rubrics at their school or have any information about them? We are researching the effectiveness of rubrics within the classroom and at the school-wide level. We have found information from the Internet mainly originating from other countries, but we're interested in finding out more about Australian usage.

However, the majority of topics did not result in sustained conversations (Capponi, 2004). Usage data confirm that most activity involved browsing discussion threads, rather than formulating replies to the threads. Ninety-two percent of pilot participants reported that they browsed but did not start a new thread or contribute to an existing thread. This is sometimes called lurking, but as Preece suggests, and Brazelton and Gorry (2003) concur, this is not always indicative of lack of engagement or of the level of quality. For example, one teacher commented:

I have enjoyed reading other teachers' stories and feeling part of a wider educational community.

However, teachers who looked for feedback from others when they posted information were disappointed when little or none was forthcoming. This may be explained by the prevailing culture of teaching as an isolated activity or the perception that the public, formal, and permanent nature of the communication is too revealing of one's shortcomings (Hartnell-Young, 2003). The Forum feature was discontinued in 2004.

While sociability is well covered through Wenger's architecture, usability, in Preece's terms, is not. This is concerned with how users interact with technology, and includes support for social interaction, information design, navigation, and access. Teacher users have a wide range of information and communication technology skills, ranging from basic to advanced. However, their skill levels were only a minor factor in their use of the NQSF Web site. In terms of usability, most pilot participants reported favorably on the simplicity of the design and navigation of the NQSF Web site (Capponi, 2004). Even those who reported difficulties persisted with use, indicating that purpose was an overriding consideration. Many commented like this:

The structure of the site has been easy to follow and when it was not I just proceeded and had a look anyway.

Copyright © 2007, Idea Group Inc. Copying or distributing in print or electronic forms without written permission of Idea Group Inc. is prohibited.

Barriers to engagement are found outside the NQSF itself, such as in the variable telecommunications infrastructure across Australia which affects participation in the online space. NQSF members commented on inhibiting factors such as slow access to the Internet, local server configuration, and personal access to a computer.

Imagination

Wenger uses the term imagination to refer to people building an image of the world and themselves. We consider that for teachers this includes the notion of being members of a profession and asking the question "Who are we?" Teachers in the NQSF reported learning about strategies that are being developed, tested, and implemented by colleagues in other schools, and stated that they shared resources on a wider scale than previously. Many teachers reported interest in what other schools were doing. One cluster's report noted:

It has also been useful to access information about other projects from around the country and see what else is happening.

A consequence of online interaction has been the desire for face-to-face use of the NQSF platform as a further springboard to community interaction, and this has occurred in several cases:

As a result of this networking, I have accompanied the Principal on a couple of visits to schools located in other parts of the State. We have discussed issues pertaining to our respective schools and offered mutual support, exchanged learnings and resources between sites.

We'd read of their work and then we'd e-mail or telephone to talk in other ways. We used NQSF as the platform to get in touch. (Capponi, 2004, p. 81)

Creating a sense of self and the profession, from local though to national scale, is not something that has been high on the minds of many teachers. However, several reported that the awareness of others raised by their membership of the NQSF led them to look at their own situations with new eyes; and for some, this new culture of networking motivated them to think more of the audience for their contribution to the Web site:

Copyright © 2007, Idea Group Inc. Copying or distributing in print or electronic forms without written permission of Idea Group Inc. is prohibited.

It was a challenge to put items that might be of interest to others on the [site].

Wenger suggests that knowledge building can be enhanced by time off for reflection and conversation, exploration and play. However, providing a Web space for sociability, or a national telecommunications infrastructure, is not enough. Teachers reported the biggest barrier to accessing the NQSF online environment is the lack of time, given the existing culture of teaching and what is regarded as important. One teacher wrote:

The site with all its functions is a wonderful attempt to create a 'community of scholars' and to rid intellectual discussion of the tyranny of distance. However, the tyranny of time retains its power.

As well, finding time to participate in synchronous rather than asynchronous activities posed difficulties for participants wanting to form communities across time zones (Australia has five time zones in summer time, and three time zones for the rest of the year).

The resulting low levels of interaction and contribution, particularly in the early stages, frustrated some members. Local factors played a role in this, particularly the level of access to reliable computers and sufficient bandwidth, which varies within and between states and school sectors. Some teachers reported that they found Internet access too slow during school hours, when they had to compete with students, so they used the site only before or after school hours. Lack of access to telephones and private, uninterrupted work spaces were also reported to be barriers to engaging in teleconferences. Similarly, participating in simultaneous online and telephonic professional learning activities was difficult where schools lack suitable equipment (such as a hands-free phone). Most teleconferences have been scheduled at the end of the school day to alleviate this problem.

Alignment

The third element of Wenger's community of practice model, alignment, is achieved by the NQSF through the broad purpose of school-based improvement. The community gives teachers a platform and an opportunity to affect the world through the evidence they provide of their own research into quality practice. Data are both collected and shared, in order to inform others, to improve schooling nationally, and to connect with others globally (30 members of the NQSF are from the UK or New Zealand). As one participant explained:

Copyright © 2007, Idea Group Inc. Copying or distributing in print or electronic forms without written permission of Idea Group Inc. is prohibited.

If you've got a purpose and you need to know something and you know the site is there...resources, people as well as information, then you use it. (Capponi, 2004, p. 74)

The Ten Key Dimensions provide a tool for alignment, acting as a boundary object as they allow members of the community to organize their experience into the areas of curriculum, assessment and reporting, professional learning, leadership and management, and so on. The Your School and Your Cluster Project documents are also tools of alignment, and increasingly provide a scaffold for data collection and analysis, leading to shared understanding within and between schools, as one school report indicated:

All of the cluster schools have realized the value of the assessment schedule that we had to provide for the duration of the project. Not only did this schedule serve the purposes of the project, but we also found that we were using the data in many of the mandatory planning tasks expected in the running of our schools...The use of the NQSF framework tools was an excellent way to review planning targets in our schools, not only the project goals, but the other goals associated with the schools' directions.

In spite of a range of experiences with the technology, over time participants have found, as Wenger et al. (2002) suggest, that quality arises from the existence of a shared practice: a common set of situations, problems, and perspectives that overrides the choice of a specific form of communication (e.g., face-to-face as opposed to Web-based) and enables members of a community to share information. Alignment is supported by the facilitation of the CAER, in particular the feedback provided through the quality assurance processes on documents submitted to the Web site.

The development of learning in communities of practice over time is well documented. In the NQSF experience, the focus of the telephonic communication shifted over time from discussion about the site (tutorials) to focus increasingly on national discussion on topics of common interest (teletopics). With less reliance on facilitators to lead conversations, and more direct exchanges between teachers, the facilitator's role has shifted from instructor to knowledge builder, entering the conversation at strategic points to clarify discussion or to introduce new knowledge. As Capponi suggests, the facilitators have a role to make strategic contributions that directly support participants' priorities. The exchange of information in recent times has been at a much deeper level, with greater sharing of practice, deeper questioning of each other, and greater consideration of the effects of practice than exchanges earlier in the project.

Copyright © 2007, Idea Group Inc. Copying or distributing in print or electronic forms without written permission of Idea Group Inc. is prohibited.

Conclusion

The NQSF is underpinned by a belief that teachers and researchers can work in partnership with others to make improvements in the quality of education. Its purpose is to build knowledge and improve practice in order to create new solutions to educational problems. We suggest that the NQSF functions as a community of practice, and in this chapter, we have described its features in light of Wenger's model of three infrastructures: engagement, imagination, and alignment. We found the model useful in evaluating the successes and weaknesses of the community, and in identifying gaps. However, we also found that the various elements of the model were intertwined, so that, for example, issues to do with time and space occupied more than one of the three infrastructures.

The NQSF provides space for engagement for educators distributed across a large continent. In spite of differential accessibility across the nation, an online environment can help counter the "tyranny of distance" that characterizes Australian geography. The pattern of registrations by state—generally a higher proportion of schools in the less densely populated states—and a higher level of engagement in non-metropolitan schools indicate that online communities of practice may provide access to the research and knowledge base, and opportunities for knowledge creation that cannot be readily accessed through conventional means. Access and usability concerns present continuing challenges. Concerns to do with the national telecommunications infrastructure in Australia include limitations of bandwidth and geographical coverage of connectivity. In such a large landmass, the variable coverage of access to broadband telecommunications impacts on access to the Internet for schools and individuals, affecting their capacity to engage in a national community. It is critical that this issue be addressed by the national government as a matter of educational and social policy.

Within the NQSF, the impending development of a two-layer entry, with the removal of the requirement for passwords for access to resources, is likely to encourage more engagement. Feedback from teachers has indicated that the need to use a password to access the NQSF is an impediment to their participation. However, access via a password will remain on the areas of the site that give access to material that has been produced by schools and personal and school contact details.

At a school level, the set-up of local area networks can also be a barrier to engagement. Australian schools typically establish their computer networks as intranets that aim to provide effective internal structures for students and teachers. In most schools, this results in constraints on access to the external Internet so that bandwidth can be allocated preferentially to internal intranet usage. The paradox is that while the site provides acceptable performance when accessed over a standard telephone line, many teachers are unable to achieve acceptable access via school intranets,

Copyright © 2007, Idea Group Inc. Copying or distributing in print or electronic forms without written permission of Idea Group Inc. is prohibited.

because the bandwidth available to a single user is less than that available over a standard telephone line.

In addition, the differential levels of capacity across school systems is one of the reasons for differential take-up of membership of the NQSF. The most up-to-date school systems have highly efficient intranets that allow schools good access to the Internet, while some others are yet to implement basic capacity measures—exemplified in some school systems by teachers not having access to personalized e-mail and not having access to a connection to the system at their desk.

A school's duty of care extends to preventing student access to undesirable Web sites, and this is also often used by schools as an explanation for constraining access to the external Internet. Alternative strategies need to be implemented to allow teachers to have efficient access to designated Internet sites. Effective policies and the provision of the required bandwidth are critical to the implementation of systems that allow schools to address these issues of duty of care and teacher access to peer-to-peer communications via the Internet.

Although there is no indication that the searchability of the NQSF Web site has constrained teacher access, it has affected the usability of the site for teachers. The current search capacity allows teachers to search only the HTML text on the Web site. A search function that allowed teachers to search deeper by interrogating the contents of documents on the site would provide greater utility for teachers. To date, the funding body has declined to fund the development of this capacity on the Web site. Recent search engine developments for documents such as those on the NQSF Web site have focused on "natural language" strategies for interrogating text material. The implementation of a strategy based on an advanced "natural language" search model would allow the development to leapfrog the expensive and ongoing cost of meta-tagging the material on the site.

In terms of imagination, we argue that a professional community must encourage a sense of the profession, and that the NQSF is contributing to this at a national level. Facilitation and management are necessary at this scale, and it is likely to be a benefit if the managers share the purpose with participants. However, this is a time-consuming activity that requires a level of content knowledge and technical expertise. The site was originally designed to be used on the basis of most schools having only one or two teachers registered on the site. The concept of participation was that teams of teachers in schools would utilize the site to gather resources, and that one or two members of the team would be assigned to this role. However, this restricts the capacity to use "push" strategies via e-mail to enhance the quality of engagement. To address this issue, a multi-user registration upload tool is being developed. This will allow schools to efficiently create multiple accounts for a single school by uploading appropriate contact details for teachers from school records. To enhance effectiveness, the registration forms will be pre-populated where possible from existing data held in the registration database—school details, for

Copyright © 2007, Idea Group Inc. Copying or distributing in print or electronic forms without written permission of Idea Group Inc. is prohibited.

example—and the information displayed for verification before adding accounts to the database.

While users were not highly involved in the development and management of the NQSF, the alternative—such as a large online community of educators emerging from the grassroots across the nation—is unlikely, given the factors discussed earlier. A range of evidence presented in this chapter supports this contention. Although the NQSF commenced from what might be seen as a top-down approach, it evolved as the logical next development from a national research study of innovation in Australian schools. A key outcome of this national study was a set of recommendations to enhance teacher access to the knowledge base and peer-to-peer communication required for effective evidence-based innovation in schools. The significant take-up across schools—a third of all schools nationally—and the increasing use of the site, the registration of schools across all school systems and sectors, and the broad range of non-teacher users of the site indicate a shared sense of the profession. Although parents have at this stage not been provided with access, the national parent bodies have expressed an interest in being able to access the site. The strategy currently being implemented to provide password-free access to the resources area will make that area of the site available to all members of the public.

Alignment is achieved through the shared purpose, the documentation framework, and the quality assurance processes, among other things. The NQSF is beginning to integrate emerging understandings of knowledge work and professional learning into the practices and processes schools are developing to address the challenge of meeting the needs of their students and the pressures of the external environment for change. The framework bridges the boundaries between practitioners and researchers. As Brazelton and Gorry (2003) found in the United States, communities of practice are not implanted in the landscape, but they grow over time where they are seen to be of quality and relevance.

There is as yet no evidence of wider effects of this work, where teachers in schools might influence national policy. However the NQSF has provided the opportunity for them to identify shared concerns and amass a body of evidence that could influence policy in the future. Development in this area could include strategies such as those used by the National College for School Leadership in the UK, particularly the use of "hot seats" to provide teachers with direct access to senior policymakers and government ministers. There is significant potential for the implementation of strategies that allows policymakers to canvas and interactively discuss critical issues with school-based practitioners. An alternative would be to provide policymakers with access to a tool that abstracts the key issues from school-generated materials that are uploaded to the site. However, we should not automatically assume that policymakers operate from a paradigm that gives prominence to the use of grounded evidence about the practices and issues that they seek to address, and certainly not assume that they would want to *interact* with the producers (teachers) of such evidence.

Copyright © 2007, Idea Group Inc. Copying or distributing in print or electronic forms without written permission of Idea Group Inc. is prohibited.

The sustainability of the NQSF community depends on the capacity of school culture to allow teachers to interact with other communities in a purposeful way, and to enable school improvement at local and national levels. To do this, there needs to be a continuing commitment to provide supportive technologies on the part of governments, coupled with a commitment by teachers to building knowledge.

References

Brazelton, J., & Gorry, G. A. (2003). Creating a knowledge-sharing community: If you build it, will they come? *Communications of the ACM, 46*(2), 23-25.

Brook, C., & Oliver, R. (2003). Exploring online community development: The relative importance of influencing factors. *Proceedings of the Australasian Society for Computers in Learning* (ASCILITE), Adelaide, Australia.

Capponi, N. (2004). *Teacher professional learning in an online community: The experience of the NQSF pilot project.* Melbourne: University of Melbourne.

Carr, W., & Kemmis, S. (1986). *Becoming critical.* London: Falmer Press.

Cuttance, P., & Innovation and Best Practice Consortium. (2001). *School innovation: Pathway to the knowledge society.* Canberra: Department of Education, Training and Youth Affairs.

Darling-Hammond, L. (1998). Teachers and teaching: Testing policy hypotheses from a national commission report. *Educational Researcher, 27*(1), 5-15.

Day, C. (1999). *Developing teachers: The challenges of lifelong learning.* London/Philadelphia: Falmer Press.

Fullan, M. (1993). *Change forces: Probing the depths of educational reform.* London: Falmer Press.

Harasim, L. (2002). What makes online learning communities successful? In C. Vrasidas & G. Glass (Eds.), *Distance education and distributed learning* (pp. 181-200). Greenwich, CT: Information Age.

Hartnell-Young, E. (2003). *Towards knowledge building: Reflecting on teachers' roles and professional learning in communities of practice.* Melbourne: University of Melbourne.

Hill, P., & Crévola, C. (1997). The literacy challenge in Australian primary schools. *IARTV Seminar Series, 69.*

Kemmis, S. (1999). Action research. In J. Keeves & G. Lakomski (Eds.), *Issues in educational research* (pp. 150-160). Oxford: Pergamon.

Kovaric, P., & Bott, A. (2000). Teacher support through virtual communities. *Proceedings of the American Educational Research Association Annual Meeting.*

Copyright © 2007, Idea Group Inc. Copying or distributing in print or electronic forms without written permission of Idea Group Inc. is prohibited.

Retrieved August 29, 2005, from www.gseis.ucla.edu/etu/kovaric/virtualcommunities.pdf

Ministerial Council on Education Employment Training and Youth Affairs. (1999). *The Adelaide declaration on national goals for schooling in the twenty-first century.* Retrieved March 20, 2005, from http://www.mceetya.edu.au/nationalgoals/natgoals.htm

Piaget, J. (1969). *Psychologie et pédagogie.* Paris: Editions Denoël.

Preece, J. (2000). *Online communities: Designing usability, supporting sociability.* Chichester, UK: John Wiley & Sons.

Preece, J. (2001). Sociability and usability: Twenty years of chatting online. *Behavior and Information Technology Journal, 20*(5), 347-356.

Rheingold, H. (2000). *The virtual community: Homesteading on the virtual frontier.* Cambridge, MA: MIT Press.

Schlager, M., Fusco, J., & Schank, P. (1999). Cornerstones for an online community of education professionals. *IEEE Technology and Society Magazine, 17*(4), 15-21.

Sergiovanni, T. (1999). *The lifeworld of leadership: Creating culture, community, and personal meaning in our schools.* San Francisco: Jossey-Bass.

Wellman, B. (2001). Physical place and cyberplace: The rise of networked individualism. In L. Keeble & B. Loader (Eds.), *Community informatics: Shaping computer-mediated social relations* (pp. 17-43). New York: Routledge.

Wenger, E., McDermott, R., & Snyder, W. (2002). *Cultivating communities of practice.* Boston: Harvard Business School Press.

Wenger, E. (1998). *Communities of practice: Learning, meaning, identity.* Cambridge, UK: Cambridge University Press.

Copyright © 2007, Idea Group Inc. Copying or distributing in print or electronic forms without written permission of Idea Group Inc. is prohibited.

Chapter XIII

Iterative Design and Evaluation of a Web-Based Experimentation Environment

Anh Vu Nguyen-Ngoc,
Ecole Polytechnique Fédérale de Lausanne (EPFL), Switzerland

Yassin Rekik,
Ecole Polytechnique Fédérale de Lausanne (EPFL), Switzerland

Denis Gillet,
Ecole Polytechnique Fédérale de Lausanne (EPFL), Switzerland

Abstract

Nowadays, Web-based experimentation environments provide an excellent instrument to add flexibility in traditional engineering curricula. This chapter presents a model for the evaluation of such environments. The proposed model relies on an iterative evaluation paradigm. It allows the integration of different analysis methods including quantitative and qualitative analysis, and social network analysis. The chapter also describes the iterative user-centered design and development of the

Copyright © 2007, Idea Group Inc. Copying or distributing in print or electronic forms without written permission of Idea Group Inc. is prohibited.

eMersion environment developed at the Ecole Polytechnique Fédérale de Lausanne (EPFL), as well as the results and analyses of the evaluation process carried out in the automatic control laboratory courses using the eMersion environment from the 2002 winter to the 2005 summer semesters at the EPFL. The evaluation was performed to study different aspects relevant for an online learning community in engineering education, such as participation, flexibility, learning performance, collaboration, and community social structure.

Introduction

Automatic control is a mandatory course offered to various engineering degree programs including electrical, mechanical, and micro-engineering curricula at the Ecole Polytechnique Fédérale de Lausanne (EPFL). In automatic control, as in other engineering domains, laboratory activities—or hands-on activities in general—play an essential role in theoretical knowledge reinforcing and know-how acquisition. Hands-on activities also help in increasing students' motivation.

For about a decade, academic institutions have tried to meet the increasing student needs for professional competencies, personal development, and career planning, including the necessary skills for teamwork and lifelong learning. Furthermore, engineering departments have had to solve the logistical dilemma of educating more students with fewer resources while maintaining the quality of education. Within this challenging context, the so-called *flexible* learning paradigm (Gillet, 2003; Kazmer & Haythornthwaite, 2005; Mosterman et al., 1994) happened to be helpful. This paradigm is leading towards the development of a hybrid-learning scheme in which the traditional courses are combined with online activities that can be carried out at anytime and from anywhere. In addition to providing students with new online resources, the flexible learning paradigm also sustains the development of a learning community. All people involved in a course, including the educators, the tutors, the teaching assistants (TAs), and the students, who synchronously and asynchronously interact with each other and with laboratory resources, form what is called an online learning community.

Web-based experimentation is one of the online activities that plays a key role in the development and deployment of the flexible education paradigm in engineering education. Web-based experimentation stands for hands-on activities carried out online using either simulators (virtual experimentation) or remote connection to real laboratory equipment (remote experimentation). Typical Web-based experimentation sessions are mediated by tutors and TAs. There might be some face-to-face (f2f) sessions in which the students work in the laboratory with the presence of the tutor and/or TA (see Figure 1 as an example), but most of the learning activities take

Copyright © 2007, Idea Group Inc. Copying or distributing in print or electronic forms without written permission of Idea Group Inc. is prohibited.

place online. This bimodal context requires special features to effectively support the online learning community.

First of all, the content delivered in online engineering courses includes not only static documents, textual presentations, or video presentations, but also computation, graphics generated on-the-fly, real devices measurements, etc. Hence, the environments supporting Web-based experimentation must provide necessary functionalities to enable monitoring, measuring, and manipulating the virtual or real experimentation resources. They also require additional software components supporting the organizational and the collaborative tasks associated with the hands-on activities.

Secondly, Web-based experimentation environments should encourage students to carry out experimentation in a flexible way. In other words, students are allowed to perform multi-session experiments. For instance, they can do the first part of the experiment at school, and pursue the rest of it at home thanks to the remote access to the laboratory equipment.

Thirdly, Web-based experimentation environments should provide shared spaces, as well as online collaboration facilities with which students can find, share, and co-construct knowledge. These components help the students actively create their own contextual meaning, rather than passively acquiring knowledge structures created by others. In an active learning perspective, students need to interact with their peers, collaborate, discuss their positions, form arguments, reevaluate their initial positions, and negotiate meaning.

Last but not least, Web-based experimentation environments should support awareness. In learning and especially in flexible learning, awareness (Dourish & Bellotti,

Figure 1. Hands-on activities in f2f learning modality

Copyright © 2007, Idea Group Inc. Copying or distributing in print or electronic forms without written permission of Idea Group Inc. is prohibited.

1992) plays a very important role for every member of the community. Tutors need awareness to have a general perception of the class activities, to monitor the class progress, and to detect problems in order to intervene in time. Students need awareness to have a perception about their progress compared with other groups. Awareness is also necessary for students to find potential collaborators for exchanging documents and ideas, or to ask for help.

As a summary, in order to effectively and efficiently support online communities in engineering education, Web-based experimentation environments have to integrate components supporting multiple interaction dimensions, including not only the interaction with the experimentation resources, but also collaboration (interaction between students), tutoring (interaction between students and TAs), and data exchange (interaction among the Web components themselves). Furthermore, awareness features should be provided explicitly. Although several institutions have recently developed Web-based experimentation environments (Atkan, Bohus, Crowl, & Shor, 1996; Faltin, Böhne, Tuttas, & Wagner, 2002; Ogot, Elliott, & Glumac, 2003; Schmid, 1998; Tzafestas, Alifragis, & Palaiologou, 2005), no one satisfies all these requirements. Such environments have mostly focused on the interaction between the students and the experimentation resources. In some cases (e.g., Faltin et al., 2002), students have been provided with a shared workspace such as BSCW (http://bscw.gmd.de). However, the collaboration, the tutoring, and the data exchange in the context of flexible engineering education are still very limited or not supported.

Flexible learning and Web-based experimentation resources have been integrated progressively within the automatic control course in the engineering curricula at the EPFL. This chapter describes the valuation scheme and results obtained between the 2000 winter and the 2005 summer semesters regarding the deployment of the flexible scenario and the associated Web-based experimentation environment called eMersion for the course mentioned previously. The next section deals with some evaluation issues concerning Web-based experimentation environments. Then the model proposed for the evaluation of such online learning environments is detailed. A section is also dedicated to the presentation of the successive designs and refinements implemented. The following section is about the evaluation instruments and results. Finally, the chapter ends with some concluding remarks.

Evaluation Issues of Web-Based Experimentation Environments

User-centered evaluation is a newly emerging facet of the Web-based experimentation environment development. Evaluation is one of the main challenges as well

Copyright © 2007, Idea Group Inc. Copying or distributing in print or electronic forms without written permission of Idea Group Inc. is prohibited.

as a prerequisite that could allow students to profitably exploit the environment. In single-user applications, it is already difficult to test the perceptual, cognitive, motor variables (Card, Moran, & Newell, 1983). It is however extremely difficult to evaluate multi-user applications (Grudin, 1988), especially to evaluate Web-based experimentation environments that support collaborative hands-on activities where many interactions take place at both a technical and a social level. Another very important point that needs to be evaluated is the learning performance of students participating in such an online course. In the traditional classroom, there are several methods that the tutor can use to evaluate students' learning process and to know about the students' progress. In an online environment, the tutor can mainly evaluate what he/she has access to.

Some initial attempts to evaluate Web-based learning environments in engineering education have been reported in Faltin et al. (2002), Ogot et al. (2003), Roppel, Hung, Wentworth, and Hodel (2000), and Tzafestas et al. (2005). These works have considered employing existing usability engineering methods applied to a small population of students. The favorite methods employed were empirical ones (Rosson & Carroll, 2002) such as field study, usability testing in a laboratory, or controlled experiments. In fact, various important aspects related to the online learning community in Web-based experimentation environments have been neglected. Actually, the evaluation should provide answers to questions about participation, learning performance, flexibility, collaboration, and social structure of the online learning community. The variety and complexity of the interaction processes and the need to consider the system from both social and technical stages of view (Nguyen-Ngoc, Rekik, & Gillet, 2005b) require mixed and integrated evaluation methods that combine different sources of data and different analysis techniques applied at different phases from the analysis to the design, and up to the exploitation stages of the environment. By using different sources and methods at various points in the evaluation process, the evaluators can build on the strength observed and minimize the weakness identified. A multi-method approach to evaluation can increase both the validity and reliability of evaluation data (Frechtling & Sharp, 1997).

The eMersion environment (Gillet et al., 2003; Gillet, Nguyen-Ngoc, & Rekik, 2005) has been iteratively designed, developed, and deployed since the year 2000 on a semester basis. A model for the evaluation of Web-based experimentation environments has emerged from this iterative process. Then it has been generalized with the aim of providing a new structured framework to cope with the specific requirements of evaluating online learning environments in engineering education. This evaluation model, the instrumentation feedback model for evaluation, is detailed in the next section.

Copyright © 2007, Idea Group Inc. Copying or distributing in print or electronic forms without written permission of Idea Group Inc. is prohibited.

Instrumentation Feedback Model for Evaluation

The term *instrumentation feedback model* was coined in the work of Leifer (1997). This term is used in the sense of observing both independent and dependent variables in an automatic feedback control environment.

Our model includes five instrumentation nodes (see Figure 2). Each one represents a phase in the process of learning using the online environment. The outcomes are differentiated into levels, and each of them is evaluated and validated through a feedback path. The output of the evaluation process at one node could provide feedback and influence the input of another node.

The input of the whole process is the online course requirements. From these requirements, the pedagogical scenario can be designed. It is important to integrate the design and the development process around scenarios. Scenarios have people built-in, they are specific, they are grounded in the real world, and they describe an existing or envisioned system from the perspective of participative and non-participative users, including a narration of their goals, plans, and reactions (Rosson & Carroll, 2002). At Node 1, the pedagogical objectives and the course requirements are already defined. Based on these definitions, the course environment is designed or redesigned. By redesigned, we mean that some fundamental concepts of the environment need to be modified or replaced. At Node 2, the tutors and the students' requirements are defined in greater detail. The system functionalities that facilitate the online learning activities are also specified at this node.

The evaluation is carried out at Node 3 and Node 4, for the innermost, formative evaluation loop from Node 3 to Node 2, or in other words, the formative evaluation process takes place during the course. The goal of the formative evaluation is to identify the aspects of the system that can be improved, and to provide guidance on what to change in the design. One big constraint in applying formative evaluation is that it must not disturb the students who are currently using the system. Thus, in general, only minor modifications of the system functionalities are allowed. The summative evaluation loop at Node 4 is aimed at measuring the acceptability of the system (Nielsen, 1993). The summative evaluation loop may lead to the modification of the pedagogical scenario (the loop from Node 4 to Node 0) or to the redesign of the environment (the loop from Node 4 to Node 1).

In the proposed model, all the analysis methods are fed with data coming from different sources, meeting the need for capturing different forms of interaction in an online engineering learning community. The basic instruments providing quantitative data are automatic data coming from the log, questionnaires, and the student's learning performance. In a Web-based experimentation environment like eMersion, the *artifact-based log* constitutes an interesting support reflecting the student hands-on

Copyright © 2007, Idea Group Inc. Copying or distributing in print or electronic forms without written permission of Idea Group Inc. is prohibited.

Figure 2. Instrumentation Feedback Model for Evaluation

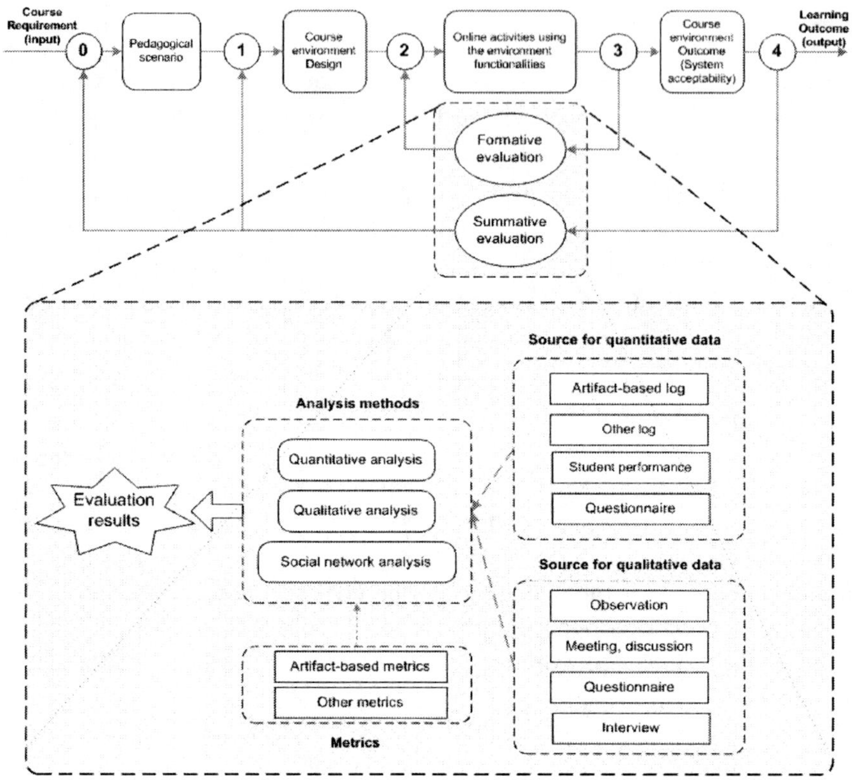

activities and interactions within the online community. The concept of artifact is used to represent any kind of data that could be saved, extracted, and analyzed during hands-on activities. It can be shared and can facilitate the interaction among members of the learning community. Because of the important role of the artifact-based log, it is separated from other forms of log. The instruments providing qualitative data are observations, interviews, and discussions directly with students and TAs.

The analysis methods include quantitative and qualitative analysis, and social network analysis. Social network analysis (SNA) methods are applied to construct the social structure and to find the interaction patterns in the learning community. SNA (Wasserman & Faust, 1994) is an approach that focuses on the study of patterns of relationships between members in a community.

Evidently, the choice of the evaluation methods may be changed from one course to the other. It depends on the pedagogical scenario as well as the evaluation objectives. Basically, the evaluation analyses are carried out to estimate predefined

Copyright © 2007, Idea Group Inc. Copying or distributing in print or electronic forms without written permission of Idea Group Inc. is prohibited.

metrics. We have proposed a set of candidate metrics that could be useful to measure the usability and the utility of the environment supporting the online engineering learning community. These metrics are briefly presented as follows:

- **Metrics for user learnability** (Shneiderman, 1998)**:** To measure the time and effort students spend to be able to use the environment and the resources provided to achieve specific tasks accurately and completely.
- **Metrics for user acceptability, participation, and satisfaction:** To see if students accept and participate in the new learning paradigm, and how satisfied they are.
- **Metrics for learning performance:** To see if there is any difference in learning performance when students carry out experimentation remotely compared with when they carry out experimentation locally.
- **Metrics for learning pattern:** To measure the possible patterns students prefer to follow in their online courses.
- **Metrics for environment comprehensiveness, effectiveness, and efficiency:** To measure if the environment provides all necessary information and functionalities to respond to the users' needs.
- **Metrics for flexibility:** To measure how often students participate in flexible sessions, how they divide tasks among members in the same group, and so forth.
- **Metrics for interaction in the community:** To measure the interaction patterns in the online engineering learning community.
- **Metrics for social structure in the community:** To measure the social relationships, the activeness, the knowledge distribution, and the mediation role of members in the online engineering learning community.

The proposed metrics are defined at a fairly high abstraction level. They can be somewhat considered as important features that need to be considered in order to evaluate an online learning environment, and more precisely speaking, a Web-based experimentation environment and the online learning community using that environment. Most of these metrics are based on the artifact analysis and calculation. Hence, they are called *artifact-based metrics*. Not all of these metrics need to be calculated. Again, the appropriate choice depends on the evaluation phase as well as on the evaluation objectives.

The following sections will be used to illustrate how this model has been applied to evaluate the automatic control laboratory course. First, we will present the course setting, and then discuss the iterative design of the eMersion environment that has been carried out for this course. Finally, the evaluation results will be presented.

Copyright © 2007, Idea Group Inc. Copying or distributing in print or electronic forms without written permission of Idea Group Inc. is prohibited.

The eMerson Design History

The Automatic Control Laboratory Course Setting

Traditional Automatic Control Course

The academic year at EPFL is divided into a winter and a summer semester. There is a strict separation between lectures, exercise sessions, and laboratory assignments set by the study programs and the course schedule. Every week, two hours of lectures are taught to the students enrolled, followed by one hour of in-class exercise supervised by a TA. The laboratory assignments, which can last for two or four hours depending on the degree program, are also completed under supervision of a TA.

Flexible Automatic Control Course

Flexible learning deployment implies some changes in pedagogical methods such as the structure, the presentation, and the organization of information. The pedagogical scenarios have been established and evaluated progressively from the year 2000. All laboratory assignments have been reorganized into two-hour modules. They are structured into three parts: introduction, experimentation, and examination. The introduction part is dedicated to the presentation of the learning objectives, the freedom offered by the flexible learning, and the learning tools. The experimentation part is split into three to seven hands-on modules depending on the degree programs in which the students are enrolled. The examination part is carried out as a laboratory test.

The hands-on modules are composed of two parts. The first one is dedicated to a preliminary analysis and design activity called the *prelab,* which has been introduced to ensure that students have the prior knowledge necessary to benefit from the hands-on experiment, and to motivate them to do preparatory work on their own. Students need to submit a prelab document to the TA to be granted the right to proceed further with the actual experimentation, called the *labwork.* The labwork consists of carrying out a real experiment and of validating the preliminary design on the physical device. No fixed schedule is imposed on the students; only the sequence of modules has to be followed. The laboratory test consists of performing a random module and then presenting the associated results to the tutor. The course lasts for 14 weeks.

The students enrolled in the course have the possibility of following different learning modalities. The modalities vary according to the presence of a TA, and according to the students' location. When group members work together in the presence of a TA, they are in f2f condition. Students can also work in flexible sessions and

Copyright © 2007, Idea Group Inc. Copying or distributing in print or electronic forms without written permission of Idea Group Inc. is prohibited.

remotely access the physical laboratory devices and/or computer simulation tools. In whichever learning modality, the students use the same Web-based experimentation environment, the eMersion environment.

The evolution history of the eMersion environment can be divided into four major periods, which started with the 2000 winter semester. These periods will be presented in the following sections.

The eMersion Evolution History

First Period, 2000 Winter Semester: Observation and Analysis

We proceeded with a classical f2f setting during the first year of the project. The students had regular f2f sessions with two TAs in a laboratory room. The laboratory workbenches were equipped with either an electrical drive or a thermal process trainer connected to a Macintosh computer through an analog/digital converter board. Several software applications were available on the computer: LabVIEW for controlling the connected device and acquiring sample data points, and SysQuake (http://www.calerga.com), which executes Matlab-compatible scripts for analysis and design.

The experts in education science observed a total of six hands-on sessions. Two hands-on sessions were slightly modified to conduct a controlled experiment for understanding the effect of distance in getting the TAs' help. For that purpose, the TAs were not present in the laboratory room, but they were accessible by telephone.

The observations have shown a cognitive overload for the students to master at the same time several user interfaces, mathematical analysis and design concepts, and the experiment itself. The students' working method was to save data produced by the LabVIEW application and/or snapshots of mathematical plots to local files that they could take home on a floppy disk and/or to print their results. The sessions with simulated distance showed that students did not use the telephone and preferred to get assistance from their co-located colleagues. They exchanged data using floppy disks and printed documents.

Second Period, 2001 Winter and 2002 Summer Semesters: The eMersion Version "Niceberg"

The main challenge of the second year was to experiment with a new organization of work. That organization was based on a mix of flexible sessions with planned f2f sessions. In flexible sessions students work without the presence of TAs, who were reachable asynchronously by telephone or by e-mail.

Copyright © 2007, Idea Group Inc. Copying or distributing in print or electronic forms without written permission of Idea Group Inc. is prohibited.

The eMersion environment was changed from a collection of standalone applications into a Web-based experimentation environment. The LabVIEW application was replaced with a Java applet, and the SysQuake application was replaced with SysQuake Remote, which is a thin-client consisting of a Web form for editing and submitting scripts to a SysQuake engine located on a server. In addition, online manuals, online experimentation protocol, bibliography, and reference documents were also available in the environment. Figure 3 shows the environment portal (available only in French) from which students can perform experiments and can use the different facilities provided.

During these semesters we introduced two preliminary versions of shared workspaces for students working online. The first one called *Niceberg* was based on a Web-based content management system. The second one called the *Lab Journal* was a Web-based shared workspace that provided various editing functionalities. Niceberg integrated a desktop with a forum, a space for accessing the submitted laboratory reports, and various facilities for supporting students working online. The TA had access to the laboratory reports submitted and could annotate these reports with structured notes. The Lab Journal provided several workspaces for structured text fragments (in forms of XML fragments) imported from other documents, for manual notes, images, and electronic messages (see Figure 4). All these documents could be combined together to form a report. Both Niceberg and the Lab Journal

Figure 3. The eMersion portal of a group

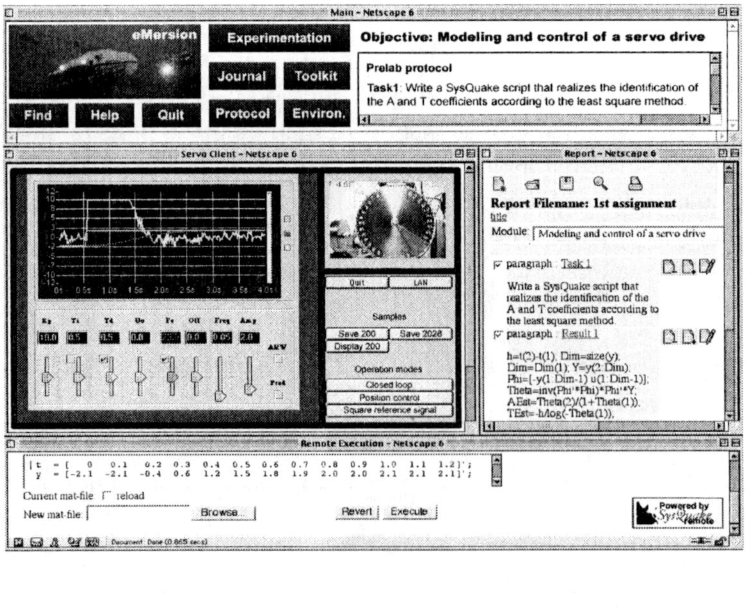

Copyright © 2007, Idea Group Inc. Copying or distributing in print or electronic forms without written permission of Idea Group Inc. is prohibited.

Figure 4. The Lab Journal user interface

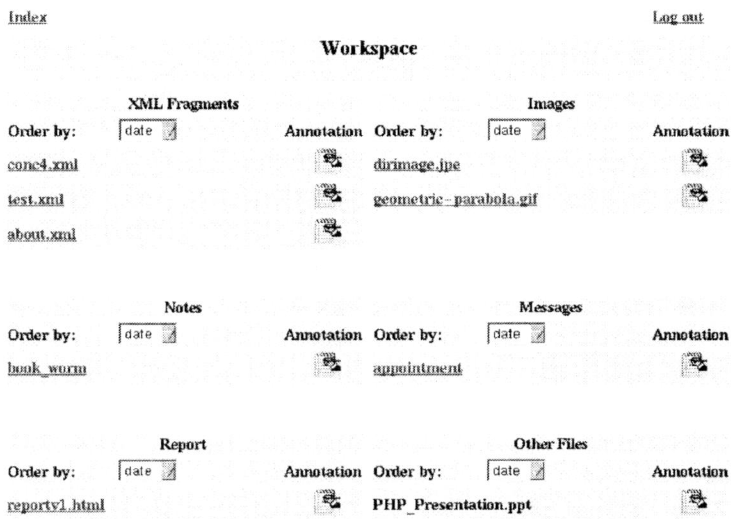

had functionalities that allowed students to submit their reports to the TA. The access to these journals was based on password identification, but everybody could see the files in other students' journals except for those that were marked as hidden by the owners.

In fact, the Lab Journal has played the role of an electronic laboratory journal for *each* group. Laboratory journals take a privileged place in engineering education (McCormack, Morrow, Bar, Burns, & Rasmussen, 1991; Myers et al., 1991). They serve as chronological repositories for experimentation resources, planning, and realization. Laboratory journals, as a special kind of document archive, are used extensively by students in the execution of their own work and to share information with others. The activity history, the details, the results of a series of experiments, and the knowledge developed can be captured in a laboratory journal and then be reused in the same or in another session by the same or by another student. The metaphor of laboratory journals can acquire the collaboration support property of paper and paper-like instruments within a community, which has been demonstrated through many empirical studies (e.g., Schmidt & Bannon, 1992; Sellen & Harper, 2002). To summarize, an electronic laboratory journal that combines the peculiarities of a paper laboratory journal with the features of database systems and Web access is an appropriate instrument for sustaining collaboration and interaction in a Web-based experimentation environment.

The observations and the focus groups gave rise to a lot of criticism on the environment. The forum that had not been used in the 2001 winter was removed for the

Copyright © 2007, Idea Group Inc. Copying or distributing in print or electronic forms without written permission of Idea Group Inc. is prohibited.

summer semester and replaced with a messaging system embedded in the students' workspaces. However this messaging system was also not used; students preferred e-mail as a means for communication within the community. In both prototypes the structured editing functionalities were not used as they were complicated, and in addition, students preferred to create reports with a real-text editor such as MS Word. For data collection, students had to cut and paste information from the Experimentation applet's output console to a text editor and save it to a local file. In fact, the students used the journals only for submitting reports to the TAs. As a result, the main goal of the journal, which was for collecting data and for supporting data sharing and exchange among students in the community, was not fulfilled at all.

We attributed the failure of the journals to a wrong choice of functionalities and to a poor design of the user interface. First, the structured notes editing functions were not appropriate. Second, it was too difficult and required many extra steps to import data into the journals from the other components such as the Experimentation applet. The difficulty of importing data into the journals and the flexible context were the source of the discontinuity of interaction (Nguyen-Ngoc, Rekik, & Gillet, 2005b), which clearly prevented the collaboration and interaction in the online engineering learning community, and also complicated the student hands-on tasks.

Third Period, 2002 Winter to 2004 Summer Semester: eMersion 1

The lessons learned from the first two periods led us to redesign the eMersion environment. The eMersion 1 environment included three main components: the Experimentation Console for experimentation activities; the Lab Journal, which was renamed *eJournal*, as a collaboration space; and the Toolkit Console, which was the SysQuake Remote component for mathematical analysis and design. In the Experimentation Console, the equipment was visualized in real time using a Web cam. The image quality was improved using virtual reality techniques that gave students more feeling of *reality*. Students could choose between different modes of connection such as LAN or ADSL. Using the eJournal, students could import/export a set of parameters, as well as save the experimentation results and snapshots displayed on the Experimentation Console. The experimentation results stored in the eJournal could then be processed using SysQuake Remote. This point was quite important since it facilitated the continuity of interaction within the community while carrying out the experiments (Nguyen-Ngoc et al., 2005b).

The interface of the eMersion 1 environment is illustrated in Figure 5.

The eJournal was completely redesigned. All complex structured text editing and asynchronous messaging functionalities were removed. Its role of supporting interaction and collaboration in the online engineering learning community was stressed. The eJournal main space looked like the mailbox of an e-mail client, except that it did not contain e-mail but rich-type documents (see Figure 6), namely *fragments*.

Copyright © 2007, Idea Group Inc. Copying or distributing in print or electronic forms without written permission of Idea Group Inc. is prohibited.

Figure 5. The eMersion 1 environment as used to remotely control an electrical drive

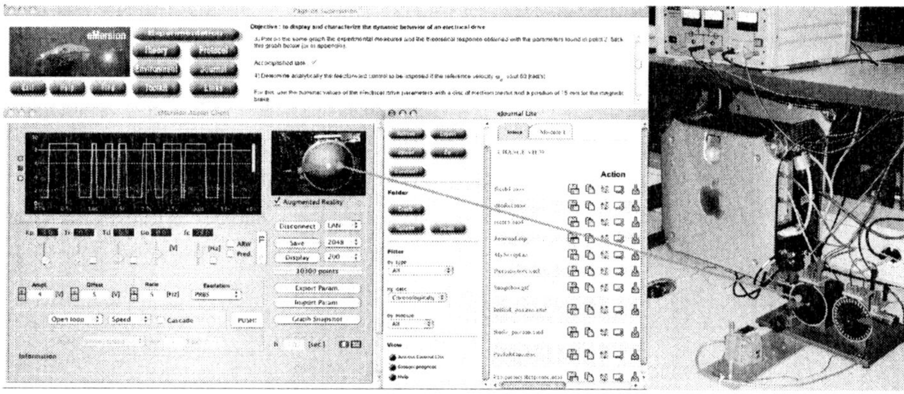

In fact the concept of fragments also plays the role of artifacts as presented in the instrumentation Feedback model for evaluation. Any fragment was typed, representing different kinds of data. The fragments with different types were handled differently. Tags could be assigned to fragments when they were created in order to ease their processing and sharing. A list of tags corresponding to the assigned tasks was automatically generated from the experimentation protocol.

Figure 6. The eJournal interface in the eMersion 1 environment

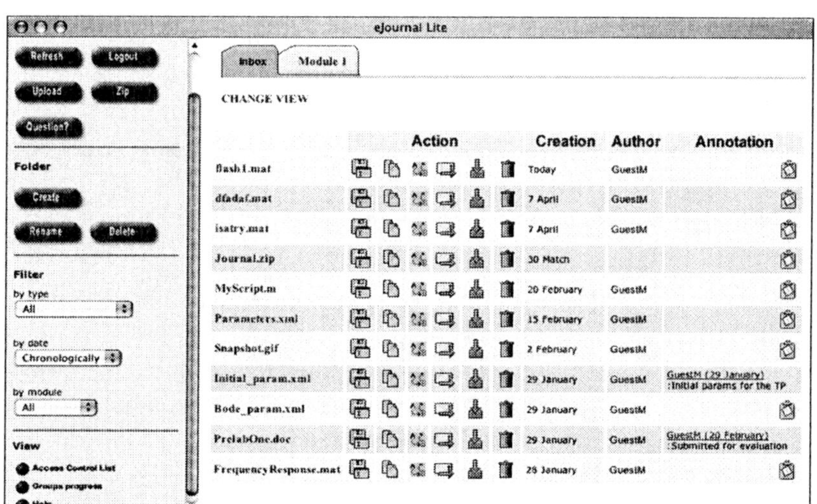

Copyright © 2007, Idea Group Inc. Copying or distributing in print or electronic forms without written permission of Idea Group Inc. is prohibited.

Using the eJournal, the members of the online engineering learning community were provided with many different ways to collaborate with one another. Students could submit their fragments to the TA. The fragments could be annotated. In the 2002 winter semester, two different annotation systems were provided: one was Wiki based, which allowed students freely to create and edit Web page content linked to the fragment, and another was based on a simple HTML form. Students could directly send fragments with associated annotations, or send questions with attached fragments to other groups or to TA via an integrated e-mail system. This mechanism was used for prelab submission, and it could be used to get contextualized support. Students could also copy/move fragments from one eJournal to another. The fragment was at the same time an instrument and a result of the interaction and collaboration process. As an example, the experimental results of a student are saved in his eJournal when he has finished his assignment, and shared with his group colleagues for further processing in the next assignment.

The eJournal enabled many services that generate awareness information. Besides the availability awareness such as the user presence and the user location, many other kinds of group awareness based on the fragment activities analysis and calculation, called *fragment-based awareness,* were also provided in an external page. Such awareness provided information about group activities, group progress, and the social structure of the community (Nguyen-Ngoc, Gillet, & Sire, 2004b).

Fourth Period, 2005 Summer Semester: eMersion 2

The eMersion 1 environment almost fulfilled all the designers' and the students' expectations. However, the incremental adaptations carried out during the course of its utilization made the code not as clean as it should have been. In addition, partner institutions mentioned their interest for using the environment for their own courses. Hence, it was decided to completely rewrite the code to make it more modular for further adaptations and for release under an open source scheme. The functionalities provided by the environment were regrouped as services, and the possibility of integrating new tools supporting the online community as plug-ins was implemented.

The resulting eMersion 2 also better integrates awareness features. Relevant information for the group and the class progresses are displayed in real time. Hence, it better supports students' self-motivation and autonomy development while using the online environment. The experimentation protocol was also redefined so that each task requires a *deliverable,* which is what the students are supposed to achieve after finishing a task. Basically, the student needs to respond and/or submit a deliverable in order to pass to the next task. Different kinds of deliverables could be defined. However, for this version a deliverable can only be a fragment. Depending on the experimentation modules, the deliverables for a task could be mandatory or elective.

Copyright © 2007, Idea Group Inc. Copying or distributing in print or electronic forms without written permission of Idea Group Inc. is prohibited.

This means that, for some tasks, the students just work for themselves. In such a case they can simply *finalize* the current task by *tagging* the fragment in an appropriate way. For this purpose, a status flag has also been added in the eJournal (which is another form of awareness). When a fragment is finalized, the flag is changed and the progress indicators are updated. When a fragment is submitted, the flag is changed, the progress indicators are updated, and the fragment is sent to the TA.

Figure 7 illustrates this new user interface of the eJournal. The two visible flags enable one to change the language of the GUI *on-the-fly*.

Figure 7. The eJournal interface in eMersion 2

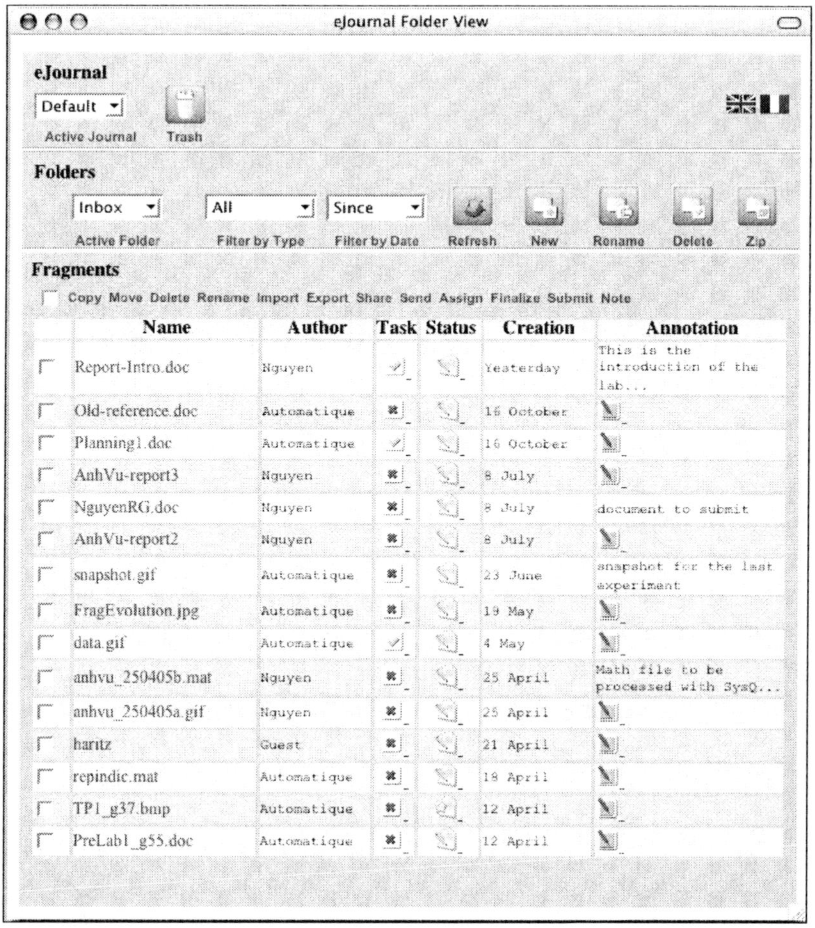

Copyright © 2007, Idea Group Inc. Copying or distributing in print or electronic forms without written permission of Idea Group Inc. is prohibited.

Evaluation of the Automatic Control Course

Evaluation Instruments

This section presents the results of a comparative evaluation study carried out from the 2002 winter to the 2005 summer semesters. The evaluation took place in an iterative process through the different loops presented with the purpose of studying the participation, learning performance, flexibility, collaboration, and social structure aspects of an online engineering learning community. Another objective was to improve the user interface design.

During the course, the developer and the evaluator were present in the laboratory with TA and students (f2f modality). By observing the behavior of the students and the TA, and by talking with them whenever they faced problems in using the environment, the evaluator could find the potential bugs of the system as well as different minor aspects of the system that could be improved. The log data also helped to facilitate this formative evaluation process. This evaluation loop (from Node 3 to Node 2 in the Evaluation Model) iterated during the whole semester.

At the end of the semester, questionnaires were distributed to the students. Our questionnaires were based on the IBM CSUQ Questionnaire (Lewis, 1993) with some extensions (Nguyen-Ngoc, Gillet, & Sire, 2004a). The questionnaires were used to measure the metrics for user acceptability, participation, and satisfaction.

The fragment-based log was also analyzed. Fragments that originated from components of the Web-based environment and which were directly imported to the eJournal were called *intra-fragments.* Fragments that were uploaded from a local user's computer were called *extra-fragments.* These were created using external applications. Fragments that were created during f2f sessions were called *f2f-fragments,* while those created during flexible learning modalities were called *flexible-fragments.* The intra-fragments helped to observe the amount of student work that took place within the Web-based environment. This measure reflected the metrics of environment comprehensiveness, effectiveness, and efficiency. The flexible-fragments measure was linked to the importance of f2f learning modalities compared with flexible learning modalities—that is, the metrics for flexibility.

The volunteer students were interviewed. The tutor also organized a meeting in which all TAs of the course could express their ideas and their comments about the environment.

One should bear in mind that the result of the summative evaluation loop could cause major modifications and improvements of the environment for the following semesters. For each evaluation loop, different analysis methods were carried out.

Copyright © 2007, Idea Group Inc. Copying or distributing in print or electronic forms without written permission of Idea Group Inc. is prohibited.

The next section shows some of the results from the evaluation process carried out in the automatic control laboratory courses during these five semesters at the EPFL.

Evaluation Population

- In the 2002 winter semester, 30 students enrolled in the fourth year of the mechanical engineering degree program participated in the course. For the sake of simplicity, this sample was called Group Winter 2002.
- In the 2003 summer semester, 96 students enrolled in the third year of the micro-engineering degree program participated in the course. This represented the Group Summer 2003.
- In the 2003 winter semester, 49 students from mechanical engineering and 6 students from electrical engineering enrolled in the course. They were fourth-year students. This represented the Group Winter 2003.
- In the 2004 summer semester, 47 students from electrical engineering, 97 students from micro-engineering, and 12 students from mechanical engineering participated in the course. They were all third-year students. This represented the Group Summer 2004.
- In the 2004 winter semester, there was no course.
- In the 2005 summer semester, 39 students from electrical engineering, 69 students from micro-engineering, and 9 students from mechanical engineering participated in the course. They were all third-year students. This represented the Group Summer 2005.

In total, during this period of five semesters, 454 students used the eMersion environment to perform hands-on activities. The evaluation results have been reported elsewhere (Fakas, Nguyen-Ngoc, & Gillet, 2005; Gillet et al., 2005; Nguyen-Ngoc et al., 2004a; Nguyen-Ngoc et al., 2005a). For the sake of simplicity, only *representative* results will be presented and discussed here.

Evaluation Results

Metrics for User Satisfaction

Among the 181 students enrolled in the course from the 2002 winter to the 2003 winter semester, 129 returned the questionnaires distributed (71.3%). In these three semesters, we encouraged students to spend some time to fill in the questionnaires and return them right after the laboratory test. In the 2004 summer semester, stu-

Copyright © 2007, Idea Group Inc. Copying or distributing in print or electronic forms without written permission of Idea Group Inc. is prohibited.

Figure 8. Mean of satisfaction (2002 winter to 2005 summer semesters)

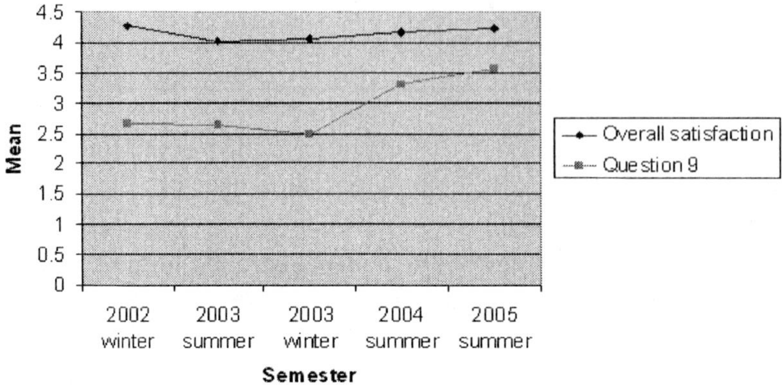

dents could return the questionnaires approximately one month after the test. In fact, this was an examination period at the EPFL, and only 22 questionnaires were returned (14%). From the experience obtained from the 2004 summer semester, we also prepared an electronic version of the questionnaire accessible to all enrolled students in the 2005 summer semester. For this semester, 74 questionnaires were filled in and returned (62.2%). Figure 8 shows the mean of overall satisfaction, and that for question 9: "The system provides error messages that clearly help me to resolve problems." This question received the worst ranking and greatly reduced the general satisfaction. In fact, as implementing a help system is quite time consuming and it was not the priority of the development team, only basic features were provided. Although this bad score was not a surprise, it was an example of the difficulty of providing an efficient help system for an online community. It is interesting to underscore that despite the fact that no help system was introduced, the 2004 and 2005 results are significantly better. This shows that a well-designed environment does not necessarily need a help system to be understood and used, while a bad one requires additional support resources.

Students were also asked to provide the three most positive and three most negative aspects (in order of importance) at the end of the questionnaires concerning the usage of the environment and the environment itself. The most frequent positive comment of the system was its flexibility. The integration of all the necessary tools in one integrated environment also appears to be important in the students' positive comments. Students also enjoyed different interactive and collaborative features provided by the eJournal. They also liked the hands-on activities that reinforced their theoretical knowledge. The majority of negative comments concerned technical problems (e.g., server and client crashes) and the complexity of the interface (many windows for many tools).

Copyright © 2007, Idea Group Inc. Copying or distributing in print or electronic forms without written permission of Idea Group Inc. is prohibited.

Metrics for Environment Comprehensiveness, Metrics for Flexibility

We carried out the analysis of fragment logs for all five semesters. On average, about 86% of the fragments were created within the environment with the Experimentation component and the SysQuake Remote component; the other 14% were fragments created with external applications and then uploaded to the environment (e.g., MS Word documents). The number of fragments created in flexible sessions corresponded to 42.6%. The intra-fragment and flexible-fragment measures of each semester are shown in Figure 9.

One should recall that the summative evaluation loop (from Node 4 to Node 1 in the evaluation model) at the end of the semester provides feedback for the system design for the next semester. The summative evaluation results may lead to fundamental modifications of the environment. During the 2002 winter semester, we proposed two annotation mechanisms; one was based on the Wiki mechanism. However, very few students used this annotation mechanism. Thus in the next version for the 2003 summer semester, this mechanism was dropped. Since the 2003 summer semester version, the possibility of sustaining the continuity of interaction has been improved. As a consequence, the intra-fragments and the flexible-fragments have increased greatly from 76.67% and 26.29% in the 2002 winter semester, to 86% and 55% in the 2003 summer semester. Since then, the flexible-fragment ratio has slightly decreased. This might be explained by the fact that more teaching assistants were available in f2f sessions. Thus students benefited more in working directly with them in the laboratory. In addition, in 2004 and 2005, enough workbenches were available for all the students to work simultaneously. This was not the case

Figure 9. Fragment measures (2002 winter to 2005 summer semesters)

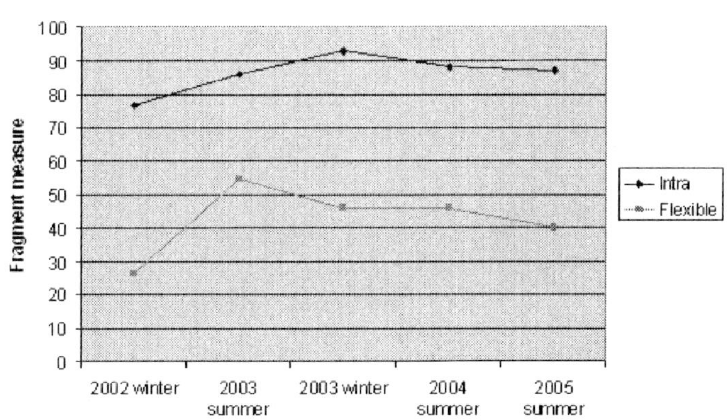

Copyright © 2007, Idea Group Inc. Copying or distributing in print or electronic forms without written permission of Idea Group Inc. is prohibited.

in 2002 and 2003. It was in fact a logistical constraint that was initially the main motivation for the development of the eMersion environment. Later, the pedagogical motivations became more important.

To have a clear view about these fragments, one should see the examples in Figures 10 and 11. In these figures, each column represents the number of created fragments by a micro-engineering group of the Group Summer 2004. In each column, the white part represents the intra-fragments. The black part represents the extra-fragments. Figure 11 represents the same data but from another perspective. The black part shows the fragments that were created in f2f sessions, while the white part is the number of fragments created in flexible sessions.

One should not forget that we applied more or less the same evaluation methods for the evaluation loops. However, the evaluation variables and parameters for the next loop (or next semester) may be modified depending on the result and on the requirements.

Metrics for Learning Performance

Since the 2003 summer semester, we started considering the group performance (via the grade of the group members). Analysis in the Group Winter 2003 and Group Summer 2004 showed that there was a statistically significant correlation between the number of created fragments and the group performance (obtained via the groups'

Figure 10. Intra- and extra-fragments produced by micro-engineering groups during 2004 summer semester

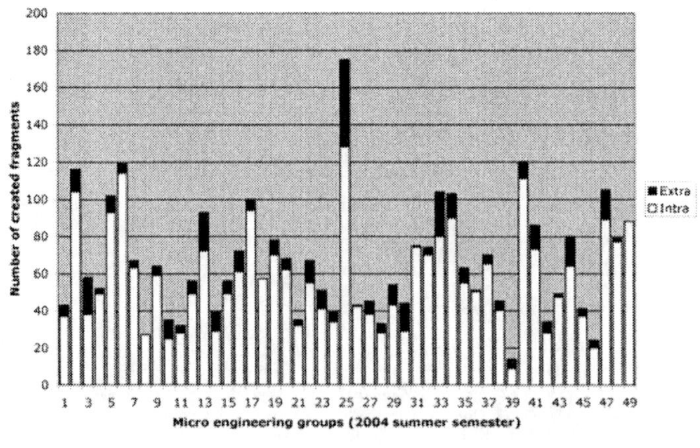

Copyright © 2007, Idea Group Inc. Copying or distributing in print or electronic forms without written permission of Idea Group Inc. is prohibited.

Figure 11. F2f- and flexible-fragments produced by micro-engineering groups during 2004 summer semester

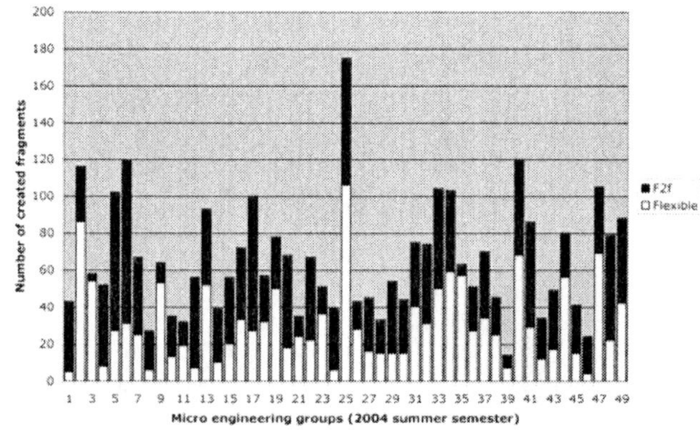

grades). The Pearson product-moment coefficient correlation between these two variables was 0.522 ($p<0.01$) for the Group Winter 2003, 0.296 ($p<0.05$) for the Group Summer 2004, and 0.3 ($p<0.05$) for the Group Summer 2005. We have found no statistical correlation between these two variables in the Group Summer 2003.

We divided all groups into two sub-groups: the first one preferred working in flexible modalities (high flexibility groups), the second one worked mostly in f2f modalities (low flexibility groups). This classification was based on the flexible-fragments of all groups. A group was classified as high flexibility if its flexible-fragments were more than or equal to 50%. Actually, for the Group Summer 2003, the grade mean of high and low flexibility groups was 5.04 over 6 (S.D.=0.58) and 5.07 (S.D.=0.6), respectively; for the Group Winter 2003, these were 5.05 (S.D.=0.69) and 5.12 (S.D.=0.56); for the Group Summer 2004, both sub-groups received the same grade mean of 4.3 (S.D.=1.05); and finally for the Group Summer 2005, these were 4.69 (S.D.= 1.1) and 4.65 (S.D.=1.12).

The results showed that there was no significant difference between the educational outcomes from students who performed the experiment remotely compared with those who preferred carrying out the experiments in f2f sessions.

Metrics for Learning Pattern

Since the 2003 summer semester, we have considered the learning pattern of students in the online engineering learning community. In the 2003 summer semester,

Copyright © 2007, Idea Group Inc. Copying or distributing in print or electronic forms without written permission of Idea Group Inc. is prohibited.

Figure 12. Cumulative number of fragments created each day of the week during the 2004 summer semester

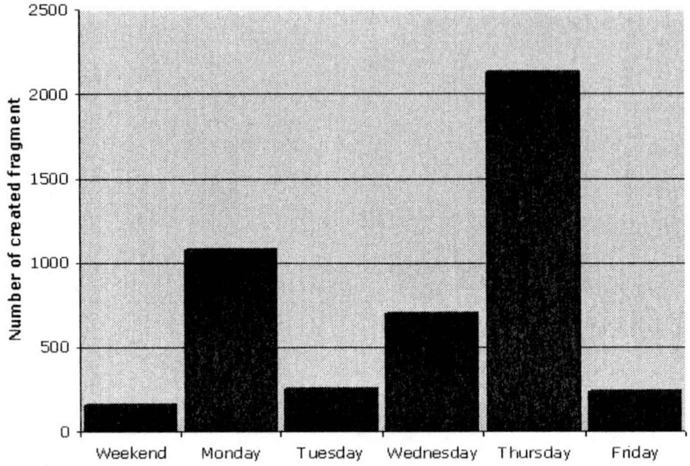

1.4% of fragments were created during weekends, and 2.5% of fragments created in the evening and at night—that is, from 6:00 p.m. to 7:00 a.m. the next day. These numbers were 6.6%-4.4% and 3.5%-17.4% in the 2003 winter and 2004 summer semesters, respectively.

We noted that students worked most actively on the days in which there were laboratory sessions. Figure 12 shows a histogram illustrating the cumulative total number of fragments created each day of the week during the 2004 summer semester. In this semester, there was one f2f session every Thursday (from 10:15 a.m. to 12:00 noon) for groups from micro-engineering degree programs, and every Monday (from 5:15-7:00 p.m.) for groups from mechanical and electrical engineering degree programs.

Metrics for Interaction and Social Structure

Last but not least, we performed different SNA methods to find the interaction patterns between different groups, as well as the social structure in the community. The SNA methods have been carried out since the 2003 summer semester. For establishing the community structure and interaction patterns, we were interested in those techniques giving information about structural properties of the network as a whole, and particularly those related to cohesion (Woodreff, 1999) such as sociogram, clique, and Freeman's centrality degree (Wasserman & Faust, 1994). These methods were applied to each semester to provide so-called *social structure awareness* for tutors and TAs (Nguyen-Ngoc et al., 2004b). As an example, Figure

Copyright © 2007, Idea Group Inc. Copying or distributing in print or electronic forms without written permission of Idea Group Inc. is prohibited.

Figure 13. Sociograms of the interactions found during the 2004 summer semester

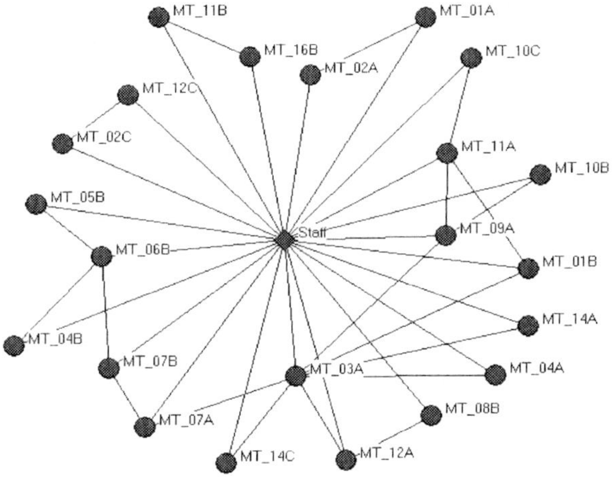

13 shows a sociogram representing the social structure established in the Group Summer 2004 community.

In a sociogram, nodes (circles) represent groups, and lines represent the interaction between groups. Different shapes and colors are used to refer to some special groups. For example, the Staff group (tutors and TAs) is represented by the central diamond.

Discussion

The metrics calculated previously help to answer most of our evaluation objectives—that is, to study various aspects of an online engineering community. We find the results satisfactory concerning the "acceptability goal" as shown by the metrics for user satisfaction. However, the mean satisfaction is not much higher than the neutral scale point, thus suggesting much room for improvement.

The participation goal is also reached as all the groups created a significant number of fragments. As a corollary, we believe that the "participation goal" contributes to the "acceptability goal" as evidence of the use of the environment.

The metrics for environment completeness and metrics for flexibility show that the students took advantage of different learning modalities. These metrics also show that the system functionalities satisfy the needs of students while performing online hands-on activities.

Copyright © 2007, Idea Group Inc. Copying or distributing in print or electronic forms without written permission of Idea Group Inc. is prohibited.

SNA contributed to identifying the interaction patterns at different levels: the community, the group, and the individual. It also shows the interaction in time—that is, the interaction between students from different semesters. In fact the metrics for interaction and social structure show that staff members still play the most important role in the knowledge distribution within the community. The SNA measure can be used not only at the evaluation phase, but also during the learning process to provide awareness information to tutors and students. It gives tutors and students a general overview of active and passive groups in the learning community, as well as the structure of the community.

The statistical analysis shows that there might be correlation between the number of created fragments and the group performance. The validation procedure should be refined to confirm this assertion. We should also consider other variables that may affect the performance, such as group motivation, previous knowledge, and experience. The result from comparing the groups who preferred working in flexible modalities (high-flexibility groups) and those who worked mostly in f2f modalities (low-flexibility groups) supports the assumption that the Web-based learning environment is an *added value* for traditional engineering education (Gillet et al., 2005).

The evaluation loops also allow us to improve the user interface of the environment. This helps us know exactly what students really want in an online environment.

Conclusion

This chapter presents the iterative design and the evaluation of a Web-based experimentation environment deployed in engineering education, namely eMersion. The eMersion environment provides an excellent support for the deployment of a flexible learning paradigm in engineering curricula.

The chapter also presents the eJournal, an extended electronic laboratory journal, which is an implementation of what we called a mediation artifact or a collaboration artifact (Nguyen-Ngoc et al., 2004b, 2005b). The deployment and evaluation of the system over a long period of time have confirmed the adequacy of the chosen metaphor. It has also confirmed the important role of the laboratory journal in supporting collaborative learning activities in an online learning community.

This chapter proposes a model, namely the instrumentation feedback model for evaluation, for the assessment of online learning communities using Web-based experimentation environments. The model encourages an iterative evaluation process. The evaluation is carried out at different stages of the learning process through different evaluation loops. At each loop, different evaluation analysis methods—including qualitative and quantitative analysis, and Social Network Analysis—could be

Copyright © 2007, Idea Group Inc. Copying or distributing in print or electronic forms without written permission of Idea Group Inc. is prohibited.

combined to provide evaluators with a maximum of data representing the different aspects of the online community. These analysis methods are fed with data coming from different sources, meeting the need for capturing different forms of interaction in the usage of a Web-based experimentation environment. The model opens up a new set of ways for evaluating online learning communities in engineering education. This model has been generalized from and validated by the experience gained from successive semesters. Although so far the model is only used for evaluating the automatic control laboratory courses and the eMersion environment at the EPFL, it is generic enough to apply to other pedagogical scenarios and other learning environments.

This chapter describes the results and analyses of the evaluation process carried out in the automatic control laboratory courses from the 2002 winter to the 2005 summer semesters at the EPFL.

Acknowledgments

The elements presented in this chapter result from various e-learning projects and activities carried out with the support of the Board of the Swiss Federal Institutes of Technology and of the European Union in the fifth and sixth framework programs (http://www.prolearn-project.org).

References

Atkan, B., Bohus, C. A., Crowl, L. A., & Shor, M. H. (1996). Distance learning applied to control engineering laboratories. *IEEE Transactions on Education, 39*(3), 320-326.

Card, S. K., Moran, T. P., & Newell, A. (1983). *The psychology of human-computer interaction.* London: Erlbaum.

Dourish, P., & Bellotti, V. (1992). Awareness and coordination in shared workspaces. *Proceedings of the Conference on Computer-Supported Cooperative Work* (CSCW), Toronto, Canada.

Fakas, G., Nguyen-Ngoc, A. V., & Gillet, D. (2005). The electronic journal: A collaborative and cooperative learning environment for Web-based experimentation. *Computer-Supported Cooperative Work (CSCW): The Journal of Collaborative Computing, 14*(3), 189-216.

Copyright © 2007, Idea Group Inc. Copying or distributing in print or electronic forms without written permission of Idea Group Inc. is prohibited.

Faltin, N., Böhne, A., Tuttas, J., & Wagner, B. (2002, August 18-21). Distributed team learning in an Internet-assisted laboratory. *Proceedings of the International Conference on Engineering Education,* Manchester, UK.

Frechtling, J., & Sharp, L. (1997). *User-friendly handbook for mixed method evaluation.* Directorate for Education and Human Resources, Division of Research, Evaluation, and Communication.

Gillet, D. (2003). Towards flexible learning in engineering education. In W. Aung, R. Altenkirch, T. Cermak, R. W. King, & L. M. S. Ruiz (Eds.), *Innovations 2004: World innovations in engineering education and research* (pp. 95-102). New York: iNEER in cooperation with Begell House Publishing.

Gillet, D., Geoffroy, F., Zeramdini, K., Nguyen-Ngoc, A. V., Rekik, Y., & Piguet, Y. (2003). The cockpit, an effective metaphor for Web-based experimentation in engineering education. *International Journal of Engineering Education, 19*(3), 389-397.

Gillet, D., Nguyen-Ngoc, A. V., & Rekik, Y. (2005). Collaborative Web-based experimentation in flexible engineering education. *IEEE Transactions on Education, Special Issue on Web-based Instruction, 48*(4), 696-704.

Grudin, J. (1988). Why CSCW applications fail. *Proceedings of the Conference on Computer-Supported Cooperative Work (CSCW)*, Portland, OR.

Kazmer, M. M., & Haythornthwaite, C. (2005). Multiple perspectives on online learning. *ACM SIGGROUP Bulletin, 25.*

Leifer, L. (1997). Design team performance: Metrics and the impact of technology. In *Evaluating corporate training: Models and issues.* Kluwer.

Lewis, J. R. (1993). *IBM computer usability satisfaction questionnaires: Psychometric evaluation and instructions for use.* Boca Raton, FL: IBM Corporation.

McCormack, J. B., Morrow, R. K., Bar, H. F., Burns, R. J., & Rasmussen, J. L. (1991). The complementary roles of the laboratory notebooks and laboratory reports. *IEEE Transactions on Education, 34*(1).

Mosterman, P., Dorlandt, A. M., Olin Campbell, J., Burow, C., Bouw, R., Brodersen, A. J. et al. (1994). Virtual engineering laboratories: Design and experiments. *Journal of Engineering Education, 83*(3), 279-285.

Myers, J. D., Fox-Dobbs, C., Laird, J., Le, D., Reich, D., & Curtz, T. (1991). Electronic laboratory notebooks for collaborative research. *Proceedings of the Proceedings of the 5th Workshop on Enabling Technologies: Infrastructure for Collaborative Enterprises,* Stanford.

Nguyen-Ngoc, A. V., Gillet, D., & Sire, S. (2004a). Evaluation of a Web-based learning environment for hands-on experimentation. In W. Aung, R. Altenkirch, T. Cermak, R. W. King, & L. M. S. Ruiz (Eds.), *Innovations 2004: World innovations in engineering education and research* (pp. 303-315). New York: iNEER in cooperation with Begell House Publishing.

Copyright © 2007, Idea Group Inc. Copying or distributing in print or electronic forms without written permission of Idea Group Inc. is prohibited.

Nguyen-Ngoc, A. V., Gillet, D., & Sire, S. (2004b, June 21-26). Sustaining collaboration within a learning community in flexible engineering education. *Proceedings of the World Conference on Educational Multimedia, Hypermedia & Telecommunications (ED-MEDIA)*, Lugano, Switzerland.

Nguyen-Ngoc, A. V., Rekik, Y., & Gillet, D. (2005a). Formal assessment of a Web-based learning environment. *Proceedings of the iNEER Conference on Engineering Education and Research,* Tainan, Taiwan.

Nguyen-Ngoc, A. V., Rekik, Y., & Gillet, D. (2005b). A framework for sustaining the continuity of interaction in a Web-based learning environment for engineering education. *Proceedings of the World Conference on Educational Multimedia, Hypermedia & Telecommunications* (ED-MEDIA), Montreal, Canada.

Nielsen, J. (1993). *Usability engineering.* San Francisco: Morgan Kaufmann.

Ogot, M., Elliott, G., & Glumac, N. (2003). An assessment of in-person and remotely operated laboratory. *International Journal of Engineering Education,* 57-64.

Roppel, A. T., Hung, Y. J., Wentworth, W. S., & Hodel, A. S. (2000). An interdisciplinary laboratory sequence in electrical and computer engineering: Curriculum design and assessment results. *IEEE Transactions on Education, 43*(2), 143-152.

Rosson, M. B., & Carroll, J. M. (2002). *Usability engineering scenario-based development of human-computer interaction.* San Francisco: Morgan Kaufmann.

Schmid, C. (1998). The virtual control lab VCLAB for education on the Web. *Proceedings of the American Control Conference,* Philadelphia, PA.

Schmidt, K., & Bannon, L. (1992). Taking CSCW seriously: Supporting articulation work. *Computer-Supported Cooperative Work (CSCW): The Journal of Collaborative Computing, 1*(1), 7-40.

Sellen, A. G., & Harper, R. H. R. (2002). *The myth of the paperless office.* Boston: MIT Press.

Shneiderman, B. (1998). *Designing the user interface: Strategies for effective human-computer interaction.* Reading, MA: Addition-Wesley.

Tzafestas, C. S., Alifragis, M., & Palaiologou, N. (2005). Development and evaluation of a virtual and remote laboratory in robotics. In *Innovations 2005: World innovations in engineering education and research* (pp. 255-270). New York: iNEER in cooperation with Begell House Publishers.

Wasserman, S., & Faust, K. (1994). *Social Network Analysis: Methods and applications.* Cambridge: Cambridge University Press.

Woodreff, E. (1999). Concerning the cohesive nature of CSCL communities. *Proceedings of the Conference on Computer-Supported Collaborative Learning (CSCL),* Standford.

Copyright © 2007, Idea Group Inc. Copying or distributing in print or electronic forms without written permission of Idea Group Inc. is prohibited.

Chapter XIV

Understanding Participation in Online Courses: A Case Study of Online Interaction

Noppadol Prammanee,
Burapha University International College, Chonburi, Thailand

Abstract

This chapter reports the results of a case study of online interaction. Prior to conducting the case study, the author conducted a pre-study to understand how students and instructors view the problems they face in online courses. After that, the author used Hillman et al. and Moore's four types of interaction, along with Henri's analytical model, as a framework to guide the investigation in order to understand the nature of interaction in an online course. The results of this study showed that a combination three of the types of interaction and the analytical model help teaching and learning become more effective. Furthermore, this study provides recommendations and practices that would be helpful for online instructors to design and deliver online courses effectively.

Copyright © 2007, Idea Group Inc. Copying or distributing in print or electronic forms without written permission of Idea Group Inc. is prohibited.

Introduction

Even after a decade of online learning, students and instructors still face problems with online learning environments. These significant problems persist with online courses: students are often reluctant to enroll, students drop out of such courses, and instructors hesitate to teach them.

These problems occur when students have limited technological skills (Bernárdez, 2003; Carnevale, 2000; Clark & Mayer, 2003; Frankola, 2001; Mamary & Charles, 2000; Nelson, 1999). Students are also dissatisfied with poor interaction and lack of timely feedback from their instructor and classmates (Hara & Kling, 1999; Kearsley, 1995; Levin, Waddoups, Levin, & Buell, 2001; Muirhead, 1999; Vrasidas & McIsaac, 1999).

Instructors may hesitate to teach online courses because they have to spend more time and effort than teaching in a traditional classroom. Online activities include facilitating students in learning by teaching and delivering course materials, providing support and feedback, and encouraging students to participate in online activities. Some instructors find promoting these activities particularly challenging because of their limited knowledge of new and emerging technology (Bennett, Priest, & Macpherson, 1999; Clark, 1993; Dillon & Walsh, 1992; Ellis & Phelps, 2000; Gunawardena, 1992; Means et al., 1993).

Design of the Study

To better understand these problems, the author conducted a pre-study and a case study. In the pre-study, the author investigated the reasons why students choose not to enroll in or drop out of the online courses and why instructors are hesitant to teach them. During the pre-study, the author observed how instructors and students interact in online learning environments, and how they view the problems they face in online courses. After understanding the problems from the pre-study, the author designed the case study to understand the nature of interaction in an online course, Technology Integration (TI), at Midwestern University in the U.S. The TI course was an online course combined with four face-to-face meetings. Figure 1 represents the relationships between the pre-study and the case study.

The *Pre-Study* is linked to two other nodes in the diagram: *Validate the Problems* and *Build the Case Study*. These two links represent how the pre-study serves a two-fold purpose—to clarify the problems identified using existing research and to set guidelines to build a case study. To validate the problems identified in current research, the author conducted the pre-study to understand the problems that students and instructors are facing with online courses. Then the author constructed

Copyright © 2007, Idea Group Inc. Copying or distributing in print or electronic forms without written permission of Idea Group Inc. is prohibited.

Figure 1. The visual representation of the connections between the pre-study and the case study

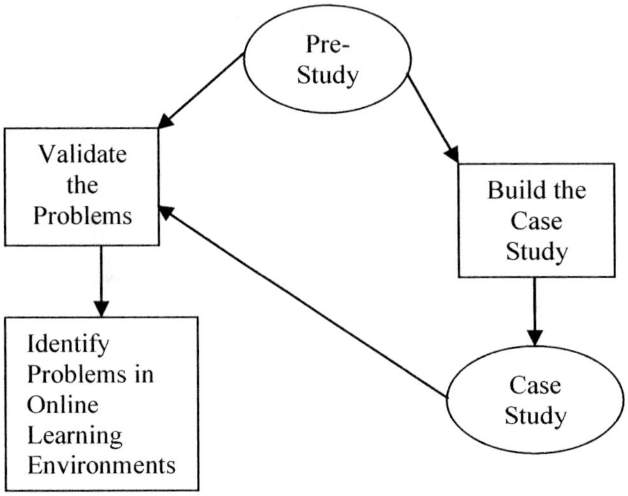

a framework based on a model of four types of interaction (Hillman, Willis, & Gunawardena, 1994; Moore, 1989) and Henri's (1992) analytical model.

Theoretical Framework of the Case Study

After observing traditional classroom environments, participating in online courses, and reading research reports, the author found that interaction is one of the most important factors determining whether students succeed in or fail at a course. Interaction is important in all forms of education (Anderson, 2003; Dewey, 1938; Moore, 1989), and it has been demonstrated to be one of the most important factors in distance education (McIsaac & Gunawardena, 1996; Moore, 1989; Wagner, 1994). According to Salomon (1981), education is a social phenomenon in which interaction must play a necessary part. Garrison asserts that education is a "collaborative experience which necessitates mediation by others as well as recognition and validation of learning" (1990, p. 41). Garrison adds that for information to become knowledge, it has to be "shared, critically analyzed, and applied" (p. 41). From these perspectives, the author found the research by Hillman et al. (1994) and Moore (1989) particularly relevant to this study. Their frameworks using the four types of interaction (learner-interface, learner-instructor, learner-learner, and learner-content interactions) help explain the nature of online interaction and the importance of each major component in distance education. The author applied their models to investigate the problems found in the current research.

Copyright © 2007, Idea Group Inc. Copying or distributing in print or electronic forms without written permission of Idea Group Inc. is prohibited.

Learner-instructor and learner-learner interaction allow students to learn better in online learning environments because some students may need to interact with their classmates and instructor in order to clarify the questions (Hillman et al., 1994). Students must interact with each other in order to learn satisfactorily (Fulford & Zhang, 1993; Hackman & Walker, 1990). Jakupcak and Fishbaugh (1998) found that one-third to one-half of the class time should be set aside for students to interact with one another. Irani (1998) also asserts that when students interact, they learn better and are more satisfied with the course. In addition, Bull, Kimball, and Stansberry (1998) assert that students gain a deeper understanding of the course's subject matter when they are allowed to interact with one another. Therefore, interaction is one of main factors in effective learning. Interaction not only impacts a student's satisfaction with the course, but also allows students to exchange their ideas and knowledge online.

Technology and tools are the main factors that allow students to interact with their instructor and classmates. Luetkehans (1999) conducted a study using groupware tools to examine learner-instructor and learner-learner interaction. Her study in-''cated participants "used the tool to share ideas and information and to maintain ..cords" (p. 498). Walther (1996) investigated how learner-learner interaction is based on learner-interface interaction, and how computer-mediated communication influences how people communicate and interact. Walther found that advance planning by instructors is important in order for students to interact significantly. To achieve the highest level of learning, instructors must realize the importance of planning their teaching strategies, employ appropriate learning tools, and promote online interaction.

The author also used Henri's (1992) analytical model to analyze the online transcripts in order to understand the instructor's and learners' messages posted on the Blackboard course management system (CMS). Henri's analytical model includes five dimensions: frequency of participation, patterns of online interactions, rate of social cues, application of cognitive skills, and use of metacognitive skills to analyze the online transcripts.

Data Collection

The author gathered data through interviews, document analysis, and observation (both online and face-to-face). The author examined four weeks of the online participants. The author did not include weeks that had lower participants because of extenuating factors. For example, the first week, students did not post at all because they had face-to-face meetings and most of them were not familiar with the CMS or other tools for the online course yet. During the midterm and final weeks, students rarely posted because they presented their midterm and final projects in class. The author began collecting the data by observing the online discussions and four face-

Copyright © 2007, Idea Group Inc. Copying or distributing in print or electronic forms without written permission of Idea Group Inc. is prohibited.

to-face meetings in the spring of 2002. Using this methodology, this study addressed the following questions:

1. In what ways do participants engage in the four types of interaction in the online course studied?
2. What was the frequency of participation (as measured by counting the total number of messages, words, lines, and sentences posted) in electronic discussions?
3. How did the participants demonstrate patterns of online interactions (chain of connected messages), social cues, cognitive skills, and metacognitive skills in the electronic discussions?

Participants

Twelve students were enrolled in the TI course. However, only seven students and one course instructor were interviewed because five of them chose not to participate in the interviews. Of the five students who were not willing to participate in the interviews, four allowed the author to review the online discussions (transcript analysis). One student did not participate in either interviews or the analysis of online discussions; this study did not include any statements from this particular student. Therefore, the total number of participants of this study was 12.

Data Analysis

Data analysis is a continuous process from the "first day the researcher arrives at the setting" (Erlandson, Harris, Skipper, & Allen, 1993; Stake 1995) until the study is complete (Stake, 1995). For this study, the purpose of data analysis is to link "data [that has] usually been derived from interviews, field observations, and documents" (Merriam 1998, p. 193). To make the data analysis more organized and effective, the author divided the data into two sections. The first section, which dealt with question 1, contained document reviews, interviews, and observations data. The second section, a transcript analysis based on Henri's five-step model analysis, addressed research questions 2 and 3.

Data Analysis Section 1

After the author completed site interviews, observations, and collected the documents, the author sorted the data into several types, transcribed the taped interviews,

Copyright © 2007, Idea Group Inc. Copying or distributing in print or electronic forms without written permission of Idea Group Inc. is prohibited.

and reviewed the observations and document data. The author transferred all of the data into Microsoft Word documents and put them into one column. The author highlighted the relationships between the different types of data and between the data and the research questions. The author entered the highlighted data into the summary table, then created a table to organize the data into specific categories.

Data Analysis Section 2

In the second section of the data analysis, this study used Henri's (1992) five-step model to organize and analyze the data. This study used four processes to manage the data:

1. Importing the data from Blackboard into a Word document and entering it into one column.
2. Printing out all the data in order to make it easy to read, mark, and code.
3. Counting and analyzing the data based on the five steps of Henri's model.
4. Transferring raw data onto an Excel document to calculate the frequency of behaviors along various dimensions within each of five categories: participation, interaction, social, cognitive, and metacognitive skills.

Transcript Analysis

The analysis of the transcripts used the five steps devised by Henri (1992) as shown in Tables 1 through 5.

As shown in Table 1, the author analyzed the total number of messages, words, lines, and sentences of the instructor's and students' messages posted on Blackboard using the "analysis of online transcripts." Using MS Word, the author imported the data and counted the number of words and lines using the "Word Count" tool to view the

Table 1. Frequency of participation (Adapted and modified from Henri, 1992, p. 125)

Dimension	**Analysis of Online Transcripts**
Participation	Discussion in four selected weeks Total number of messages Total number of words Total number of lines Total number of sentences

Copyright © 2007, Idea Group Inc. Copying or distributing in print or electronic forms without written permission of Idea Group Inc. is prohibited.

Table 2. Patterns of online interactions (Adapted and modified from Henri, 1992, p. 127)

Dimension	Analysis of Online Transcripts	Example
Interaction	Direct response (DR)	"In response to Nick's message 1"
	Direct commentary (DC)	"I agree with Nick's answer that…"
	Indirect response (IR)	"I think the answer is…"
	Indirect commentary (IC)	"I agree with the answer…"
	Independent statement (IS)	The statements that relate to subject under discussion, but do not lead to any future or prior statements

number of the words and lines. The author counted the number of messages manually. The author counted the number of the sentences by arranging the data into one column in MS Word. Using the one-column format, the author categorized different items for the next analysis: social cues, cognitive skills, and metacognitive skills.

Table 2 shows patterns of online interaction. To analyze patterns of interaction, this study examined the individual words and sentences in each document. Using "chains of connected messages" (Henri, 1992, p. 125), the author analyzed the pattern of interactions on the discussion boards. In discussion boards, the participants might respond to a question that has been posted with a "direct response" or post a comment to someone's messages on the discussion board with a "direct commentary." Moreover, the participants who interact using "direct response" and "direct commentary" will indicate these in their reply message. Moreover, some participants might respond to an "indirect response" with an "indirect commentary"—a message that does not refer to the person who posted it. The author used Table 2 as a framework to record the data to answer research question 2.

Table 3 illustrates how the author analyzed the data within a document (with data divided into one column) to find the social cues. The author analyzed the data using Henri's recommendations, such as self-introduction, expression of feeling, and

Table 3. Rate of social cues (Adapted from Henri, 1992, pp. 125-126)

Dimension	Analysis of Online Transcripts	Example
Social Cues	Self-introduction Expression of feeling Greetings Emoticons	"Hello, my name is…" "I'm feeling great…" "Hi everyone" ☺, :X, and :{}:

Copyright © 2007, Idea Group Inc. Copying or distributing in print or electronic forms without written permission of Idea Group Inc. is prohibited.

greetings to categorize social cues. Next, the author transferred the raw data into an Excel document in order to analyze the average number of social cues for the four selected weeks. This study used Table 3 as a framework to record the data the author analyzed in order to answer part of question 3.

Table 4 shows how the author analyzed the cognitive skills as the author did with social cues; that is, the author read the data line by line. In addition, the author analyzed the indicator of each dimension to find out which indicators were more frequently used and for what reasons. This table shows the framework the author used to help answer research question 3.

Table 4. Rate of cognitive skills

Dimension	**Definition**	**Analysis of Online Transcripts (Indicators)**
Elementary clarification	Observing a problem, identifying its elements, and observing their linkages in order to come to a basic understanding	• Identifying relevant elements • Reformulating the problem • Asking a relevant question • Identifying previously stated hypotheses
In-depth clarification	Analyzing and understanding a problem to develop an understanding which sheds light on the underlying values, beliefs, and assumptions	• Defining the term • Identifying assumptions • Establishing referential criteria • Seeking out specialized information
Inference	Introduction and deduction, admitting or proposing an idea on the basis of its link with propositions already admitted as true	• Drawing conclusions • Making generalizations • Formulating a proposition which proceeds from previous statements
Judgment	• Making decisions, statements, appreciations, evaluations, and criticisms • Sizing up	• Judging the relevance of the solution • Making value judgments • Judging inferences
Strategies	Proposing coordinated actions for making decision	• Making a decision on the action to be taken • Proposing one or more solutions • Interacting with those concerned

Source: Analytical Model: Cognitive Skills (Adapted from Henri, 1992, p. 129)

Copyright © 2007, Idea Group Inc. Copying or distributing in print or electronic forms without written permission of Idea Group Inc. is prohibited.

Table 5. Rate of metacognitive skills (Adapted from Henri, 1992, p. 132)

Dimension	**Definition**	**Analysis of Online Transcripts (Indicators)**
Evaluation	• Assessment, appraisal, or verification of one's knowledge and skills • Effectiveness of a chosen strategy	• Asking whether one's statement is true • Commenting on one's manner of accomplishing a task
Planning	Selecting, predicting, and ordering an action or strategy necessary to complete an action	• Predicting the consequences of an action • Organizing aims by breaking them down into secondary objectives
Regulation	Setting up, maintaining, and supervising the overall cognitive task	• Redirecting one's efforts • Recalling one's objectives • Setting up strategies
Self-awareness	Ability to identify, decipher, and interpret correctly the feelings and thoughts connected with a given aspect of the task	• "I'm pleased to have learned so much…" • "I'm discouraged at the difficulties involved…"

Table 5 explains how the author analyzed the metacognitive skill data line by line, as used with the social cues and cognitive skill data. The author used this table to record the metacognitive skill data that the author used to answer the last part of research question 3.

Results and Discussion

The results of this study illustrated that Henri's (1992) five-step model supported Moore's (1989) three types of interaction (learner-instructor, learner-learner, and learner-content). The author agrees with Anderson's (2003) idea that he does not address learner-interface interaction separately because he considers it to be a component of the other three types of interaction, rather than a distinct form of interaction itself. In addition, Henri's model can be used to improve upon Moore's interaction types; for example, frequency of participation and social cues encourage learner-instructor and learner-learner interaction. The results of this study indicate that students tended to post more messages when they were required to contribute as a part of the course grade. More important, these online activities in TI course increased because the instructor employed social cues with the students in order to build rapport with them at the beginning of the course. This finding indicates that once students become familiar with their instructor and their classmates, they feel

Copyright © 2007, Idea Group Inc. Copying or distributing in print or electronic forms without written permission of Idea Group Inc. is prohibited.

more comfortable exchanging ideas and knowledge. For the learner-content interaction, using cognitive and metacognitive skills in assignments and course-related activities helped learners to think critically and develop skills they can use outside of the classroom.

As a result, the author synthesized the findings from these models in the following sections: learner-instructor interaction, learner-learner interaction, and learner-content interaction. Based on these findings, this study provides recommendations and practices that would be helpful for online instructors to design and deliver online courses effectively.

Learner-Instructor Interaction

Moore's (1989) original model of learner-instructor interaction involves the motivation and feedback provided by the instructor and dialog between the instructor and the students. The results of this study illustrated that the facilitator role of the instructor influenced learning a great deal by being organized, requiring students to participate, generating social cues, posting questions to the class, providing help with other issues related to the course goals, and providing feedback.

Teaching in online format requires that the instructor be more organized than in the traditional classroom. The results of interviews and observations showed that students want the instructor to organize the online discussion, including an area for announcements, a place for class discussion, and a place to submit assignments. Mary expressed her feelings:

"I think it would be nice to have a posting place. It's good to have one place set up for questions and answers. I never figured how to get in that place [the discussion areas]. I think instructors have to be more organized. Instructions need to be clear, easy to understand, and more accessible."

Vrasidas and McIsaac (1999) found that requiring students to participate in course activities increased interaction. Vrasidas and McIsaac's findings were similar to Henri's model (the frequency of interaction) in terms of supporting the interaction between the learner and instructor. My findings confirm the results of these studies—that is, when students were required to participate, such as posting assignments on the discussion board as part of their grade, their interaction increased.

The evidence in Table 6 shows that the level of participation increased when students were required to submit their assignments. For example, Week 3 contained more messages than Week 5, but the number of words, lines, and sentences were slightly lower because of the general nature of the discussion topics. The discussion

Copyright © 2007, Idea Group Inc. Copying or distributing in print or electronic forms without written permission of Idea Group Inc. is prohibited.

Table 6. The results of the frequency of participation

Week	Number of Posts	Number of Words	Number of Lines	Number of Sentences	Discussion Period
3	51	6,809	537	358	2/13–2/20
5	43	7,329	685	370	2/27–3/6
8	36	5,421	565	267	3/20–3/27
11	30	5,508	573	289	4/10–4/17
Total	160	25,067	2,360	1,284	

topics (such as technology and how to integrate it into the classroom) of Week 3 provided the opportunity for (but did not require) discussion. In Week 5, students were required to post their own KnowQuest assignments onto the discussion board. According to the assignment handout, one of the KnowQuest assignments in Week 5 required students to choose four educational Web sites to examine, think about how they could use the Web sites in their own classrooms, and post their thoughts on the discussion board. Because of the specific nature of the assignments, Week 5 activities contain more words, lines, and sentences. Week 3 actually had more posts than Week 5, but fewer words, lines, and sentences. Because Week 3 was earlier in the semester, students were not as familiar or comfortable with the technology. As a result the posting of shorter messages was actually more related to social interaction and getting to know one another. Besides the discussions required for the class, some of the messages in Week 3 contain greetings, self-introductions, personal inquiries, and other information. This finding indicated that in the early weeks of an online course, the instructor should allow students to build rapport with their classmates and instructor as well as discuss the course content.

In Week 11, students were required to post their CreateQuest assignments onto the discussion board. When comparing the number of the posts between Week 8 and Week 11, the author found that Week 8 covered the Learn Quest Assignment and contained more posts, but there were fewer words, lines, and sentences in Week 8 than in Week 11. Even though similar assignments were required in Weeks 8 and 11, the number of words, lines, and sentences posted during Week 11 was still greater than Week 8. This study shows that these items increased because in Week 11, students not only submitted their assignments in a timely manner, but they also made the effort to discuss their final projects online. Another possible reason there were fewer posts in later weeks, such as Week 11, is that most students were very involved in completing their final projects. The results of this finding implied that in the latter weeks instructors should not overwhelm the students with assignments and course activities because students need to spend time completing their final projects or preparing for the final exam.

Another issue influencing online interaction was social cues. The result of the

Copyright © 2007, Idea Group Inc. Copying or distributing in print or electronic forms without written permission of Idea Group Inc. is prohibited.

Table 7. The results of the rates of social cues

Week	Number of Social Cues
3	13
5	9
8	2
11	0

transcript analysis shows that students used more social cues in the early weeks of class than in the later weeks because the students wanted to get to know their classmates. During Week 3 students were still introducing themselves to the class. This is why the messages in Week 3 contained more social cues than in Weeks 5, 8, and 11 (see Table 7). For example, in a Week 3 discussion, Brenda introduced herself to the class saying, "Hello: I am a sixth grade teacher in [school name] school district…" (Posted Friday, February, 15, 2002, 9:27 pm). This finding is similar to another study by Hara, Bonk, and Angeli (2000), which claims that the number of social cues decreased as the semester progressed. This finding suggested that online instructors need to allow students to become familiar with their classmates and instructor in the beginning of the course.

In the traditional teaching format, the instructor is physically present in the class so that students can interact with their instructor through verbal or non-verbal communication. However, these interactions may be missing in an online learning environment. To compensate for this, instructors must post questions and require students to contribute. Instructor-mediated discussion increases online participation. Most participants in this study admitted that the instructor led the online activities by posting the questions and asking them to answer. During her interview, Mary stated:

"The instructor encouraged active learning by proposing questions and asking us to search for the answers. After we searched for the answers and found them, we had to process the information and then post the responses. So, through the questions and the assignments he set up for us, he facilitated learning."

The instructor can encourage online interaction by offering help with other issues related to the course. The data from interviews and observations showed that the instructor offered help with both content and technology. During four face-to-face meetings, the author observed the instructor helping students with the course content and technology before class began, during the break, and after class as well. Fay discussed how the instructor helped her in learning, though she had problems with the technology:

Copyright © 2007, Idea Group Inc. Copying or distributing in print or electronic forms without written permission of Idea Group Inc. is prohibited.

"When I was frustrated, he encouraged me. He told me that I was not the only one having problems, and that it was not going to affect my grade, it was not going to count against me. I think I was at a frustration level where almost no learning could have taken place, if it had not been for his good attitude. I would have otherwise just said, 'I have to get out of this class.' I was putting in hours of trying, and I'm not computer savvy...I just felt like this is awful. If Ian had not been as reassuring as he had been, there is no way I would have completed this class."

According to Fay's comments, instructors need to act as a good mentor, especially online instructors who may never see students face-to-face. If online instructors are not acting as good mentors, students may feel uncomfortable expressing problems because they think it may affect their grade.

Another issue that appeared to influence interaction in this course was feedback. Several educators, such as Acker and McCain (1993), Levin et al. (2001), Muirhead (1999), and Wagner (1994), claim that feedback is important in motivating students to learn because it helps them know whether they are making progress or not. In this study, participants felt that lack of timely feedback discouraged them from participating in online activities. To illustrate, Mary explained her frustration with the lack of feedback from the instructor:

"Well, it was frustrating because I posted something and then checked to see if he responded back. There was no response back. So, you know, it was a little disappointing, I guess. The lack of participation lowered the quality of the interaction...I would like to have been drawn into a conversation with him on the computer...when I e-mailed him, it took so long to get a response. Then I was left wondering if I was doing the right thing. To improve the online instruction, the instructor needed to be more available—even if it's just e-mail. I kind of wonder if he only checked the e-mail on the weekends...It would have been nice to have feedback about the work we did because I could have been completely wrong, barking up the wrong tree and I just continued because I never had any feedback."

Patty explained:

"I got frustrated because the other time when I was trying to post something, I wasn't sure if I was in the right place. So I think if I had not had that frustration, I would have contributed more."

These comments indicated that instructors must provide timely feedback to encourage students to achieve in online learning.

Copyright © 2007, Idea Group Inc. Copying or distributing in print or electronic forms without written permission of Idea Group Inc. is prohibited.

Learner-Learner Interaction

Moore's (1989) original model of learner-learner interaction is helpful in terms of resource sharing. The findings in this study were confirmed in Moore's original model: the participants collaborated online about the course-related goals with their classmates and instructor. This study found that learner-learner interaction is helpful when the instructor required students to collaborate in class activities, assist one another with assignments, participate in weekly activities, and be familiar with technology and tools.

Collaboration also influences interaction in the TI course. This finding is also similar to another online learning model by Salmon (2002), who states knowledge sharing is a part of "information exchange." Students felt that collaboration assisted them in terms of brainstorming and decision making when they performed group projects. For example, students could assist group members by discussing topics, content, and resources for their projects. In addition, collaboration helped students obtain information from various sources. For example, group members could help each other locate the information either from libraries or online. After that, they could summarize, prepare, and present the project together. The participants (Brenda and Ian) in this study agreed that they produced better work together than when working alone. Researchers (Cavalier & Klein, 1998; Hathorn & Ingram, 2002; Jonassen, 2003; Lamb, 2003; Weller, 2002) agree that collaboration is very important. To help students learn from one another in an online course, the instructor should provide the opportunity for students to work together, encourage students to collaborate with their classmates. The instructor may need to require students to participate as a part of their grade, because sometimes merely encouraging students to participate may not be enough to motivate students to interact.

Working as a group enhances cooperative learning. According to Bailey and Cotlar (1994), cooperative learning should involve "small groups of students working together to maximize their own and each others' education" (p. 186). The author observed that most of the groups contained two to three members. Since groups were relatively small, the students agreed that each member shared tasks equally; this enabled them to explore and learn to the fullest extent. When assigning group projects, the instructor should consider group size; too many members in a group can make working together difficult for all.

Learner-learner interaction is important for students to assist one another with assignments. The results of this study revealed that learners interacted with their classmates by clarifying assignments and asking for help about the course-related questions. Some participants felt that the lack of help from their classmates, both with content and technology, discouraged them from participating in this course. When students do not receive help from their classmates, they are more likely to drop out of the courses. Mary said:

Copyright © 2007, Idea Group Inc. Copying or distributing in print or electronic forms without written permission of Idea Group Inc. is prohibited.

"We learned from one another and we helped one another. Vanessa's very good with the technology and content. So, the three of us kind of worked together in the same school district and helped one another. So, that was a good thing, but if I had been the only one in this building, taking a class, it would have been a nightmare because this class was hugely frustrating. I put so many hours into this class, so many hours. I can't even begin to tell you. And then, it was so frustrating. So, if I have not had them also here and Vanessa to help me when I had a computer problem...I think I would have dropped the class. And I've never ever in my whole life dropped a class."

This finding indicated that learner-learner interaction is still important in online learning environments. Therefore, if possible, instructors should group students who work and live near each other so that they can assist one another. Instructors must consider students' knowledge and skills, and organize groups that balance the strengths of each student. Moreover, online instructors should provide adequate training to help students become familiar with the technology. This training should include all technologies related to the course, such as real-time chat, asynchronous tools, and the telephone. Using these tools helps students to communicate effectively. For example, if Mary does not know how to send an e-mail attachment, she could call Jason for help. Jason could ask Mary to turn on the computer and walk her through the process during the phone call. Real-time chat helps for students in brainstorming and decision making for their group project because the chat offers the immediate response.

Weekly participation and contribution in online activities are important for students to learn. When students do not participate, they do not know what is happening in the class discussions. During interviews with the participants, I asked, "How does lack of student participation in the weekly discussion affect the quality of learning?" Some participants said that the quality of learning was affected because they were not observing what was going on (Brenda, Jandra, and Mary). Fay said, "I was one of those who did not keep up with the weekly online discussion. I really ran into a lot of problems and I just did not know where to go and what to do." Since the number of interactions affects the amount of learning, the instructor should require students to participate regularly in weekly discussion.

In the online learning environment, students must use technology and tools in order to access the content, communicate with the instructor, and interact with other students. According to Bailey and Luetkehans (2001), Duffy and Cunningham (1996), Honebein (1996), and Pallof and Pratt (1999), online instructors should employ both synchronous and asynchronous tools to communicate with students. The results of this study showed that the instructor used both synchronous and asynchronous tools to promote online interactions.

Copyright © 2007, Idea Group Inc. Copying or distributing in print or electronic forms without written permission of Idea Group Inc. is prohibited.

The use of synchronous tools increases online interaction. One synchronous tool used in this class was real-time chat. During the interviews, participants explained that using real-time chat helped them receive a quick response from their group members (Mary and Vanessa). The real-time chat helped participants to discuss and respond immediately when they were involved in the group project. The research of Lara, Howell, Dominguez, and Navarro (2001) concurs with the author's findings. They found that using synchronous discussion provides "immediate and simultaneous responding" (p. 63). Mary and Vanessa stated that the real-time chat allowed them to brainstorm in order to make a decision related to project task. Mary also praised the benefits of chat because it allowed her to read the archives when she could not attend the chat session.

Other tools that seemed to influence interaction in this course were asynchronous tools, such as e-mail and discussion board. These offer students ample time to think and post messages. The instructor used the discussion board to lead the discussions, and the discussion board helped students to exchange ideas and share information with each other and the instructor. Jandra said the discussion board was one of the significant tools that helped her exchange ideas because she could take time to think before posting her own questions and responding to her classmates' questions. During the online observations, students indicated that they interacted with their classmates by replying to other messages on the discussion board. For instance, some students asked other classmates to clarify answers or ask for more information related to the answers.

E-mail also helped students to communicate and collaborate online. The participants that the author observed and interviewed commented that e-mail was helpful for them in contacting one another, sending messages, or attaching class assignment files (Betty, Fay, Patty, and Vanessa). This study found that students like using e-mail to attach working files so that other team members could add their findings for group projects and return these edited files. Accordingly, e-mail is a very useful communication tool that provides privacy. One participant stated that without e-mail, she could not have conveyed her personal messages directly to the instructor; she would have felt uncomfortable about posting messages about embarrassing problems. Another advantage of e-mail is that it reaches a whole group of recipients at one time. The instructor used e-mail to inform students of any changes in case Blackboard was down or not accessible. Without e-mail, the instructor would have to spend more time calling each student to inform them of course situations. To take advantage of e-mail, online instructors must reply to students' messages instantly. To take advantage of e-mail, online instructors must reply to students' messages instantly. Brenda said, "I am happy that the instructor was very patient with us and provided timely feedback."

Familiarity with technology was also important for students to learn in online courses. Hara and Kling (1999) found that students became frustrated with online learning

Copyright © 2007, Idea Group Inc. Copying or distributing in print or electronic forms without written permission of Idea Group Inc. is prohibited.

because they did not have adequate technology skills and did not receive technical support. In this study, students with limited technological skills felt that they did not want to participate in any online interactions. For example, Fay stated:

"Sometimes I felt like, 'Wow, what they said was over my head.' And there was one time when I'd lost two of my assignments. I lost them. I typed them. I pushed a little button. This computer was broken. This one was really sick for two weeks. And so I was using that one. I pushed the button. I swear I saw the little thing over here changed...I had wanted to edit it and I posted it without editing it. Again there was something I wanted to change, and I could not figure out how to do it. And I want to go back and do it because I found out how to do it after we posted. I wanted to go back and do it but I could not find it. Two assignments were gone."

This finding is consistent with another scholar (Wilken, 1999) who claims that when students became frustrated with technology, they stopped participating. Therefore, training students to use technology tools at the beginning of the class should be mandatory in all online courses.

Learner-Content Interaction

Moore (1989) discusses the learner-content interaction in terms of interacting with the "content or the subject of the study" in a way that helps students to learn. The results of this study revealed that the instructor assisted students by providing assignments relevant to learners' professions and assigning an assignment involving cognitive and metacognitive skills.

Relating assignments to the students' professions motivates them to engage in learning. The results of interviews, observations, and document analysis showed that assigning WebQuest assignments encouraged students to learn in this course because they could apply the value of this assignment to their own classroom teaching. Keller (1987) concurs that "relevance" deals with the instructional designer's and educator's attempts to make instruction seem "relevant" to present and future career opportunities for the students. The importance of relevance is apparent in another study by Levin et al. (2001) which states that relevance in online learning should be "thought of as helping teachers prepare curriculum and develop practice directly relevant to their teaching, while also expanding their ideas about what is and should be relevant in their professional practice" (Relevant and Challenging Section, para. 4). Therefore, in order to encourage students to learn, the instructor must design a curriculum that is relevant to their professions. For example, when designing the curriculum, educators should identify the students' knowledge and skills, and develop assignments related to those skills. The author observed that

Copyright © 2007, Idea Group Inc. Copying or distributing in print or electronic forms without written permission of Idea Group Inc. is prohibited.

the instructor in this study asked students to complete the technological survey in the first week of class. Then, after learning that students were K-12 teachers, the instructor designed assignments that the students could adapt for their own classrooms. Online course assignments should allow students to use problem solving and critical thinking; the assignments can be done both in groups and individually. The group assignments should require every member to contribute in the activities. For example, student A searches for information, student B reads and summarizes, and student C puts the project together. After that, all students should review the final project together to make sure that it meets the requirements of the assignment.

After analyzing transcripts, the author found that students used cognitive skills to think critically, especially when they were doing assignments. For example, the data in Table 8 shows that Week 5 contains a greater amount of elementary clarification because students consulted their instructor and classmates about their first WebQuest assignments.

This study used four indicators under elementary clarification to identify which skills the students used: (1) identifying relevant elements, (2) reformulating the problem, (3) asking a relevant question, and (4) identifying the previously stated hypotheses. The author found that students demonstrated five indicators of elementary clarification in order to complete the WebQuest assignments in Week 5. According to the Week 5 assignments (KnowQuest), the students were required to choose four education Web sites they could apply to their classroom. After that, students were required to post their thoughts to the discussion board about the four Web sites they chose. While fulfilling these requirements students first demonstrated identifying relevant elements when they identified the educational Web site and thought about how they might apply it in their classroom setting. After that, students used reformulation of the problem to consider it again before they decide to use those Web sites in the classroom. Next, if students were not confident about the Web site, they might have demonstrated their uncertainly by asking a relevant question when they qualified their answers by asking questions of their classmates or instructor. Finally, some students

Table 8. The results of the rate of cognitive skills

Week	Elementary Clarification	In-Depth Clarification	Inferencing	Judgment	Strategies	Total Number of Instances
3	15 (20.5%)	20 (27.4%)	32 (43.8%)	3 (4.1%)	3 (4.1%)	73
5	24 (32.9%)	11 (15.1%)	26 (35.6%)	10 (13.7%)	2 (2.7%)	73
8	15 (29.4%)	5 (9.8%)	14 (27.5%)	13 (25.5%)	4 (7.8%)	51
11	8 (28.6%)	7 (25%)	6 (21.4%)	5 (17.9%)	2 (7.1%)	28

Copyright © 2007, Idea Group Inc. Copying or distributing in print or electronic forms without written permission of Idea Group Inc. is prohibited.

demonstrated identification of the previously stated hypotheses when they identified the previous questions and answers before making a final decision. Using these steps shows that cognitive skills helped students do better on their assignments, and they could apply these skills in the real-life situations when they need to think critically. To encourage students to use cognitive skills, instructors could design the course assignments that involve critical thinking, collaborating, and constructivism. For instance, the course assignments not only ask students to answer yes/no questions, but also ask students to answer, "Why is this correct or incorrect?"

Not only did students demonstrate cognitive skills on the online discussion board, but my transcript analyses indicated that students expressed metacognitive skills. The metacognitive skills consist of four categories: evaluation, planning, regulation, and self-awareness. The author found that in Week 3, students expressed more on the evaluation category (see Table 4) than other weeks because Week 3 discussed "Engaged Learning with Technology." This discussion allowed students to express ideas and opinions about using technology and integrating it into classroom teaching. The author found that when students exchanged ideas and opinions, they had to assess and verify their own knowledge and skills, as well as the accuracy of statements that classmates had posted. This finding could be useful to help instructors plan courses that ultimately help students hone their skills.

The result of this study showed that the planning category was used in every week of the discussion, but Week 3 has fewer instances of planning than any other week. This is because Week 3 was still early for some students to worry about predicting and organizing their assignments. This finding showed that in the first week of the online courses, instructors should allow students to know their instructor and fellow classmates, and familiarize themselves with the course requirements.

It is interesting to note that the data in Table 9 shows that the instances of the planning dimension category tended to increase as the semester progressed. For instance, during Weeks 5, 8, and 11, students began to submit their assignments, but not during Week 3. However, when comparing Week 5 to Week 8, Week 8 contains

Table 9. Rate of metacognitive skill use

Week	Evaluation	Planning	Regulation	Self-Awareness	Total Occurrences
3	7 (87.5%)	1 (12.5%)	0	0	8
5	0	5 (41.7%)	3 (25%)	4 (33.3)	12
8	0	4 (57.1%)	0	3 (42.9%)	7
11	0	8 (72.7%)	1 (9.1%)	2 (18.2%)	11

Copyright © 2007, Idea Group Inc. Copying or distributing in print or electronic forms without written permission of Idea Group Inc. is prohibited.

less of a "planning dimension" because the assignments required similar activities; so after they had experience from Week 5, the students found it unnecessary to keep submitting questions about the assignment. From this finding, it is important for instructors to consider having a variety of assignments so they can learn in a variety of ways.

Finally, Week 5 contains more of a "regulation dimension" than Week 8 and Week 11, because in Week 5 the students were required to submit their first assignments. In submitting assignments, some students may need to consult other classmates to reach their objectives. In Weeks 5, 8, and 11, there were fewer instances of the regulation category because the course had several assignments with similar instructions. Week 8 did not contain any instances of regulation category, but Week 11 contains one because in Week 11, students not only submitted their assignments, but they also started discussing their final projects. Therefore, the online instructors should assign less work when students begin working on their final projects because then they will have more time to interact with one another.

Recommendations for Future Practice

This study defines the role instructors should play in online courses. For example, how do instructors promote online interaction in order to increase students' participation in the online courses? The following practical recommendations are provided for faculty members who are teaching online courses or who are planning to teach online courses.

Identify learners' backgrounds as early as possible. During the first week of the online class, instructors should ask their students to provide information about their prior experiences and backgrounds. Discovering the students' backgrounds before planning lessons can help ensure the instructors provide appropriate training for those who are less technologically adept. Also, knowing students' backgrounds and areas of interest can help the instructors when dividing students into groups for class assignments or other class activities.

Provide technological orientation as early as possible. Before the semester begins or during the first week of the class, the instructors should send online orientation materials to students, so they can explore how to interact with the course activities. An instructor should give students their usernames before the class begins. After that, the instructor should instruct students how to log on to the online course and provide step-by-step procedures on how to use Blackboard, post messages, participate in real-time chat, and reply to other messages.

Plan ahead when assigning group projects. When dividing students up for group projects, instructors should start this division in the early weeks to allow ample time for them to prepare for the lessons. Another important strategy to help students feel

Copyright © 2007, Idea Group Inc. Copying or distributing in print or electronic forms without written permission of Idea Group Inc. is prohibited.

comfortable with their group members is to let students get to know one another before they collaborate with their group members. Moreover, groups should be small (three or four members) and consist of students with a range of skills; this way, students can communicate easily and share tasks equally. When working as a group, students need to log in daily to see what their fellow group members have posted and check their e-mail often as well. Instructors may need to assist students to ensure that they know their responsibilities in the group.

Post course content and course information gradually. The author recommends that instructors post course content gradually. This way, students will not feel overwhelmed with information. The instructor should release materials gradually and on a need-to-know basis to keep the students focused. The instructors should post the course content weekly (perhaps one week in advance) to help students form a habit of checking the discussion board often. Likewise, the course information, such as course announcements and course agendas, should be available online one week in advance, if possible. To make sure that students receive course information, instructors may need to send a brief summary of the course information via e-mail as well.

Provide several types of contact information. Several students informed the author that they were glad to have multiple ways of contacting the instructor when problems arose. Instructors should provide students with several types of contact information, such as an e-mail address and telephone number. E-mail is helpful for students to send and receive attachment files to and from their instructor. Having the instructor's telephone number is useful for students when they need detailed information that can only be clarified by lengthy discussion (such as technology issues).

Provide assistance and search for additional information. Instructors should provide assistance, give consistent and timely feedback, and spend time searching for additional information for students. The author observed that students were more satisfied with the course when instructors provided timely feedback.

Require students to participate as much as possible. The instructor should also require students to actively participate. The author recommend that instructors require students to participate often as a substantial part of their grade. More importantly, the instructors need to have online office hours when they will be available for students, reply to students' e-mail, and post messages to the discussion board.

Provide the opportunity to express social cues as early as possible. Social cues may be one of the most important factors that help students get to know their classmates. Without knowing one another, students may not feel comfortable sharing knowledge and information with their classmates. Therefore, online instructors need to focus on the social cues in addition to content in the beginning of the course.

Introduce, facilitate, and summarize online discussions to maximize students' participation. To encourage students to participate and contribute in online discussion, the instructors should participate in every discussion. In the author's study, the author

Copyright © 2007, Idea Group Inc. Copying or distributing in print or electronic forms without written permission of Idea Group Inc. is prohibited.

observed that the instructor did not participate in online discussions as much as the students would have liked. The author recommended that the instructor lead a discussion each week by starting the topic, highlighting examples of insightful online discussion, posting relevant comments to student messages, and giving some ideas for critical thinking. Moreover, after the end of the discussion, the instructors need to wrap it up by making a conclusion. By wrapping up, the instructor can organize the overall concept so that students can easily grasp the main ideas of what has been discussed. This makes it much easier for the class to advance to the next topic.

Require students to lead online activities. In addition to leading discussions themselves, instructors should also require students to post topics for discussion, so they can practice interacting with the instructor and other students. The instructor should require students to participate in online discussions at least two or three times per week. As I observed, the students appreciated receiving relevant feedback from their instructor. This has an added benefit of making it easier for the instructor to enforce the weekly posting requirement. Since online discussions allow for unlimited length or quantity of messages, some students may post very long and detailed messages. As a result, without requiring students to log on regularly to read and reply to other messages, some students may not frequently participate in these discussions. When they do log on to the online course, they may feel overwhelmed with the messages waiting.

Be more organized and conscientious than conventional instructors. The instructors have to be more organized than traditional classroom instructors because students may not have a chance to meet with the instructor if they are confused with the online course features. For example, the instructor should set up a specific discussion area for each topic, such as course information, course discussion, and course assignments, and make sure that the information stays current.

Promote cognitive and metacognitive skills. The instructors should provide assignments that require students to use their cognitive and metacognitive skills. The assignments can be in the form of multiple choice questions, short-answer questions, and essays. To complete the multiple-choice questions, students need to use their thinking processes to recall the information from lectures, readings, and in-class activities. While completing the short-answer questions, students need to use their critical thinking, such as "how to solve this problem and how to explain it clearly." Essays require students to research various sources—either online or in books—to find information to support their ideas.

Conclusion

Overall, the pre-study helped the author to understand the problems that instructors and students face when participating in online courses. The results of the pre-study

Copyright © 2007, Idea Group Inc. Copying or distributing in print or electronic forms without written permission of Idea Group Inc. is prohibited.

were similar to, and some were different from, the existing literature. From the case study, the author discovered that the three types of interaction helped students to learn when they interact with this instructor and classmates, and also when they access the course content. To enhance interaction, instructors need to encourage or require course attendance and provide social cues. Moreover, to help students think critically, instructors should provide exercises that require students to use their cognitive and metacognitive skills. All in all, the three types of interaction help measure how students advance their knowledge and learning skills. Henri's analytical model provides a means for the author to quantify the data using Moore and Hillman et al.'s model, so the author can more accurately interpret the data and provide useful recommendations.

Once the instructors and educational institutions are well prepared to handle the technology and provide adequate assistance for students, the author believes that more students will enroll in online courses or degree programs. Moreover, when the institutions adequately prepare faculty to use the technology and insure their workloads would not become a problem, it will encourage more instructors to teach online courses. The author also encourages scholars to continue conducting research on online learning. As online learning grows, it should become easier to access, handle, and understand so that it will encourage students to continue to enroll in online courses and complete them.

References

Acker, S. R., & McCain, T. A. (1993). *The contribution of interactivity and two-way video to successful distance learning applications: A literature review and strategies positioning.* Columbus: Ohio State University Center for Advanced Study in Telecommunications.

Anderson, T. (2003). Model of interaction in distance education: Recent developments and research questions. In M. G. Moore & W. G. Anderson (Eds.), *Handbook of distance education* (pp. 129-144). Mahwah, NJ: Lawrence Erlbaum.

Bailey, E. K., & Cotlar, M. (1994). Teaching via Internet. *Communication Education, 43,* 184-193.

Bailey, M., & Luetkehans, L. M. (2001). Practical guidelines for Web-based training. In B. H. Khan (Ed.), *Web-based instruction* (pp. 235-243). Englewood Cliffs, NJ: Educational Technology Publications.

Bennett, S., Priest, A., & Macpherson, C. (1999). Learning about online learning: An approach to staff development for university teachers. *Australian Journal of Educational Technology, 15*(13), 207-221. Retrieved January 5, 2002, from http://ascilite.org.au/ajet/ajet15/bennett.html

Copyright © 2007, Idea Group Inc. Copying or distributing in print or electronic forms without written permission of Idea Group Inc. is prohibited.

Bernárdez, M. (2003). From e-training to e-performance: Putting online learning to work. *Educational Technology, 43*(1), 6-11.

Bull, K. S., Kimball, S. L., & Stansberry, S. (1998*). Developing interaction in computer-mediated learning.*

Carnevale, D. (2000). What makes an online course succeed? Not everyone agrees, a study finds. *Chronicle of High Education,* (October 12). Retrieved August 7, 2002, from http://www.chronicle.com/free/2000/10/2000101201u.htm

Cavalier, J. C., & Klein, J. D. (1998). Effects of cooperative versus individual learning and orienting activities during computer-based instruction. *Educational Technology Research and Development, 46*(1), 5-17.

Clark, R. C., & Mayer, R. E. (2003). *E-learning and the science of instruction.* San Francisco: Pfeiffer.

Clark, T. (1993). Attitudes of higher education faculty toward distance education: A national survey. *The American Journal of Distance Education, 7*(2), 19-23.

Dewey, J. (1938). *Experience and education.* New York: Collier Macmillan.

Dillon, C. L., & Walsh, S. M. (1992). Faculty: The neglected resource in distance education. *The American Journal of Distance Education, 6*(3), 5-21.

Duffy, T. M., & Cunningham, D. J. (1996). Constructivism: Implications for the design and delivery of instruction. In D. H. Jonassen (Ed.), *Handbook of research for educational communications and technology* (p. 177). New York: Simon & Schuster Macmillan.

Ellis, A., & Phelps, R. (2000). Staff development for online delivery: A collective, team-based action learning model. *Australian Journal of Educational Technology, 16*(1), 26-44. Retrieved January 5, 2002, from http://ascilite.org.au/ajet/ajet16/ellis.html

Erlandson, D. A., Harris, E., Skipper, B., & Allen, S. (1993). *Doing naturalistic inquiry: A guide to methods.* Newbury Park, CA: Sage.

Frankola, K. (2001). *The e-learning taboo—High dropout rates: Best practices for increasing online course completion rates.* Retrieved August 28, 2001, from http://www.nyuonline.com/vn_3/inside/articles/learning_taboo.html

Fulford, C. P., & Zhang, S. (1993). Perceptions of interaction: The critical predictor in distance education. *The American Journal of Distance Education, 7*(3), 8-21.

Garrison, D. R. (1990). Communication technology. In D. R. Garrison & D. Shale (Eds.), *Education at a distance: From issues to practice* (pp. 41-52). Malabar, FL: Krieger.

Gunawardena, C. N. (1992). Changing faculty roles for audiographics and online teaching. *The American Journal of Distance Education, 6*(3), 58-71.

Copyright © 2007, Idea Group Inc. Copying or distributing in print or electronic forms without written permission of Idea Group Inc. is prohibited.

Hackman, M. Z., & Walker, K. B. (1990). Instructional communication in the televised classroom: The effects of system design and teacher immediacy on student learning and satisfaction. *Communication Education, 39,* 196-206.

Hara, N., Bonk, C. J., & Angeli, C. (2000). *Content analysis of online discussion in an applied educational psychology.* Report No. 2-98, Center for Research on Learning and Technology, USA.

Hara, N., & Kling, R. (1999). Students' frustrations with a Web-based distance education course. *First Monday, 4*(12). Retrieved February 25, 2001, from http://firstmonday.org/issues/issue4_12/hara/index.html

Hathorn, L. G., & Ingram, A. L. (2002). Online collaboration: Making it work. *Educational Technology, 42*(1), 33-40.

Henri, F. (1992). Computer conferencing and content analysis. In A. R. Kaye (Ed.), *Collaborative learning through computer conferencing* (pp. 115-136). New York: Springer.

Hillman, D. C., Willis, D. J., & Gunawardena, C. N. (1994). Learner-interface interaction in distance education: An extension of contemporary models and strategies for practitioners. *The American Journal of Distance Education, 8*(2), 31-42.

Honebein, P. C. (1996). Seven goals for the design of constructivist learning environments. In B. G. Wilson (Ed.), *Constructivist learning environments: Case studies in instructional design* (pp. 11-24). Englewood Cliffs, NJ: Educational Technology Publications.

Irani, T. (1998). Communication potential, information richness and attitude: A study of computer-mediated communication in the ALN classroom. *ALN Magazine, 2*(1). Retrieved December 14, 2003, from http://www.aln.org/alnweb/magazine/vol2_issue1/irani.htm

Jakupcak, J., & Fishbaugh, M. S. (1998). *A horse of a different color: Distance education: Making it effective.*

Jonassen, D. H. (2003). The vain quest for a unified theory of learning. *Educational Technology, 43*(4), 5-3.

Kearsley, G. (1995). The nature and value of interaction in distance learning. In M. Koble (Ed.), *Proceedings of the American Center for the Study of Distance Education Invitational Research Conference in Distance Education: Towards Excellence in Distance Education: A Research Agenda* (pp. 366-374). University Park, PA: Penn State.

Keller, J. M. (1987). Development and use of the ARCS model of instructional design. *Journal of Instructional Development, 10*(3), 2-10.

Lamb, A. (2003). Extreme thinking transforming traditional student projects into effective learning environments. *Educational Technology, 43*(4), 31-40.

Copyright © 2007, Idea Group Inc. Copying or distributing in print or electronic forms without written permission of Idea Group Inc. is prohibited.

Lara, L., Howell, R., Dominguez, J., & Navarro, J. (2001). Synchronous and asynchronous interaction of bilingual Hispanic pre- and in-service teachers in distance learning. *The American Journal of Distance Education, 15*(3), 50-67.

Levin, S. R., Waddoups, G. L., Levin, J., & Buell, J. (2001). Higher interactive and effective online learning environments for teacher professional development. *International Journal of Educational Technology, 2*(2). Retrieved June, 26, 2001, from http://www.outreach.uicc.edu/ijet/v2n2/slevin/index.html

Luetkehans, M. (1999). *A case study of using groupware to support collaborative activities in a distance learning course.*

Mamary, E. M., & Charles, P. (2000). On-site to online: Barriers to the use of computers for continuing education. *Journal of Continuing Education in the Health Professions, 20,* 171-175.

McIsaac, M. S., & Gunawardena, C. N. I. (1996). Distance education. In D. H. Jonassen (Ed.), *Handbook of research for educational communication and technology* (pp. 403-437). New York: Simon & Shuster Macmillan.

Means, B., Blando, J., Olson, K., Middleton T., Morocco, C. C., Remz, A. R., & Zorfass, J. (1993). *Using technology to support educational reform.* U.S. Department of Education, Office of Educational Research and Improvement, under Contract No. RR91172010. Retrieved August 5, 2003, from http://www.ed.gov/pubs/EdReformStudies/TechReforms/title.htm

Merriam, S. B. (1998). *Qualitative research and case study applications in education.* San Francisco: Jossey-Bass.

Moore, M. G. (1989). Three types of interaction. *The American Journal of Distance Education, 3*(2), 1-6.

Muirhead, B. (1999). *Attitude toward interactivity in a graduate distance education program: A qualitative analysis.* Retrieved September 9, 2001, from http://www.dissertation.com/library/1120710a.htm

Nelson, L. M. (1999). *Increasing retention of adult learners in telecourses through the incorporation of learning-centered instructional strategies and the use of multiple modalities for content delivery and interaction.* EdD Practicum Report, Nova Southeastern University, USA.

Palloff, R. M., & Pratt, K. (1999). *Building learning communities in cyberspace.* San Francisco: Jossey-Bass.

Salmon, G. (2002). *E-tivities: The key to active online learning.* London: Kogan Page.

Salomon, G. (1981). *Communication and education.* Beverly Hills, CA: Sage.

Stake, R. E. (1995). *The art of case study research.* Thousand Oaks, CA: Sage.

Vrasidas, C., & McIsaac, M. (1999). *Principles of pedagogy and evaluation for Web-based learning.* Retrieved January 31, 2002, from http://seamonkey.

Copyright © 2007, Idea Group Inc. Copying or distributing in print or electronic forms without written permission of Idea Group Inc. is prohibited.

ed.asu.edu/~mcisaac/ICEM99/pedagogymss.html

Wagner, E. D. (1994). In support of a functional definition of interaction. *The American Journal of Distance Education, 8*(2), 6-2.

Walther, J. (1996). Computer-mediated communication: Impersonal, interpersonal, and hypersonal interaction. *Communication Research, 23*(1), 3-43.

Weller, M. (2002). *Delivering learning on the Net: The why, what & how of online education.* London: Kogan Page.

Wilken, C. S. (1999). Computer-mediated interaction in distance education courses. *Kappa Omicron Nu FORUM: Technology, 11*(1). Retrieved March 19, 2003, from http://www.kon.org/archives/forum/11-1/forum11-1_print.html

Copyright © 2007, Idea Group Inc. Copying or distributing in print or electronic forms without written permission of Idea Group Inc. is prohibited.

Chapter XV

Exploring the Influence of Instructor Actions on Community Development in Online Settings

Christopher Brook, Edith Cowan University, Australia

Ron Oliver, Edith Cowan University, Australia

Abstract

This chapter presents an exploration of the community experience in online settings where the development of a learning community was a key instructional aim. The inquiry used the learning community development model (Brook & Oliver, 2003) to guide the study and measured the individuals' community experience using the Sense of Community Index (Chavis, Hogge, McMillan, & Wandersman, 1986) supported by observations and open-ended questions. The chapter reports the findings of a multi-case study that explored instructor actions in the process of community development in online settings.

Copyright © 2007, Idea Group Inc. Copying or distributing in print or electronic forms without written permission of Idea Group Inc. is prohibited.

Introduction

Many scholars assert that the social phenomenon of community might be put to good use on the support of online learning (Bonk & Wisher, 2000; Hiltz, 1998; Palloff & Pratt, 1999). This assertion is well supported by theories of learning that highlight the importance of social interactions in the construction of knowledge (Bruner, 2001; Dewey, 1929; Vygotsky, 1978). Further support is found in the works of scholars who explore the community construct. These scholars posit that community is characterized by a willingness of members to seek new members, involve all participants, and share knowledge and the results of their endeavors (Moore & Brooks, 2001). Benefits associated with community membership include an increase in intellectual capital (Stewart, 1997), an increase in social capital including the norms of reciprocity (Putnam, 2000), and the satisfaction obtained through membership (Lott & Lott, 1965). It has also been suggested that sense of community is characterized by a phenomenon of the whole being greater than the sum of its parts (Hawley, 1950). These characteristics afford members clear advantage over non-members, but it remains unclear in what ways these characteristics might be purposefully developed in online settings (Bonk & Wisher, 2000). It is clear, however, that the decision to join some communities and not others rests with the *will* of the individual (Tönnies, 1955). Factors that influence this decision remain unclear, although it is generally accepted that individuals seek community membership because it is beneficial for them to do so (McMillan, 1996).

While a definitive definition of community remains elusive (Puddifoot, 1996), a number of generally accepted characteristics have been suggested. Community is distinct from family and society (Tönnies, 1955), and it exists in a geographic and relational sense (Gusfield, 1975) including online settings (Surratt, 1998) in the form of virtual communities. It has been suggested that community is a sense rather than a tangible entity (Wiesenfeld, 1996). Sense of community exists in many forms including those associated with neighborhoods, fraternities, sport, and religion, and an individual is likely to belong to more than one community at a time (Sarason, 1974). Sense of community has been represented as a four-dimensional framework comprising the elements of membership, influence, fulfillment of needs, and shared emotional connection (McMillan & Chavis, 1986), although these elements might be present at varying levels in different community settings (McMillan, 1996). Individual community member's experience of these elements can be measured using the Sense of Community Index (SCI) (Chavis et al., 1986), a measurement tool that has been shown to have validity across contexts (Chipuer & Pretty, 1999) and data gathering techniques sensitive to the realities of members (Sonn, Bishop, & Drew, 1999). However, it is not clear in what ways the individual's experience of each of these discrete elements might be promoted in online settings.

Copyright © 2007, Idea Group Inc. Copying or distributing in print or electronic forms without written permission of Idea Group Inc. is prohibited.

The Learning Community Development Model

Following an expansive review of contemporary literature, Brook and Oliver (2003) developed the learning community development model (LCDM). The model describes three components in the process of community development in online settings—those that exist prior to any instructor actions, identified as presage factors. Instructor actions, identified as process teaching and learning strategies, and the various outcomes including sense of community, identified as the product. Figure 1 shows the three components of the LCDM.

Those factors that exist prior to any action from the instructor are described as presage factors. These factors are presented in three categories of system, learning context, and student characteristics. Process factors describe the forms of engagement and activity employed by the instructor to promote community development. These are presented in the categories of establishing a reason and context for communication, enabling communication, supporting communication, and moderating communication. The final component of the LCDM describes the product of the interrelationship between presage factors and process teaching and learning strategies, and includes—among other outcomes—sense of community.

The suggested interrelationship between presage factors and process teaching and learning strategies in developing a sense of community among learners gives rise to the question: *In what ways do process teaching and learning strategies employed by instructors influence community development in online settings?*

Figure 1. The Learning Community Development Model (Brook & Oliver, 2003)

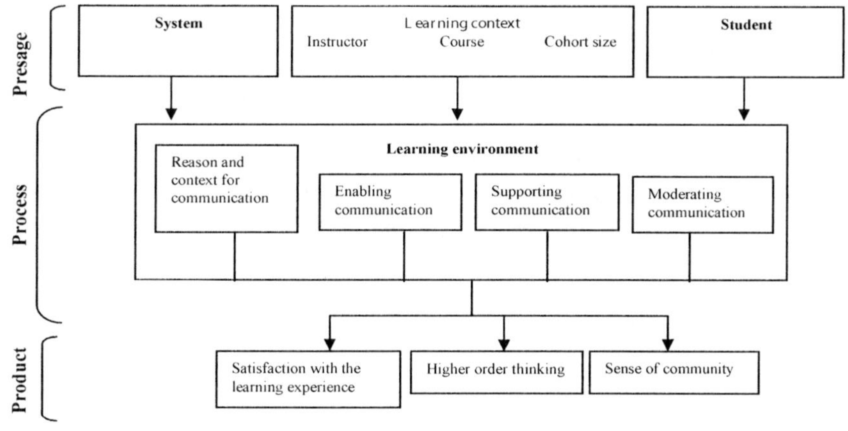

Copyright © 2007, Idea Group Inc. Copying or distributing in print or electronic forms without written permission of Idea Group Inc. is prohibited.

Methodology

The context-specific nature of the community experience (Sonn et al., 1999) and the desire to ensure congruence between the goals of the researcher and those of the practitioner (Reeves, 1999, 2000) influenced the methodology developed for this study. In accordance with these factors, a grounded theory (Strauss, 1987) approach was chosen due to the inductive nature of generating theory from close contact with the empirical world (Patton, 1990). In the tradition of Grounded Theory, data collection strategies were embedded in the experiences, actions, and behaviors of the actors involved, requiring a case study approach to the inquiry (Willig, 2001). This approach accounted for the context-specific nature of the community experience, providing for the generation of theory from the actions of expert practitioners. A multi-case approach (Burns, 1996) involving multiple instances of the development of an online learning community was used. This approach allowed for refinement and further development of findings based on multiple instance of the same phenomenon under different conditions (Willig, 2001). Five instrumental cases considered exemplar models (Willig, 2001), selected on a replication logic (Burns, 1996), were chosen for this study.

Data Collection

The selection of data collection methods was guided by the nature of case study research that requires a certain level of *triangulation* (Willig, 2001) and the context-specific nature of the community experience (Hill, 1996). In accordance with these conditions, it was necessary to adopt data collection mechanisms that allowed participants to describe their experience, allowed an objective interpretation of the community experience, and provided a way to quantify the community experience. Data collection methods included the following.

Interviews

Interviews were used to account for the forms of engagement and activity the instructors adopted to promote community development. Interview methods were sensitive to the instructor's understanding and interpretation of the forms of engagement and activity employed (Willig, 2001). Interviews were conducted in the early and latter stages of course delivery.

Copyright © 2007, Idea Group Inc. Copying or distributing in print or electronic forms without written permission of Idea Group Inc. is prohibited.

Observations

Potential incongruence between what the interviewee says and what actually happens was explored through the inclusion of an observational data collection strategy (Becker & Blanch, 1970). Observations were made of all participant online interactions throughout the various courses.

Questionnaire

A demographic questionnaire was employed to collect data on individual characteristics that appeared likely to influence community development including cultural influence, communication patterns, and perceptions of self as connected or separate. Participating students were asked to complete the questionnaire at the beginning of the various courses.

Sense of Community Index

The SCI was the principal source of data gathered to facilitate exploration of the community experience. Respondents were required to rate their experience of the four discrete elements of sense of community on a five-point scale (1 = low and 5 = high). These ratings were then combined to provide the individual's total sense of community experience (4 = minimum and 20 = maximum). The index was completed at the beginning of the course to establish the early sense of community experience and toward the end to ascertain any variation.

Results

The reporting of each case study begins with an overview of the course, including presage and process factors that appeared to influence community development. This is followed by an investigation of participant responses to the SCI. The chapter concludes with a presentation of factors that emerged as supports or limitations in community development, and any emergent trends in the interrelationship between the presage and process components of the model.

Copyright © 2007, Idea Group Inc. Copying or distributing in print or electronic forms without written permission of Idea Group Inc. is prohibited.

Case Study 1: Alexander's Course

Introduction

In his course, Alexander was delivering a teaching and learning skills program for higher education instructors working in the university setting. The course operated over a five-week period and included 27 participating students. The course was delivered in the online setting and included one face-to-face meeting scheduled at the beginning of the course.

Process Teaching and Learning Strategies

Investigation of the reason and context established by the instructor revealed that a sense of advantage motivated individuals to engage in collaborative activity. All the reports required as an outcome of group activity were completed, indicating that students engaged in some form of cooperative endeavor. Many students reported that learning activities that reflected the lived-in world motivated their participation.

Many students reported benefits associated with a free choice of communication tools. Manipulating the cohort to develop small-group and whole-class settings was seen to reduce the risk associated with communication in public forums for some students, while ensuring critical mass required for a satisfactory group experience. However, the pace of learning was a commonly cited impediment to meaningful interactions with students perceiving a lost opportunity to engage in critical discussion.

The instructor took intentional action to support communication in various ways. Technical training provided to students at the beginning of the course assisted 97% of the students engage in online interactions in a timely manner. Peer support networks were active and there was ample evidence of knowledge sharing. Student written communication adhered to social norms and while there was an awareness of the potential for misunderstanding, there was little evidence that students were discomforted by communications. Group activities were managed by the students, requiring them to engage in self-regulatory behaviors.

Alexander used a warm, friendly, and accepting tone in his written communication that transferred to student behaviors. His timely contributions to discursive activity were seen to motivate continued student participation.

An overview of the conditions seen to influence community development in this setting is presented in Table 1. A positive or negative symbol is used to describe an instance where predominant factors were seen to be either positive or negative.

Table 1 shows that instructor actions were generally supportive of community development. in Alexander's course but were predominantly unsupportive, however.

Copyright © 2007, Idea Group Inc. Copying or distributing in print or electronic forms without written permission of Idea Group Inc. is prohibited.

Table 1. Process factors influencing community development (Alexander's course)

Instructor	Process Teaching and Learning Factors			
	Reason and Context	Enabling	Supporting	Moderating
Alexander	+	-	+	+

Student Responses to the Sense of Community Index

The overall sense of community experienced by participants is indicated as an aggregation of the ratings given to each of the four discrete elements. The minimum rating possible is four and the maximum is 20. Of the 27 students participating in the course, eight volunteered to complete the SCI.

The student responses to the SCI indicate that in many instances the student's perceived sense of community altered as a consequence of course participation. Table 2 shows that of the eight respondents, six perceived an increased sense of community and two indicated that this sense reduced. This suggests that process factors tended to overcome many of the limiting aspects of presage factors present in this setting. However, this was not the case for all students, suggesting factors that suppressed aspects of the community experience for some individuals continued throughout the course. The SCI does not indicate in what ways these factors influenced community development, however it does suggest that sense of community was reduced for these two students.

It is useful to further explore the extent to which students experienced each of the four discrete elements of sense of community described in the SCI. Table 3 shows

Table 2. The sense of community experienced by participants in Alexander's course

Student	Sense of Community		
	1st	2nd	Diff.
Bridgett	14.33	15.33	+1.00
Maurice	12.33	13.33	+1.00
Marianne	9.66	12.66	+3.00
Yvonne	11.66	13.00	+1.34
Jim	6.00	7.33	+1.33
Valerie	6.66	5.33	-1.33
Brenda	9.66	11.33	+1.67
Natalie	11.00	10.33	-0.67
Average	**10.16**	**11.08**	**+0.92**

Copyright © 2007, Idea Group Inc. Copying or distributing in print or electronic forms without written permission of Idea Group Inc. is prohibited.

Table 3. Discrete elements of sense of community experienced by participants in Alexander's course

Students	Sense of Fulfillment of Needs			Sense of Membership			Sense of Influence			Sense of Shared Emotional Connection		
	1st	2nd	Diff.	1st	2nd	Diff.	1st	2nd	Diff.	1st	2nd	Diff.
Bridgett	3.66	4.00	+0.34	3.33	3.33	even	3.66	4.00	+0.34	3.33	2.66	-0.67
Maurice	3.00	3.33	+0.33	2.33	2.66	+0.33	3.00	3.33	+0.33	4.00	3.66	- 0.34
Marianne	2.00	3.66	+1.66	1.66	3.00	+1.34	3.00	3.00	even	3.00	3.33	+0.33
Yvonne	3.33	4.00	+0.67	2.33	2.66	+0.33	2.66	2.66	even	3.33	3.33	even
Jim	1.00	2.00	+1.00	1.00	1.33	+0.33	2.00	1.66	-0.34	3.00	2.66	-0,34
Val	1.33	1.33	even	1.00	1.00	even	1.66	1.00	-0.66	2.66	2.00	-0.66
Brenda	2.66	4.00	+1.34	1.33	1.66	+0.33	2.33	3.00	-0.67	3.33	3.00	-0.33
Natalie	2.33	3.33	+1.00	2.33	1.33	-1.00	2.66	2.33	-0.33	3.66	3.33	-0.33
Average	**2.51**	**3.20**	**+0.69**	**1.96**	**2.25**	**+0.29**	**2.70**	**2.62**	**-0.08**	**3.66**	**3.08**	**-0.58**

the student experience of each of the discrete elements of sense of community and indicates variation.

Table 3 shows that in general terms, respondents indicated an increased sense of fulfillment of needs (+0.69) and membership (+0.29). Of the eight respondents, seven showed an increased sense of fulfillment of needs and six indicated an increased sense of membership. As presage factors remained constant, it appears that process factors overcame limiting aspects of presage factors and promoted a sense of fulfillment of needs and membership among participants. However, this was not the case for all four discrete elements of sense of community. Five students reported a reduced sense of influence (-0.08) and six a reduced sense of shared emotional connection (-0.58). This suggests that aspects of process factors were not useful in promoting a sense of influence and shared emotional connection among students.

Most students reported that the excessive pace of learning served to limit their participation in collaborative activity. Those students who commented on the limiting nature of the pace of learning referred to a decreased opportunity to engage in meaningful interactions and thoughtful reflections. In addition, some students expressed dissatisfaction with the role of online instructor, arguing that this limited their communication opportunities.

In this setting it appears that in the process component of the model, in the event the instructor established a more suitable pace of learning and made more direct contributions to discursive activity, community development would have been further supported.

Copyright © 2007, Idea Group Inc. Copying or distributing in print or electronic forms without written permission of Idea Group Inc. is prohibited.

Case Study 2: Philip's Course

Introduction

The course in which Philip participated was an undergraduate education program for students studying how to teach in online settings. The course operated over a 12-week period, included 12 students, and was delivered exclusively in the online setting.

Process Factors

Students in this setting indicated that their motivation to engage in collaborative activity came from the advantage received for doing so and the authentic nature of learning activities. The majority of reports required as an outcome of small-group activity were produced; however, one group was seen to be dysfunctional, with only one active member and the report was not produced. The flexible nature of group membership ensured that the active student in this small-group setting was able to continue participation through seeking membership in a more active setting. Rotated membership in small-group settings ensured that all active students shared the burden of non-participating students. The use of small-group and whole-class settings resulted in an increased opportunity for all students to contribute in meaningful ways, and the provision of a meeting schedule resulted in an appropriate pace of learning. However, many students perceived that, as a consequence of the restrictions placed on the use of CMC (computer-mediated communication) technologies, this setting did not meet their communication needs.

Technical difficulties were not cited as impediments to participation in this setting, suggesting that stating technical expectations and requirements was a useful strategy in preparing students for learning in online settings. In addition, there was scant evidence that students were discomforted by online interactions, suggesting that they were aware of the protocols for communicating in written forms. In addition, many students were seen to undertake various roles and responsibilities, and regulate their own learning experience.

Many students responded well to the warm and friendly tone of communication established by the instructor and mirrored this behavior. The peer support and social discussion forums were well used, with many students taking advantage of the opportunity to post or respond to questions and engage in non-course-related discussion. However, many students cited the level of instructor participation in discursive activity as a limiting aspect of this course.

Copyright © 2007, Idea Group Inc. Copying or distributing in print or electronic forms without written permission of Idea Group Inc. is prohibited.

Table 4. Process factors influencing community development (Philip's course)

Instructor	Process Teaching and Learning Factors			
	Reason and Context	Enabling	Supporting	Moderating
Philip	+	-	+	-

An overview of the conditions seen to influence community development in this setting is presented in Table 4, indicating those factors of a presage or process nature that were supportive or limiting of community development. A positive or negative symbol is used to describe an instance where predominant factors were seen to be either positive or negative.

Interestingly, in Philip's course there were several process teaching and learning factors that appeared to be unsupportive of community development.

Student Responses to the Sense of Community Index

Table 5 shows student responses to the sense of community index and indicates variation.

Data presented in Table 5 reveals that two students indicated an increased sense of community, and two indicated a reduction in their sense of community. It is noteworthy that while Angela, a student in Philip's course, experienced a relatively strong increase in her sense of community (+2.00), Miriam, who reported the greatest reduction in her community experience, reported a negative influence at almost the same level (-1.67). This polarity of experience suggests that instructor actions tended to overcome limiting aspects of presage factors for some participants but not others. Once again, the SCI does not indicate in what ways these factors influenced community development; however, it does suggest that two students experienced a reduced sense of community, while two others experienced an increased community experience.

Table 5. Results of the sense of community index (Philip's course)

Student	Sense of Community		
	1st	2nd	Diff.
Angela	12.00	14.00	+2.00
Kathleen	13.33	14.00	+0 .67
Mary Liz	14.33	13.66	-0.67
Miriam	15.33	13.66	-1.67
Average	**13.74**	**13.83**	**+0.09**

Copyright © 2007, Idea Group Inc. Copying or distributing in print or electronic forms without written permission of Idea Group Inc. is prohibited.

Table 6. Discrete elements of sense of community experienced by participants in Philip's course

Students	Sense of Fulfillment of Needs			Sense of Membership			Sense of Influence			Sense of Shared Emotional Connection		
	1st	2nd	Diff.	1st	2nd	Diff.	1st	2nd	Diff.	1st	2nd	Diff.
Angela	4.00	3.33	-0.67	1.66	3.33	+1.67	2.33	4.00	+1.67	4.00	3.33	- 0.67
Kathleen	4.66	3.66	-1.00	2.00	3.66	+1.66	3.33	4.00	+0.67	3.33	2.66	- 0.67
Mary Liz	4.33	2.66	-1.67	2.66	3.33	+0.67	3.66	4.33	+0.67	3.66	2.66	-1.00
Miriam	4.33	2.33	-2.00	3.00	3.66	+0.66	4.33	4.66	+0.33	3.66	2.33	-1.33
Average	**4.33**	**2.99**	**-1.42**	**2.33**	**3.35**	**+1.02**	**3.41**	**4.25**	**+0.84**	**3.66**	**3.08**	**-0.58**

The extent to which students experienced each of the four distinct elements of sense of community described in the SCI provides further insight into the individual sense of community experience. Table 6 shows at an individual level the student experience of each of the four discrete elements of sense of community and indicates variation.

The data shows that the individual experience of each of the four discrete elements of community altered and that some reasonably consistent trends appeared to emerge.

The individual experience of sense of fulfillment of needs is noteworthy. Initially, respondents reported a strong expectation that their needs would be met through their participation in this setting (4.33). However, all respondents reported a reduction in this sense at the end of the course (2.99). While this response remains positive, it suggests that actualities did not reflect student expectations. This is a strong indication that respondents perceived that their needs had not been met through their participation in this setting. In addition, respondents indicated a decreased sense of shared emotional connection, but an increased sense of membership and influence.

This finding suggests that in some way instructor actions appeared to promote a sense of membership and influence among students, but contribute to a reduced sense of fulfillment of needs and shared emotional connection.

Instructor actions that are likely to have contributed to a reduced sense of fulfillment of needs and shared emotional connection were revealed in the process component of the model. In this component it was revealed that many students were aggrieved at the restrictions placed on the use of CMC technologies, believing this to have suppressed communication opportunities. In addition, many students were critical of the level of instructor participation in course-related activities, believing this to have suppressed their learning opportunities. While the SCI provides scant insight into the influence these factors had on the sense of community experienced by students, it is likely that the influence was negative.

Copyright © 2007, Idea Group Inc. Copying or distributing in print or electronic forms without written permission of Idea Group Inc. is prohibited.

This outcome suggests a reasonably consistent trend in the influence that instructor actions had on the sense of community developed in this setting. It is likely that in the event the instructor was more engaged in discursive activity and allowed unrestricted access to CMC technologies, conditions supporting community development would have been enhanced.

Case Study 3: Cathleen's Course

Introduction

Cathleen was the instructor in a post-graduate program for professional teachers studying special education. The course operated over a 12 week period, included 44 students, and was delivered exclusively in the online setting.

Process Factors

Once again, the advantage received for participating in collaborative activity served as a primary factor motivating student participation. Many students took the opportunity to share knowledge and understanding derived from their workplace. Reports required as an outcome of group activity were produced, and there was scant evidence that individuals had not contributed in appropriate ways.

Students took advantage of the opportunity to use communication tools of their choosing to engage in frequent communications. The planned meeting schedule ensured an appropriate pace of learning and fostered a sense of continuance among participants. There was strong evidence in this setting that students were comfortable in communicating online, and were prepared to undertake various roles and responsibilities. However, technical problems were cited as the most inhibiting factor to participation, and there was a strong suggestion that the help desk facility did not fully meet student technical needs.

The tone of communication throughout the course mirrored the warm and welcoming tone established by Cathleen. There was little evidence that any students were dissatisfied with Cathleen's contributions, despite these being largely didactic in nature. Many students took advantage of the opportunity to engage in non-course-related discussion through the social discussion forum.

An overview of the conditions seen to influence community development in this setting is presented in Table 7, indicating those factors of a presage or process nature that were supportive or limiting of community development. A positive or negative symbol is used to describe an instance where predominant factors were seen to be either positive or negative.

Copyright © 2007, Idea Group Inc. Copying or distributing in print or electronic forms without written permission of Idea Group Inc. is prohibited.

Table 7. Process factors influencing community development (Cathleen's course)

Instructor	Process Teaching and Learning Factors			
	Reason and Context	Enabling	Supporting	Moderating
Cathleen	+	+	-	+

Table 7 shows that instructor actions were largely supportive of community development in this setting.

Student Responses to the Sense of Community Index

Completion of the SCI was voluntary, and 13 of the available 35 students chose to respond to the index. Table 8 shows student responses to the SCI at the beginning and end of the course, and indicates variation in the community experience.

The data reveals that overall, students reported a marginally increased sense of community. Of the 13 responses, eight reported an increased sense of community, four reported a reduced sense of community, and one reported that the sense of community remained static. These responses suggest that process factors overcame limiting aspects of presage factors for some participants but not others.

Table 9 shows the individual experience of each of the four discrete elements of sense of community and indicates variation. Although it continues to be difficult to draw definitive conclusions from such a small data set, some reasonably consistent

Table 8. Results of the sense of community index (Cathleen's course)

Student	Sense of Community		
	1st	2nd	Diff.
Melanie	7.33	8.33	+1.00
Louise	9.00	9.66	+0.66
Lisa	10.00	10.66	+0.66
Jennifer	11.00	12.00	+1.00
Wendy	11.33	13.66	+1.33
Janine	12.00	11.00	-1.00
Karin	12.33	12.00	-0.33
Ludmilla	11.66	12.66	-1.00
Tony	11.00	11.00	even
Tania	12.33	12.00	-0.67
Samantha	13.33	13.66	+0.33
Bridget	11.66	12.33	+0.67
Anonymous	12.00	12.33	+0.33
Average	**11.15**	**11.65**	**+0.48**

Copyright © 2007, Idea Group Inc. Copying or distributing in print or electronic forms without written permission of Idea Group Inc. is prohibited.

trends are evident. Table 9 shows that of the 13 respondents, nine reported a reduced sense that their needs had been met through their participation in this setting, two indicated that their sense of fulfillment of needs had not altered, and only two indicated that this sense had increased. In addition, 10 of the 13 respondents indicated a reduced sense of shared emotional connection, only two indicated that this sense had increased, and one indicated no change. In contrast, all 13 respondents indicated an increased sense of membership and 12 reported an increased sense of influence, with one respondent indicating no change.

This finding suggests a reasonably consistent trend in the way that instructor actions influenced sense of community development in this setting. In some way, instructor actions appeared to contribute to an increased sense of membership and influence among participants, while leading to a reduction in the sense of shared emotional connection and fulfillment of needs.

The instructor actions that are likely to have contributed to a reduced sense of fulfillment of needs and shared emotional connection were seen in the process component of the model. In this component it was revealed that many students were aggrieved at the nature of technical support available, believing this to have discouraged their participation. In addition, students were critical of the instructor's limited capacity to resolve technical problems, believing that the instructor had in some way been neglectful of her responsibilities. It was also seen that many students experienced delayed access to early online interactions, a situation that resulted in feelings of isolation and dissociation.

Table 9. Discrete elements of sense of community experienced by participants in Cathleen's course

Student	**Sense of Fulfillment of Needs**			**Sense of Membership**			**Sense of Influence**			**Sense of Shared Emotional Connection**		
	1st	2nd	Diff.	1st	2nd	Diff.	1st	2nd	Diff.	1st	2nd	Diff.
Melanie	2.33	2.33	even	1.33	2.00	+0.67	1.33	2.33	+1.00	2.33	1.66	+0.67
Louise	3.00	2.66	-0.34	1.33	2.00	+0.67	2.33	3.00	+0.67	2.33	2.00	-0.33
Lisa	3.33	3.00	-0.33	1.33	2.00	+0.67	2.33	2.66	+0.33	3.00	3.00	Even
Jennifer	3.33	3.00	-0.33	2.00	2.66	+0.66	2.66	3.66	+1.00	3.00	2.66	-0.34
Wendy	3.33	3.33	even	2.00	2.33	+0.33	3.00	4.00	+1.00	3.00	4.00	+1.00
Janine	3.33	2.33	-1.00	3.00	3.33	+0.33	2.66	3.00	+0.34	3.00	2.33	-0.67
Karin	3.00	2.66	-0.34	2.33	3.33	+1.00	3.33	3.66	+0.33	3.66	2.33	-1.33
Ludmilla	3.00	3.33	+0.33	2.33	3.00	+0.67	2.33	3.66	+1.33	4.00	2.66	-1.34
Tony	3.00	2.66	-0.34	2.00	2.66	+0.66	2.33	3.00	+0.67	3.66	2.66	-1.00
Tania	3.66	3.33	-0.33	2.00	2.66	+0.66	3.00	3.33	+0.33	3.66	2.66	-1.00
Samantha	3.66	4.00	+0,34	2.33	2.66	+0.33	3.33	3.66	+0.33	4.00	3.33	-0.36
Bridget	3.66	2.66	-1.00	1.00	2.66	+1.66	3.33	3.66	+0.33	3.66	3.33	-0.33
Anonymous	3.33	2.66	-0.67	1.33	2.66	+1.33	3.66	3.66	even	3.66	3.33	-0.33
Average	**3.23**	**2.92**	**- 0.31**	**1.87**	**2.61**	**+0.74**	**2.74**	**3.33**	**+0.59**	**3.30**	**2.76**	**-0.54**

Copyright © 2007, Idea Group Inc. Copying or distributing in print or electronic forms without written permission of Idea Group Inc. is prohibited.

It appears that in the event the instructor developed a stronger technical skill set and provided technical support to students, conditions supporting community development would have been enhanced. In addition, it appears that in the event the instructor facilitated more timely access to early online interactions, the feelings of isolation and dissociation experienced by students would have been lessened and the high rate of withdrawal might have been avoided.

Case Study 4: Jim's Course

Introduction

Jim taught a post-graduate education program for students studying the principles of online instruction. The course operated over a 12 week period, included nine students, and was delivered exclusively in the online setting.

Process Factors

All students participated in collaborative activity, even those who were usually unwilling to do so, indicating that the benefits provided for participation were well suited to the needs of individual students. Although two students expressed dissatisfaction with the nature of learning activities, the majority of students were satisfied that the authentic nature of learning activities motivated their participation and supported knowledge sharing. All reports required as an outcome of group activity were received, indicating that students engaged in some form of collaborative activity.

One student expressed dissatisfaction with the available communication tools; however, this was an isolated incident, with all other students taking advantage of the opportunity to use communication tools of their choosing. The regular meeting schedule established by the instructor appeared useful in keeping students engaged, with many students citing this as a factor that sustained their participation. Students cited the availability of small-group and whole-class settings as a factor that encouraged a sense of togetherness, providing the opportunity for experienced individuals to mentor others.

In one case, a technical difficulty appeared to result in a student withdrawing from the course. However, this was the only instance where a student appeared dissatisfied with the timeliness of the technical support provided by the instructor. The majority of students were active in discursive activity, and there was little evidence that any students were discomforted by the nature of online communications.

Copyright © 2007, Idea Group Inc. Copying or distributing in print or electronic forms without written permission of Idea Group Inc. is prohibited.

Table 10. Process factors influencing community development (Jim's course)

Instructor	Process Teaching and Learning Factors			
	Reason and Context	Enabling	Supporting	Moderating
Jim	+	+	+	+

Student communications mirrored the warm and welcoming tone of communication established by the instructor. The 100% completion rate of group activities reflected the willingness of individual students to undertake various roles and responsibilities. The leadership role was shared among participants, although the timely contributions made by the instructor were valued.

An overview of the conditions seen to influence community development in this setting is presented in Table 10, indicating those factors of a presage or process nature that were supportive or limiting of community development.

Jim's course was characterized by a setting where process factors were supportive of community development.

Student Responses to the Sense of Community Index

Eight of the nine students participating in this setting volunteered to complete the SCI. Table 11 shows student responses to the sense of community index at the beginning and end of the course, and indicates the variation at completion.

The student experience of sense of community appeared to increase as a consequence of participating in this setting, although this increase was not consistent for all students. Clare and Katrina, who reported the greatest increase in sense of community (+3.00), exemplify this outcome. Meanwhile, Michael—who reported

Table 11. Results of the sense of community index (Jim's course)

Student	Sense of Community		
	1st	2nd	Diff.
Clare	6.66	9.33	+3.00
Michael	7.33	7.33	even
Katherine	9.66	10.33	+0.67
John	10.66	11.66	+1.00
Athina	11.33	13.33	+2.00
Rodney	13.33	15.00	+2.00
Megan	15.33	16.00	+1.67
Katrina	14.00	17.00	+3.00
Average	**11.03**	**12.49**	**+1.46**

Copyright © 2007, Idea Group Inc. Copying or distributing in print or electronic forms without written permission of Idea Group Inc. is prohibited.

Table 12. Discrete elements of sense of community experienced by participants in Jim's course

Student	**Sense of Fulfillment of Needs**			**Sense of Membership**			**Sense of Influence**			**Sense of Shared Emotional Connection**		
	1st	2nd	Diff.	1st	2nd	Diff.	1st	2nd	Diff.	1st	2nd	Diff.
Clare	2.00	2.33	+0.33	1.00	2.33	+1.33	1.66	2.66	+1.00	2.00	2.00	even
Michael	2.00	2.33	+0.33	1.00	1.00	even	1.66	1.66	even	2.66	2.33	-0.33
Katherine	3.00	3.33	+0.33	1.66	1.66	even	2.33	2.33	even	2.66	3.00	+0.34
John	3.00	3.66	+0.66	2.00	2.33	+0.33	2.66	3.33	+0.67	3,00	2.33	-0.67
Athina	3.00	3.66	+0.66	2.33	2.66	+0.33	2.66	3.33	+0.67	3.33	3.66	+0.33
Rodney	4.00	4.33	+0.33	2.33	3.00	+0.67	3.33	3.33	even	3.66	4.00	+0.34
Megan	5.00	4.66	-0.34	2.33	3.33	+1.00	4.00	3.66	-0.34	4.00	4.33	+0.33
Katrina	4.00	5.00	+1.00	2.00	3.66	+1.66	4.00	3.66	-0.34	4.00	4.33	+0.33
Average	**3.25**	**3.66**	**+0.41**	**1.83**	**2.50**	**+0.67**	**2.79**	**3.08**	**+0.29**	**3.16**	**3.25**	**+0.09**

one of the lower sense of community experiences (7.3)—revealed no change in his sense of community experience.

Table 12 shows the individual experience of students in each of the four discrete elements of sense of community, and indicates variation between the beginning and end of the course.

Within this limited data set, some reasonably consistent trends appeared to emerge.

It appears that for the majority of students, instructor actions appeared to contribute to an increased sense for each of the discrete elements of sense of community. However, this was not the case for all students, with some perceiving no change in discrete elements of sense of community and others perceiving a reduction. Megan perceived a reduced sense of fulfillment of needs and influence, Katrina perceived a reduced sense of influence, and Michael reported a reduced sense of shared emotional connection. There was little evidence to suggest in what way conditions in this setting had influenced the sense of community experience for Katrina and Megan. These students were seen to engage in discursive activity and made no disparaging remarks regarding the setting or the actions taken by the instructor. However, it appears that the sense of community experienced by these respondents was suppressed in some way. As previously described, Michael made strong comment on what he perceived to be weakness in the actions taken by the instructor that contributed to his feeling of meaningless activity. It appears that in the event the instructor made minor modifications to the nature of collaborative activities, the participant sense of community experience would have been stronger.

Copyright © 2007, Idea Group Inc. Copying or distributing in print or electronic forms without written permission of Idea Group Inc. is prohibited.

Case Study 5: Elaine's Course

Introduction

Elaine presented a professional development program for registered training authorities (RTOs) working in the field of vocation education and training (VET) in principles of online teaching. The course was intended to operate over a six-month period with an initial active component of five weeks and included seven students. The course was delivered in the online setting with one face-to-face meeting scheduled for the end of the initial five-week period. The course did not progress beyond the initial five-week period.

Process Factors

Extremely low levels of student participation marked this course. There was scant evidence that actions taken by the instructor motivated students to engage in collaborative activity. Although students were given unrestricted access to communication tools, the instructor revealed that students preferred to communicate on a one-to-one basis with the instructor via the telephone. As might be expected, the students were unprepared to direct their own learning experience, preferring to take leadership from the instructor. The strong leadership role undertaken by the instructor was seen to reflect a traditional didactic approach to instruction and to promote passive behaviors among learners.

There was little evidence that students were discomforted by online communication, although their rate of participation was extremely low. Those students who did contribute to discursive activity adopted a warm and welcoming tone similar to that of the instructor.

An overview of the conditions seen to influence community development in this setting is presented in Table 13, indicating those factors of a presage or process nature that were supportive or limiting of community development. A positive or negative symbol is used to describe an instance where predominant factors were seen to be either positive or negative.

Table 13. Process factors influencing community development (Elaine's course)

Instructor	Process Teaching and Learning Factors			
	Reason and Context	**Enabling**	**Supporting**	**Moderating**
Elaine	-	-	-	+

Copyright © 2007, Idea Group Inc. Copying or distributing in print or electronic forms without written permission of Idea Group Inc. is prohibited.

Elaine's course was characterized by process factors being largely unsupportive of community development.

Student Responses to the Sense of Community Index

Of the seven participating students in this setting, only two volunteered to complete the SCI. Table 14 shows student responses to the sense of community index at the beginning and end of the course and indicates variation.

These responses suggest that conditions in this setting were not supportive of community development. Despite respondents indicating a reduced sense of community experience, there was little evidence that students were aggrieved with actions taken by the instructor. However, data analysis suggested that the instructor dominated discursive activity and tended to adopt a didactic approach to instruction. The aggregated sense of community index does not indicate in what ways these factors influenced community development, but it does suggest that the influence was negative.

Table 15 shows the individual experience of each of the four discrete elements of sense of community and indicates variation between the beginning and end of the course.

The difficulty in drawing definitive conclusions from a small data set is exemplified in this setting. However, it appears that the individual experience of each of the discrete elements of community altered and that some reasonably consistent trends emerged.

Table 14. Student responses to the Sense of Community Index (Elaine's course)

Student	**Sense of Community**		
	1st	**2nd**	**Diff.**
Meredith	7.00	5.00	-2.00
Robin	11.66	7.66	-4.00
Average	**9.33**	**6.33**	**-3.00**

Table 15. Discrete elements of sense of community experienced by participants in Elaine's course

Student	**Sense of Fulfillment of Needs**			**Sense of Membership**			**Sense of Influence**			**Sense of Shared Emotional Connection**		
	1st	**2nd**	**Diff.**	**1st**	**2nd**	**Diff.**	**1st**	**2nd**	**Diff.**	**1st**	**2nd**	**Diff.**
Meredith	2.00	1.33	-0.67	1.00	1.00	even	1.66	1.33	-0.33	2.33	1.33	-1.00
Robin	3.00	2.33	-0.67	2.00	1.33	-0.67	3.66	2.66	-1.00	3.00	1.33	-1.67
Average	**2.5**	**1.83**	**-0.67**	**1.50**	**1.16**	**-0.34**	**2.66**	**1.99**	**-0.67**	**2.65**	**1.33**	**-1.32**

Copyright © 2007, Idea Group Inc. Copying or distributing in print or electronic forms without written permission of Idea Group Inc. is prohibited.

Table 15 shows that in the majority of cases, respondents reported a decreased experience of each of the four discrete elements of sense of community. The only exception to this trend was Meredith, who reported a low but static sense of membership. This finding suggests that the actions taken by the instructor failed to promote a sense of community experience for the participants in this setting. It appears that in the event the instructor took more intentional action to establish a reason and context for communication, enabling, supporting, and moderating communication, the participant sense of community experience would have been stronger.

Exploring Process Teaching and Learning Strategies, and Community Development

The learning community development model provided a framework for exploring the development of sense of community in online settings. The study has revealed that many instructor actions were seen to support community development, while others were not. Trends in the data suggest a correlation between instructor actions described in the process component of the model and the participant sense of community experience. Table 16 shows the limiting and supporting aspects of process teaching and learning strategies in each setting, and the number of discrete elements of sense of community developed. A positive or negative symbol is used to describe predominant factors.

The data presented in Table 16 reveals that participants reported an increased experience of the discrete elements of sense of community in settings where the instructor demonstrated strong actions in each of the process elements of the Learning Community Development Model. In contrast, participants reported a reduced experience of two or more of the discrete elements of sense of community in settings characterized by weak instructor actions in one or more of the process elements.

Table 16. Trends in the influence of instructor actions on the sense of community experience

Instructor	Reason and Context	Enabling Communication	Supporting Communication	Moderating Communication	SOC Elements Increased
Alexander	+	-	+	+	+2
Philip	+	-	+	-	+2
Cathleen	+	+	-	+	+2
Jim	+	+	+	+	+4
Elaine	-	-	-	+	0

Copyright © 2007, Idea Group Inc. Copying or distributing in print or electronic forms without written permission of Idea Group Inc. is prohibited.

This finding suggests that those instructors who develop strong practices in each of the process elements of the Learning Community Development Model are likely to support community development.

Conclusion

The learning community development model identifies a number of important process factors, which can influence community development. In this study it was revealed that instructors used, and others failed to use, a variety of strategies to promote communication and participation. Analysis of the data collected revealed the following strategies were frequently successful in promoting conditions for community development. Using the model, this study has identified factors across all process elements that can support community development. Table 17 shows the process factors and elements that were seen to support community development across the five courses included in this study.

An analysis for the findings suggested instructors often used a variety of strategies to successfully promote community development in online settings.

As technology such as videoconferencing continues to develop, it might be interesting to explore the manner in which instructors use these technologies to support community development in online settings.

Table 17. Process factors and elements that can support community development

Process Factor	Element
Reason and Context for Communication	• Starting online interactions in a timely manner • Establishing real-world contexts • Providing incentives • Requiring a collaborative product • Establishing an onerous workload
Enabling Communication	• Using small-group and whole-class settings • Managing group membership • Establishing schedules • Using communication tools
Supporting Communication	• Encouraging self-regulation and leadership • Providing technical training and support in the immediate setting • Developing skills for communicating in text
Moderating Communication	• Humanizing the text-based setting • Engaging actively • Participating in a timely manner • Accepting all contributions

Copyright © 2007, Idea Group Inc. Copying or distributing in print or electronic forms without written permission of Idea Group Inc. is prohibited.

Limitations of the Study

The findings of this study provide strong evidence that the Leaning Community Development Model affords a framework that encapsulates the essential design principles for online learning communities. However, several factors can limit the generalizability of the findings.

The SOC experience is context specific and is an extra individual variable (Hill, 1996); as such, it is difficult to generalize the findings from one case study to another. A multi-case study approach was adopted to address this limitations; however, findings continue to be difficult to generalize due to the context-specific nature of the community experience and the small sample size.

The nature of human research that requires voluntary participation resulted in a small number of students participating in the study. This eventuality makes it difficult to claim with any degree of conviction that findings reflect the experiences of all participants.

Finally, the rich descriptions developed through qualitative research are simultaneously the strength and weakness of this approach. Such descriptions are derived from the observations of the researcher, and while every effort was made to ensure objective conclusions were drawn, it is not possible to avoid the subjective nature of interpretations drawn from observations.

References

Becker, H., & Blanch, G. (1970). Participant observation and interviewing: A comparison. In W. J. Filstead (Ed.), *Qualitative methodology*. Chicago: Markham.

Bonk, C. J, & Wisher, R. A. (2000). *Applying collaborative and e-learning tools to military distance learning: A research framework*. Retrieved July 2, 2002, from http://www.publicationshare.com/docs/Dist.Learn(Wisher).pdf

Brook, C., & Oliver, R. (2003). Online learning communities: Investigating a design framework. *Australian Journal of Educational Technology, 19*(2), 139-160.

Bruner, J. (2001). *Constructivist theory*. Retrieved May 10, 2001, from http://tip.psychology.org/bruner.html

Burns, R. B. (1996). *Introduction to research methods*. South Melbourne, Australia: Addison-Wesley Longman Australia.

Chavis, D. M., Hogge, J., McMillan, D., & Wandersman, A. (1986). Sense of community through Brunswick's lens: A first look. *Journal of Community Psychology, 14*, 24-40.

Copyright © 2007, Idea Group Inc. Copying or distributing in print or electronic forms without written permission of Idea Group Inc. is prohibited.

Chipuer, H. M., & Pretty, G. M. H. (1999). A review of the sense of community index: Current uses, factor structure, reliability and further development. *Journal of Community Psychology, 27*(6), 643-658.

Dewey, J. (1929). *The sources of a science of education.* New York: Liveright.

Gusfield, J. R. (1975). *The community: A critical response.* New York: Harper Colophon.

Hawley, A. H. (1950). *Human ecology: A theory of community structure.* New York: Ronald Press Company.

Hill, J. L. (1996). Psychological sense of community: Suggestions for future research. *Journal of Community Psychology, 24*(4), 431-437.

Hiltz, S. R. (1998). Collaborative learning in asynchronous learning environments: Building learning communities. *Proceedings of the WebNet 98 World Conference of the WWW, Internet and Intranet Proceedings,* Orlando, FL.

Lott, A. J., & Lott, B. E. (1965). Group cohesiveness as interpersonal attraction: A review of relationships with antecedents and variables. *Psychological Bulletin, 64,* 259-309.

McMillan, D. W. (1996). Sense of community. *The Journal of Community Psychology, 24*(4), 315-325.

McMillan, D. W., & Chavis, D. M. (1986). Sense of community: A definition and theory. *Journal of Community Psychology, 14,* 6-23.

Moore, A. B., & Brooks, R. (2001). Learning communities and community development: Describing the process. *International Journal of Adult and Vocational Learning.*

Palloff, R., & Pratt, K. (1999). *Building learning communities in cyberspace.* San Francisco: Jossey-Bass.

Patton, M. Q. (1990). *Qualitative evaluation and research methods.* Newberry Park, CA: Sage.

Puddifoot, J. E. (1996). Some initial considerations in the measurement of community identity. *The Journal of Community Psychology, 24*(4), 327-334.

Putnam, R. D. (2000). *Bowling alone.* New York: Simon and Schuster.

Reeves, T. (1999). *A research agenda for interactive learning in the new millennium.* Retrieved July, 29, 2001, from http://it.coe.uga.edu/~treeves/EM99Key.html

Reeves, T. (2000). Enhancing the worth of instructional technology research through design experiments and other development research strategies. *Proceedings of the International Perspectives on Instructional Technology Research for the 21st Century,* New Orleans, LA.

Sarason, S. B. (1974). *The psychological sense of community.* San Francisco: Jossey-Bass.

Copyright © 2007, Idea Group Inc. Copying or distributing in print or electronic forms without written permission of Idea Group Inc. is prohibited.

Sonn, C., Bishop, B., & Drew, N. (1999). Sense of community: Issues and considerations from a cross-cultural perspective. *Community, Work & Family, 2*(2), 205-218.

Stewart, T. A. (1997). *Intellectual capital.* New York: Doubleday/Currency.

Strauss, A. L. (1987). *Qualitative analysis for social scientists.* New York: Cambridge University Press.

Surratt, C. G. (1998). *Internet citizens and their communities.* New York: Nova Science.

Tönnies, F. (1955). *Community and association* (C. P. Loomis, Trans.). London: Routland & Kegan Paul.

Vygotsky, L. S. (1978). *Mind in society: The development of higher psychological processes* (M. Cole, V. John-Steiner, S. Scribner, & E. Souberman, Trans.). Cambridge, MA: Harvard University Press.

Wiesenfeld, E. (1996). The concept of 'we': A community social psychology myth? *The Journal of Community Psychology, 24*(4), 337-346.

Willig, C. (2001). *Introducing qualitative research in psychology adventures in theory and method.* Buckingham: Open University Press.

Copyright © 2007, Idea Group Inc. Copying or distributing in print or electronic forms without written permission of Idea Group Inc. is prohibited.

Chapter XVI

Promotion of Self-Assessment for Learners in Online Discussion using the Visualization Software

Toshio Mochizuki, The University of Tokyo, Japan

Hiroshi Kato, National Institute of Multimedia Education, Japan

Satoru Fujitani, Mejiro University, Japan

Kazaru Yaegashi, Fukuyama University, Japan

Shin-ichi Hisamatsu, The University of Tokyo, Japan

Tomoko Nagata, Hyogo University of Teacher Education, Japan

Jun Nakahara, The University of Tokyo, Japan

Toshihisa Nishimori, The University of Tokyo, Japan

Mariko Suzuki, Shiga University, Japan

Abstract

This chapter describes a method of self-assessment for learners in a collaborative discussion. The authors propose this method of self-assessment in an online discussion and examine its effectiveness through the development and evaluation of a software program in order to visualize the discussion on a bulletin board system.

Copyright © 2007, Idea Group Inc. Copying or distributing in print or electronic forms without written permission of Idea Group Inc. is prohibited.

The software, referred to as the "Bulletin board Enrollee Envisioner" (i-Bee), can visually display the co-occurrence relation between keywords and learners. Thus, i-Bee can display content-wise contributions made by each learner to the discussion. In addition, i-Bee can display the recent level of participation of each learner and the frequency of the learner's use of each keyword. Through the evaluation, the authors revealed that i-Bee enables students to assess and reflect upon their discussion, understand the condition, and reorganize their commitment in a discussion that reflects their learning activity.

Introduction

The study of computer-supported collaborative learning (CSCL) is a challenge with regard to producing an environment that is conducive to mutual learning among learners who use computers. Recent research in e-learning has highlighted the significance of building an online learning community, which plays a role in the sustenance of a fruitful online learning experience (Palloff & Pratt, 1999). At present, the importance of promoting communication among learners via computer-mediated communication (CMC) is rapidly increasing.

However, there are some difficulties faced by learners in mutually recognizing the status of a learning activity in the CSCL environment—this constitutes the most important research issue (Gutwin, Stark, & Greenberg, 1995; Kato, Mochizuki, Funaoi, & Suzuki, 2004). Japanese communication researchers Kimura and Tsuzuki (1998) pointed out that group communication in the CMC tends to be disorganized and lacks in cohesion due to decreased interpersonal pressure, given the nature of the CMC. Briefly, learners are sometimes confused about what they should and should not discuss. This raises the question of the way in which CSCL environments assist learners in recognizing their commitment and reorganizing their discussion in a content-wise manner; if not, it may lead to a failure in the organization of a fruitful discussion for the purpose of learning.

In order to address this issue, the authors propose a method to self-assess the online discussions in electronic forums or bulletin board systems (BBSs). Self-assessment is very effective for learners seeking to improve their knowledge and learning strategy (Shaklee, Barbour, Ambrose, & Hansford, 1997), particularly in a collaborative learning setting. By helping learners realize that their activities are contributing to the community, learners will be self-motivated to cooperate with each other much more during online learning (Chapter V, this volume). Learners are required to monitor the actual status of their discussion, the learning process, and their interpersonal relations. This is to improve their learning community and plan the course of their education, which will enable them to make learning a significant experience.

Copyright © 2007, Idea Group Inc. Copying or distributing in print or electronic forms without written permission of Idea Group Inc. is prohibited.

Messages exchanged in the electronic forums are useful in the assessment of collaborative learning, given that they are visualized resources of interaction among learners in a collaborative learning setting. In other words, the messages exchanged during a discussion are reflective of the learner's ability in the context of the activity (*in situ*) (Pea, 1993; Palincsar, 1998). According to the social constructivism perspective, the learner's ability in a collaborative learning setting emerges socially; therefore, the ability should be assessed on the basis of a visualized interaction among the learners and circumstances including artifacts and social factors. The qualitative assessment of the interaction between and among learners in CSCL records has always comprised a content analysis of all messages in order to detect any substantial change in them (Chi, Slotta, & de Leeuw, 1994; Oshima, 1997; Hmelo-Silver, 2003). However, a manual assessment of these messages by the learners is impractical given the tremendous effort that is required of them.

In light of this, some researchers have attempted to extract the keywords (Simoff, 1999) and abstracts of messages (Fujitani & Akahori, 2000) from the discussions by using the quantitative method. However, certain problems persist in these studies:

1. As a result of employing the probabilistic method to show the co-occurrence relations, the sentences were generally too short to contain adequate information that could be used in a collaborative learning context, raising the question of reliability.
2. As a result of presenting only the summaries, these studies do not go as far as to indicate the contribution of individual learners to the discussion, so it was of little help in assessing individual learners, although the overall message was comprehensible.
3. This method could be useful in helping learners, who did not participate in the discussion from the start, to grasp the situation; however, it is unclear how it could benefit active participants.

In this study, the proposed method of content-wise visualization of the communication produces a mapping of coordinates, which indicates how strongly each learner relates to each keyword in his/her messages. Mapping reveals the entire structure of communication in the learning community—the manner in which each learner participates in the communication and the organization of group communication.

In order to examine the validity and usefulness of the proposed method, the authors developed a software referred to as "i-Bee," (Bulletin board Enrollee Envisioner), which can visualize the relationship between learners and keywords in online messages in real time. This software also provides snapshots of past discussions and animations, which display the trajectory of change from a given period. Thus, i-Bee aims to enable learners to have a perception of their discussion in its entirely and to encourage them to assess their discussion.

Copyright © 2007, Idea Group Inc. Copying or distributing in print or electronic forms without written permission of Idea Group Inc. is prohibited.

The purpose of this study is to examine the effectiveness of self-assessment of online discussions through the development and evaluation of i-Bee based on the proposed method. With regard to learners' self-assessment, this study primarily focuses on and discusses the experience of learners in order to recognize and improve a discussion using i-Bee.

Visualizing Online Conversation

Several recent studies have focused on the visualization of learner activities in CSCL in order to create an awareness among learners. For example, Nakahara, Hisamatsu, Yaegashi, and Yamauchi (2005) developed a software that could visualize the status of the interaction and activeness of electronic forums on a mobile phone screen, in order to promote participation awareness and encourage learners to participate in the discussion at any time. Other researchers have attempted to visualize activeness (Yamauchi, Nakahara, Nagai, Kato, & Nagaoka, 2002) and social networks (e.g., Martínez, Dimitriadis, Rubia, Gómez, & de la Fuente, 2003) in the community by confirming the status of communities in CSCL. However, to date, little previous research focused on the visualization of contents of the discussion among learners. Puntambekar and Luckin (2003) have indicated that it could be worthwhile to allow learners to view the contents of the discussion and learn through reflection over the process.

In this study, the authors propose a visualization method using a text-mining technique in order to assess conversations among learners on the BBS.

Application of Text-Mining Technique

Research in the field of text mining has progressed only recently. Numerous methods have been developed for extracting applicable keywords from the text data. In addition, multivariate analyses, such as the multivariable dimension scale (MDS) and correspondence analysis (CA), are generally used to visualize the relationship of individual keywords to the entire text (Greenacre, 1984).

CA is a graphically descriptive method that facilitates an intuitive understanding of the relationship by presenting two or more discrete variables in a complex data matrix. For instance, when the matrix is based on the frequency with which each keyword is used for each person or group, frequently co-occurring variables are placed in close proximity to each other. It is considered suitable for learners to recognize the content-wise contribution made by each learner to the discussion as clusters (of keywords and persons); these clusters refer to related elements in the

Copyright © 2007, Idea Group Inc. Copying or distributing in print or electronic forms without written permission of Idea Group Inc. is prohibited.

text data (Li & Yamanishi, 1999). In addition, as compared to the Latent Semantic Analysis (Landauer, Laham, & Derr, 2004), which is suitable for analyzing vast amounts of data, CA is a more appropriate method by which to analyze a small amount of statistical data, such as messages on the BBS, since CA is independent of statistical assumptions.

Visualizing Discussion using CA

According to the method proposed in this study, if n learners discuss a relevant number of m keywords, which totals $n \times m$ for a cross-tab of **N**, then CA yields a mapping of a row vector **F** and a column vector **G**. In other words, the generalized singular value decomposition of matrix **P**, which is the relative frequency matrix of **N**:

$$\mathbf{P} = \mathbf{A}\,\mathbf{D}_{\mu}\,\mathbf{B}^{T}$$

yields a left generalized singular vector **A** and a right generalized singular vector **B**. The use of these two vectors:

$$\mathbf{F} = \mathbf{D}_{R}^{-1}\,\mathbf{A}\,\mathbf{D}_{\mu}$$

and

$$\mathbf{G} = \mathbf{D}_{C}^{-1}\,\mathbf{B}\,\mathbf{D}_{\mu}$$

results in the standardized principal coordinates **F**, **G**, which construct a mapping (Greenacre, 1984).

In this mapping, $\mathbf{D}_{\mu}$ is a diagonal matrix leading to the generalized singular value diagonal vector, $\mathbf{D}_{R}$ is the diagonal matrix that makes matrix **P** the diagonal vector, and $\mathbf{D}_{C}$ is the diagonal matrix of the sum of the columns of matrix **P**. In addition, **F** and **G** correspond with the coordinates of learners and keywords, respectively.

The Significance of Mapping Generated by the Analysis

Generally, when a CA is conducted using the relative frequency matrix **P**, **F** and **G** are distributed in proximity to each other if coordinates of **F** and **G** have a strong co-occurrence relation. In contrast, if coordinates of **F** and **G** do not have a co-occurrence relation, there is a greater dispersion between them. In addition, a relatively

Copyright © 2007, Idea Group Inc. Copying or distributing in print or electronic forms without written permission of Idea Group Inc. is prohibited.

high value in matrix **N** represents a coordinate that is located closer to the original point, and a relatively low value represents a coordinate that is located far from the original point.

Thus, it is believed that: (1) the distribution of coordinates indicates the co-occurrence relation between each learner and each keyword in his/her messages, and (2) all the data of (1) represents the topics in the discussions. Hence, a CA can display the status of an overall discussion in the BBS as well as that of each learner's involvement in that discussion. Although other aspects of the discussion, such as meaning and context, are not taken into consideration in the analysis, CA is simple and applicable to incomplete and fragmental sentences as seen in BBS messages.

The authors have already conducted a pilot study to examine the suitability of CA in order to visualize the discussion and to examine the effectiveness of mapping for learners' self-assessment. The result indicates the possibility of learners focusing more on certain topics of participation, planning their participation in topics of lesser interest, and following up on members who are unable to fully participate in discussions (Mochizuki, Fujitani, Isshiki, Yamauchi, & Kato, 2003).

Development of i-Bee

Based on the method proposed earlier, the authors developed a CSCL software—i-Bee (Bulletin board Enrollee Envisioner)—in order to visualize small-group (mainly asynchronous) discussions on BBS in real time. i-Bee is a plug-in tool that works with discussion forums of exCampus and its databases; exCampus is an e-learning module developed and distributed free of charge by the National Institute of Multimedia Education in Japan (Nakahara & Nishimori, 2003). It encompasses numerous functions that are necessary to build an e-learning site in a university—course management, learning management, interfaces for video streaming, discussion forums, and so forth.

The four features of i-Bee include: (1) the visualization of the relationship among keywords and learners in real time, (2) the visualization of a time-series trajectory and snapshots of certain past periods, (3) the visualization of the recent levels of participation of learners and of the frequency of keywords, and (4) the location of messages containing corresponding keywords, depicted as flowers, to be clicked by a learner on i-Bee.

Copyright © 2007, Idea Group Inc. Copying or distributing in print or electronic forms without written permission of Idea Group Inc. is prohibited.

Real-Time Visualization of Content-Wise Discussion

When a learner logs onto the BBS on exCampus, i-Bee pops up as an additional window (Figure 1) and displays the participating learners (bees) and keywords (flowers) selected by teachers. The distribution of the bees and flowers is based on the results of the CA conducted at that time. Each bee and flower is drawn with its name, which represents what is being described. i-Bee refreshes the status not only when the learner logs in, but also each time the learner accesses an article; therefore, i-Bee can display the updated status.

While visualizing the coordinates, i-Bee displays each bee inclined toward the flowers as an indication of the number of times a learner uses the corresponding keywords.

The angles of the bees are calculated based on the frequency and location of the flowers (see Table 1).

i-Bee was developed so that learners could recognize their statuses in the forums. Furthermore, it aimed at encouraging learners to reflect on their attitudes in a discussion in a content-wise manner. In order for learners to appropriately assess their discussion, it was necessary to design a visualized image for them to easily recognize the overall image and their level of involvement in the discussion.

In order to address this issue, the authors adopted the "bees and flowers" metaphor to explain the co-occurrence relation between the learners and keywords in the

Figure 1. Outline of i-Bee (Arrows, circles, and English translations are not included in the original; these are only included here for explanatory purposes.)

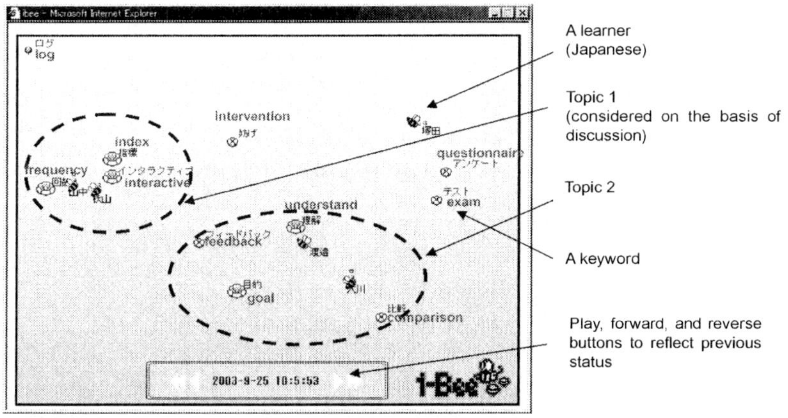

Copyright © 2007, Idea Group Inc. Copying or distributing in print or electronic forms without written permission of Idea Group Inc. is prohibited.

Table 1. Expressed information and its indexes, targets, and facial expressions

Information	Index	Target	Facial Expression
What each learner talks	Coordinates calculated by CA	Distance between bees and flowers	The more a learner uses a certain keyword, the shorter the distance between the learner and the keyword.
Recent trend of keywords used by each learner.	Weighted coordinate value of keywords calculated with the number of times each learner used the corresponding keywords recently.	Head direction of bees	The more frequently a learner uses a certain keyword, the more the corresponding bee turns toward the corresponding keyword (however, the display is limited to angles of 45, 135, 180, 225, and 315 degrees)
Activeness of each learner	$i = \frac{\text{number of the learner's articles at a certain period}}{\text{average number of the learner's articles per a period}}$	Bee	$i \geq 1$: active bee $1 \geq i \geq$ threshold: normal flying bee threshold $> i$: sleeping bee
Activeness of each topic (keyword)	$i = \frac{\text{frequency of the keyword used by all learners at a certain period}}{\text{average frequency of the keyword used by all learners per a period}}$	Flower	$i \geq 1$: full bloom $1 \geq i \geq$ threshold: flowering period threshold $> i$: bud of flower

discussion. Based on the algorithm of the CA, strongly related elements should be located as coordinates in close proximity to each other. A comparison of the algorithm with the metaphor exhibits quite a resemblance—bees get drawn toward attractive flowers out of a need to suck their nectar, while flowers require the bees to distribute their pollen. Thus, the learners can view the content and status of their discussion in the forum.

Visualization of the Discussion Process

Previous research indicated that learners can effectively reflect upon their learning experience when a learning support system provides trajectories or snapshots of their learning abilities at several points (Collins & Brown, 1988). Therefore, in order to promote an increased level of reflection by learners upon their discussion, the authors developed i-Bee to allow them to view their previous status and the process of change during the discussion.

When a learner accesses i-Bee, it displays a trajectory of the learner's coordinates from the unit time t–1 to t before providing a snapshot at time t (t is the number of unit time, which is calculated from the beginning until a certain point of time). Using the configuration tool, moderators such as teachers or teaching assistants are required to appropriately configure the unit of time in accordance with the learning activity. For example, if the course is conducted once a week, the teacher may set the unit time as one week.

Copyright © 2007, Idea Group Inc. Copying or distributing in print or electronic forms without written permission of Idea Group Inc. is prohibited.

Furthermore, learners can view their previous status at every unit of time. In other words, learners can view their discussion status as snapshots for a week before, a unit of time before, a unit of time after, or a week after, by clicking on the operation buttons provided within the i-Bee window.

While displaying the animation and snapshots, i-Bee fixes the coordinates of the flowers (keywords) and mobilizes those of the bees (learners) so as to naturally indicate the trajectory of the way in which each learner (bee) has related to the keywords (flowers) and other learners (bees).

Visualization of Activeness

Since it does not display the recent level of learner participation and that of the appearance of the keywords in the discussion, learners and moderators should experience difficulties in understanding the status of the discussion on the basis of the simple coordinates of bees and flowers produced by the CA.

In order to visualize their activeness at certain points, i-Bee displays the bees and flowers at three levels (refer to Table 1): "sleeping bee," "normal flying bee," and "active flying bee" represent the possible facial expressions of the learner's recent level of participation. "Flower bud," "flowering period," and "full bloom" represent the recent appearance of keywords, indicating their frequency. i-Bee calculates each learner's activeness as the proportion of his/her messages within the recent unit time to its average per unit of time. In the case of certain keywords, i-Bee calculates their activeness as the proportion of frequency of the use of keywords by all learners within the recent unit time to its average per unit of time.

Cooperation with exCampus Discussion Forums

i-Bee was developed to be compatible with the exCampus discussion forums. Learners can launch a search for messages containing certain keywords that are depicted as flowers on i-Bee. In this way, learners can easily locate interesting messages while viewing i-Bee by clicking on the corresponding flower. Thus, i-Bee assists learners in locating interesting or surprising articles from a large number of messages.

Implementation

Figure 2 shows the workflow of i-Bee. It requires a morpheme analysis system, such as "ChaSen" for Japanese text (Matsumoto et al., 2000), in order to calculate the frequency of each word from the text of the discussion.

Copyright © 2007, Idea Group Inc. Copying or distributing in print or electronic forms without written permission of Idea Group Inc. is prohibited.

In order to use i-Bee in a course, moderators are required to set keywords using the configuration tool because the automatic keyword selection, which is based on a statistical analysis, cannot select the appropriate words that are representative of a discussion. The configuration tool permits only the moderators to modify the settings (the unit of time to organize the frequency matrix, users whose articles are analyzed, users who use i-Bee, keyword selection, etc.). These keywords are stored in the condition database.

The frequency of the use of keywords and the indexical information in the discussion are stored in the keyword database, and this database will reflect the condition database. A database records the appearance of each keyword based on the following information:

- the speaker/author of the message in a certain period, and
- the total frequency of each keyword used in the messages by each speaker/author until a certain period.

The CA uses these data to construct a graphical display of the discussion profiles by using Ox. Ox is a formula processing environment, which is an object-oriented matrix programming language with a comprehensive mathematical and statistical function library (Doomik, 2001).

i-Bee procedure is as follows: first, the learners or the moderators open the visualizer (Figure 1), which was developed by using Macromedia Flash MX, and the calcula-

Figure 2. Workflow of i-Bee

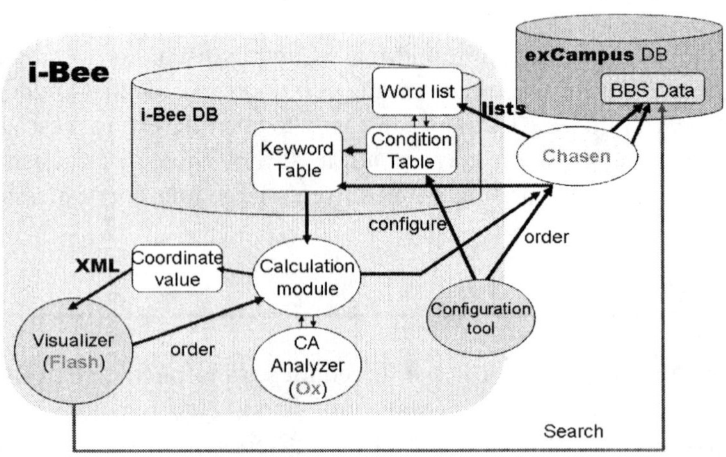

Copyright © 2007, Idea Group Inc. Copying or distributing in print or electronic forms without written permission of Idea Group Inc. is prohibited.

tor orders the morpheme analysis system to calculate the appearance frequency of the use of each keyword by each learner for a given period of time. Upon receiving the result, the keyword database stores the frequency matrix. In order to display the status at a certain period or the previous status, the CA calculates a matrix that conjugates a status at time t and another at the previous period t–1, as mentioned earlier. In other words, when n (l, t, w) is the accumulated frequency with which learner l uses keyword w until the unit time t, ***Nt*** is organized as:

$$\underset{2L\times W}{N_t} = \begin{bmatrix} n(1,t-1,1) & \cdots & n(1,t-1,k) & \cdots & n(1,t-1,W) \\ \vdots & \ddots & \vdots & ⋰ & \vdots \\ n(l,t-1,1) & \cdots & n(i,t-1,w) & \cdots & n(i,t-1,W) \\ \vdots & ⋰ & \vdots & \ddots & \vdots \\ n(L,t-1,1) & \cdots & n(L,t-1,w) & \cdots & n(L,t-1,W) \\ n(1,t,1) & \cdots & n(1,t,w) & \cdots & n(1,t,W) \\ \vdots & \ddots & \vdots & ⋰ & \vdots \\ n(l,t,1) & \cdots & n(i,t,w) & \cdots & n(i,j,W) \\ \vdots & ⋰ & \vdots & \ddots & \vdots \\ n(L,t,1) & \cdots & n(L,t,w) & \cdots & n(L,t,W) \end{bmatrix}, \text{where} \quad l = 1,\cdots,L, t = 1,\cdots T, w = 1,\cdots,W$$

The calculator commands the Ox to analyze the data using the CA. However, if a learner does not use any keyword or if a keyword does not appear at all, the operation is conducted with a matrix that omits the corresponding row or line from ***Nt*** since the operation cannot be completed due to the zero-line or -row. The analysis yields some value of the axis, and the coordinates **F** and **G** are elected as the first and second axis of the result, respectively. The calculator transforms the value of the coordinates to an XML format, and the visualizer receives the data from the calculator.

The graphical display produced by the CA displays the co-occurrence relation among participants and keywords. Learners can reflect upon not only their condition in the group, but also the flow of the discussion.

Evaluation

Method of Evaluation

As described earlier, the authors developed i-Bee to promote an understanding among learners of their current condition and to enable them to reflect upon the discussion in its entirety. The majority of us agree that it is extremely difficult to grasp higher-

Copyright © 2007, Idea Group Inc. Copying or distributing in print or electronic forms without written permission of Idea Group Inc. is prohibited.

order thinking processes in humans, such as reflection or meta-cognition. Protocol analysis is one of the methods of revealing the internal condition—for example, what the subject recognizes and how he/she feels under a certain circumstance (Ericsson & Simon, 1993). Some researches in collaborative learning conducted protocol analyses through constructive interaction among their subjects to reveal the manner in which they recognized and reflected (Roschelle, 1992; Miyake, 1986; Shirouzu, Miyake, & Masukawa, 2003). Thus, the authors assigned weight to the ideas spoken by the subjects in order to understand how their cognition worked while they used i-Bee.

Course Outline

The class prepared for an evaluation of i-Bee, referred to as "Preservice Training 7," which was a winter term prerequisite course comprising 10 lectures in an undergraduate course for interns in elementary or junior high school in Japan. Nine seniors participated in the course. They underwent internship during the summer semester. The ultimate goal of the course was for them to reflect upon their internship by preparing their teaching portfolios on the basis of discussions of their experiences during the internship and exchanging feedback regarding their teaching portfolios via the BBS. The teacher, who laid emphasis on online discussions, requested that students reflect on their own opinions regarding the discussion in their portfolios.

Discussions on the BBS were conducted for approximately 15 to 30 minutes at the beginning and end of seven out of the 10 classes. In the first four out of the seven discussions, the students discussed their experiences during the internship; in the next three discussions, they exchanged feedback on each other's portfolios. Each topic was discussed in different forums and was independently analyzed by i-Bee.

Data Collection

The authors observed two students, Alice and Betty (fictitious names), using video cameras. They were both preparing their portfolios based on their internship in junior high schools while they had been in both elementary and junior high schools. In class, they usually sat adjacent to each other, as shown in Figure 3. Their computer screens were also recorded using video cameras.

Although the BBS supports asynchronous communication (i.e., threaded discussion board), the students used the BBS synchronously during class hours. The reason for this is that their verbal data can be collected in natural situations when they sat together and verbally shared comments regarding what they observed on each of their i-Bee windows. However, the communication mode was partly asynchronous because the discussion was conducted across the lectures.

Copyright © 2007, Idea Group Inc. Copying or distributing in print or electronic forms without written permission of Idea Group Inc. is prohibited.

Figure 3. A scene from the case (Left: Alice; Right: Betty)

The first author participated in the course as a teaching assistant and recorded the data in five out of the 10 classes. In the first class, the author sought the students' permission for data collection only for the purpose of evaluating i-Bee; they granted permission. The first author also explained that the students were not required nor forced to make any remarks, although they were recorded by video cameras.

The keywords for i-Bee analysis were selected on the basis of a consensus drawn between the teacher and the first author. The keywords were selected from messages based on the educational purpose, learning context, and meaning of the keywords depending on the context of use. They altered the keywords based on the manner in which the discussion progressed. The selection process was conducted mainly during intervals between the lectures and also during class hours. The thresholds for measuring the activeness of learners and keywords were 0.4 and 0.6, respectively.

Results and Discussion: Learners' Assessment using i-Bee

The authors analyzed the videos and prepared transcripts based on them, including each utterance made by the students. A comparison of the screens with the utterance allowed the authors to study Alice and Betty's experience in recognizing the representation of i-Bee and the manner in which their recognition led to the progress of their discussion.

Copyright © 2007, Idea Group Inc. Copying or distributing in print or electronic forms without written permission of Idea Group Inc. is prohibited.

The results showed that: (1) i-Bee can be a cognitive resource for learners to assess the conditions, and (2) it can encourage learners to reflect and reorganize their learning activity on i-Bee by comparing their present status with their past status.

In this study, the authors present two cases that prove the findings summarized previously. For reasons of privacy, fictitious names have been assigned to the subjects used in the transcripts and figures. In the transcripts, the codes ":," "h," and empty double parentheses represent prolonged sounds, exhausted sounds, and unrecognizable utterances, respectively. Words enclosed in brackets indicate nonlinguistic actions.

Providing Opportunities for Assessment of the Status of Commitment in the Discussion

In this section, the authors describe the experience of the subjects in understanding their commitment as compared to that of other students. Alice observed that she shared a common commitment with another student, as described next; this assisted her in communicating with a student she had not previously interacted with (see Box 1).

Figure 4. Status of i-Bee at the time of Fragment 1 (Japanese words are the original expressions; English translations are attached to each element.)

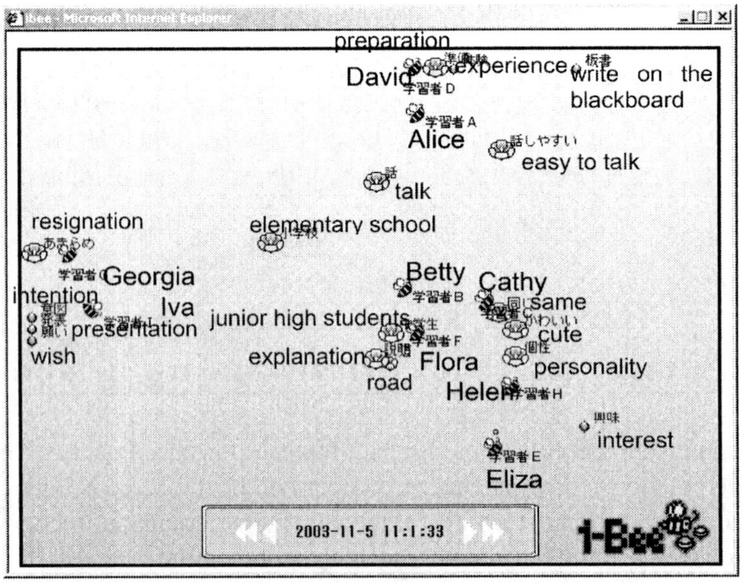

Copyright © 2007, Idea Group Inc. Copying or distributing in print or electronic forms without written permission of Idea Group Inc. is prohibited.

Box 1.

[Fragment 1]

[2006] Alice: Ah, here it is!

[2006] Betty: (( )) same place as everyone else.

[2007] Alice: Yeah, I am near by David

[2009] Betty: You're right. (( ))

[2011] Alice: Cathy is blurring again...hh...why is that? Why is it blurring?

[2017] Cathy: It's really sucking a lot of honey.

[2018] Alice: huhu hh: h

[2020] Alice: Might be poisoned!

[2021] Cathy: What should I do...it has a full stomach.

[2024] Alice: Hhhhh, this isn't good. (0.5) Eliza is still asleep.

[2029] Cathy: Ha hhhhh

[2030] Alice: And Flora is, too. Wake up, wake up!

[2032] ? : (( ))

[2033] Alice: Ahahahahaha

[2034] Alice: Really?

[2038] Alice: "Preparing" and "experience" are there

[2043] Alice: I'm friends with David

[Alice switches screen to check David's remarks and reads his messages.]

Figure 4 provides a representation of the i-Bee screen during the earlier-mentioned online discussion. In this fragment, Alice's observation that her bee's location on the i-Bee screen was closer to David's is expressed by her statement, "Yeah, I am near by David" [2007]. She then began reading David's messages, which is expressed by her statement, "I'm friends with David" [2043], although she did not pay much attention to his messages before this time.

At this point, we must pay attention to one of Alice's statements, "'preparing' and 'experience' are there" [2038], which was made before she began reading David's messages. Alice shifted her attention to "preparation" and "experience," although one observes the use of other phrases such as "easy to talk" and "talk," which are located near her bee on this screen. It appears reasonable to assume that she recognized a commonality with David based on these two keywords. In other words, she began reading his messages because she recognized a commonality with him.

Copyright © 2007, Idea Group Inc. Copying or distributing in print or electronic forms without written permission of Idea Group Inc. is prohibited.

Stating that such an activity is a type of assessment of the discussion is not an exaggeration. Other similar fragments were observed in our research. Viewed in this light, i-Bee can be regarded as a cognitive resource for learners to recognize their levels of commitment, which encourages them to conduct assessments, particularly in cases where they are less attentive.

Providing Opportunities for Reflection upon the Discussion by Comparison with Past Status

Fragment 2 describes Alice and Betty's experience in reflecting upon their statements in a content-wise manner by understanding the change in their position on i-Bee. Figure 5 shows the status of i-Bee at that time (see Box 2).

As shown in Figure 5, Alice's bee was located at a distance from the others, at a periclinal part of the mapping.

Alice stated "I can't say I'm happy with where it is," "I'm in a slightly awkward location" [4366], and "I'm so lonely" [4373], moving her mouse cursor between her bee and others very quickly, immediately after finding her location [4366].

Figure 5. Status of i-Bee window at the time of Fragment 2 (Japanese words are the original expressions; English translations are attached to each element.)

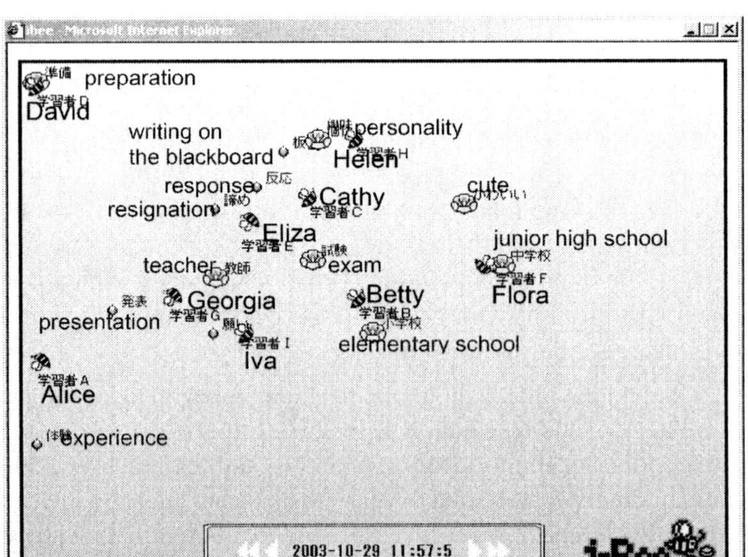

Copyright © 2007, Idea Group Inc. Copying or distributing in print or electronic forms without written permission of Idea Group Inc. is prohibited.

Box 2.

[Fragment 2]

[4355] Betty: It's interesting.

[4356] Betty: I'm starting here. [clicking on an icon on i-Bee with the mouse]

[4363] Alice: Where am I? Oh, my bee is here.

[4366] Alice: It's here, but…I can't say I'm happy with where it is. (1.5) I'm in a slightly awkward location…

[4373] Alice: Aww…My bee has become further away from the others. I'm so lonely.

[4377] Alice: Hey, don't you think my bee is lonely and distant from the others?

[4378] Betty: Where?

[4380] Betty: I can't find you?

[4384] Betty: Oh, here you are, I see.

[4385] Alice: Yeah.

[4386] Betty: I'm here. As I predicted, I'm still at the "elementary school." I have to move on to "junior high school."

[4390] Alice: My location changed from the last time. It's near "experience" now.

[4394] Betty: Oh, you're right, you're near "experience." h, h, hh

[4396] Alice: …but, the flower is wilted.

[4397] Betty: Big trouble for you!

— syncopation —

[4444] Betty: [She began to write a message titled "about junior high school students."]

At this point, it should be noted that Alice stated, "My bee has become further away from the others" [4373] and "my location changed from the last time" [4390] in the transcript. These words "become further away" and "changed" are significant in terms of the speaker's recognition of her change in status. In brief, it would not be possible for her to make such a statement without comparing her present status on i-Bee with her past status.

Therefore, it is clear that Alice used negative phrases such as "a slightly awkward location," "lonely and distant from the others" [4377], and so forth as a result of

Copyright © 2007, Idea Group Inc. Copying or distributing in print or electronic forms without written permission of Idea Group Inc. is prohibited.

her recognition of her change in status. These phrases are considered as an assessment of her bee that was now located in a relatively undesirable position than it was before; this showed that she did not commit well to the discussion.

Betty also assessed her location on i-Bee in this fragment of conversation. It is noteworthy that she attempted to improve her condition expressed on the i-Bee screen by herself. At that time, as shown in Figure 5, her location was closer to the "elementary school" and somewhat further away from "junior high school."

She confirmed her location and stated, "As I predicted, I'm still at the 'elementary school.' I have to move on to 'junior high school.'" [4386]. She then began writing a message titled "about junior high school students," which included her impression of the junior high school internship [4444].

In this case, similar to Alice's, it may be stated beyond doubt that Betty remembered the previous location of her bee as being closer to the "elementary school." She then "predicted" that its present location scarcely differed from its previous one and confirmed this as mentioned previously. She then engaged herself in writing messages regarding "junior high school."

Why did Betty state that she had "to move on to 'junior high school'"? At this point, we may recall their learning context—that is, they prepared their portfolios based on their internship in junior high school. Her position on i-Bee expressed a lack of association between her commitment in the discussion and her practice in this course. Consequently, she became aware of this disjunction and thereafter changed her statement. It can be stated that such an activity on Betty's part is indicative of the self-assessment and improvement of her statement in the discussion.

All these statements clarify that i-Bee can be a cognitive resource for learners to recognize a time-series change of state, which encourages them to assess their level of commitment to the topics or the entire discussion. Such recognition and assessment encourages learners to consider their level of participation at the meta-level.

Conclusion and Future Issues

This study deals with self-assessment during a discussion, wherein learners can view the discussion, reflect in a content-wise manner, and reorganize their attitude to the discussion. The authors propose a method by which to visualize learners' commitments to the content of a discussion and develop the i-Bee software, which is implemented in the algorithm to encourage learners to assess their discussion. The evaluation elucidates that the visualization of the discussion based on its contents should be a cognitive resource for learners to assess their learning through a discussion, along with an observation of the difference between their current and past statuses.

Copyright © 2007, Idea Group Inc. Copying or distributing in print or electronic forms without written permission of Idea Group Inc. is prohibited.

Thus, the authors conclude that providing opportunities for such assessments and reflection encourages learners to improve their learning by comparing their learning context even in a collaborative learning setting.

Our final points focus on future issues to address. The first issue is a more precise analysis of the effects of i-Bee, particularly in the asynchronous situation, in order to reveal more concrete results that indicate the manner in which i-Bee supports students. The second issue regards the selection of keywords. In order to assist even moderators such as teachers or assistants, a new method should be developed. This method should be able to satisfactorily select keywords for learners and teachers based on the learning context and from the viewpoint of social constructivism, which constitutes the basis of the collaborative learning theory. The third issue addresses the information provided by CSCL and e-learning environments like i-Bee. It can be said that providing awareness of both the discussion and other social activities is likely to encourage learners to assess and improve their activities in the CSCL and e-learning environments. In order to support learners by teaching staffs such as teachers, mentors, moderators, and so forth (e.g., Ueno, 2003), recent studies in e-learning have tried to develop data mining systems to extract and provide comprehensive information of learning activities from LMS (learning management system). However, these studies have not contributed to learners' self-assessment in online learning. At this stage, the possibility of awareness for self-assessment is a mere conjecture; we would like to empirically discuss this issue in our future works.

Acknowledgments

Portions of this chapter were presented at CSCL'05 (Mochizuki et al., 2005) and granted the right to be re-used here by the International Society of the Learning Sciences. A part of this research has received the assistance of Grant-in-Aid for JSPS Fellows for Toshio Mochizuki, Grant-in-Aid for Exploratory Research (No. 15650171, Representative: Hiroshi Kato), Grant-in-Aid for Scientific Research (B) (No. 16300280, Representative: Hiroshi Kato), Grant-in-Aid for Specific Field (No. 15020103; No 17011042, Representative: Mariko Suzuki), and Grant-in-Aids for Young Studies (B) (No. 17700607, Representative: Toshio Mochizuki; No. 16700560, Representative: Tomoko Nagata) from the Japanese Ministry of Education, Culture, Sports, Science, and Technology.

Copyright © 2007, Idea Group Inc. Copying or distributing in print or electronic forms without written permission of Idea Group Inc. is prohibited.

References

Chi, M. T. H., Slotta, J. D., & de Leeuw, N. (1994). From things to processes: A theory of conceptual change for learning science concept. *Learning and Instruction, 4,* 27-43.

Collins, A., & Brown, J.S. (1988). The computer as a tool for learning through reflection. In H. Mandi & A. Lesgold (Eds.), *Learning issues for intelligent tutoring systems* (pp.1-18). New York: Springer-Verlag.

Doomik, J. A. (2001). *Ox: An object-oriented matrix language* (4th ed.). London: Timberlake.

Ericsson, K., & Simon, H. (1993). *Protocol analysis—Verbal reports as data.* Cambridge, MA: The MIT Press.

Fujitani, S., & Akahori, K. (2000). A summary extraction method of e-mail discussion and its Web-based application to mailing list review. *Educational Technology Research, 23*(1-2), 1-12.

Greenacre, M. J. (1984). *Theory and applications of correspondence analysis.* London: Academic Press.

Gutwin, C., Stark, G., & Greenberg, S. (1995). Support for workspace awareness in educational groupware. *Proceedings of CSCL'95* (pp. 147-156).

Hmelo-Silver, C. E. (2003). Analyzing collaborative knowledge construction: Multiple methods for integrated understanding. *Computers & Education, 41,* 397-420.

Kato, H., Mochizuki, T., Funaoi, H., & Suzuki, H. (2004). A principle for CSCL design: Emergent division of labor. *Proceedings of ED-MEDIA 2004* (pp. 2652-2659).

Kimura, Y., & Tsuzuki, T. (1998). Group decision making and communication mode: An experimental social psychological examination of the differences between the computer-mediated communication and the face-to-face communication. *The Japanese Journal of Experimental Social Psychology, 38*(2), 183-192.

Landauer, T. K., Laham, D., & Derr, M. (2004). From paragraph to graph: Latent semantic analysis for information visualization. *Proceedings of the National Academy Sciences* (Vol. 101, suppl. 1, pp. 5214-5219).

Li, H., & Yamanishi, K. (2001). Mining from open answers in questionnaire data. *Proceedings of the 7th ACM SIGKDD International Conference on Knowledge Discovery and Data Mining* (pp. 443-449).

Martínez, A., Dimitriadis, Y., Rubia, B., Gómez, E., & de la Fuente, P. (2003). Combining qualitative evaluation and social network analysis for the study of classroom social interactions. *Computers & Education, 41*(4), 353-368.

Copyright © 2007, Idea Group Inc. Copying or distributing in print or electronic forms without written permission of Idea Group Inc. is prohibited.

Matsumoto, Y., Kitauchi, A., Yamashita, T., Hirano, Y., Matsuda, H., Takaoka, K. et al. (2000, December 20). *Morphological Analysis System ChaSen version 2.2.1 manual*. Retrieved December 22, 2005, from *http://chasen.aist-nara.ac.jp/chasen/doc/chasen-2.2.1.pdf*

Miyake, N. (1986). Constructive interaction and the iterative process of understanding. *Cognitive Science, 10*(2), 151-177.

Mochizuki, T., Fujitani, S., Isshiki, Y., Yamauchi, Y., & Kato, H. (2003). Assessment of collaborative learning for students: Making the state of discussion visible for their reflection by text mining of electronic forums. *Proceedings of E-Learn 2003* (pp. 285-288).

Mochizuki, T., Kato, H., Hisamatsu, S., Yaegashi, K., Fujitani, S., Nagata, T. et al. (2005). Promotion of self-assessment for learners in online discussion using the visualization software. *Proceedings of Computer Supported Collaborative Learning 2005* (pp. 440-449).

Nakahara, J., Hisamatsu, S., Yaegashi, Y., & Yamauchi, Y. (2005). iTree: Does the mobile phone encourage learners to be more involved in collaborative learning? *Proceedings of Computer Supported Collaborative Learning 2005* (pp. 470-478).

Nakahara, J., & Nishimori, T. (Eds.). (2003). *E-Learning: New challenges of the Japanese universities*. Tokyo: Ohmu.

Oshima, J. (1997). Students' construction of scientific explanations in a collaborative hyper-media learning environment. *Proceedings of CSCL 1997* (pp. 187-197).

Palincsar, A. S. (1998). Social constructivist perspectives on teaching and learning. *Annual Review of Psychology, 49,* 345-375.

Palloff, R., & Pratt, K. (1999). *Building learning communities in cyberspace: Effective strategies for the online classroom*. San Francisco: Jossey-Bass.

Pea, R. D. (1993). Practices of distributed intelligence and designs for education. In G. Salomon (Ed.), *Distributed cognitions* (pp. 47-87). New York: Cambridge University Press.

Puntambekara, S., & Luckin, R. (2003). Documenting collaborative learning: What should be measured and how? *Computers & Education, 41*(4), 309-311.

Roschelle, J. (1992). Learning by collaborating: Convergent conceptual change. *The Journal of the Learning Sciences, 2*(3), 235-276.

Shaklee, B. D., Barbour, N. E., Ambrose, R., & Hansford, S.J. (1997). *Designing and using portfolio.* Boston: Allyn and Bacon.

Shirouzu, H., Miyake, N., & Masukawa, H. (2002). Cognitively active externalization for situated reflection. *Cognitive Science, 26*(4), 469-501.

Copyright © 2007, Idea Group Inc. Copying or distributing in print or electronic forms without written permission of Idea Group Inc. is prohibited.

Simoff, S. J. (1999). Monitoring and evaluation in collaborative learning environment. *Proceedings of the CSCL 1999 Conference* (an omitted paper in the printed proceedings). Retrieved December 16, 2003, from http://kn.cilt.org/cscl99/A83/A83.html

Ueno, M. (2003). LMS with irregular learning processes detection system. *Proceeding of E-Learn 2003* (pp. 2486-2493).

Yamauchi, Y., Nakahara, J., Nagai, Y., Kato, H., & Nagaoka, K. (2002, June). *The design concept of life metaphor: User interface of Web-based discussion board.* Paper presented at ED-MEDIA 2002, Denver, Colorado.

Copyright © 2007, Idea Group Inc. Copying or distributing in print or electronic forms without written permission of Idea Group Inc. is prohibited.

About the Authors

Niki Lambropoulos is a PhD student at the Center for Interactive Systems Engineering, London South Bank University, with Dr. Xristine Faulkner, Professor Fintan Culwin, and Mike Parker. Now she works as an HCI education consultant. She started working as a Greek language teacher in Greece in 1989. In 1999 she moved to London, where she worked as a Greek language and ICT teacher, and as an ICT coordinator. In 2002 she started working as a project manager, became an expert in the field of online learning and online communities, and published widely in the field. She holds two BAs, a diploma in education from the University of Athens, and an MA in ICT in education from the Institute of Education, University of London. Her interests are in HCI, and in particular in the design, use, and evaluation of systems in working places; strategy and information architecture; understanding target audiences needs, tasks, and goals, and translating them into interactive concepts; and user/learner research. She lives and works in London.

Panayiotis Zaphiris is a senior lecturer at the Center for Human-Computer Interaction Design, City University, UK. Before joining the university in 2002, he was a researcher at the Institute of Gerontology at Wayne State University, from where he also earned his PhD in industrial engineering specializing in human-computer interaction (HCI). His research interests lie in HCI, with an emphasis on issues related to the elderly and people with disabilities. He is also interested in Internet-related research (Web usability, mathematical modeling of browsing behavior in hierarchical online information systems, online communities, e-learning, computer-aided language learning (CALL), and social network analysis of online human-to-human interactions). Dr. Zaphiris was the principal investigator of the JISC Information Visualization Foundation Study, and a co-investigator on the DRC Formal Investigation into Web Site Accessibility (managing the automatic testing of 1,000 Web sites) and the JISC Usability Studies for JISC Services and Information Environment projects.

* * *

Copyright © 2007, Idea Group Inc. Copying or distributing in print or electronic forms without written permission of Idea Group Inc. is prohibited.

Patricia Barbanell serves as museum/school education coordinator for Project VIEW. She has worked for more than 20 years developing integrated programs that serve both museums and schools. Her specialties are integrated arts, multicultural programming, and technology integration. She is past-president of New York State Art Teachers and the New York Council of Educational Associations, and she helped to write the NYS Learning Standards for the Arts. Dr. Barbanell has presented scores of presentations at professional conferences and has published several papers in professional journals.

Frances Bell is a senior lecturer at the Information Systems Institute of the University of Salford, UK. Her research interests include virtual organizing and the use of information and communication technologies in teaching and learning. Professor Bell is particularly interested in the bridge between information systems and educational research, specifically the use of theories of online communities in educational research, as well as the use of educational research in organization-based research. She has published more than 30 articles in conferences and journals, including the *International Journal of Web-Based Communities, Education Media International,* IFIP 8.2, UKAIS, and ALT-C.

Chris Brook is a post-doctoral research scholar in the School of Education at Edith Cowan University, Australia. He has extensive experience in education settings including primary, secondary, and tertiary settings. He has worked as an instructional designer in tertiary settings, and has been actively engaged in the design and development of online learning materials. Current research includes the exploration of online learning communities and the use of ICT in school settings, blended learning and teacher education, and the use of video to support learning.

Kin Fai Cheng is a research assistant in the Center for Learning Enhancement and Research at the Chinese University of Hong Kong. He has a background in psychology and has been working on a number of Web-based education development and evaluation projects. His main duty at the center is to facilitate practical aspects of the various projects and ensure smooth operations.

Peter Cuttance was professor of education and head of the School of Educational Psychology, Measurement, and Technology at the University of Sydney, Australia, from 1996-1998. He then moved to professor of education in the School of Educational Psychology, Literacies, and Learning at the university, before taking on the role of professor and director of the Center of Applied Educational Research at the University of Melbourne in 2000. His current research interests focus on Web-based strategies for school development; teacher learning; schooling for the knowledge society; innovation, accountability, and school improvement; integration of tech-

Copyright © 2007, Idea Group Inc. Copying or distributing in print or electronic forms without written permission of Idea Group Inc. is prohibited.

nology into teaching and learning in schools; school leadership for the knowledge society; and choice and diversity in school systems.

Ben K. Daniel has a broad research interest in Artificial Intelligence in Education (AIED), currently; his active research focuses on virtual learning communities, distributed communities of practice, knowledge management, and the Bayesian Belief Network. He works with the GKN project as a research associate. He is also a member of the Virtual Learning Communities Research Laboratory in Educational Communications and Technology, and the Laboratory for Advanced Research in Intelligent Educational Systems (ARIES) in the Department of Computer Science. In the two research laboratories, he works under the supervision of Dr. Richard A. Schwier, professor of educational communications and technology, and Dr. Gordon McCalla, professor of computer science, both at the University of Saskatchewan, Canada. Mr. Daniel is currently pursuing his PhD.

John Falco is director of the New Era for Leadership Institute at the College of Saint Rose, USA, and served as principal investigator of Project VIEW while superintendent of Schenectady City Schools, New York. Dr. Falco has led several transformational projects including the Schenectady Schools' Capital Region Science Education Partnership (CRSEP), a multi-district Local Systemic Change Initiative funded by the National Science Foundation. He has been named NYSCATE Superintendent of the Year for outstanding leadership in integrating technology. His major research interests center on improving reading skills for struggling emergent readers and developing leadership initiatives.

Satoru Fujitani is an assistant professor of educational technology and ICT education at Mejiro University, Japan. He earned his BE degree from Osaka University in 1994. His MS and PhD degrees in educational technology were earned from the Tokyo Institute of Technology in 1996 and 2000, respectively. His current research areas include educational technology—in particular, computing in education and science communication. He is also a museum interpreter at the National Museum of Emerging Science and Innovations, Tokyo, Japan.

Denis Gillet received his diploma in electrical engineering and his PhD in control systems from the Ecole Polytechnique Fédérale de Lausanne (EPFL), Switzerland, in 1988 and 1995, respectively. He is currently an associate professor at EPFL. His research interests include optimal and hierarchical control systems, distributed e-learning systems, and sustainable interaction and real-time Internet services. Dr. Gillet received the 2001 Recognition Award for Innovations and Accomplishments in Distance and Flexible Learning Methodologies for Engineering Education from the International Network for Engineering Education and Research (iNEER).

Copyright © 2007, Idea Group Inc. Copying or distributing in print or electronic forms without written permission of Idea Group Inc. is prohibited.

Elizabeth Hartnell-Young is an educational researcher and writer with particular interest in professional learning and the use of technologies. Her doctoral thesis looked at emerging communities of practice in schools, and she has written frequently, from the user's point of view, on e-portfolios and mobile learning. She was previously national research manager in the Center for Applied Educational Research at the University of Melbourne, and is now a research fellow in the Learning Sciences Research Institute at the University of Nottingham, UK.

Jen Harvey is head of lifelong learning at the Dublin Institute of Technology, Ireland, where she has been involved in a number of projects working with Irish community and teacher groups. Since moving to Dublin from the Institute for Computer-Based Learning, Heriot Watt University, Scotland, she has been involved in establishing a learning and teaching center, a learning technology team, as well as various associated post-graduate programs addressing the use of ICTs. Her main research interests relate to the evaluation of ICTs, the use of e-assessment, and the creation of communities to support learning.

Shin-ichi Hisamatsu received his BA and MA degrees from Keio University in 2003 and 2005, respectively. In 1999, he joined the WIDE (Widely Integrated Distributed Environment) Project and contributed to the development of Internet infrastructure, particularly Internet Protocol version 6. He is also interested in the field of educational technology. He has joined a TV program production team at NHK (the Japan Broadcasting Corporation) to promote ICT education at the high school level. In addition, in collaboration with colleagues, he developed an e-learning system referred to as "exCampus," which is a well-known open source system in Japan.

Ebba Thora Hvannberg is an associate professor in the Computer Science Department, University of Iceland. Dr. Hvannberg holds a BS in computer science from the University of Iceland, and an MS and a PhD from Rensselaer Polytechnic Institute, USA. Her main research areas include human-computer interaction, software science, distributed systems, multimedia, and formal methods. She has participated in a number of international and Icelandic research projects. She has been an active member of the research community by publishing papers, reviewing proposals, and papers. Dr. Hvannberg holds several administrative duties, including as a board member of three companies, as well as in research and educational programs.

Anne Jelfs is e-learning development manager and a member of the learning and teaching development team within the Institute of Educational Technology at the Open University, UK. Her research interests are the application and evaluation of educational technologies in education, and her PhD was on stakeholders' conceptions

Copyright © 2007, Idea Group Inc. Copying or distributing in print or electronic forms without written permission of Idea Group Inc. is prohibited.

of quality in distance higher education. The research used a qualitative approach termed "phenomenological phenomenography", and she is particularly interested in qualitative research methods. She has presented at conferences and published in numerous refereed conference proceedings, journal articles, and book chapters on the use and quality assurance of learning technologies in tertiary education.

Ann Jones is a senior lecturer and convenor of the Computers and Learning Research Group at the Institute of Educational Technology of the Open University, UK. There she has carried out educational technology research since 1978 and has also published extensively. Her research areas include the evaluation of ICT, including her recent work on a project evaluating the use of tablets in schools; social and affective uses of computers, where she recently published a review; and mobile learning, where she recently researched the potential of mobile technology for supporting informal learning in science.

Hiroshi Kato is an associate professor at the National Institute of Multimedia Education (NIME), Japan. He received his BE and ME from Keio University, and a PhD in educational technology from the Tokyo Institute of Technology. While working at NEC Corporation, he stayed at the Center for the Study of Language and Information, Stanford University, USA, as a visiting scholar from 1989 to 1990. He received the Outstanding Research Paper Award from the Japan Society of Educational Technology twice. In 2000, he began his academic career at NIME. His majors are educational technology and cognitive science.

Andrew Laghos is a PhD student in the Center for HCI Design at City University, UK; he is studying towards a degree in computer-aided language learning and computer-mediated communication. He holds an MSc in interactive multimedia, a BSc in computer science (with emphasis in information management), and a certificate in Web site development. His research interests include e-learning, Web site design, HCI, music (both computerized and live), and communication via the Web.

Paul Lam is a research assistant professor in the Center for Learning Enhancement and Research at the Chinese University of Hong Kong. He has extensive experience in English language teaching at the school level, and this education experience has been applied in several education development projects in Hong Kong universities. His current focus is on the design, development, and evaluation of Web-assisted teaching and learning, and on case-based teaching and learning.

Effie Lai-Chong Law is an IT research fellow affiliated with the Swiss Federal Institute of Technology (ETH Zurich) and the University of Leicester, UK. Dr. Law

Copyright © 2007, Idea Group Inc. Copying or distributing in print or electronic forms without written permission of Idea Group Inc. is prohibited.

holds a Master of Social Sciences in Psychology degree from the University of Hong Kong and her PhD in psychology from the University of Munich, Germany. Her research interests include human-computer interaction, technology-enhanced learning, cognitive theories, and creativity. Her research activities are highly interdisciplinary, synergizing ideas from psychology, technology, and education. She has presented and published a number of papers in international conferences, books, and journals. Currently, she is chairing and participating actively in several international and national research projects on usability evaluation and e-learning.

Keryn McGuinness works as an accredited school reviewer and educational consultant in Australia. After 24 years of teaching and school leadership in high schools in Australia and Japan, she was seconded in 2001 to the University of Melbourne as project manager of the National Quality Schooling Framework Project. Her current work also includes facilitation and management of virtual communities of practice and quality assurance of Improvement Project Reports for the National Boys Education Lighthouse Schools' Project (52 clusters, 350+ schools).

Carmel McNaught is professor of learning enhancement in the Center for Learning Enhancement And Research (CLEAR) at the Chinese University of Hong Kong. She has more than 30 years of experience in teaching and research in higher education, and has held appointments in eight universities in Australasia and southern Africa, working in the discipline areas of chemistry, science education, second language learning, e-learning, and higher education curriculum and policy matters. Current research interests include evaluation of innovation in higher education, strategies for embedding learning support into the curriculum, and understanding the broader implementation of the use of technology in higher education. She has more than 220 academic publications. Additional information is available at http://www.cuhk.edu.hk/clear/staff/staff7.htm

Toshio Mochizuki is an assistant professor at Kobe University, Japan. He received his BA and MA degrees in media and governance from Keio University in 2000 and 2002, respectively, and a PhD in educational technology from the Graduate University for Advanced Studies, Japan, in 2004. His major is educational technology, particularly computer-supported collaborative learning (CSCL). He received the Young Scholars and Outstanding Research Paper Awards from the Japan Society of Educational Technology. He is currently interested in cognitive effects with visualization of collaborative learning. He is also interested in the assessment and evaluation of education with ICT such as e-learning.

Miranda Mowbray is a technical contributor at HP's European research laboratories in Bristol, UK. She received a PhD degree in algebra from London University. Dr.

Copyright © 2007, Idea Group Inc. Copying or distributing in print or electronic forms without written permission of Idea Group Inc. is prohibited.

Mowbray co-authored *Online Communities: Commerce, Community Action, and the Virtual University,* published by Prentice-Hall in 2000, and she was one of the founders of e-mint, the Association of UK Online Community Professionals, which has been listed as one of the most-cited influences on the industry. She has advised many projects on the design of online communities.

Tomoko Nagata is an assistant professor at the Hyogo University of Teacher Education, Japan. She received her BS, MS, and PhD degrees from Osaka University in 1993, 1995, and 2000, respectively. She received the Young Scholars Award from the Japan Society of Educational Technology. In 2005, she resided in the Department of Curriculum and Instruction, University of Wisconsin, USA, as a visiting scholar. Her majors are educational technology and teacher education. Her current interest is digital teaching portfolios, because she is engaged in the pre-service training program for undergraduate students at her university, both as teacher and researcher.

Jun Nakahara is an assistant professor at the University of Tokyo, Japan. He received his BA in education from the University of Tokyo in 1998, and his MS and PhD in educational technology from Osaka University in 2000 and 2003, respectively. He received the Outstanding Research Paper Award from the Japan Society of Educational Technology thrice and the Fulbright Grant from the Japan-United States Educational Commission. In 2004, he resided at the Center for Educational Computing Initiative at MIT as a visiting scholar. His majors are educational technology and learning sciences. His current interest is CSCL for higher and continuing education.

Dianna L. Newman is associate professor at the University at Albany/SUNY, USA, and director of the Evaluation Consortium at Albany; she served as principal evaluator of Project VIEW. Dr. Newman has served on the board of directors for the American Evaluation Association; assisted in writing the "Guiding Principles for Evaluators," which function as the professional guidelines for practice; and served on the national Joint Committee for Standards in Educational Evaluation. She has been an evaluator for several federal- and state-funded technology-based curriculum integration grants, and currently she is developing an innovative model of evaluation that will document systems change resulting from technology-based curriculum integration in K-12 and higher education settings. Dr. Newman is widely published in the areas of technology innovation and K-12 curriculum practices.

Anh Vu Nguyen-Ngoc earned his BSc in computer science from the Vietnam National University in 1997. He is currently working toward a PhD at the School of Engineering, Ecole Polytechnique Fédérale de Lausanne (EPFL), Switzerland. His research interests include e-learning, collaboration and interaction systems, computer-supported cooperative work (CSCW), human-computer interaction (HCI),

Copyright © 2007, Idea Group Inc. Copying or distributing in print or electronic forms without written permission of Idea Group Inc. is prohibited.

and Web engineering. Mr. Nguyen-Ngoc was awarded a two-year federal scholarship from the Swiss Confederation in 1999. He also received an Outstanding Paper Award from the ED-MEDIA conference in 2004.

Toshihisa Nishimori is an assistant professor at the National Institute of Multimedia Education, Japan. He received his BS and MS degrees in educational technology from Osaka University in 1995 and 1997, respectively. He received the Outstanding Research Paper Award from the Japan Society of Educational Technology. His major is educational technology, and his current interest is computer-supported collaborative learning (CSCL), particularly when making effective use of roles and the division of labor in collaborative learning. With his colleagues, he developed some networked collaborative learning software and an open source e-learning system called "exCampus," which has been used in many Japanese universities.

David O'Brien, a PhD candidate, is the manager of international research at the University of Saskatchewan, Canada. His interest in collective action problems has led to research on communities and interest groups, and their effect on policy development and social service delivery. His interaction with his chapter co-authors has taken his research interests in the temporal world into the virtual domain. He also holds an MPhil from Sussex University, UK.

Ron Oliver is professor of interactive multimedia in the School of Communications and Multimedia at Edith Cowan University, Australia. He has a research background in multimedia and e-learning, and currently leads a major research team at ECU in this field. He has experience in the design, development, and evaluation of multimedia and computer-based learning materials. Current research projects involve explorations and investigations of effective online teaching and learning in higher education, exploring scalability and reusability of e-learning materials.

Noppadol Prammanee holds a BA from Burapha University, Thailand, an MS from Fort Hays State University, USA (majoring in instructional technology), and an EdD from the Department of Educational Research and Assessment at Northern Illinois University, USA (majoring in instructional technology). His research interests include instructional design computer-mediated communication, human-computer interaction, and engaging learning with technology. He is currently serving as a faculty member at Burapha University International College, Thailand.

Yassin Rekik earned his PhD in computer science from the Ecole Polytechnique Fédérale de Lausanne (EPFL), Switzerland, in 2001. He is a senior research associate at the EPFL and a professor at the University of Applied Sciences Western

Copyright © 2007, Idea Group Inc. Copying or distributing in print or electronic forms without written permission of Idea Group Inc. is prohibited.

Switzerland (HES-SO). His research interests include Web-based learning, mobile learning, collaborative and group-oriented learning, and online experimentation and laboratory activities. Dr. Rekik is currently involved in several national and international initiatives and projects, including the European Network of Excellence ProLEARN.

Maria Rigou holds a diploma in computer engineering and informatics from the University of Patras, Greece, as well as an MSc and PhD in computer science. Her PhD dissertation was entitled: "Effective Personalization Algorithms Based on Web Usage Mining." Her current research interests lay in the areas of adaptive hypermedia, Web personalization, and Web semantics. She has publications in several journals and conference proceedings, and she is the co-author of five book chapters and two books. Her professional background includes technical coordination of R&D projects with national and EU funding, and S/W development for the private sector.

Asit Sarkar is professor of management and marketing, and director of the International Center for Governance and Development, both at the University of Saskatchewan, Canada. Spanning a career of more than 30 years, Dr. Sarkar held a variety of academic and administrative appointments at the University of Saskatchewan and other institutions in Canada and abroad. He served as the first director of the University of Saskatchewan International (USI) and special advisor to the president of the University of Saskatchewan.

Richard A. Schwier is a professor of educational communications and technology at the University of Saskatchewan, Canada, where he coordinates the graduate programs of study. He is the senior researcher in the Virtual Learning Communities Research Laboratory, which is currently investigating the characteristics of formal online learning communities. His other research interests include instructional design and social change agency.

Ben Shneiderman is a professor in the Department of Computer Science, founding director (1983-2000) of the Human-Computer Interaction Laboratory, and a member of the Institute for Advanced Computer Studies and the Institute for Systems Research, all at the University of Maryland at College Park, USA. He previously taught at the State University of New York and at Indiana University. He was made a fellow of the Association for Computing Machinery (ACM), the American Association for the Advancement of Science, and received the ACM CHI (Computer-Human Interaction) Lifetime Achievement Award in 2001. Dr. Shneiderman is the author of the books *Software Psychology: Human Factors in Computer and Information Systems* (1980); *Designing the User Interface: Strategies for Effective*

Copyright © 2007, Idea Group Inc. Copying or distributing in print or electronic forms without written permission of Idea Group Inc. is prohibited.

Human-Computer Interaction (first published in 1987), co-authored in its 4th edition (2004) with Catherine Plaisant; *Hypertext Hands-On!* with Greg Kearsley; and *Leonardo's Laptop: Human Needs and the New Computing Technologies* (2002), which won the IEEE 2003 Award for Distinguished Literary Contribution. He also edited the Ablex Publishing Company book series on "Human-Computer Interaction." In addition he has co-authored two textbooks, edited three technical books, and published more than 200 technical papers and book chapters. He has been on the editorial advisory boards of nine journals. Dr. Shneiderman is the originator of the Hyperties hypermedia system, a member of the board of directors (1996-2001) of Spotfire for information visualization, and a computer science advisor (1999-2002) to Smartmoney built on his treemap concept. He is an advisor for treemap supplier HiveGroup and for ClockWise3D, as well as a member of the Technical Advisory Board for ILOG. He has consulted and lectured for many organizations including Apple, AT&T, Citicorp, GE, Honeywell, IBM, Intel, the Library of Congress, Microsoft, NASA, NCR, and university research groups.

Spiros Sirmakessis graduated from the Department of Computer Engineering and Informatics at the University of Patras, Greece, in 1992 and received his PhD on computational geometry and multidimensional data structures in 1997. Today he is the head of the Databases and Information Systems Sector and director of the E-Business and Human-Computer Interaction Lab in Applied Informatics in Administration and Economy at TEI of Messolongi. He works in the area of software engineering, Web mining, Web engineering, and distance learning, and he has several publications in international journals and conferences. Additional information is available at http://www.hci-course.gr/bio.htm

Dimitris Stavrinoudis received his diploma degree and PhD from the Computer Engineering & Informatics Department of the University of Patras, Greece. The main research field of his PhD dissertation was software quality assurance. He teaches in the Computer Engineering & Informatics Department of the University of Patras and in the Civil Engineering Department of the Technological Educational Institute of Patras. He has participated as a computer engineer and project manager in research and development projects of the Research Academic Computer Technology Institute, and Hellenic Open University. He is a member of the Technical Chamber of Greece.

Mariko Suzuki is an associate professor at Shiga University, Japan. She received her BS in natural science from Nara Women's University in 1983, and her MS and PhD degrees in human sciences from Osaka University in 1993 and 2003, respectively. She received the Young Scholars Award from the Japan Society of Educational Technology. In 2004, she resided at University of Maryland and Uni-

Copyright © 2007, Idea Group Inc. Copying or distributing in print or electronic forms without written permission of Idea Group Inc. is prohibited.

versity of California, Berkeley as a visiting scholar. Her fields are science education and educational technology. Her current interest is CSCL for pre-service training because she engaged in the training program at her university, both as teacher and researcher.

Michalis Xenos has been holding teaching and research positions since 1991 in the departments of Computer Engineering & Informatics and Mathematics of the University of Patras, and the Research Academic Computer Technology Institute, Greece. Currently he is assistant professor in the Computer Science Department of the School of Sciences and Technology of the Hellenic Open University. Dr. Xenos has authored or co-authored six books and more than 60 papers in international journals and conferences. His current research interests include software quality and educational technologies.

Kazaru Yaegashi is an assistant professor of media design and production at Fukuyama University, Japan. He received his BA degree from Musashino Art University in 1997 and his MA in interdisciplinary information studies from the University of Tokyo in 2005. His majors are design informatics and ICT education through information design. His current interest is visual communication design. He is also interested in the development and design of educational systems.

Elena Zaitseva was involved in online teaching and learning in Russia and Japan for more than 15 years. Currently she is a research assistant for the CAB project, with particular interest in intercultural aspects of computer-mediated discussion. Her general research interests include using collaborative learning environments for the support of foreign language acquisition and cultural awareness.

Danuta Zakrzewska is an assistant professor at the Institute of Computer Science Technical University of Lodz. Her research interests focus on information management in organizations as well as intelligent methods that may improve it, including techniques such as data warehousing and data mining. She published more than 30 articles in conferences, journals, and books. In the CAB project, she is involved in the investigation of language issues in student collaboration and the sustainability of the project communities.

Copyright © 2007, Idea Group Inc. Copying or distributing in print or electronic forms without written permission of Idea Group Inc. is prohibited.

Index

Copyright © 2007, Idea Group Inc. Copying or distributing in print or electronic forms without written permission of Idea Group Inc. is prohibited.

D

E

Copyright © 2007, Idea Group Inc. Copying or distributing in print or electronic forms without written permission of Idea Group Inc. is prohibited.

Copyright © 2007, Idea Group Inc. Copying or distributing in print or electronic forms without written permission of Idea Group Inc. is prohibited.

M

N

O

P

Copyright © 2007, Idea Group Inc. Copying or distributing in print or electronic forms without written permission of Idea Group Inc. is prohibited.

Copyright © 2007, Idea Group Inc. Copying or distributing in print or electronic forms without written permission of Idea Group Inc. is prohibited.

T

U

V

W

Y

Copyright © 2007, Idea Group Inc. Copying or distributing in print or electronic forms without written permission of Idea Group Inc. is prohibited.

Looking for a way to make information science and technology research easy?
Idea Group Inc. Electronic Resources are designed to keep your institution up-to-date on the latest information science technology trends and research.
Information Technology Research at the Click of a Mouse!
InfoSci-Online
Instant access to thousands of information technology book chapters, journal articles, teaching cases, and conference proceedings
Multiple search functions
Full-text entries and complete citation information
Upgrade to InfoSci-Online Premium and add thousands of authoritative entries from Idea Group Reference's handbooks of research and encyclopedias!
IGI Full-Text Online Journal Collection
Instant access to thousands of scholarly journal articles
Full-text entries and complete citation information
IGI Teaching Case Collection
Instant access to hundreds of comprehensive teaching cases
Password-protected access to case instructor files
IGI E-Access
Online, full-text access to IGI individual journals, encyclopedias, or handbooks of research
Additional E-Resources
E-Books
Individual Electronic Journal Articles
Individual Electronic Teaching Cases
IGI Electronic Resources have flexible pricing to help meet the needs of any institution.
www.igi-online.com
Sign Up for a Free Trial of Our Databases!